T0299049

This study approaches the subject of tax reform from basic economic principles. The objectives are to develop guidelines for the design of tax policy; to show how the principles can structure systematic research into tax reform in terms of the consequences for households, producers and government; and finally, to combine the guidelines and applied research into a practical tax package for Pakistan, where tax reform has become an urgent priority. Dr Ahmad and Professor Stern provide a coherent framework to show how principles can be formulated, applied research structured, and policies developed and appraised in a systematic manner.

The majority of developing countries are currently facing severe budgetary pressures with rising demands for expenditures and limited scope for raising extra government revenues. In addition, the revenue systems which are in place may themselves generate strong impediments to efficiency, the expansion of the economy, the growth of the tax base, equity and the achievement of development objectives. Tax reform should therefore be central to public policy and development planning and is seen as such by many governments. It has also moved to the forefront of discussion in international agencies.

The theory and practice of tax reform in developing countries

The theory and practice of tax reform in developing countries

Ehtisham Ahmad

Nicholas Stern

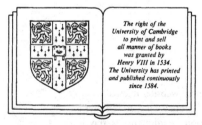

The right of the
University of Cambridge
to print and sell
all manner of books
was granted by
Henry VIII in 1534.
The University has printed
and published continuously
since 1584.

CAMBRIDGE UNIVERSITY PRESS
Cambridge
New York   Port Chester
Melbourne   Sydney

CAMBRIDGE UNIVERSITY PRESS
Cambridge, New York, Melbourne, Madrid, Cape Town,
Singapore, São Paulo, Delhi, Mexico City

Cambridge University Press
The Edinburgh Building, Cambridge CB2 8RU, UK

Published in the United States of America by Cambridge University Press, New York

www.cambridge.org
Information on this title: www.cambridge.org/9780521265638

First published 1991

A catalogue record for this publication is available from the British Library

Library of Congress Cataloguing in Publication Data

Ahmad, Ehtisham.
  The theory and practice of tax reform in developing countries / Ehtisham Ahmad,
Nicholas Stern.
    p.   cm.
  Includes bibliographical references.
  ISBN 0-521-26563-0 – ISBN 0-521-39742-1 (pbk.)
  1. Taxation – Developing countries.   I. Stern, N. H. (Nicholas Herbert)   II. Title.
  HJ2351.7.A35   1991
  336.2′05′091724 – dc20   90-33156 CIP

ISBN 978-0-521-26563-8 Hardback
ISBN 978-0-521-39742-1 Paperback

To our parents

Contents

Preface

This study approaches the subject of tax reform from basic economic principles. The objectives are to develop guidelines for the design of tax policy, to show how the principles can structure systematic research into tax reform in terms of the consequences for households, producers and government and finally to combine the guidelines and applied research into a practical tax package for Pakistan, where tax reform has become an urgent priority. Our work on tax reform in developing countries was first concerned with India when in 1980 we embarked on a research project as a central part of the initial research programme of the Development Economics Research Centre (DERC) at the University of Warwick. This was an academic programme funded first by the Nuffield Foundation and then by the Social Science Research Council (SSRC). Whilst it was an academic programme we were careful to maintain close contact with the Planning Commission and Ministry of Finance in Delhi and with the central revenue authorities. Further we had detailed and wide-ranging discussions with those responsible for tax policy and administration in the state of Karnataka, where Stern was based for much of the field work in 1981–2.

Our work on India soon attracted the attention of the World Bank and in the mid-1980s a research programme was undertaken, funded by the Economic and Social Research Council (ESRC) and the World Bank, to develop and extend our ideas to a more detailed analysis of Pakistan. This second programme, which began in 1983, was organised through the Warwick DERC and two divisions of the World Bank, the Public Economics Division of the Development Research Department, whose chief was David Newbery, and the Resource Mobilisation Division of the Country Policy Department, whose chief was Lyn Squire. The research funded by the World Bank envisaged an extension of our work to Pakistan and Mexico. The work on Pakistan was, in this second programme, accompanied by the work on Mexico, which was the responsibility of our colleague at Warwick, Jesus Seade. The research on methods and their application to India in the first programme led not only to the Pakistan–Mexico programme but also to the commissioning of a set of studies on the theory of taxation in developing countries which was organised by Newbery and Stern. The papers which ensued, including an account of our India work, were presented at a conference in Washington in 1984 and eventually published in Newbery and Stern (1987a).

During the second programme, 1983–7, the Pakistan desk at the World Bank and the Pakistan government took a helpful interest in our work and we benefited from interaction with officials at the Planning Commission, the Ministry of Finance and the tax administration authorities at the Central Board of Revenue. We were asked to present some of the results of our work to the National Taxation Reform Commission (NTRC), under the chairmanship of Qamar-ul Islam, and this we did in 1986. As a result of our research the Pakistan government and the World Bank asked us to prepare some background work on fiscal issues in connection with the Seventh Five-Year Plan (1988–93) and this was completed in the autumn of 1987. Hence, whilst our work remained essentially academic research, there was continual liaison with tax policy makers, advisers and administrators. Only after the second programme came to an end were we directly involved (as advisers) with the Pakistan government and then only in the preparation of background papers for the medium term. The programme transferred from the DERC at Warwick to the Suntory-Toyota International Centre for Economics and Related Disciplines (STICERD) at the London School of Economics where Stern took a chair in 1986 and Ahmad became Director of the Development Economics Research Programme.

We have accumulated a long list of debts over the years, intellectual, institutional, as well as personal. An incalculable debt is owed to Mahnaz Ahmad. During the first phase of the work to 1983, thanks go to the Nuffield Foundation and the Economic and Social Research Council (formerly the SSRC) for the initial grants in 1980 that made the research possible. The University of Warwick supported the establishment of the DERC and provided a personal grant to Ahmad to finance an extended stay in India during 1981–2, and generally encouraged and facilitated our work. The Overseas Development Administration (ODA) subsequently provided resources to support programming for the analysis of the large quantity of data.

In India, Dharma and Lovraj Kumar provided us with intellectual stimulation and personal comfort, and did much to make the stay of the Ahmads and the Sterns so enjoyable. Rosaleen and Sudhir Mulji were most generous in permitting us to house-sit at Malcha Marg. Bina Agarwal and

S. M. Agarwal were sources of kindness and guidance, and Naseem Gore went out of his way to make us feel at home.

Stern was a Visiting Professor at the Indian Statistical Institute (ISI) during 1981–2 funded by the Ford Foundation. N. S. Iyengar and the staff of the ISI Bangalore, Nikhilesh Bhattacharya of ISI Calcutta and V. K. Chetty and the staff of ISI Delhi were very kind and helpful in hosting Stern's visit and brief visits by Ahmad during 1982 and 1983. Ahmad was a Visiting Fellow at the National Institute of Public Finance and Policy (NIPFP) during 1981–2, and we are greatly indebted to Raja Chelliah, Amaresh Bagchi and the staff of NIPFP for their hospitality. Arvind Gupta and M. N. Murty worked with us tirelessly in Delhi, and Vijay Nayak and P. Sudarshan in Bangalore. Mallika Gopalakrishna and Shailaja Rao were a great support in Bangalore.

We are grateful for the advice and guidance of many people in India. We are particularly indebted to: Manmohan Singh, S. P. Gupta, Rakesh Mohan, and the staff of the Planning Commission; Montek Ahluwalia, Mahfooz Ahmed and the Economic Adviser's staff of the Finance Ministry; Idrak Bhatty and the staff of the National Council of Applied Economic Research; the Ministry of Law; the National Sample Survey Organisation and the staff of the Statistics Division; and the Bureau of Industrial Costs and Prices. The kindness and advice of M. Bhaktavatsala, B. K. Chandrasekhar, I. S. Gulati, the Hegdes, Jairaj, Indira Rajaraman and N. P. Singh in Bangalore were greatly appreciated as was the welcome of the Bangalore Club.

We met Jean Drèze in India in 1981, and he came to Warwick subsequently as a visitor. He has since become a colleague, initially at Warwick and then at the LSE, and is a source of constant inspiration. At Warwick we were fortunate to be able to benefit from the advice of Jeff Round on National Accounts and the intricacies of handling input–output data in numerous forms, and the visits of Sweder van Wijnbergen and François Laisney. John Humphries, who joined our team in 1982, did much to lay the programming and data-handling foundations of our work, which are still in use today. Liz Thompson was crucial in the smooth organisation and administration of the DERC, and in the transfer of our work to the LSE, and for endless moral support.

A substantial increase in our activities was made possible by a major programme grant from the ESRC in 1983, an additional grant from the ODA, and funding from the World Bank (under RPO 673-13). This permitted expansion of our team (working on Pakistan and India), to include Sue Barratt, David Coady, Hing-Man Leung, Simon Musgrave and Vijay Nayak. David Coady transferred to the LSE, where he has continued work on Pakistan for his doctoral dissertation. He was replaced by Stephen Ludlow in 1986. We have been very fortunate in the quality and dedication of the research team. We were again fortunate that Jenny Johnson was able to join Liz Thompson in keeping the organisation together in a cheerful and efficient way.

The transfer in 1986 of the programme to the LSE and its subsequent development were made possible by the generosity and hospitality of STICERD, and we are most grateful to both the Chairman and the Administrative Officer at that time, Tony Atkinson and Prue Hutton respectively. The programme at STICERD was most ably run first by Leila Alberici and Sue Coles, and then by Kerrie Beale who has held things together magnificently in the last year. Leila Alberici, Kerrie Beale, David Coady and Jenny Lanjouw have taken special responsibility in the preparation of the final typescripts.

The extensions of our work owe much to the encouragement and intellectual support of David Newbery, Tony Atkinson, Angus Deaton, John Holsen, Shahid Husain, Azizali Mohammed and Vito Tanzi. After Newbery's departure from the World Bank, our Pakistan–Mexico World Bank funding was managed by Pradeep Mitra and Zmarak Shalizi, under the supervision of Lyn Squire and subsequently Javad Khalilzadeh-Shirazi. We are very grateful to them. Nizar Jetha, Bill McCleary, Mieko Nishimizu and Lorene Yap, all of the Pakistan country desk of the World Bank, spent time and effort to comment on our work and offer encouragement. Vivian Couchoud and Peggy Pender did much to facilitate its organisation.

In Pakistan, Anwar Kamal worked with us throughout the project, researching the legal intricacies of the Pakistan tax system, and its evolution over time. We are particularly grateful to Moeen Baqai, Meekal Ahmed and the staff of the Planning Commission for their encouragement. Arshad Zaman and the staff of the Economic Adviser's Wing of the Ministry of Finance were most helpful at crucial moments of the research. Our work would not have been possible without the support of the Ministry of Statistics and the Federal Bureau of Statistics. Habeeb Hussain, the Secretary, and his successor, Akhtar Mahmood, were most unusually supportive. We have also had extensive discussions with the Central Board of Revenue, and are grateful to the staff and the Chairmen, Fazlur Rahman and I. A. Imtiazi. We have had many helpful discussions with Asghar Qadir who has commented in detail on our work over the years and has also been most hospitable. And N. A. Seyal and the Muizuddin Ahmads have always looked after us well. Notwithstanding all this kind assistance and guidance we must emphasise that we must be held responsible for all errors and opinions.

Material in a number of chapters in this book has been published in earlier incarnations elsewhere: chapter 3 draws on Stern (1987) and Ahmad and Stern (1984); chapter 5 on Ahmad and Stern (1984) and Ahmad and Stern (1987b); chapter 6 on Ahmad, Coady and Stern (1988) and Ahmad and Stern (1986); and chapter 7 on Ahmad and Stern (1990 and 1987b) and Ahmad and Ludlow (1989). Parts of a number of the other chapters are based on discussion papers from the DERC at Warwick and the DERP at the LSE. Chapter 10 utilises our 1987 paper for the Pakistan Planning Commission (see Ahmad and Stern, 1987b).

The book is intended to be helpful to a variety of readers. Graduate students, academic economists, and other professional economists from international organisations, governments and elsewhere are likely to use it in different ways. We have tried to show how principles can be formulated, applied research structured, and policies developed and appraised in a systematic manner. The careful application of the ideas presented can, we think, lead to real improvement in the development of policy and we hope they may lead to further empirical and theoretical research. The test will be whether others are able to use these ideas and methods productively.

1 Issues and methods

1.1 Introduction and issues

Most developing countries appear to face severe budgetary pressures with rising demands for expenditures and limited scope for raising extra government revenues. In addition the revenue systems which are in place may themselves generate strong impediments to efficiency, the expansion of the economy, the growth of the tax base, equity and the achievement of development objectives. Tax reform should therefore be central to public policy and development planning and is seen as such by many governments. It has also moved to the forefront of discussion in international agencies (World Bank, 1988). The major purpose of this book is to develop principles and methods which allow the systematic and practical analysis of potential reforms. In so doing we put these methods to work to produce recommendations for revenue reforms for Pakistan. We also briefly assess evidence from a number of other countries in terms of the lessons of their tax experience, similarities and contrasts with Pakistan and the generality of the approach we have adopted.

Whilst there is a strong emphasis in this book on economic principles, they cannot by themselves yield policy prescriptions. They have to be combined with an understanding of the economic, political, legal and administrative systems of the country under study. Accordingly we shall be discussing the history of the tax structure in South Asia from the common background of British rule and paying particular attention to previous attempts at reform. And our proposals will take careful account of the legal and administrative difficulties facing the tax authorities. At the end of the day, policies will be selected by those who hold political power and we have not sought to conceal the political difficulties of different strategies. Our task has not, however, been to resolve these difficulties. We have sought to characterise promising options in the light of economic principles and legal and administrative constraints and then analyse the economic gains and

1

losses, relative to the status quo, of these options. The analysis of the net economic advantage and of the likely political fate or viability of any particular policy or programme share this one basic informational requirement – the identification of gains and losses and to whom they accrue. It is this part of the analysis which requires the hard work and the detailed economic analysis.

Our applied work on the Indian sub-continent originated with an academic research project on the Indian tax system which began in 1980. In the mid-1980s the focus of our research shifted to Pakistan and it is in this context that we have taken our methods and analysis furthest. Accordingly, the applied work reported here is mainly concerned with Pakistan although we shall also draw on examples from India and, to a lesser extent, Bangladesh. This background, together with our emphasis on the development and testing of methods, means that some parts of the book will be on economic theory, others on the history and practicality of policies, but that mostly it will be a mixture.

We shall argue that it is important to take a broad and integrated view of possible sources of government revenue. For example, the level and structure of indirect taxes which would be desirable will vary greatly for different levels and structures of direct taxes and transfers. Thus the analysis will consider taxes, tariffs, duties, subsidies, pricing, transfers, land taxes, corporate and personal income taxes and so on. However, our theoretical and particularly our applied work will be focused on the indirect taxes, which have contributed greatest revenue in the past and are likely to occupy this role over the medium term.

The central question in our study has been the reform of indirect taxation. Tax reform, as opposed to tax design, concerns the search for, and analysis of, systems which are improvements on the existing state of affairs. The analysis of reform therefore involves special emphasis on the initial position and we began our applied work with a systematic description of the existing system, particularly in terms of its effects on the prices of final goods. This is especially important and difficult when, as in the sub-continent, much of taxation (through import tariffs, excise duties or sales taxes) falls on productive inputs. Tax design on the other hand is concerned more with the specification of an appropriate tax structure *ab initio*. The principles of tax design should inform those of tax reform and we shall, in later chapters, set out some of the important ideas and draw out their basic lessons in terms of guidelines.

Examples of the questions we shall be asking are as follows: How can the balance of taxation across goods or types of taxes be adjusted so as to raise the same revenue at less cost to households and producers? Where should extra revenue come from? Can the tax system be reformed in a way which maintains or increases revenue whilst improving income distribution and incentives for efficiency? And, finally, given a country's objectives over the medium term, what package of measures would we recommend? Our central example is Pakistan. Thus, whilst we wish to develop and demonstrate methods of analysis, we also want to directly address real and immediate policy issues.

In the next section we indicate some of the analytical methods we shall be using. The main tax issues facing Pakistan will be described briefly in section 1.3 and placed in international perspective in section 1.4. The structure of the book is summarised in section 1.5.

1.2 Principles and methods

We shall pay considerable attention to the theory of taxation. The purpose here is not the pursuit of pure theory as such, although that has its own value and interest, but the drawing out of principles and methods to guide the applied research. Thus we shall first try to distil the central messages of the theory in a form that points to direct lessons for tax policy. We shall then develop particular methods for structuring the detailed applied research.

The central issues in the theory of taxation have been equity, efficiency and revenue. How does the government finance its activities in such a way as to cause minimum damage? And what should be the level of these activities? Such questions require criteria and many or most commentators would want to base these criteria on the consequences of policies for the standard of living of the households and individuals of the community, now and in the future. It is the working out of these consequences that poses the greatest difficulties for economic analysis, but ultimately it is these consequences which should be characterised and evaluated. The last stage of such an analysis is the evaluation of policy which implicitly or explicitly sets the gains to some households against the losses to others. Where, of course, there are policies which allow everyone to gain, then matters of value judgement are considerably eased, but such opportunities may be rare.

Where the calculation of the consequences of policies for households is not possible then policy choice is less firmly grounded. One has to fall back on principles and guidelines which indicate the kinds of policies that are likely to produce generally favourable consequences. These guidelines may be derived from simple or stylised models which can be analysed in full. In these simple models one can make the trade-offs explicit and work out the appropriate policies with respect to social objectives which aggregate gains and losses across households. This is the theory of optimal taxation.

We must make absolutely clear at the outset that there has been no attempt to calculate optimal taxes either in this book or in our research programmes. Whilst such an activity may have some interest and provide some lessons, it generally requires knowledge that is not available, and it is not the route we have chosen. In contrast we have tried to identify improvements to the existing system, i.e. we have been asking about tax reform. In carrying out this task we have been concerned with the implications of changes for equity, efficiency, revenue and production, as should any serious attempt to analyse reform. We have attempted to use theory to structure enquiry in a systematic way.

The role of the theory of optimal taxation in our work has been in developing the basic principles of taxation. What are the appropriate ways of reconciling equity and efficiency? What types of taxes produce particular inefficiencies and should be avoided? What combinations of taxes should be selected for which problems? The understanding of these problems requires a basic grammar of the subject and the theory of optimal taxation provides an essential ingredient in that it examines directly the central issues of equity, revenue and efficiency in production and distribution (see, for example, Stern, 1984, and chapter 3 below).

As we have emphasised, it is important to take a broad view of sources of revenue and government instruments and the techniques we shall develop can be applied to pricing as well as taxation policy. One can think of raising a public-sector price as being closely analogous to raising a tax. Similarly, reducing a subsidy is formally identical to increasing a tax so that price, subsidy and tax reform should be seen as part of the same set of policy questions both conceptually and practically.

We shall pay special attention to the analysis of marginal reform, i.e. small movements from the status quo. A major advantage of such analysis is that it requires less information than that for non-marginal changes since the money impact of a small change in the price of a good on a household is given by the quantity consumed of the good, whereas for a larger change one needs to know something about the demand response. A disadvantage, however, is that one *is* interested in larger changes and hence our analysis will treat both marginal and non-marginal reforms. With their different strengths and weaknesses the two approaches should be seen as complementary.

An important part of our analysis of marginal reforms will be the social marginal cost of revenue associated with a particular instrument, e.g. a tax on a particular good or a range of goods, as with a sales tax or class of tariffs. One would then obtain extra revenue from the source with lowest marginal cost and rearrange existing revenue from higher to lower marginal cost sources. The calculation of social marginal costs requires knowledge both of the distribution of consumption within the population, in order to measure the social impact of a tax change, and of the responsiveness of revenue to a tax change, so as to calculate how much the tax in question has to be changed to raise an extra rupee. An estimate of tax responsiveness requires an estimate of both an aggregate demand system and the level of taxation of each good.

Estimation of the level of taxation of a final good in a system where many taxes fall on intermediate goods can be a complex process which requires knowledge of the input–output system. We have called the element of tax in the price of a final good the effective tax and the calculation of effective taxes has formed a major part of our applied work. The effective taxes are themselves of interest as descriptive statistics in a complex tax structure and they can be valuable in helping a government understand its own tax system.

The simple social marginal cost, as we have described it, represents a useful tool but can provide immediate guidelines only where production distortions are minimal; formally where social opportunity costs of goods, or shadow prices, coincide with producer prices. Where they do not then we have to take account of the implications of reform for the pattern of production and not simply for government revenue. We shall use shadow prices extensively in the analysis of these production implications. Distortions on the production side of an economy, and these are pervasive in most developing countries, should force us to consider explicitly the implications of production rearrangement. Shadow prices are a powerful tool for doing this, whether or not the adjustment of production occurs as the result of a tax reform.

Just as the effective taxes are useful summary statistics in their own right as well as an input into the reform analysis, so also are shadow prices. Hence a major by-product of our work is a set of shadow prices for India and Pakistan. The shadow prices have a very wide range of potential applications in reform problems (see Drèze and Stern, 1988; Ahmad and Stern, 1989; and Ahmad and Ludlow, 1989).

Our approach will therefore be based on both the economic principles of tax design and the analytical methods for the examination of tax reform which we shall develop. Whilst the applications will be primarily to Pakistan, the principles and methods could be applied in a wide range of circumstances and countries. We should emphasize that our approach should not be seen as a radical new departure from the public finance tradition or competitive with it. As we shall see in chapter 3 we are simply developing and applying those themes such as efficiency, equity, revenue and allocation of production which have been central to the subject from Dupuit and Wicksell to Marshall and Pigou to Musgrave and Samuelson.

1.3   Tax issues in Pakistan

In Pakistan the dominant source of tax revenue is indirect taxes. These account for around 80% of total revenue with about half of indirect tax revenue coming from customs. Over the last ten years or so the proportion of tax revenue coming from indirect taxes has fluctuated between 79% and 86% with an upward trend in recent years. The proportion of total revenue coming from customs has varied around 40% (see chapter 2 for further details). The recent past has seen a big increase in surcharges of various kinds as the potential of other sources has become stretched.

Rising current expenditure by the government together with an inadequate tax system has led in the 1980s not only to *ad hoc* tax measures such as surcharges but also to a substantial increase in borrowing and cuts in capital (development) expenditure. From 1980–1 to 1986–7, a period during which growth rates were between $6\frac{1}{2}$ and 7%, current expenditure as a proportion of GDP rose from $15\frac{1}{2}$ to 24% whereas the proportion of tax revenue in GDP fell from 14 to 13% (see chapters 2 and 10 for further details). Whereas in 1980–1 total (tax and non-tax) revenues at 18% exceeded current expenditure by $2\frac{1}{2}$%, thus allowing a contribution to the financing of development expenditure (then around 9%), by 1986–7 a deficit on the government current account of $3\frac{1}{2}$% of GDP had appeared and development expenditure had been cut back to $7\frac{1}{2}$%.

Pakistan has therefore reached a position where tax reform is a matter of some urgency. The tax system is excessively reliant on indirect taxes in general and on customs in particular. It was inherited at independence and has developed through the accretion of *ad hoc* measures in response to pressures for revenue and from particular interests. It is now a system which has little logical coherence, is full of administrative complication and difficulty, and is not delivering the required revenue. If it is not subject to major reform in the near future its deficiencies may become a substantial brake on the impressive growth rates Pakistan has achieved in the last quarter of a century. Hence, whilst we are concerned to develop principles and methods which can be of general usefulness, we are also interested in providing proposals which might help in confronting the difficulties which Pakistan is now facing.

The major research questions to be examined are dictated by a combination of the practical potential of instruments, and data availability. Our principal investigation is of indirect taxation. We begin the applied work by examining the existing structure. In the analysis, we use information on tax collections and rate structures, by commodity group, at a reasonably disaggregated level. Given the extensive taxation of inputs these have to be matched with data on inter-sectoral flows using input–

output tables. In this way we arrive at an analytic description of the current tax system. The evaluation of potential reforms also requires estimates of household responses as well as an assessment of the relation between market prices and opportunity costs. Much of our research programme was therefore directed towards constructing the 'building blocks': describing the tax system; estimating demand responses; and preparing a system of shadow prices. Not all of this work is reported in this book, however, and interested readers will be directed to papers describing the 'building blocks', which have some interest in their own right.

As much less information exists in Pakistan on the direct taxes, including the personal income tax and the corporate income, or corporation, tax, we have had to fall back on fairly general economic principles in guiding the discussion and in organising our recommendations. A major set of recommendations involves the use of presumptive methods for hard-to-tax groups and where income estimates are likely to be unreliable. The direct taxation of land, and income from land, is a major topic of interest in Pakistan. We have again used a combination of historical analysis and economic principles in organising the discussion around the limited data on land ownership that are available.

1.4 International perspectives

The revenue systems of countries of the sub-continent have a number of features in common with those of many other developing countries. These are, notably, low shares of taxation in GDP compared to developed and many developing countries, increasing demands on revenue, low contribution of income taxes and a heavy dependence on indirect taxes, particularly trade taxes. There is, however, enormous variety within developing countries in their taxation sources and one must be wary of generalisations. For example, Trinidad and Tobago raises around 34% of its GDP in taxes and around 84% of this revenue comes from income taxes (see Tanzi, 1987). But even here there are similarities with other developing countries in that most of the income tax revenue comes from the corporate income tax rather than the personal income tax.

The diversity is illustrated by an analysis of the sources of revenue of eighty-six developing countries in Tanzi (1987). Tanzi identifies a number of broad relationships within this diversity. First, there is a tendency for tax to GDP ratios to increase with GDP per capita. Second, the tax structure is also related to GDP per capita with the income tax to GDP ratio increasing with GDP per capita. The import tax to GDP ratio, on the other hand, declines with GDP per capita, notwithstanding the positive relation between the import to GDP ratio and GDP per capita. There is also a negative relation between the use of trade taxes and domestic indirect taxes (as measured by tax to GDP ratios).

It will be interesting (see chapter 9) to compare the picture for Pakistan with that for India. Both were subject to the same tax system prior to partition in 1947. The two tax systems still have a number of features in common, with a similar legal basis, and a heavy dependence both on indirect taxes, and within indirect taxes, on customs/trade taxes and excises on domestic production. Both customs and domestic excises involve heavy taxation of productive inputs with important cascading effects through the system and associated efficiency problems. The two countries have also a concern to protect domestic industries.

There are, however, important differences. First, as India's productive base has grown the importance of the excises on domestic production has increased, and they now raise more revenue than the tariffs. Second, India has a stronger system of regional finance than Pakistan, with the Indian constitution giving a clear demarcation of certain taxes to the States and others to the Centre. In India, in contrast to Pakistan, the constitution has represented a tight constraint on governmental fiscal strategies. In particular the excise tax in India is a federal tax, whereas responsibility for sales taxation is with the States. Because of this political division, the growth of domestically based taxation, which has been driven by the Centre, has shown a concentration on excise taxes relative to sales taxes. The economic advantage of sales taxes, that they do not fall so heavily on inputs, would have pointed the other way. Third, India has begun, in a small way, a process of reform with the introduction of MODVAT or modified value-added tax which allows some rebating of the domestic excise paid on inputs. Fourth, India has increased the proportion of tax to GDP to higher levels than Pakistan. Fifth, India has resorted to domestic and foreign borrowing substantially less than Pakistan.

The problems and issues that we shall be examining are common to many developing countries and where, as in the centrally planned economies, the issue of tax and price reform is of central importance. And the economic principles and techniques of analysis we shall use are general. Hence we trust that our approach and conclusions will also be of interest outside the sub-continent.

1.5 The purposes and plan of the book

Our first purpose in this book, as already indicated above, is to develop, and demonstrate at work, a set of economic principles and methods for the applied analysis of tax problems. The second is to provide a set of proposals for tax reform in Pakistan. The combination of these two purposes requires a close involvement with the detail of the theory and with the tax systems and economy of Pakistan, and, to a lesser extent, India. We have tried to avoid unnecessary detail but have not omitted technical discussion where we regard it as an essential part of our purpose. We believe that all of the book should be easily accessible to the professional economist and graduate student. Those with less familiarity with technical economics should be able to understand most of the discussion and certainly the essence of the arguments and conclusions, which we have tried to explain using intuitive economic reasoning throughout.

The issues with which we have been concerned are central to policy, and it is these that have generated the detailed analysis. The aspects on which we have focused, that is, efficiency, equity, revenue and production, are inescapable for any serious analysis of taxation and the difficulties and complexities that arise flow from trying to establish the consequences of policies in these terms. We have, however, tried to find ways of cutting through these wherever we can.

The structure of the book follows from its purposes: first, to present a set of general principles and methods for the analysis of reform and, second, to examine possible strategies for reform of the tax system in Pakistan. The next chapter describes the tax system of Pakistan, its development and its problems. The following three chapters provide principles and methods. Chapters 6 to 8 describe the empirical analysis. Chapter 3 contains a review and development of the basic principles of taxation. We show how these may be put to work both in terms of organising a framework for data for applied investigations and as pointers to problems of the existing structure together with guidelines for new structures. We pay particular attention to the trade-offs between equity and efficiency, the appropriate relationship between direct and indirect taxation, and the arguments for and against the uniformity of indirect taxation. A second major theme is the effect of tax reform on the productive structure, and the concept, and use, of social opportunity costs or shadow prices in the analysis. We discuss dynamic aspects of taxation and contrast our methods with those of others. The chapter concludes with a set of simple canons for taxation which arise from the theory.

Chapter 4 is concerned with an application of the principles of taxation to agriculture and a consideration of the special difficulties raised. We focus on the role of the pricing of agricultural inputs and outputs as tools of taxation, the problems and desirability of income and land taxation and the role of the exchange rate.

In chapter 5 we examine the specific problems of the direct use of the theory presented in chapters 2 and 3 in applied work. We develop the concept of 'effective taxes', which summarise the impact of the taxation of intermediate goods on final goods, and describe the method adopted for the calculation of shadow prices. We show how household data can be put to use in the examination of the distributional impact of tax changes. The social marginal cost of public funds is examined in detail and we show how it can be applied to different classes of taxes. The problems of measuring the impact of non-marginal reforms are examined and we set out some problems for further work.

The concepts and techniques developed in chapter 5 are applied in chapter 6 where we present calculations of effective taxes for Pakistan and a set of shadow prices. These calculations provide tools of substantial interest in their own right, whether or not they are applied to tax reform, and some of their implications are discussed. Their application to tax reform is presented in chapter 7 where we first employ the concept of the social marginal cost of funds to identify improving directions of marginal reform for indirect taxes. We go on to develop and analyse non-marginal reforms of indirect taxes in terms of different versions of a VAT for Pakistan.

Chapter 8 is devoted to a particular, but important, problem – the taxation of land. We analyse the relative decline of revenue from this source and the problems for the general tax system associated with the treatment (or rather exclusion) of agricultural income in the tax base. We then develop a number of possible schemes for the taxation of land, describe their possible impact and assess their advantages and disadvantages.

In chapter 9 we contrast the position of Pakistan with that of a number of other countries on which we have worked, particularly India, Bangladesh and Mexico. We also set the problems of Pakistan in a broader international context. In so doing we attempt to bring out the similarities as well as the differences in a way which can help in preparing proposals for reform for Pakistan. Chapter 10 contains an analysis of alternative sources of revenue for Pakistan in the medium term. To do this we assemble a package of reforms which arise naturally from the detailed analysis of particular problems in earlier chapters. We show that there are indeed ways of overcoming many of the incentive, distributional and administrative problems of the existing system whilst at the same time raising sufficient revenue to alleviate the severe and growing budgetary problems. In chapter 11 we identify problems for further research and draw together the lessons concerning general principles, practical methods of tax analysis and the reform of Pakistan's tax system.

2 The structure of taxation in Pakistan and its historical background

2.1 Introduction

In Pakistan, as in the other countries of the sub-continent, there is a tension between the expenditures that have evolved over some forty years of independent governance and the ability of successive administrations to raise the requisite revenues. This has much to do with the limitations of the tax instruments inherited from the immediate colonial past. These instruments may have been appropriate for a government with low revenue requirements, concentrating on administration and defence. The independent governments, however, had more ambitious objectives, particularly concerning the promotion of development. 'Development investment' became an important concept and claim on public funds.

In the post-colonial period, with the unabated emphasis on defence and administration, the perceived requirements of development investment have placed growing pressure on an increasingly inadequate set of revenue instruments. Indeed, as we shall see, excessive reliance on convenient tax 'handles' to raise revenue, such as import duties, can have a perverse impact on the promotion of the activities the expenditure was designed to promote. In this chapter we examine the evolution of the set of existing tax instruments. Further, we look at some of its problems and ask how it could bear the burden of raising additional revenues. We go on to assess how it might be reformed, from the point of view of equity, incentives and production, and administrative feasibility. These are not necessarily objectives that might be espoused by a colonial administration. Unfortunately, given inertia and special pressure groups, it is by no means certain that the systematic development of a tax strategy with respect to these objectives would be pursued by independent governments either.

In section 2.2 we examine how the tax system evolved prior to independence. The importance of the land tax declined and there was increasing use of other tax instruments: customs, excises and taxes on sales

Table 2.1. *National income and public expenditure and revenue in British India, 1900–1 to 1946–7*

	Public expenditure (Rs million)[b]	Total revenues (Rs million)	As percentage of national income[a]			
			Public expenditure	Total current revenues	Tax revenues	Non-tax revenues
1900–1	958	817	10	8	6	3
1917–8	2 845	1 397	16	8	5	3
1921–2	2 132	1 516	8	6	5	1
1930–1	2 086	1 692	12	10	7	2
1940–1	2 149	2 061	11	10	7	3
1946–7	7 973	5 942	16	12	9	3

Notes: [a] The national income of British India has been calculated from the per capita national income at current prices for undivided India given by S. Sivasubramoniam and the population of British India given by K. N. Reddy.
[b] Public expenditure is the total of central and state government expenditure on current and capital account, as shown in the budget. The figures include interest payments and retirement of the public debt, but exclude the bulk of expenditure on the railways (for which there was a separate budget after 1925).
Source: Kumar (1982), table 12.6, p. 926.

and on income. We also discuss the question of multi-level finance and the allocations of tax instruments to provincial governments to meet expenditure requirements. The historical background is then contrasted in section 2.3 with the pattern of taxation that has evolved in Pakistan since independence. The present position differs in some important aspects from the inherited system, although that pattern still exerts a dominant influence. Section 2.4 contains concluding comments.

2.2 Historical background

During the nineteenth century, and until independence in 1947, with the exception of the period of the two world wars, tax revenues in British India were of the order of 5 to 7% of the national income (see Kumar, 1982). The colonial administration was loath to increase direct taxation, and was especially sensitive to the interests of particular groups such as landowners, on whom it relied for support and whom it considered its allies. In this section we examine the evolution of the tax system over the past century or so, and trace the development of tax instruments as a response to perceived and changing needs.

As table 2.1 indicates, whilst tax revenues were between 5 and 7% of national income from 1900 to 1940, public expenditures were higher, and fluctuated more, at around 10% of national income over this period. In the twenty-five years prior to independence, expenditure increased substantially and consequent budgetary difficulties led to a change in the pattern of financing, with a greater reliance on customs duties and excises. The resort to customs and excises in the face of budgetary difficulties was repeated again and again by the independent governments later in the century. Further, with the devolution of certain revenue categories, particularly land revenue, to the Provinces following the Government of India Act of 1919, there was a continued decline in land revenue collections. This accelerated following the Government of India Act of 1935, which led to elected provincial governments for the first time. These governments were keen to mitigate the effects of the Depression, and also to out-manoeuvre their colonial masters at the Centre in the 'popularity' game. This led to a further erosion in the land revenue base. We discuss land revenue, customs, income taxes, domestic commodity taxes and multi-level finance in turn.

2.2.1 Land taxation

From a European perspective (see Habib, 1982) the Mughal kings 'owned' the land and took their 'land revenue' (or *mal*) as their rent. 'The *mal* essentially represented a claim on behalf of the state to a share of the actual

Table 2.2. *The distribution of central and provincial revenue for selected years, 1900–1 to 1946–7[a]*

	Total tax collections[b] (Rs million)	Percentage of total tax revenues					
		Land revenue[c]	Customs[d]	Taxes on Excise	income	Salt	Others
1900–1	575	53	9	10	3	16	9
1917–8	914	36	18	17	10	9	10
1921–2	1 269	27	30	14	15	5	10
1930–1	1 310	23	36	13	12	5	11
1940–1	1 424	19	28	16	19	5	13
1946–7	4 420	7	22	22	37	2	9

Notes: [a] Including the provincial revenue for stamps.
[b] Central and provincial.
[c] Including provincial rates.
[d] A small amount of provincial income tax is included in 'customs'.
Source: Kumar (1982), table 12.7, p. 929.

crop' (Habib, 1982, p. 235). The share was often one-half. In practice, in northern India, the basic unit of assessment was the village and the intermediary, generally the *zamindar*, was given a particular amount to collect. The *zamindar* received in return, revenue-free, large areas of land (Habib, 1982, p. 240).

The *mal* was different from its successor, the British land revenue, at least in principle, in that under the British the rent was fixed on a piece of land irrespective of what was grown. In many districts of Bengal presidency, the land revenue was 'permanently settled' in that it was fixed in 1793 in perpetuity at the level which *zamindars* had paid previously (Kumar, 1982). In contrast most of the Madras presidency was under the '*raiyatwari* system' with settlements made periodically with the *raiyat* or landowner. Land revenue under this system was initially fixed as a share of gross output per acre of land, adjusted according to quality and with remissions for bad harvests. Subsequently, however, in the Madras presidency during the 1850s, it was transformed into a tax of around 35–50% on net produce. In such areas periodic revisions were to be carried out every 20–30 years. In these 'temporarily settled' areas, constant revisions and assessments were considered to be costly in terms of administrative effort and political goodwill. There was thus a consideration of a move towards a form of permanent settlement on Bengal lines, with its fixed cash assessments, throughout British India. It was felt that price changes were not particularly relevant, and even if there were price rises, additional sources of revenue could be found easily. None the less, the idea of permanent settlement throughout the country was dropped in 1883, and in Bengal a recommendation was made in 1938 to abolish permanent settlement. This was not implemented until after the Second World War.

As indicated in table 2.2, the relative importance of land revenue declined from over half the total collections at the turn of the century, to around 7% at the time of independence in 1947. Not only is this decline associated with the increasing importance of other tax instruments, but also it suggests a falling incidence as a proportion of gross agricultural output. While land taxation had remained more or less constant at around 5% of gross agricultural output (which is, incidentally, the rate suggested by the *ushr* legislation in Pakistan in 1980–1; see chapter 8), the incidence declined precipitously when elected provincial assemblies came to power in 1937, and fell to around 2% in 1946–7 (table 2.3). In Pakistan, for 1980–1, land revenue collections were a third of 1% of gross output (see chapter 8, table 8.3 for details).

The discussion of an agricultural income tax is postponed to chapter 8, although we note here that agricultural incomes were not initially exempt when the income tax was introduced in 1860. The income tax is the subject of the next subsection.

Table 2.3. *Land revenue collections in British India*

	Collections (Rs million)	% of gross agricultural output
1900–1	263	5
1921–2	347	3
1931–2	330	5
1937–8	266	4
1940–1	276	3
1946–7	313	2

Source: Kumar (1982), table 12.5, p. 918.

2.2.2 The income tax

The income tax was introduced in the sub-continent, as in the UK, as a temporary measure to meet a financial emergency, for a period of five years from 1860 (see Kumar, 1982, details in this subsection). As mentioned above, agricultural incomes were not exempt, and assessments on land-holders accounted for half of the collections. While there were over 1 million assessees, the administrative costs imposed by bringing in small assessees were thought to have contributed to the experiment's 'administrative and financial failure' (Kumar, 1982, p. 924).

After another brief period of experimentation, 1869–72, the income tax was finally reimposed as a permanent measure in 1886. The rate structure was 2% on incomes above the Rs 500 exemption limit, and 2½% on incomes above Rs 2000. Agriculture was exempted on the grounds that the land tax and cesses already constituted a sufficient burden. Income taxes accounted for 4% of tax collections in 1914.

During the First World War, with a greater need for revenues, higher rates were introduced, but the highest rate, on incomes above Rs 25 000 per annum, was still only 6%. Company profits were also brought into the net. At the end of the war in 1919, income tax collections accounted for 12% of revenues, not substantively different from the 14% of total tax revenues achieved in Pakistan in 1985, with considerably higher rate structures (see section 2.3 for details). During the Second World War, an excess profits tax of 50% was introduced in 1940–1, and this was raised to 66% later.

The 1922 income tax law, which was most detailed in its manifestations and legal provisions, remained in force until 1979, the main changes being in terms of frequent adjustments to rate structure. The essential features however continue to this day. In section 2.3 we describe the rate structure for Pakistan for our reference year, 1984–5, and point to some of the difficulties that have evolved, particularly with respect to administration and coverage of non-salary incomes.

2.2.3 Taxation of trade

With the financial problems of the East India Company and the war of 1857, tariffs were introduced but with more favourable treatment of British suppliers than others. Thus, in 1857, there was a 10% general tariff on manufactured imports, but British manufacturers were liable only to a 5% rate. There was a reversion in 1882 to free trade with the abolition of all import duties except those on salt and alcohol (see Kumar, 1982).

Despite the broadly free trade policy, foreign trade was a major source of revenue in the nineteenth century. This was on account of export duties and monopoly profits on the export of opium to China. This, however, was stopped in 1912–13. A further source of revenue was salt, roughly 30% of consumption being imported and subject to 'countervailing' import duties to match the excise levied on domestic production.

With the reappearance of a budgetary deficit during the First World War, a general tariff of 11% was reintroduced. Continuation of budgetary difficulties in the post-war period led to a proposal in 1921%2 for an increase in the general tariff structure to 15%. By now a Legislative Assembly (under the Government of India Act 1919) was in place. The proposal to increase general tariff rates was rejected by the Assembly on the grounds that the increased revenues were likely to be used to finance increased defence expenditures. A more explicit 'defence surcharge' proposed on imports was, after public pressure, to be withdrawn by the Zia administration in Pakistan almost 65 years later.

Subsequent to the 1919 Government of India Act, the principle of encouraging domestic industry, which had received a fillip during the global interruption of trading patterns during the Great War, was conceded with the establishment of an Indian Fiscal Commission to consider the question of protective tariffs. The commission recommended 'discriminating protection' guided by three criteria: (i) that there should be natural advantages for a particular good; (ii) that the protection should lead to more rapid growth; and (iii) that the protection should be for a predetermined period. The commission sought to allay the fears of the colonial administration with the observation that 'India for many years to come is likely to concentrate on the simpler forms of manufactured goods, and these are precisely those in which the UK has the smallest interest.' A tariff board, established in 1923, examined numerous claims for protection. This was granted to nine industrial sectors for a ten-year period (1929–39). These sectors were: steel, cotton textiles, sericulture, paper, sugar, silver thread and wire, magnesium chloride, heavy chemicals and matches.

It was, however, realised very quickly that tariffs were an attractive and simple tax handle for governments with revenue shortfalls. An increase in the general tariff level led to greater protection in 1930. The sub-continent subsequently became embroiled in a trade war between the UK and Japan. In 1931, non-UK cotton textiles were subjected to a 31.25% tariff, against 25% for UK imports. During the subsequent year discriminating tariffs on non-UK textile imports were raised to 50%, and again to 75% following a depreciation of the yen. All these events tended to reinforce the expectation of a protected environment, as far as domestic manufacturers were concerned.

2.2.4   Excises

In the latter half of the nineteenth century, salt taxes contributed around 10% of revenues and excises 5% (Kumar, 1982, p. 916). Collections from opium contributed around 15% of revenue but declined in the early twentieth century after exports to China were stopped in 1912–13. During the twentieth century revenue from salt taxes declined (see table 2.1) and excises rose. The rise in excises during the two wars was particularly sharp.

The main source of revenue from excises in the nineteenth century was alcohol. Countervailing duties on domestic production of cloth were introduced at the end of the nineteenth century largely as a result of pressure from the Lancashire industry against the Indian import tariffs. During the Second World War there was a substantial contraction in imports, and thus in customs revenue, which the government tried to make up by levying excises on protected industries: cloth, sugar, matches and steel. The levy on motor spirits, introduced to curtail consumption, became permanent. The excise revenue from alcohol continued to grow along with consumption. Excise revenue surged again during the Second World War, as with the First, and replaced lost customs duties. Tobacco taxes were not imposed until 1943 because the prevailing method of production was small scale and the government saw administrative problems in collection.

2.2.5   Intergovernmental finance

Arrangements for the devolution of taxation came in the train of the Government of India Act of 1919, which led to the establishment, in 1921, of legislative assemblies (LAs) at the Centre and in the Provinces. Further elaboration and modifications were introduced in the Government of India Act of 1935, which formed the basis for the charge of various taxes.

Under the Government of India Act of 1919, the central LA was to be concerned with defence and external trade. The central LA was empowered to meet military expenditures for the defence of the realm and sources of revenue for the central government were to be the income tax and contributions from the Provinces. With respect to external trade, the main policy instruments were to be tariffs and exchange rates.

Provincial LAs were given control over education, health and agricultural development as well as protective irrigation and famine relief. Revenue instruments under the provincial legislatures included land revenue, since this was closely associated with rural administration, excises on liquor, stamp duties and irrigation charges.

A feature of the 1919 Act was the set of *provincial contributions* to central revenues. The Meston Settlement of 1920 defined these contributions in terms of capacity to pay based on population and wealth, after deducting from contribution liability the receipts of income tax already incurred. Punjab, UP and Madras accounted for 78% of the provincial contributions and Bombay and Bengal 75% of the income tax collections.

The 1935 Government of India Act, while maintaining the distribution of powers between the Centre and the Provinces over various tax instruments, none the less led to important variations in the inter-governmental flow of resources. The proceeds of the central taxes, income taxes and export duties were to be divided between the Centre and Provinces according to an allocation to be determined by the Centre. This arrangement has continued in independent India, where under the Constitution, a Finance Commission is constituted every five years to determine the allocation of the divided taxes, grants-in-aid and other financial arrangements.

In order to safeguard its expenditures, under the Government of India Act of 1935, the central government was entitled to a lump-sum from the income tax and railway contributions before the sharing arrangements came into play. Of the divided taxes, the income tax was the most important, with 50% of the proceeds being distributed to the Provinces in fixed proportions, depending on the allocation of taxpayers, total population, inequalities in benefits and incidence of other taxes. The export duties on jute were apportioned such that the jute-growing provinces received 62.5% of such revenues. Further, a system of subsidies was instituted for a number of backward provinces for periods ranging from five to ten years. These provinces included Sind, NWFP, Orissa, Assam and UP.

The Government of India Act of 1935 came in the wake of the recession, which had had a major impact on revenue sources. There had been a precipitous drop in land revenues, as well as in provincial excises and the income tax, all of which formed the base for provincial budgets. On the other hand, there had been an increase in imports and associated customs duties, with the result that central revenues had remained buoyant. The imbalance in provincial finances was exacerbated by the coming to power, for the first time under colonial rule, of popularly elected ministries at the provincial level in 1937. There was a concerted move to cancel arrears on account of land revenue that had built up since the recession and to reduce payments. This reduced provincial revenues considerably. Further, the provincial governments were in large measure part of an independence movement in opposition to the 'colonial' central government. Thus the provinces were not particularly inclined to impose additional taxation of any sort.

There are political tensions involved in a multi-level system of government, particularly when the governments concerned are of differing political persuasions, with an incentive to maximise transfers or grants-in-aid from the federal level. This perhaps explains the decline in the relative importance of the land revenue, and the reluctance of 'popularly elected' representatives to impose a tax with clear incidence on their constituencies, when it would be politically more desirable to wheedle funds from the Centre. Further, colonial administrations and military governments have been wary of taxation that might erode support from powerful interest groups. Given the complexion of successive governments and military administrations in post-independence Pakistan, the influence of the landed classes is hard to overestimate. And whilst Finance Commissions in India are required to reconsider central–provincial finances every five years, and the deliberations and recommendations are made public, the system in Pakistan is very much more *ad hoc* and secretive, and without clear guidelines or a consensus of opinion. Intergovernmental finance is not a major focus of this book, but we recognise its importance, and some of our recommendations, particularly with respect to the devolution of the land tax to the local level (there is more on this subject in later chapters), are likely to have implications for the system of local responsibilities and federal transfers.

2.3 The structure of taxation in Pakistan in the mid-1980s

The basis for the tax system of Pakistan remains the Government of India Act of 1935, and the tax instruments inherited from the British. The one major change was the transfer to the central government, soon after independence, of the power to tax sales. This has remained a provincial prerogative in India and, as we shall argue later, has proved to be a straitjacket restricting the adaptation of the tax system to the needs of a modern economy in India. Notwithstanding this constraint, there have been serious attempts at identifying and rectifying the deficiencies of the inherited tax system in India, which Pakistan has failed to undertake. The Pakistan tax system has evolved as a series of *ad hoc* measures dictated largely by short-term pressures and the immediate convenience and relative ease with which extra revenues can be generated. Despite some additional complications relating to the trade regime and the structure of protection, the Pakistan tax system retains the essential characteristics and problems of the framework arising from the Government of India Act of 1935.

In the following subsections, we trace the effects of various tax instruments and their manifestations in the recent past. In so doing we do not wish to replicate the descriptive details which may be found, for instance, in the Reports of the Taxation Commissions of, say, the mid-1970s or the mid-1980s (see Government of Pakistan, Ministry of Finance, 1974, and National Taxation Reform Commission, 1986). Our purpose is to focus on the background so as to provide the basis for the analytical discussion of the system in later chapters.

In subsection 2.3.1 we describe the overall structure, with particular reference to recent years, how revenues have moved over time, problems of collection and particular events. Individual tax handles are considered in successive subsections: the taxation of income, customs duties, and domestic indirect taxes, including excises and the sales tax. A brief discussion of multi-level finance is followed by some comments on tax buoyancy in Pakistan and on the prospects for revenue.

2.3.1   *Revenues over time and in an international context*

At independence, Pakistan had a relatively low level of tax collections as a proportion of national income (see table 2.1 above). The increase of collections from 9% in 1960–1 to 12.5% by 1970–1 was closely related to the changing structure of the economy, permitting higher collections from excises and particularly from customs duties.

Collections have, however, stabilised at around 12–13% of GDP over the last two decades. This can be seen in table 2.4, although the overall figures mask a changing composition of taxation in Pakistan. Striking features during the 1980s have been the declining contributions of income taxes (down from 21% of tax collections in 1981–2 to 14% in 1985–6) and of domestic taxation (excises declined from 31% of tax collections to 23% in the same period). The fact that tax collections have nevertheless remained constant as a proportion of GDP is largely because of a greater reliance on customs duties, the contribution of this tax instrument

Table 2.4. *Pakistan*: *Total tax/GDP ratio, 1975–6 to 1986–7*

	GDP (market prices) (Rs million)	Total tax revenue[a] (Rs million)	Tax revenue/GDP (%)
1975–6	121 423	15 544	12.8
1976–7	149 748	17 759	11.9
1977–8	176 419	21 585	12.2
1978–9	195 109	25 008	12.8
1979–80	234 528	32 507	13.9
1980–1	277 961	38 846	14.0
1981–2	321 840	43 003	13.4
1982–3	362 165	49 029	13.5
1983–4	418 201	53 646	12.8
1984–5	477 982	55 963	11.7
1985–6	547 126[b]	68 900[b]	12.5
1986–7	608 145[b]	79 000	12.9

Notes: [a] Total tax revenue refers to the consolidated tax revenues of the federal and provincial governments.
[b] Estimates reported in World Bank (1989a), Pakistan, *Medium-Term Economic Policy Adjustments*.
Source: Government of Pakistan, Ministry of Finance, *Economic Survey*, 1986–7.

increasing from 38% of tax collections to 42% over the same period (in 1987–8 customs duties were still 41% of revenues, or Rs 38.3 billion, as reported in the Budget Speech of 5 June 1989).

The reliance on import duties for raising extra revenue has led to a number of problems. Frequent rate increases have made it difficult for producers and officials to understand and forecast the structure of protection and incentives. They have also encouraged evasion and thereby weakened intended protection. The narrow base of domestic indirect taxation and the inadequacies of direct tax instruments have limited the degree of manoeuvre of the government in raising revenue in response to increasing expenditures, thus leading to a resort to customs as an apparently easy option. As we shall argue, it is a response which is short-sighted, will not be feasible indefinitely and is already damaging.

This introduction to the current tax system suggests major questions for the analysis of reform. Domestic indirect taxes and the set of direct taxes should be examined closely to see whether they can provide an administratively more buoyant and efficient framework for equitable sources of revenue. The structure of customs duties and trade taxes should also be examined with respect to similar criteria. In this regard, the experience of

Table 2.5. *Federal tax structure of Pakistan, 1976–7 to 1985–6*

	1976–7	1977–8	1978–9	1979–80	1980–1	1981–2	1982–3	1983–4	1984–5	1985–6
	(Rs million)									
Tax revenue										
Direct taxes	2 569	2 733	3 349	5 121	7 148	8 449	8 949	9 497	9 619	9 880
Income and corporate	2 497	2 655	3 266	5 000	7 000	8 250	8 750	9 292	9 400	9 712
Wealth tax	36	40	42	80	100	150	152	160	172	108
Gift tax	7	8	9	9	10	6	12	10	12	
Estate duty	7	6	7	5	5	5				
Workers welfare tax	23	24	25	27	33	38	35	35	35	60
Indirect taxes	12 930	16 558	19 642	25 214	29 986	31 235	38 421	46 864	48 002	58 508
Customs	5 696	7 945	10 000	12 600	14 385	14 999	19 002	21 700	22 605	28 586
Sales tax	1 270	1 614	1 846	2 331	3 188	3 250	3 400	4 100	4 752	5 038
Federal excise	4 889	6 184	6 792	9 483	10 709	12 150	13 373	16 333	15 705	15 700
Stamps			3	4	5	7	11	16	9	13
Surcharges	1 075	816	1 001	796	1 699	829	2 635	4 715	4 932	9 171
Total tax revenue	15 499	19 291	22 990	30 335	37 134	39 684	47 370	56 361	57 621	68 388
Percentages of total tax revenue										
Direct taxes	17	14	15	17	19	21	19	17	17	14
Income and corporate	16	14	14	16	19	21	18	16	16	14
Indirect taxes	83	86	85	83	81	79	81	83	83	86
Customs	37	41	43	42	39	38	40	39	39	42
Sales tax	8	8	8	8	8	8	7	7	8	7
Federal excise	32	32	30	31	29	31	28	29	27	23
Surcharges	7	4	4	3	5	2	6	8	9	13

Source: Government of Pakistan, Ministry of Finance, *Economic Memoranda to the Budget* (various years).

Table 2.6. *Pakistan's tax collection in an international context*

| | Pakistan | All countries in sample | Per capita income ($) | | | |
			0–349	350–849	850–1699	1700+
% of GDP						
Customs	5.46	5.02	4.94	6.62	5.31	3.19
Sales and VAT	0.91	2.07	1.87	1.43	1.89	3.10
Excises	2.99	1.97	1.64	2.24	1.91	2.16
Income and corporate	1.90	5.60	2.66	5.50	5.75	8.08
	11.26	14.66	11.11	15.79	14.86	16.53
% of total taxes						
Customs	42	31	39	38	29	15
Sales and VAT	7	12	15	9	10	13
Excises	23	12	13	16	11	10
Income and corporate	14	29	20	30	30	36

Note: The data are for the early to mid-1980s.
Source: Table 2.5, Pakistan; Tanzi (1987), international comparisons.

other countries may be a useful guide in the identification of feasible possibilities. It is important not to be mechanistic here – the average outcome for other countries is not necessarily an indication of good directions for Pakistan. If, however, other poor countries manage to overcome difficulties in collection and raise significant revenues under certain heads, one should ask whether it is possible for Pakistan to do the same.

In table 2.6 we set out the contributions of various tax heads to total tax revenue (early to mid-1980s) for groups of developing countries ranked by per capita GNP (from Tanzi, 1987) and compare them with the structure operating in Pakistan in the mid-1980s. A comparison with the average for the poorest group of countries ($0–349 per capita GNP) shows that Pakistan, with a per capita GNP of $350 in 1981 (World Bank, 1983), has a tax/GDP ratio which is not far from the mean of the group. Note that actual ratios may be even lower if GDP is underestimated. This is, however, some way below the 18–19% ratios achieved by India by the late 1970s. The proportion of domestic excises in GDP in Pakistan at 3% is somewhat higher than the average for the poorest group, which stands at 1.6%. On the other hand other poor countries appear to be collecting a substantially higher   proportion   in   both   sales   tax/VAT   and   income/

corporation tax. On this basis there would appear to be scope for considerable improvement under these two heads.

The 'imbalance' *vis-à-vis* customs duties in Pakistan is also highlighted in table 2.6 in that this head contributes more as a proportion of GDP than is the case for the average of the poorest countries. It appears that, for richer developing countries, customs tend to form a lower proportion of total revenues, as there is a greater level of domestic activity that can be brought into the tax net, as well as a more effective system of direct taxation. This is a pattern noted by Hinrichs (1966) and Tanzi (1987). One would expect, however, indirect taxes to remain the predominant source of revenue in a country like Pakistan in the medium term, given the apparent difficulties of collection of direct taxes (see the following subsection). However, there are strong distributional advantages to raising revenue through direct taxes and, in the longer term, there may be administrative advantages as well. As the economy develops, and as formal employment increases and accounting practices improve, it is desirable that greater emphasis be placed on income taxes, and careful forward planning in this direction would be sensible. The reform and expansion of domestic indirect taxes and of direct taxes form the central issues for consideration in the analysis of the Pakistan tax system.

2.3.2 Income and corporation tax and direct taxes

A number of direct taxes have been in place in Pakistan during the past forty years. *Estate duties* were introduced in 1950 but have since been withdrawn. The *gift tax* was imposed as a federal charge in 1963, but was made a provincial tax under the 1973 Constitution; it was abolished in 1985. While *capital gains* remain taxable in principle, the provisions are in abeyance. Thus, the major extant direct taxes are the income and corporation tax and the wealth tax. In this book we concentrate on the former.

While there have been a number of changes in the income tax provisions, these relate mainly to rate structure and exemptions, and the current law under the Income Tax Ordinance of 1979 is not dissimilar in principle to the Income Tax Act of 1922 which it replaced. The tax is intrinsically global and applies to the total income of a person from all sources, unless specifically exempted, at rates to be specified in annual Finance Acts. A person is defined to include an individual, a firm, an association of persons, a body of individuals whether or not incorporated, a company or any other juridical person. One of the main exemptions, in place since the British days (with the exception of an experiment in 1977; see chapter 8), relates to income from agricultural activities and land.

Table 2.7. *Rate structure of the income tax, fiscal years 1984 and 1985*

	Range (Rs)	Marginal rate (%)
Fiscal year 1984		
Basic exemption limit	18 000	0
Band 1 (taxable income)	< 10 000	10
Band 2	≥ 10 000 < 15 000	20
Band 3	≥ 15 000 < 20 000	25
Band 4	≥ 20 000 < 25 000	30
Band 5	≥ 25 000 < 30 000	35
Band 6	≥ 30 000 < 45 000	45
Band 7	≥ 45 000 < 70 000	50
Band 8	≥ 70 000 < 100 000	55
Band 9	≥ 100 000	60
Fiscal year 1985		
Basic exemption limit	24 000	0
Band 1 (taxable income)	< 25 000	5
Band 2	≥ 25 000 < 50 000	15
Band 3	≥ 50 000 < 100 000	25
Band 4	≥ 100 000 < 200 000	35
Band 5	≥ 200 000	45

Source: Government of Pakistan, Ministry of Finance, *Economic Memoranda to the Budget*, 1984 and 1985.

The combined income and corporation tax collections, as shown in table 2.5, have been of the order of 14% of tax collections, or around 1% of GDP during the mid-1980s. Within this tax head, however, the personal income tax forms a relatively small proportion of revenue collections. While the breakdowns have not been published on a regular basis since the early 1980s, the 1986 National Taxation Reform Commission (NTRC) suggested that for the assessment year 1983–4, 83.4% of the income tax collection (of Rs 10.2 billion) was on account of corporate bodies (NTRC, 1986, p. 21).

Table 2.8. *Summary statement of income and corporation tax, assessment year 1983–4*

Income group Rs	Assessees		Total tax	
	No.	%	Rs million	%
1–25 000	321 287	66.4	70	0.68
25 001–50 000	118 551	24.5	292	2.86
50 001–100 000	28 656	5.9	377	3.69
100 001–	15 594	3.2	9 477	92.77
Total	484 088	100.0	10 216	100.00

Source: National Taxation Reform Commission (1986), table 3.1, p. 21.

The personal income tax laws are among the most complex for any tax instrument, and the rate structure is highly differentiated. Clearly, there is a problem with implementation and revenue collections. The 1986 NTRC estimates (pp. 103–4) that, on the basis of the National Accounts (which themselves are likely to be biased downwards), Rs 50.8 billion escaped assessment as against the Rs 19.3 billion which was covered by the tax net. Whilst this kind of estimate must be treated with some caution it does seem likely that the degree of evasion is very high.

It has been argued that part of the problem with personal income taxation in Pakistan is that there have been too many taxable bands and that the top marginal tax rates have been too high, thus encouraging evasion and increasing administrative complexity. In fiscal year (FY) 1984, there were nine bands, in addition to an exemption limit of Rs 18 000, with the top marginal rate at 60%. A simplification during FY 1985 reduced the top marginal tax rate to 45%, with five bands and an exemption limit of Rs 24 000. While we would agree that a simplification of rate structures is desirable in principle, by itself it is unlikely to lead to greater compliance when the local culture is one that encourages tax evasion. The two most substantial issues appear to be the exemptions, which severely reduce the tax base, and compliance and administration, which are probably of over-riding importance. Both of these aspects were covered in some detail by the 1986 NTRC. Whilst administrative reform is not our major topic, here we share the concern of the NTRC and commend their discussion.

The distribution of income and corporation tax payments for the assessment year 1983–4 has been described by the NTRC. Of the total tax collections 92.8% were realised from the 3.2% of assessees whose taxable incomes were above Rs 100 000. The majority of taxpayers, 90.9%, fell below the Rs 50 000 level and contributed only 3.5% of the total tax

Table 2.9. *Incidence of income taxes on individuals, assessment year 1983–4*

Income group Rs	Assessees		Total tax	
	No.	%	Rs million	%
1–25 000	313 855	71.2	61	5.0
25 001–50 000	101 360	23.0	236	19.5
50 001–100 000	18 925	4.3	285	23.5
100 001–	6 748	1.5	630	52.0
Total	440 888	100.0	1 212	100.0

Source: National Taxation Reform Commission (1986), table 3.10, p. 24.

collection (see table 2.8). For the personal income tax, the 1.5% of the assessees whose incomes were above Rs 100 000 contributed over half of the assessments (see table 2.9). On the other hand 94% of assessees had incomes below Rs 50 000, contributing only 24% of the revenue, but generated considerable bother and cost in terms of tax administration.

It is clear then that income and corporation tax collections are largely on account of the tax liabilities of companies. Table 2.10a shows that over 11 000 companies were assessed in 1984–5 for a tax liability of Rs 9.4 billion, 64% of the collections being on account of domestic public and foreign companies or around 11.2% of the assessments. As table 2.10b suggests, almost half of the collections were from only 175 companies, the majority (136) being public limited companies or multinationals. Thus a major proportion of the combined income and corporation tax collections may be ascribed to a handful of companies – the elaborate legal superstructure notwithstanding.

The 1986 Finance Bill also introduced modifications in the corporate tax structure. The basic rate of income and supertax for companies quoted on the stock exchange was reduced from 55 to 40%. Further, dividends from such companies were exempted from the personal income tax (although subject to the 40% corporate rate). Private companies, however, were not affected by these changes. Their income was subject to tax at the 55% rate, and dividends were also subject to the personal income tax rate of the recipient.

An important loophole in the operation of the income tax is the *de facto* suspension of the capital gains tax. It was (correctly) perceived that in the absence of proper indexation, the tax had become iniquitous and open to much abuse, but rather than modifying the provisions to allow for proper

Table 2.10a. *Tax assessment of companies, assessment year 1984–5*

	Assessments		Total tax	
	No.	%	Rs million	%
Domestic Public Companies (including Ltd. Companies)	947	8.3	5 272	56.1
Foreign Companies	368	3.2	747	7.9
Domestic Private Ltd. Companies	9 866	86.7	3 286	34.9
Others	194	1.8	101	1.1
Total	11 375	100.0	9 406	100.0

Source: Computer Wing of the Income Tax Department; NTRC (1986), table 3.2, p. 22.

Table 2.10b. *Tax contribution by major taxpayers, assessment year 1984–5*

		Total tax		Average tax contribution (Rs million)
	No.	Rs million	%	
Multinational companies	23	381.0	9.7	16.5
Public companies (inclusive of 42 govt. sponsored)	113	3 143.2	80.2	27.8
Private companies	39	401.1	10.2	10.3
Total	175	3 925.3	100.0	

Source: Computer Wing of the Income Tax Department; NTRC (1986), table 3.3, p. 23.

indexation, it was decided to suspend the tax altogether. Thus income can be legally converted into capital gains to avoid the payment of income tax. This is used by those with sufficient funds and knowledge, thus accentuating the incidence of the tax on the middle class. On the other hand, it must be recognised that the taxation of capital gains is problematic in most countries and one cannot count on large revenues from this source.

Another major loophole is the exemption of agricultural incomes. This is less common from an international perspective, seems to be widely exploited and, if the will is there, can be closed. It provides an opportunity for those with land to declare non-agricultural incomes as accruing from

Table 2.11. *Pakistan major imports*

Sector	1969–70	1974–5	1975–6	1976–7	1977–8	1978–9	1979–80	1980–1	1981–2	1982–3	1983–4	1984–5	1985–6
							(Rs million)						
Chemicals	91	392	483	550	648	815	895	2413	2699	3423	4587	5604	6610
Drugs and medicines	62	253	272	348	513	601	751	936	1222	1390	1800	1974	2245
Dyes and colours	54	266	280	281	363	311	392	462	493	578	613	682	729
Chemical fertiliser	282	1022	558	624	1048	2808	2711	3537	893	2117	1539	1790	2079
Electrical goods	219	1187	1189	1302	1594	1699	1804	1915	1687	2079	2391	2477	3114
Machinery (non-electrical)	709	2071	2797	3312	4147	4251	5590	5684	6845	9312	10828	13437	14955
Transport equipment	340	1227	1353	2016	1635	2474	4903	4686	5170	5424	6307	7816	9178
Paper, board and stationery	35	522	270	341	378	493	608	741	922	1054	1172	1559	1626
Tea	1	664	617	752	1258	1000	954	1184	1091	1676	2567	3507	2175
Sugar (refined)	—	—	—	1	1	3	494	473	1	14	—	—	930
Art-silk yarn	3	173	127	117	804	1138	1547	1301	1570	1607	1586	1586	1321
Iron, steel and manufactures thereof	361	2054	1699	1881	2660	2668	2992	2779	4163	4475	4096	3935	4355
Non-ferrous metal	67	416	119	339	344	327	484	582	638	647	677	934	862
Petroleum and products	208	3334	3744	4083	4918	5247	10685	15199	18046	20529	19161	21763	16775
Edible oils	77	1360	1047	1478	1553	2953	2295	2625	3450	3670	6516	6954	6129
Grains, pulses and flours	56	2470	1792	665	1339	3507	1050	637	806	880	866	2910	5067
Other imports	720	3514	4118	4922	4612	6093	8774	8390	9786	9276	12000	12845	12795
Total	3285	20925	20465	23012	27815	36388	46929	53544	59482	68151	76707	89778	90946

Source: Government of Pakistan, Federal Bureau of Statistics, *Monthly Statistical Bulletin* (various).

agriculture. Plugging this loophole should not only provide direct collections from agriculture but also improve income tax collections outside agriculture. Steps were taken in the 1988 Finance Bill to discourage declaration of non-agricultural income as if it were from agriculture.

The incomes of those working in the agricultural sector are, in one way or another, subject to different forms of taxation or subsidy (see also chapter 4). These involve subsidy (or taxation) of inputs, control of the price of outputs (in part through the exchange rate for those goods which are traded on world markets), and through indirect taxes on expenditures arising from income. These kinds of considerations apply also to those whose income arises from the non-agricultural sector, but there are, in addition, taxes on the corporate and personal incomes arising in this sector. Hence, if for agriculture there are low taxes (and sometimes subsidies) on inputs, and outputs are not taxed more heavily than elsewhere, then someone whose income arises from agriculture is unduly favoured relative to someone whose income arises elsewhere. Further, as we have seen, the exemption of agricultural incomes leads to significant evasion of tax on non-agricultural income.

The question is not, therefore, whether or not agricultural incomes are taxed (one way or another they will be, albeit at times at a negative rate), but by what method and to what extent. At present it seems that the level of taxation operating through the price of output is not significant (although in earlier years there is some evidence that such taxation was prevalent). And there seem to be substantial subsidies operating through certain inputs (e.g. water). On equity grounds, therefore, there seems to be a strong case for raising taxation on incomes accruing from agriculture. And, particularly since the Green Revolution (late 1960s), high incomes from large land holdings are not uncommon in agriculture. Equity suggests that high income in one sector should not be exempt from tax, while lower incomes in other sectors of the economy are subject to fairly high rates of tax. This issue is pursued further in later chapters.

2.3.3   The pattern of trade and customs duties

Particularly since the start of the Second Five-Year Plan at the beginning of the 1960s, Pakistan has followed a policy of import-substituting industrialisation. This has involved the use of direct controls on trade (for a detailed description of the evolution of controls in Pakistan to 1970, see Islam, 1981) in conjunction with the use of tariffs on permitted imports. The pattern of imports that has evolved is thus largely composed of capital goods, intermediate goods, raw materials and essential food items such as grain, edible oils and tea (see table 2.11).

Table 2.12. *Protection structure in Pakistan, 1986*

4-digit product category	Prohibited	Partly prohibited	Restricted	Free of restriction	Total
1 Live animals			1	5	6
2 Meat	6				6
3 Fish	3				3
4 Dairy products	4		3		7
5 Animal products not elsewhere specified	15				15
6 Live trees and plants	4				4
7 Vegetables	6				6
8 Fruits and nuts	11		2		13
9 Coffee and tea	1		9		10
10 Cereals	3		4		7
11 Milling industry products	4	1	2		7
12 Oil seeds		1	8		9
13 Vegetable saps		2			2
14 Vegetable plaiting		1		3	4
15 Fats and oils	1	3	1	10	15
16 Meat preparations	5				5
17 Sugar	1	1		1	3
18 Cocoa preparations	1	1		4	6
19 Cereal preparations	4		1	1	6
20 Vegetable preparations	7				7
21 Miscellaneous edibles	4	1		1	6
22 Beverages	9	1			10
23 Food residues	1	1		5	7
24 Tobacco	1			1	2
25 Salt		1		28	29
26 Metallic ores		2		2	4
27 Mineral fuels			2	14	16
28 Inorganic chemicals				51	51
29 Organic chemicals		10		30	40
30 Pharmaceuticals	1	2		2	5
31 Fertilisers			2	3	5
32 Tanning and dyeing extracts		1		11	12
33 Perfumery		1		2	3
34 Soaps	1	3		3	7
35 Glues		4		3	7
36 Explosives	1	2		3	6
37 Photographic goods			4	3	7

Table 2.12. (*cont.*)

4-digit product category	Prohibited	Partly prohibited	Restricted	Free of restriction	Total
38 Miscellaneous chemicals	1			15	16
39 Plastic materials		7			7
40 Rubber		6	6	4	16
41 Hides and skins				9	9
42 Leather and products	5			1	6
43 Furskins	4				4
44 Wood articles	8	2		15	25
45 Cork articles				4	4
46 Straw manufacture	2				2
47 Paper making materials				2	2
48 Paper and paperboard	3	5	1	8	17
49 Printing materials	2	3		6	11
50 Silk		1		6	7
51 Synthetic fibres		3	1		4
52 Metallised textiles	1	1			2
53 Wool	1	1	1	9	12
54 Flax	1			4	5
55 Cotton	2	1		6	9
56 Synthetic fabrics	1	2	1	3	7
57 Vegetable textiles	1	1	1	4	7
58 Carpets and rugs	9	1			10
59 Ropes	2	8		6	16
60 Knitted goods	6				6
61 Apparel	10				10
62 Other made-up textiles	4	1			5
63 Rags		1		1	2
64 Footwear	6				6
65 Headgear	6	1			7
66 Umbrellas	2			1	3
67 Prepared feather	4				4
68 Stone articles	1	5	2	7	15
69 Ceramic	3	4	3	4	14
70 Glass	2	4	4	10	20
71 Precious stones	10	5	1		16
72 Coin	1				1
73 Iron and steel		11	10	17	38
74 Copper	1	2	2	10	15
75 Nickel				6	6
76 Aluminum		3		11	14
77 Magnesium				3	3

Table 2.12. (*cont.*)

4-digit product category	Prohibited	Partly prohibited	Restricted	Free of restriction	Total
78 Lead				6	6
79 Zinc				5	5
80 Tin				6	6
81 Other base metals				4	4
82 Tools	4	1	7	2	14
83 Misc. articles of base metal	4	4	1	4	13
84 Boilers		11	8	47	64
85 Electrical machinery			10	18	28
86 Railway			1	9	10
87 Vehicles	4	5	2	3	14
88 Aircraft				5	5
89 Ships	1			4	5
90 Optical goods		4	1	24	29
91 Clocks and watches	1	3		7	11
92 Musical instruments		3		9	12
93 Arms	3	4			7
94 Furniture	2	2		4	8
95 Carved articles	1	1			2
96 Brooms, etc.	1	1	1		3
97 Toys	5	3			8
98 Misc. manufactures	4	4		7	15
99 Art	4	1		1	6
Total	227	165	103	519	1012
Share in total (%)	22	16	10	51	100

Source: Government of Pakistan, Central Board of Revenue (1986).

As table 2.12 indicates, of around 1000 types of products at the 4-digit level, 22% are on the prohibited list, and 51% are importable without restriction. It also indicates that even within each 4-digit product category there are commodities which differ in the level of restriction faced, reflecting the fact that there are restrictions which introduce quotas by particular types of users and sources. Thus the scope for import revenue collections is quite circumscribed, not only by the items on the prohibited list, but also by the quotas and duty-free items that are permitted.

The resulting pattern of statutory tariffs is described in table 2.13, for a broad classification of goods. Note that of the nine groups listed in the under-10% tariff category, seven were such that more than 98% of these

Table 2.13. *Summary of Pakistan tariff structure*

Tariff rate (%)	Major items	% of imports
0 to less than 10	Wheat[a]	2.0
	Vegetable oil[a]	9.1
	Crude petroleum[a]	17.0
	Petroleum product[a]	1.3
	Fertiliser[a]	3.6
	Jute fibre	0.9
	Aircraft/parts[a]	2.5
	Insecticides[a]	1.4
	Medicaments	1.7
		39.5
10 *to less than* 50	*Tea*	4.2
	Tallow	1.1
	Organic chemicals	2.7
	Machinery (mechanical)	12.8
	Machinery (electrical)	4.6
	Paper	2.0
	Misc. chemical products	2.0
	Others	2.2
		31.6
50 to less than 100	Artificial resin	2.0
	Rubber	1.3
	Continuous fibre	1.8
	Discontinuous fibre	1.4
	Iron and steel	4.6
	Vehicles	7.4
	Optical–medical equipment	1.6
	Others	1.8
		21.9
100 and over	Betel nuts and betel leaves	0.5
	Others	0.1
		0.6

Note: [a] More than 98% of sectoral imports duty-free.
Source: National Taxation Reform Commission (1986), annexure I, p. 73.

types of imports were duty-free, e.g. wheat, vegetable oils and fertilisers. In all, 57% of all imports into Pakistan in 1983–4 were duty-free.

The consequence of this pattern of prohibition, quotas and duty-free items is that the number of goods which yield import revenues is limited and the level of statutory tariffs is higher than it might otherwise be. Thus, in the case of machinery, import duty rates range from 20 to 80%, for electrical

Table 2.14. *Nominal import duties by sector, 1984–5*

	Import value (Rs million)	Duty collected (Rs million)	Nominal duty %
Meat, fish and prep.	1.37	1.73	126.28
Dairy products	533.45	12.49	2.34
Fruits, nuts, vegetables	570.86	180.70	31.65
Coffee, tea, spices	3 689.16	762.29	20.66
Oilseeds, fruits	275.92	379.68	137.60
Animal, vegetable oils	8 207.91	217.83	2.65
Sugar, confectionery	31.04	18.55	59.76
Cereal, vegetable preps.	3 052.33	79.21	2.60
Beverages, spirits	14.30	2.57	17.97
Tobacco	13.36	55.77	417.50
Mineral, fuels, oils	22 489.34	267.42	1.19
Chemicals and products	10 049.54	742.61	7.39
Pharmaceutical products	1 973.95	5.77	0.29
Dyes, colours, pigments	682.15	474.34	69.54
Perfumery, soap	140.35	107.51	76.60
Matches, explosives	21.99	4.88	22.19
Photo, cinema equipment	273.19	262.80	96.20
Rubber and products	1 010.87	506.53	50.11
Leather and products	107.61	8.14	7.56
Wood pulp, paper	1 817.68	528.38	29.07
Silk yarn, fabrics	29.27	39.45	134.80
Man-made yarn, fabrics	2 541.24	1 585.07	62.37
Cotton yarn, fabrics	436.96	0.68	0.16
Wool, veg. yarn, fabrics	1 179.98	14.97	1.27
Textile articles	586.88	143.46	24.44
Carpets, tapestries	130.42	1.95	1.50
Glass, earthenware	839.01	163.85	19.53
Precious metals, stones	4.72	6.62	140.34
Base metals	933.95	402.03	43.05
Iron, steel manufacture	3 204.77	1 949.82	60.84
Cutlery, tools	943.64	197.45	20.92
Mechanical machinery	13 437.45	1 826.02	13.59
Electrical machinery	2 476.84	1 259.79	50.86
Railway machinery	284.30	20.58	7.24
Transport vehicles	4 551.98	2 153.72	47.31
Ships, boats, aircraft	2 979.49	248.64	8.35
Timepieces and parts	115.56	64.62	55.92
Arms and ammunitions	30.57	17.72	57.97
Toys, games, sport goods	37.03	7.37	19.90
All other articles n.e.s.	1 986.57	5 145.04	258.99

Source: Government of Pakistan, Federal Bureau of Statistics, *Monthly Statistical Bulletin*, September 1986; Government of Pakistan, Federal Bureau of Statistics, *Foreign Trade Statistics*, June 1986.

Table 2.15. *Permissible articles available in smuggled markets*

Betel nuts
Coffee
Cinnamon
Cloves
Cardamom
Tyres and tubes
Hacksaw blades
Spanners, drill wrenches, glass cutters, pliers and pincers
Door locks
Hardware, such as door handles, hinge fittings, door closers
Fuel injection pump parts
Air-conditioners
Crankshafts
Dry battery cells
Spark plugs
Electric bulbs
Crown wheels and pinions
Clutch plates, 12″ and 13″
Rear axle shafts
Master cylinder kits
Clocks
Cassette recorders
Audio cassettes
Revolvers and pistols
Non-prohibited bore guns
Ammunition for non-prohibited bore arms
Toothbrushes
Ballpoint pens and pencils
Gas-lighters

Source: National Taxation Reform Commission (1986), annexure IX, p. 90.

machinery 20 to 125%, and for chemicals 40 to 80%. Nominal rates of duty (defined as the actual duty collected as a proportion of imports), as distinct from statutory rates, are described in table 2.14. We distinguish statutory, nominal and effective when we discuss taxes, tariffs and duties and reserve the last term for cases where allowance is made for input taxes. Nominal rates provide an indication of the extent to which a particular category of goods is taxed allowing for the range of statutory duties, exemptions, actual administration and so on. The pattern in table 2.14 confirms the high tariffs on capital and intermediate goods, as well as on particular final goods such as textiles, clocks, arms and ammunition, rubber products, coffee, spices and betel nuts. It is not surprising that these items were among the 'permitted' articles also available in smuggled markets in Pakistan, as

Table 2.16. *Customs receipts*

	1976–7	1977–8	1978–9	1979–80	1980–1	1981–2	1982–3	1983–4	1984–5	1985–6
					(Rs million)					
Total import duty	5 567	7 890	10 170	12 280	13 939	15 419	17 659	19 965	20 188	21 976
Chemicals and products	240	298	350	388	436	506	579	618	734	753
Dyes, colours, paints	115	147	180	236	246	368	413	404	513	425
Iron, steel and products	700	1 150	1 360	1 993	2 252	2 072	2 361	1 623	1 872	1 903
Machinery	933	1 375	1 530	1 370	1 521	1 793	2 040	2 498	3 196	4 486
Metals other than gold	128	200	250	296	352	294	343	290	418	389
Minerals, fuels, oils	323	208	260	391	440	503	571	222	280	237
Rubber and rubber goods	123	255	260	371	416	517	586	456	521	492
Vehicles	712	770	1 180	964	1 060	1 666	1 900	1 902	2 380	2 580
Wood, pulp and products	128	147	180	262	295	298	357	393	518	486
Yarn and fabric	540	800	1 100	1 694	2 094	2 133	2 448	1 913	1 671	1 385
Other items	1 626	2 540	3 520	4 317	4 827	5 271	6 062	9 647	8 085	8 840
Surcharge on imports							2 650	3 480	4 240	4 218
Iqra surcharge[a]										4 168
Export duty	189	135	130	220	750	310	331	450	425	818
Molasses	20	20	20	40	66	50	27	47	58	28
Raw cotton	1	0	0	0	500	150	250	265	300	669
Hides and skins	100	100	100	10	90	50	27	54	55	32
Rice	58	0	0	0	90	0	0	0	0	0
Other items	10	15	10	170	94	60	27	84	11	89
Sea and land misc.	90	90	100	500	396	470	335	305	412	464
Gross receipts	5 846	8 115	10 400	13 000	15 085	16 199	20 975	24 200	25 265	31 644
Less refunds, etc.	150	170	400	400	700	1 200	1 973	2 500	2 660	3 058
Rebates of import duty	65	100	130	180	350	850	1 315	1 667	2 497	2 871
Other rebates	85	70	270	220	350	350	658	833	163	187
Net receipts	5 696	7 945	10 000	12 600	14 385	14 999	19 002	21 700	22 605	28 586

Note: [a] 'Iqra' surcharge is an earmarked levy to finance education expenditures.

reported by the 1986 NTRC (see table 2.15). The NTRC estimated that smuggling led to around Rs 20 billion in evaded imported duties (during the mid-1980s), 60% of which involved gold. The high rates of duty concentrated on a limited group of commodities constrain the flexibility of the import tariff instrument as an additional source of revenue. Still higher rates are likely to encourage smuggling, and evasion measures such as incorrect invoicing.

Given the pattern of imports into Pakistan (see table 2.17), it is not surprising that the major revenue earners are commodities in the raw materials and intermediate goods sectors. In 1986–7, seven sectors yielded over half a billion rupees each in customs receipts (source as table 2.16). These were (in order of importance) machinery, vehicles, iron and steel and manufactures, yarn and fabrics, chemicals and products, rubber, and wood, pulp and stationery. They accounted for over Rs 11 billion or just under half of the import revenues. Further, of the Rs 8 million collected on account of the *iqra* surcharge (an import surcharge in 1986 earmarked for education) and the other import surcharges, some part must have been due to the above-named sectors. The cumulative effect of this type of import structure and taxation is that the users of such goods, to a large extent other domestic manufacturers (except in the case of vehicles), pass on the costs through higher output prices. Users have to pay more, and exporters in particular, are penalised. Attempts to correct the obvious disadvantages to exporters, through duty drawbacks and the export subsidies, have led to considerable abuse, as noted by the NTRC (1986).

Given the pattern of Pakistan's industrialisation and the heavy reliance on the taxation of imported inputs and intermediate goods, it is no surprise that the pattern of exports is strongly oriented towards rice and raw cotton, with cotton yarn and textiles and carpets and rugs forming the bulk of processed exports. In order to mitigate the effects of the taxation of inputs, compensatory export rebates have been available in the 1979–85 period at rates of 7.5%, 10% and 12.5%. However, the eligibility of a category of items for a given rebate has varied. The award of export rebates, see table 2.18, does not appear to have been based on calculations of the 'effective taxation' through imported or other inputs.

Export duties have not been a major source of government revenues, and have been deployed to capture windfall profits due to occasional sharp increases in international prices. For example, in 1987, fortuitous increases in international prices for rice and cotton provided an opportunity for the government to impose export duties. This helped to reduce an otherwise alarming budget deficit. It would be an error, however, to consider that export duties could remain as a major contributor to government finances over the medium or long term. If such duties are to be matched by subsidies

Table 2.17. Major exports

	1974–5	1975–6	1976–7	1977–8	1978–9	1979–80	1980–1	1981–2	1982–3	1983–4	1984–5	1985–6
						(Rs million)						
Fish and fish preparations	157	279	381	341	462	531	559	790	897	1007	1231	1335
Rice	2304	2479	2478	2409	3380	4179	5602	4128	3683	5688	3340	5527
Hides and skins	46	30	2	—	—	—	23	6	2	5	4	4
Raw wool	20	66	76	73	100	95	50	112	169	171	261	274
Raw cotton	1544	981	292	1102	655	3321	5203	2938	3897	1772	4368	8291
Cotton waste	19	10	24	16	15	19	19	12	82	195	137	85
Leather	367	596	647	637	1247	1264	892	1152	1195	1972	2325	2900
Cotton yarn	851	1422	1172	1060	1956	2038	2050	2075	3146	2931	3974	4511
Cotton thread	57	40	43	71	58	70	101	81	162	116	72	61
Cotton cloth	1313	1359	1603	1741	2135	2416	2390	2949	3579	4856	4638	5082
Petroleum products	139	192	269	626	608	1764	1675	2047	985	543	525	507
Synthetic materials	22	34	36	154	65	54	1272	248	2798	1452	636	802
Footwear	126	66	89	72	97	106	101	100	148	214	248	248
Animal castings	21	35	33	26	31	41	60	57	53	56	69	99
Cement and products	280	51	6	3	—	—	—	—	1	—	—	—
Gur and products	164	197	182	203	273	333	287	305	288	322	341	444
Oil cakes	—	—	2	99	72	41	34	9	9	45	104	37
Paint and varnishes	7	8	10	8	8	9	14	—	—	—	18	10
Tobacco, raw and manufactured	133	160	164	126	101	81	54	106	123	143	158	195
Ready-made garments and hosiery	245	328	418	139	377	731	745	1294	2025	2950	2662	4214
Drugs and chemicals	116	133	134	146	131	122	149	125	128	157	127	84
Surgical instruments	129	131	134	161	211	240	264	252	287	430	774	842
Carpets and rugs	456	719	912	1171	1765	2198	2243	1679	1913	2323	2031	2693
Sports goods	205	189	199	195	212	245	312	320	442	665	674	787
Other exports	1565	1748	1988	2401	2966	3512	5181	5485	8430	9326	9262	10560
Total	10286	11253	11294	12980	16925	23410	29280	26270	34442	37339	37979	49592

Source: Government of Pakistan, Federal Bureau of Statistics, Monthly Statistical Bulletin, various years.

Table 2.18. *Rates of rebate (compensatory) on exportables, 1984–5*

7.5%	10.0%	12.5%
Grey Jersey cloth	Cotton textiles	Artificial leather
Poultry	Canvas goods	Leather goods
Flowers	Blended textiles	Canvas footwear
Fresh fruits	Synthetic textiles	Engineering goods
Acetate yarn		Plastic goods
		Sports goods
		Cutlery
		Surgical instruments
		Carpets
		Canned fruits
		Marble products
		Wooden launches
		Fibre glass
		PVC products

Source: Government of Pakistan, Federal Bureau of Statistics, *Foreign Trade Statistics*, 1985.

when the price is low there will be no long-run revenue. If they are not, then we have essentially an inefficient method of taxing agriculture. For the commodities in question, world markets are quite competitive and it is unlikely in the long term that there is an argument for an export duty to exploit any inelasticity of demand.

One of the major arguments for raising revenue from customs duties is administrative rather than protective. The protection argument should be subjected to very careful scrutiny, as to why the industry in question is likely to show much greater learning-by-doing than others. Given Pakistan's weak administrative record with domestic taxes, customs duties are likely to remain a major source of revenue in the medium term. This is, however, unsatisfactory and the intention should be to reduce the relative importance of customs as revenue from domestic taxation grows.

2.3.4 Excises and surcharges

Excises are the second largest head of revenue in Pakistan, but have declined in relative importance from 29% of total tax revenues in 1983–4 to around 21% in 1986–7 (see Government of Pakistan, 1988a). This tax is more narrowly based than the customs duty, and the top six commodities (in order of importance: tobacco, sugar, oil and petroleum products,

Table 2.19. *Federal excises and surcharges*

	1976-7	1977-8	1978-9	1979-80	1980-1	1981-2	1982-3	1983-4	1984-5	1985-6
					Federal excises (Rs million)					
Vegetable products	601	700	852	1335	1070	733	715	957	985	726
Beverages	105	120	180	300	376	500	700	721	970	857
Tea	64	0	0	0	0	0	0	0	0	0
Sugar	845	904	995	900	1100	1530	1850	2400	2480	2300
Tobacco	1557	1900	2100	2768	3362	3820	4240	5100	5556	5200
Cement	150	436	813	1626	1764	2171	2276	3127	1600	1800
Natural gas	295	320	321	535	700	770	833	800	800	850
Crude oil	0	0	0	0	0	0	0	37	110	360
Petroleum, oil and lubricant products	740	900	950	1090	1112	1218	1330	1542	1500	1700
Paints and varnishes	60	70	75	105	148	160	170	197	200	200
Cosmetics	38	40	45	49	57	165	70	77	80	100
Soap and detergents	65	100	110	114	170	205	210	255	250	300
Soda ash	10	10	10	10	15	16	18	17	20	20
Tyres and tubes	30	20	13	18	22	20	23	27	30	50
Bank cheques	13	14	15	15	18	24	25	20	15	15
Cotton yarn	120	100	0	215	265	290	270	308	300	320
Man-made yarn	79	60	28	40	51	56	100	146	175	250
Woollen fabric	45	38	32	34	43	50	45	50	22	30
Woollen carpets	0	0	0	0	0	0	0	0	18	12
Electric batteries	50	39	33	45	59	67	65	60	70	60
Electric bulbs	24	20	23	40	51	80	60	77	50	75
Fluorescent tubes	0	0	0	0	0	0	0	0	12	0
Matches	14	25	30	25	30	25	28	31	30	35

Services, hotels	45	43	56	62	73	100	105	124	130	85
Fabrics of man-made fibre	43	70	0	0	0	0	0	0	0	0
Arrears	53	409	0	0	0	0	0	0	0	0
Other items	146	172	133	173	223	150	250	260	302	355
Gross total	5 189	6 508	6 812	9 500	10 709	12 150	13 383	16 333	15 705	15 700
Refunds	20	20	21	17	0	0	10	0	0	0
Transfer to provinces	280	304	0	0	0	0	0	0	0	0
Net total	4 889	6 184	6 792	9 483	10 709	12 150	13 373	16 333	15 705	15 700
Surcharges (Rs million)										
Total surcharges	1075	816	1 001	796	1 699	829	2 635	4 715	4 932	9 171
Fertiliser	206	197	177	172	368	371	631	961	963	347
Natural gas	516	365	413	414	525	458	385	1 216	1 030	2 989
Petroleum	353	253	412	211	806	0	1 620	2 538	2 939	5 835

Source: Government of Pakistan, Ministry of Finance, *Economic Memoranda to the Budget,* various years.

cement, natural gas, and beverages – see table 2.19) accounted for Rs 14 billion of the Rs 16 billion gross collected in 1986–7. There is some cascading caused by the excise tax, principally through cement, gas, oil and petroleum products. However, the tax on cement is one way of taxing the construction industry and luxury housing. Taxing oil and petroleum products is one of the few feasible mechanisms for taxing the transport industry. Such taxation would appear particularly desirable given the damage to roads, pollution and congestion.

The major surcharges, on petroleum products and gas, have similar effects to the domestic excises. These surcharges have risen very rapidly in the past few years and have now led to fuel prices which are high by international standards. Whilst some case can be made for increasing surcharges on the grounds of revenue and externalities, such arguments cannot justify indefinite increases. The surcharges are, in their economic effects, essentially part of the excise tax system and over the medium term should, for analytical and public clarity, be integrated with them.

2.3.5   The sales tax

The sales tax in Pakistan until the late 1980s has been a single-stage manufacturers tax imposed on imports and on domestic production, at a standard rate of 12.5% (with rates of 5% and 10% on 'necessities'). Revenue collections have remained at around 7% of total tax collections (0.9% of GDP in 1986–7) for a number of years, and throughout the Sixth Plan period (see table 2.5). There are numerous exemptions (300 tariff headings and 19 broad categories of domestically produced goods) with the consequence that the tax base is extremely narrow. Effectively, the sales tax operates much like a surcharge on the excise tax or the import tariff. The bulk of the sales tax collections accrue on the imports side, with only 22% arising from domestically produced goods (see table 2.20).

Some experience has been accumulated in administering a system of sales tax credits to avoid the cascading effects of taxing inputs to domestic manufacturing. The system of granting rebates to exported goods has, however, been open to much corruption and abuse. This is partly due to the fact that the assessment of rebates operates on a case by case basis, allowing too much leeway for *ad hoc* evaluations. This system of sales taxation is very weak and, given our discussion of customs and excise above, a major objective should be the shifting of indirect taxation away from customs and towards final sales.

Given the current weaknesses of domestic indirect taxation, the desirability of shifting away from customs duties and the limited potential in the short run from direct taxes, the reform of sales taxation should be the

Table 2.20. *Sales tax*

	On imports	On excisable goods	On non-excisable goods	Total sales tax
		(Rs million)		
1978–9	1 476	241	130	1 846
1979–80	1 935	256	140	2 331
1980–1	2 488	400	300	3 188
1982–3	2 734	337	330	3 400
1984–5	3 724	499	528	4 752
1985–6	3 653	729	656	5 038

Note: Data for 1981–2 and 1983–4 are incomplete and these years are omitted.
Source: Government of Pakistan, Ministry of Finance, *Economic Memoranda to the Budget*, various years.

centrepiece of tax policy in Pakistan in the medium term. The objectives of a reform of the taxation of sales should be:
(i)   to widen the tax base
(ii) to ensure an initial increase in revenues
(iii) to avoid the cascading effects associated with the taxation of intermediate goods and raw material inputs
(iv) to provide a correct assessment of the rebates that should be allowable to exporters on account of the taxation of inputs
(v)   to provide a mechanism which permits some cross-checking of returns between taxpayers and assists in the checking of corporate income statements.
The wider base should yield revenues which grow at least as fast as GNP.
   The possibilities appear to be:
(i)   a sales tax at the wholesale or retail stages
(ii) retention of the existing system of the manufacturers sales tax with fewer exemptions
(iii) some variant of the VAT.
On (ii), the 1986 NTRC calculated (on the basis of industrial output and imports) that the elimination of exemptions would lead to a sales revenue that could be ten times greater than at present (see table 2.21). However, such a tax would be close to a turnover tax and would have undesirable cascading effects. Options (i) and (iii), a retail sales tax and a VAT, or a general sales tax with rebates, are discussed further in later chapters; see specifically chapter 7.

Table 2.21. *Estimates of sales tax collections assuming no exemptions*

	1982–3	1983–4
	(Rs million)	
(1) Local manufacturers		
(a) Domestic industrial output	134 396	163 644
(b) Calculated sales tax assuming no exemption (@ 12.5%)	16 800	20 456
(c) Actual sales tax collection	698	924
(d) Actual/calculated ((c) as percentage of (b))	4.2%	4.5%
(2) Imports		
(a) Value of imports	68 151	70 707
(b) Import duty (actual)	20 901	24 771
Total base for sales tax	89 052	101 478
(c) Calculated sales tax assuming no exemption (@ 20.0%)	17 810	20 296
(d) Actual sales tax collection	2 791	3 700
(e) Actual/calculated ((d) as percentage of (c))	15.7%	18.2%
(3) Total		
(a) Calculated sales tax assuming no exemptions (1(b)+2(c))	34 610	40 752
(b) Actual sales tax collection (1(c)+2(d))	3 489	4 624
(c) Actual/calculated ((b) as percentage of (a))	10.1%	11.4%

Note: The table presents an estimate of the sales tax that would have been collected if there had been no exemptions. This is compared with actual collections.
Source: Based on National Taxation Reform Commission (1986), p. 91.

2.3.6 Multi-level finance

Pakistan has not managed to institute an administrative machine comparable to the Indian Finance Commissions, and this is partly because of the lengthy interregnums of military rule. The issue of multi-level finance in Pakistan remains problematic and politically sensitive. None the less there are some advantages in Pakistan's current state of affairs, relative to that of India, which may make both tax reform and revenue sharing an easier proposition in the longer term. These advantages relate to (i) the central responsibility for sales taxes; and (ii) greater prospects for local financial reform of both expenditures and revenues, for instance through the use of earmarked instruments such as *ushr*.

The sales tax advantage is clearly seen in the difficulties faced in India with State-level jurisdiction over sales taxes and in the introduction of the MODVAT (see chapter 10). Pakistan is not so constrained, and is in a better position to overhaul indirect taxes to ensure revenues over time, as well as to encourage efficiency and fairness.

The financing of local expenditures is a major area of research and is likely to be of great importance in the longer term. While this is not the focus of our work, suggestions in this book (see chapter 8) can have major implications for revenue-sharing possibilities in the future.

2.3.7   Tax buoyancy and prospects for revenue

It is common, in the tax literature, to consider future revenue possibilities in relation to past trends. A method which is frequently used is to measure the buoyancy of a tax. The buoyancy of a tax describes the relationship over time between percentage changes in tax collections and percentage changes in incomes. If, for a given tax, its buoyancy is less (greater) than one then the revenue from that tax has been rising more slowly (quickly) than income. Whilst the buoyancy does not add greatly to a simple examination of the series for collections and GDP, or tax shares in total revenue or GDP, it can be a useful summary statistic. These are also calculated in most conventional tax analyses, and we estimate the relation

$$\ln T_t = a + b \ln Y_t + \varepsilon_t$$

where T_t is the collection from the tax head in question, Y_t is GDP at market price, and ε_t a random term. Notice that in the estimated relationship many things may intermediate between income and collections, including changes in the base or rates, avoidance, evasion, administration and so on. The parameter b represents the buoyancy.

In table 2.22 we present buoyancy estimates for the period 1976–7 to 1985–6 for direct taxes (including the income tax, land revenue, and provincial direct taxes), income and corporation tax, customs, sales and excise taxes, surcharges and indirect taxes. The OLS estimates confirm autocorrelation. To correct for this, we use (i) the Cochrane–Orcutt two-step procedure based on first differences, (ii) the Hildreth–Lu search procedure, and (iii) maximum likelihood estimates (using a joint normal distribution for $(\varepsilon_t, \varepsilon_{t-1})$). These are all standard methods of correcting for autocorrelation.

We observe that the parameter estimates vary substantially according to the method of estimation. Thus, for instance, the buoyancy of sales taxes is greater than 1 for OLS and ML estimates, but 0.95 for the Cochrane–Orcutt and Hildreth–Lu formulations. Similarly excise buoyancy is 0.95 for OLS and ML, but around 0.67 for the others. The highest buoyancy is for surcharges, reflecting their rapid increase in recent years.

While some may be tempted to argue that taxes with a high buoyancy are

Table 2.22. *Buoyancy estimates, 1976–7 to 1985–6*

Variable (ln)	OLS	Cochrane– Orcutt	Hildreth– Lu	Maximum likelihood
Direct taxes	1.19	0.66	0.62	1.12
$\bar{R}^2$	0.89	0.052	0.0078	0.98
DW	0.55	0.78	0.79	0.69
Income and corporation tax	1.19	0.67	0.62	1.12
$\bar{R}^2$	0.89	0.062	0.0098	0.98
DW	0.55	0.78	1.08	0.69
Indirect tax	0.978	0.929	0.930	0.982
$\bar{R}^2$	0.984	0.980	0.979	0.970
DW	1.631	2.41	2.432	1.751
Customs	1.13	1.00	1.01	1.16
$\bar{R}^2$	0.965	0.959	0.962	0.974
DW	1.23	2.47	2.45	1.61
Sales tax	1.06	0.954	0.947	1.07
$\bar{R}^2$	0.972	0.927	0.918	0.982
DW	1.13	2.00	2.05	1.589
Federal excise	0.957	0.679	0.661	0.947
$\bar{R}^2$	0.94	0.623	0.583	0.989
DW	0.89	2.09	2.14	1.48
Surcharges	1.75	2.20	2.18	1.74
$\bar{R}^2$	0.698	0.737	0.745	0.644
DW	1.54	2.30	2.23	1.756

Note: The equation estimated is ln (tax collection)$=a+b\ln \text{GDP}+\varepsilon$, and the estimate of b is shown in the table. DW is the Durbin]Watson statistic.

Dependent variables are the (logarithm of) tax revenue collections on account of (i) direct taxes (inclusive of the income and corporation tax and provincial direct taxes); (ii) the income and corporation tax; (iii) all indirect taxes; followed by its individual components; (iv) customs; (v) sales tax; (vi) excises, and (vii) surcharges.

promising candidates for future revenue, however buoyancies based on past behaviour will not be good indicators for future revenues if major changes have taken place. For example, although all estimates suggest that the buoyancy of surcharges is greater than unity, and this head has grown roughly twice as fast as GDP in the period considered, this has arisen from a series of additions to the rates and types of surcharge, a source of growth which cannot continue. Rather, as we shall argue, the major reform efforts should be focused on the taxation of income and sales, for which the buoyancy coefficients are less than unity.

Similar estimation problems and ambiguities would apply to 'elasticities' where one attempts to estimate the relationship between collections and incomes for constant tax schedules. One attempts to control for 'discretionary changes' and this adds considerably to the complication. Without very detailed information these estimates are generally quite arbitrary. Even if successfully carried through, the useful guidance from such analyses is limited: we shall not pursue 'buoyancies' or 'elasticities' any further here.

2.4   Concluding comments

These brief descriptions of the development of the tax system during the colonial period and the system as it stood in the mid-1980s indicate that the current system has changed little in its basic legal structure. The tax revenues and public expenditure as a percentage of national income were 8% and 10% at the turn of the century, 10% and 11% at the beginning of the Second World War and over 13% and 20% in the mid-1980s. Independence has seen public expenditures as a fraction of national income more than double whereas the fraction of tax revenue in national income has risen only 3 percentage points. It would appear that the combination of the colonial legal structure, the current tax administration, and the successive political regimes and pressures has proved incapable of financing the public expenditures desired by an independent Pakistan. The result has been heavy borrowing, to which we shall return in chapter 10.

Land revenue declined from 53% of government revenues in 1900 to 20% at the outbreak of the Second World War and less than 10% by independence. Its contribution now is minimal. Other direct taxes have not grown to take its place and they contributed, in the mid-1980s, only 14% of revenue, compared to 21% in 1981. The major source of revenue in the recent past, some 80–85%, has been indirect taxes, with around half of this revenue coming from customs duties. The pressures on revenue in the 1980s have led to a steady rise in surcharges, mostly acting like additions to existing indirect taxes.

The indirect taxes are of a form which create important distortions to the price mechanism. The customs duties are heavily focused on capital and intermediate goods, which puts the users of these goods at a disadvantage and artificially encourages the production of these goods in Pakistan. High duties and a long list of prohibited imports together lead to great problems of smuggling without necessarily leading to efficient domestic production. The domestic sales tax is very weak (most sales tax revenues come from an addition to customs duty classified as sales taxation) and domestic excises are focused in revenue terms on a small group of goods, principally tobacco, sugar, petroleum products and cement.

The picture then is of an antiquated system under severe pressure and replete with problems and idiosyncracies. The requirement for reform in terms of a more rational, efficient, equitable, productive and easily administered system is urgent. The primary focus in the short and medium term will have to be indirect taxes with an emphasis on building a domestic indirect tax base so that the dependence on customs can be reduced. In the longer term the direct tax base should be expanded, including the more effective taxation of agricultural incomes. The remainder of this book is devoted to the principles that should guide such a reform and an analysis of the directions that reform might take.

3 Theory

3.1 Issues

An analysis of the design or reform of a tax system should look at revenue, the distribution of welfare across households or individuals, and at incentives and production. Economic theory helps us to structure this analysis, and the models we shall examine provide an integrated framework for examining these issues. In all applied economic policy problems, and particularly in public finance, the economic analysis must be combined with political and administrative considerations before recommendations can be made and these aspects have played a major role in the policies we shall suggest later in the book. The importance of these other factors does not, however, provide a justification for casualness in economic analysis, and it is unfortunate that policy advice is often offered in ignorance of the basic economic theories concerning taxation.

Economic theory can play a number of (related) roles in tax analysis. First, it can provide basic principles for the design and reform of taxes, by pointing to the appropriate bases for taxation and indicating which taxes are likely to cause efficiency problems, and by giving guidance on how to set rates. Second, it can provide benchmarks in terms of simple models in which policy implications are clear. This allows a focus for comparison around which complications can be introduced. This procedure can often guide us as to the appropriate policy tools for dealing with those complications. Third, it can provide methods for organising data and making calculations. All three roles will be important for the work described in this book.

Our major focus will be indirect taxes. These generally constitute the most important source of revenue in developing countries and are also the taxes for which theory is best developed. A central theme, however, in our theoretical analysis, and itself an important lesson which is often overlooked, is that one tax should not be examined in isolation from another. The appropriate base and rate structure for an indirect tax system will, as we shall see, depend critically on the availability of direct taxes and income transfers and how these are structured. Thus rules for, or specific policies on, indirect taxes should not be proposed without clear statements concerning other taxes and income transfers. Extensive differentiation for the VAT may be difficlt to implement. Desired differentiation of the indirect tax system could be achieved by a judicious use of different instruments, including subsidies, excises, tariffs and sales taxes/VAT.

The theory of the design and reform of indirect taxes is set out in section 3.2 where we concentrate on models where the only imperfections of the economy lie in the need to raise revenue and the absence of an attractive system of lump-sum taxation. We draw out the lessons of the theory for both trade and domestic taxes. In section 3.2 and section 3.4 we consider theoretical arguments concerning the uniformity of indirect taxation and in section 3.4 we also examine some considerations outside the theory. In section 3.3 we consider what theory has to say about the different kinds of indirect taxes relating to Pakistan. In section 3.5 we extend this analysis to economies with additional distortions in the sense that markets do not work perfectly. Dynamic issues form the subject matter of section 3.6. Many of them can be incorporated in the standard models, with suitable reinterpretation, but important additional difficulties arise. We examine direct taxes in section 3.7 focusing on their purpose and their relation to indirect taxes. Alternative tools of analysis such as computable general equilibrium models and effective rates of protection are examined in section 3.8 in relation to the theories set out earlier in the chapter. We summarise the main conclusions of the analysis in section 3.9 in the form of some basic principles for taxation.

3.2   Theory and basic principles

3.2.1   *Optimality*

The development of basic principles requires an analytical foundation so that we can understand the circumstances in which they apply and the critical assumptions in their justification. In this subsection we shall, therefore, sketch the outline of the standard models of normative tax theory and then ask what lessons they offer for taxation in developing countries. Those who wish to avoid the technical detail can examine the principles themselves set out in section 3.9 where we draw together the main lessons in the form of simple and intuitive rules.

As a benchmark and to keep things simple at the beginning we take two of the standard frameworks in the theory of taxation: first, where revenue can be raised in a lump-sum manner directly from households; and, second, where revenue has to be raised by the taxation of transactions between consumers and producers. In the former case, if there are no externalities, and indifference curves and isoquants have the usual convex shape, then any Pareto-efficient outcome can be achieved as a competitive equilibrium, in which the government raises revenue and redistributes purchasing power using the appropriate set of lump-sum taxes. The policy is clear: there should be no taxes of any kind (neither on commodities nor on income) except those which are lump-sum. Whilst the model is presented mainly as a benchmark it does immediately generate a general principle which is of value in guiding policy: revenue should be raised and redistributed in ways which, as far as possible, are lump-sum. There are relevant examples such as some forms of land or poll taxes which come fairly close, but generally governments will also have to consider taxes which are clearly not lump-sum.

In the second case we retain the competitive framework and the assumption of no externalities but now revenue has to be raised by the taxation of commodities bought and services supplied. The standard theory in the tradition of Pigou, Ramsey, Samuelson, Boiteux and Diamond and Mirrlees is to formulate the problem as the choice of indirect taxes to maximise a Bergson–Samuelson social welfare function whilst raising a given revenue. The use of a Bergson–Samuelson welfare function is not *per se* restrictive since it simply says that our judgements of welfare are conducted basically in terms of the living standards of the households in the community (current and future). Neither does it presuppose a benevolent all-knowing government. We ask simply how a commentator interested in raising living standards and in the distribution of welfare would evaluate policy in this simple framework. An absence of understanding of the logic of policy in this example would preclude us from generalising to more complicated worlds.

Notice that the commentator could be self-interested or concerned with the welfare only of a narrow group. This would simply be a special case. Those who wish to analyse taxes in terms of the competing interests of different groups would need to know what structure of indirect taxes corresponds to the interests of the different groups in order to understand how the different groups could or should try to influence the outcome. Hence an understanding of the solution to these problems is basic to any approach to taxation in terms of who will gain and who will lose. In other words it should form part of the foundations of many different kinds of analyses of taxes.

3.2.2 A model of taxation and public sector pricing

The problem is to raise a given level of revenue using commodity taxes whilst lowering the welfare of households as little as possible. Formally we choose a tax vector **t** to

Maximise $\qquad\qquad V(\mathbf{g})$ $\qquad\qquad\qquad\qquad$ (3.1)

subject to $\qquad\qquad R(\mathbf{t}) = \mathbf{t}'\mathbf{X}(\mathbf{q}) \geqq \bar{R}$ $\qquad\qquad\qquad$ (3.2)

where: primes denote row vectors; **p** are the prices faced by producers; **q**, equal to (**p** + **t**), are the consumer prices; the level of household welfare corresponding to **q** is $v^h(\mathbf{q})$ and household demands are $\mathbf{x}^h(\mathbf{q})$; $\mathbf{X}(\mathbf{q})$ is the aggregate demand vector, and $V(\mathbf{q})$ is social welfare arising from those prices ($V(\mathbf{q}) \equiv W(v^1(\mathbf{q}), v^2(\mathbf{q}), \ldots, v^H(\mathbf{q}))$) where W is a Bergson–Samuelson social welfare function; $R(\mathbf{t})$ is indirect tax revenue and $\bar{R}$ the required revenue. Notice that we are assuming that there are no lump-sum incomes, so that the demands and welfare of households (and thus social welfare) depend only on the prices which they face for the goods and services which they buy and sell. The aggregate demand vector **X** is the sum of the demands of the individual households $\mathbf{x}^h$. The assumptions on production are essentially that all production is either by the government or by competitive private firms, with constant returns to scale, all trading at the same prices. We are assuming that there is no taxation on transactions between producers but that all final sales to the consumer can be taxed. One can show that these assumptions allow us to conduct the analysis as if producer prices are fixed (see, for example, Diamond and Mirrlees, 1971).

The formulation of the problem should make it clear that the same model applies to public-sector pricing of good i where we interpret p_i as the marginal cost (assumed constant for simplicity although this is not essential) and t_i as the excess over marginal cost. Thus it is immediately obvious that the final price of a good sold directly to the final consumer by the public sector should *not* be marginal cost since optimal t_i would only exceptionally be zero. Public-sector prices should include an element of taxation for goods sold to the final consumer, i.e. there should be a contribution to resource mobilisation or revenue raising.

The solution to the problem (3.1) and (3.2) gives us the many-person Ramsey rule for optimal commodity taxation. It is useful to set this out since it is the simplest embodiment of the basic trade-off between equity and efficiency in taxation. The rule is derived straightforwardly from the first-order conditions for the Lagrangean, $V + \lambda R$, for the above maximisation problem; λ is the Lagrange multiplier on the revenue constraint, i.e. the social marginal utility of government income. We have

$$\frac{\partial V}{\partial t_i} + \lambda \frac{\partial R}{\partial t_i} = 0 \qquad (3.3a)$$

We then substitute

$$\partial V/\partial t_i = -\sum_h \beta^h x_i^h \quad \text{and} \quad \partial R/\partial t_i{}^{A6334} \partial X/\partial t_i$$

where β^h is the social marginal utility of income of household h (i.e. $\partial W/\partial u^h . \alpha^h$ where α^h is the private marginal utility of income). We then use the Slutsky decomposition of demand derivatives for housethis income derivative is evaluated at $m^h = 0$ here) to yield

$$\frac{\sum_k t_k \sum_h s_{ik}^h}{X_i} = -\sigma_i \qquad (3.3b)$$

where

$$b^h \equiv \frac{\beta^h}{\lambda} + \mathbf{t}' \frac{\partial \mathbf{x}^h}{\partial m^h} \qquad (3.3c)$$

and

$$\sigma_i \equiv 1 - \sum_h \frac{x_i^h}{X_i} . b^h \qquad (3.3d)$$

In deriving (3.3b) and (3.3c) we have used the symmetry ($s_{ik}^h = s_{ki}^h$) of the compensated (Slutsky) demand derivative for household h f income, b^h, of household h, where 'net' means there is an adjustment to the social marginal utility, β^h, for the marginal propensity to spend on taxes out of extra income. Thus from (3.3c) and (3.3d) we see that σ_i is higher the higher is the fraction of the good consumed by those who have a low net social marginal utility of income b^h.

We may now interpret (3.3) in terms of a trade-off between efficiency and equity. If there is a single household then we may think of the problem well be an option and, if it is, it provides the best way of raising revenue. If, however, we are confined to commodity taxes then, for a single household, σ_i is simply $(1-b)$ which is independent of i. Equation (3.3b), with one household and thus σ_i independent of i, is the Ramsey rule. This is often interpreted as saying that (for small taxes) the proportional reduction in compensated demand arising from taxes should be the same for all goods (t_k measures the price change anwith distribution in the special sense that b^h is independent of h. Crudely speaking, the efficiency result is to tax goods which are in inelastic demand, although as we have seen the correct expression is in terms of quantity reductions and compeutional concerns are explicitly ignored.

Where we *are* concerned with distribution then (3.3) tells us that the reduction in compensated demand should be greater for goods consumed relatively more by those with a low net social marginal utility of income (b^h). We might think of those with low b^h as the rich and it is in this sense that we orient taxes towards the consumption of the better-off. Thus (3.3) captures the essential elements of the trade-off between equity and efficiency in the standard analysis of optimal commodity taxation.

3.2.3   Uniformity of indirect taxes and its relation with direct taxes

The expression (3.3b) is known as the many-person Ramsey rule and it allows us to investigate the relationship between indirect taxation and other tax or subsidy instruments and the appropriate balance between them. Suppose, for example, we can make lump-sum transfers which depend on the demographic characteristics of the household – an example would be a subsidised rice ration where the amount depends on household composition. The model of (3.1) and (3.2) is then augmented to include the influence of the grants on household welfare and demands and we take off their costs from $t'X$ in (3.2). The optimality condition for the transfers can then be combined with (3.3) to analyse the appropriate construction of policies. Commodity taxes should be at the same proportional rate if the grants are set optimally and if the following conditions apply (see Deaton and Stern, 1986). These are: (i) the Engel curves are linear and parallel (i.e. the marginal propensities to consume each commodity are constant across incomes of households), although the intercepts can vary with household composition, and (ii) factors supplied are separable in the utility function from consumption goods (changes in factors do not alter marginal rates of substitution between goods). Intuitively, all the redistribution that is desirable is carried out through the lump-sum grants which are financed by uniform commodity taxation, and there is no justification for further redistribution through differentiation of commodity taxes since everyone has the same marginal propensity to spend on each good. To put it another way, efficiency points us towards taxing necessities and distribution towards luxuries; under special assumptions about the shape of preferences and the setting of direct taxes the two effects cancel, and the role of indirect taxes is simply to raise revenue for the grants which act as a basic income guarantee related to household composition.

The above uniformity result was first stated by Atkinson (1977) for the linear expenditure system and then generalised by Deaton (1979, 1981) to linear Engel curves although in these models households are identical except for differences in wages. Atkinson and Stiglitz (1976) analysed the case of non-linear income taxation (again where individuals differ only in the wage), and one finds that the more subtle form of income taxation allows one to dispose of the assumption concerning the linearity of the Engel curves (whilst retaining separability). We have focused on the Deaton and Stern (1986) treatment since it allows demands to vary with household composition and deals with direct tax tools of some empirical relevance for developing countries – we do see transfers related to household composition, but there is no empirical evidence of the so-phisticated non-linear income taxes required in the Atkinson–Stiglitz theory.

The formal results of the last few years have allowed a better understand-ing of both indirect taxation and of the balance between direct and indirect taxation than was possible from previous discussions which simply listed some of the things to be borne in mind. Having seen the assumptions which are used in establishing the results we are in a position to see how far they help in analysing the problems of developing countries.

In our judgement they make three types of contribution. First, they train the intuition to understand what is important in an argument about the structure of taxes and thus help in organising practical enquiry and in using empirical results. Second, they help in further research because they provide a basis of comparison for modified models which are more appropriate for developing countries and for judging results. Third, they lead rather naturally to the theory of reform which allows one to devise practical checks on optimality conditions and on desirable directions of movement. There is no suggestion, here, that formula (3.3) provides a practical basis for calculating what taxes should be. The model is a benchmark, not a workable description, and the amount of information on the demand structure which would be required might not be available (see Deaton, 1987). We give examples of the first type of contribution below and discuss examples of the other two contributions in the following two subsections.

An example of the first contribution concerns the level of the lump-sum grant which emerged in the special model considered by Deaton and Stern (1986) as the central redistributive tool. This leads us to ask whether a system of lump-sum grants related to household structure is possible. In many developing countries one does find some transfers through rationing systems (particularly for food) which are rather like lump-sum grants, the rations often being related to family structure. Where rations are resaleable then from the formal point of view they are just like lump-sum transfers (and even if they are not resaleable they are like lump-sum transfers if the level is lower than total purchases of the commodity). Thus a prominent feature of an argument concerning whether indirect taxes should be uniform is a judgement concerning the optimality or otherwise of the rations. This judgement can itself be structured since we have an explicit condition for the optimality in terms of the net social marginal utilities of income, the b^h; the average value of these net social marginal utilities in terms of public income should be unity (if the average value were greater, for example, the transfer should be increased). With explicit value judgements (the welfare weights β^h), a knowledge of taxes t, and an estimate of the demand system, this can be checked (see, for example, Ahmad and Stern, 1984, for India). More generally the results tell us that the inter-relations between different parts of a tax system will be crucial in that the design of one part depends sensitively on the existence of options and the choice of policy elsewhere. Thus it is of special importance in developing countries to scrutinise carefully the availability of a wide range of instruments and to ask whether those that are used have been appropriately adjusted. For further discussion see Stern (1990).

3.2.4 Adaptations of the model for LDCs

The second class of lessons involves the relaxation of some of the assumptions of the simple model to better describe developing countries. There should be no delusion that one can specify a single model for all developing countries – see Newbery and Stern (1987a) for a collection of models. There are, however, at least two common features of poor countries which should be accommodated. Production often takes place in units which cannot be described adequately as (competitive) firms facing prices distinct from those of consumers and producing under constant returns to scale. Peasant agriculture is an obvious and central example. Further, one cannot reasonably assume that all goods can be taxed. Whilst models which deal with these features in a direct way can be, and have been, constructed, it is important to recognise that they do not require us to jettison immediately all of the standard model and its lessons. Thus, for example, if production goes on in the peasant household which faces consumer prices for its purchases and sales then the model is formally unaffected and one simply interprets demands and demand responses as being net of household production. And the optimal tax rules (3.3) are first-order conditions for those taxes which can be chosen and thus apply for the subset of taxes which are set optimally.

What does change if either production takes place in households, or there is a restriction on those goods which can be taxed, are the results generally known as production efficiency theorems. Diamond and Mirrlees (1971) showed that if private production takes place under perfect competition and constant returns to scale (one need not assume that producer prices are fixed) then, at an optimum for indirect taxes, aggregate production should be efficient. Thus marginal rates of transformation (MRT) should be the same for public and private sectors, and public-sector shadow prices (which will be equal to public MRTs at the optimum) and private market prices (which will be equal to private MRTs given the competitive assumption) should coincide. One can allow diminishing returns to scale if profits are optimally taxed. If some production is conducted by households facing consumer prices q, whilst firms transact at prices p, then clearly overall production will not be efficient, although the Diamond–Mirrlees analysis shows that production in the public sector and private firms taken together should be efficient. When some goods cannot be taxed then one would want to consider taxing inputs into those goods as a surrogate for taxing final goods (see Stern, 1984, and Newbery, 1986). This would violate efficiency. Where aggregate efficiency is desirable then goods sold by the public to the private sector should be priced at marginal cost. Notice the difference here between private producers and consumers; for the latter the appropriate price will generally include a tax element over and above marginal cost.

There has been some analysis of restricted taxation in models of the Arrow–Debreu and Diamond–Mirrlees variety, with n goods which are numbered $1, 2, \ldots, n$ and not immediately associated in the model with particular commodities such as corn or manufactures (see, for example, Stiglitz and Dasgupta, 1971 – or Drèze and Stern, 1987, who in addition consider rationing and non-market clearing). However, for the most part, studies which attempt to take account of peasant production and restricted taxation deal with models which have an explicit distinction between agricultural and other sectors. Then particular relative prices such as the terms of trade between agriculture and industry and the structure of certain markets, especially that for labour, take a central place. Examples of public policy analysis in such models (often of the dual economy variety) include Dixit (1971), Dixit and Stern (1974), Newbery (1974), Srinivasan and Bhagwati (1975), and a number of chapters in a volume edited by Newbery and Stern (1987a) – for example, chapters 7 and 13, Newbery; chapter 15, Heady and Mitra; and chapter 16, Sah and Stiglitz. The latter volume may also be consulted for further references.

The main results from these models continue to have the general form of a trade-off between efficiency and equity (such as (3.3)). For example, the appropriate price for an agricultural input will depend on its marginal social cost of production, the elasticity of net demand and the pattern of use by different types of farmer. Broadly speaking the higher the social cost, the less elastic the demand and the richer the users, the higher should be the price. There are two further specific features which often play a role: the structure of labour markets and any premium on government revenue. Thus if a tax reduces the rural demand for labour it may have the deleterious effect of increasing migration if urban wages are fixed. Or it may reduce both urban and rural wages where these are endogenous. Clearly the calculation of the effects and their welfare consequences are going to depend on the precise structure of the labour market (see Williamson (1988) for some discussion of the evidence).

The shadow value of government revenue, λ, is an interesting concept in its own right – it is the opportunity cost of public funds. Early writers on development suggested this was particularly high since the government had pressing needs for revenue to finance investment. As we shall shortly see, it is a natural tool when we come to discuss tax reform.

The shadow value, λ, of government revenue is endogenous in the model of (3.1) and (3.2). It will depend, *inter alia*, on the revenue requirement $\bar{R}$. In terms of the Lagrangean for the problem $\bar{R}$ plays no explicit role (it comes into the solution, of course, since the constraint must be satisfied) but we can think of a desire for revenue being reflected in a higher λ. Thus one can write government objectives to include a term expressing the value of government revenue (i.e. λR), suppress the constraint containing $\bar{R}$, specify λ and then think of the eventual revenue as being endogenous. Then the weight on revenue can be discussed in terms of λ, and, for example, a government that attached a high value to public investment would have a high λ. In the dynamic context the value of investment is itself endogenous and this is discussed in section 3.6. Generally, as should be obvious, the higher is λ the higher are taxes and the lower subsidies.

3.2.5   Directions of reform

The third class of lessons from the standard optimisation models concerns extensions to the analysis of marginal reform. Our focus here is on marginal reform, i.e. small movements from an initial position. We shall be concerned to identify those directions of movement which are feasible and welfare-improving. An important advantage of the analysis of marginal reform, as we shall see, is its parsimony in terms of data and assumptions. The study of marginal reform may be contrasted with that of non-marginal reform where we compare the outcome from a different set of (feasible) taxes with the initial position. A central purpose of a welfare analysis of non-marginal reform is the identification of gainers and losers. Methods for doing this are set out in chapter 5. Whilst that analysis will require stronger assumptions and more extensive data and estimates, it has the advantage of being specific about the direction and extent of movement. The marginal analysis is not specific about step length and generally identifies a whole class of directions for improvement. The different strengths and weaknesses of the two approaches make them complementary and both are pursued in our applied work below.

Suppose we start from a status quo which is not an optimum and try to identify improving directions of reform. We show how such an investigation may be usefully structured. We retain the notation and model of (3.1) and (3.2) but no longer assume optimisation. We define

$$\lambda_i = -\frac{\partial V}{\partial t_i}\bigg/\frac{\partial R}{\partial t_i} \qquad (3.4)$$

We can interpret λ_i as the marginal cost in terms of social welfare of raising an extra unit of revenue from increasing the taxation of good i; $-\dfrac{\partial V}{\partial t_i}$ represents the welfare cost of a unit change and the inverse of $\dfrac{\partial R}{\partial t_i}$ tells us the magnitude of the change in t_i required to raise one rupee. What matters for policy then is the relative size of the λ_i, i.e. if $\lambda_i < \lambda_j$ then we increase welfare at constant revenue by increasing the tax on good i and decreasing it on good j (optimality would require λ_i to be independent of i). The analysis places the status quo in a central position and asks, 'Given where we are, in what direction should we move?' It seems quite likely (and it is confirmed by our experience) that the type of language involved is more easily understood by the policy-maker than the notion of a large move towards some optimum which may emerge from a model of which he is suspicious. This may be an advantage for the applied worker who is collecting data, although much of his underlying model is the same (but he can assume rather less; see below). We assume here that producer prices are fixed. The assumptions are examined further in section 3.3.

As we shall see (section 3.3) an advantage of this approach is that it uses less information than is required for optimality – essentially we need only 'local' information (demand responses around the status quo), rather than 'global' information (a full description of demand functions for all price vectors) which is required for the analysis of optimality. Further, it allows considerations which are not captured in the model to be set alongside the calculated welfare increase in an appraisal of the costs and benefits of change. This type of discussion is less straightforward when the full optimum is computed since both considerations are not easily integrated into a calculation whose output is a specific set of optimal rates. A disadvantage is that directions only, and not step size, are identified. And there will usually be a choice between many welfare-improving directions which, like that for step size, must be made using criteria outside the model. Examples of relevant considerations might be (i) administrative convenience, e.g., which directions are easily achievable using existing tools, or (ii) political acceptability which may limit how far one can go, or (iii) confidence, or the lack of it, in estimates of the critical parameters which are indicating a particular direction. Such questions are typically ignored in the optimality calculation.

The investigation of the theory of marginal reform was begun by Guesnerie (1977); see also Drèze and Stern (1987). It was developed for detailed application by the present authors (for example, Ahmad and Stern, 1984, 1987a) and its use is illustrated in chapter 6 below. In order to see what is involved we write out equation (3.4), the expression for the marginal social cost of revenue arising from an adjustment of the ith tax, more fully,

$$\lambda_i = \frac{\sum_h \beta^h x_i^h}{X_i + \mathbf{t}' \dfrac{\partial \mathbf{X}}{\partial q_i}} \tag{3.5}$$

Intuitively the numerator represents the money cost (x_i^h) to households of a unit price change weighted by the welfare weight β^h and aggregated across households. The denominator measures the response of revenue to the tax change and involves the vector of demand responses $\partial \mathbf{X}/\partial q_i$. Note that only the *aggregate* demands and demand responses appear in the denominator and, with our assumption of fixed producer prices, derivatives with respect to q_i and t_i are the same. An alternative way of writing (3.5) is as the distributional characteristic D_i divided by a tax elasticity,

$$\lambda_i = \frac{\rho_i D_i}{\eta_i} \tag{3.6}$$

where

$$D_i = \frac{\sum_h \beta^h x_i^h}{X_i}, \quad \rho_i = \frac{t_i X_i}{R}, \quad \text{and} \quad \eta_i = \frac{t_i}{R} \frac{\partial R}{\partial t_i}. \tag{3.7}$$

The distributional characteristic is the sum of the x_i^h weighted by the β^h divided by the unweighted total, ρ_i is the share of the ith good in tax revenue and η_i is the elasticity of tax revenue w.r.t. the ith specific tax. One may see λ_i therefore as the product of a distributional term and an 'efficiency' term since distributional judgements do not enter ρ_i and η_i.

The expression (3.5) tells us about the data requirements: we need the welfare weights β^h, the consumptions x_i^h, the tax rates $\mathbf{t}$, and the aggregate demand responses. The β^h are the value judgements which can be discussed directly and can be varied to allow for more or less egalitarian viewpoints. The x_i^h come from household surveys, the demand responses from estimates of consumer demand systems and t is the vector of taxes in terms of their impact on final goods. Methods of applying the theory, and some of the problems which may be encountered, are discussed in chapters 5 and 7.

3.3 Forms of indirect taxation

Indirect taxation can take a number of different forms and theory can enlighten us on their merits and defects. We briefly discuss here the implications of the theory for tariffs (and quotas), domestic excises, sales taxes and VAT. In general, trade quotas are inferior to tariffs. One could improve on a quota/licence system by auctioning the licences; the auction price is then the equivalent of a tariff – the value of the quota licence goes to the government rather than the firm getting the licence. Further, one can argue that tariffs are inferior to taxes (such as sales taxes or VAT) which are levied on final consumption goods (irrespective of whether domestically produced or imported) since tariffs distort the allocation of resources in favour of the domestic production of the good under tariff (see Dixit, 1985). More formally one can show that if lump-sum taxes are impossible then the optimal indirect tax system (with respect to a Bergson–Samuelson welfare function) in an open economy is to have taxes on final sales, with domestic and imported goods treated equally. A tariff in conjunction with an equal excise on domestic production would have the same effect as a sales tax on goods which are for final consumption only. This is essentially an application of the Diamond–Mirrlees (1971) efficiency theorem (see Dixit and Norman, 1980, chapter 6, for an explicit formal argument).

3.3.1 Tariffs

Arguments in favour of tariffs as against taxes (on final sales) would generally be associated with administration or with the desire to protect a particular domestic industry. There is no doubt that the administrative considerations pointing towards tariffs are of substance for many developing countries with weak internal revenue systems. It is important for revenue growth over time, however, to build up an efficient internal tax administration and to encourage formal accounting in the private sector, so one would not want to hold fast to an administrative argument in favour of tariffs over the indefinite future.

The protection argument would have to be examined directly in terms of a particular industry; whether the industry was likely to grow and whether it should grow, whether or not there were better ways of encouragement than the tariff and so on. Thus one should first scrutinise very carefully the argument that a particular industry should be promoted relative to others.

Generally speaking, the encouragement of one industry implicitly implies the discouragement of another. For example, a protective tariff on an industry puts up prices to the users of that industry's output and works to increase the exchange rate, thus discouraging export industries and other import-substituting activities. In many developing countries agriculture has been penalised in this way. One must therefore be convinced that there are genuine arguments for encouraging a particular industry which do not apply (or apply with less force) to other industries. Such arguments may work in terms of learning-by-doing, training, externalities or regional distributional considerations (see, for example, Ahmad, 1987). All too often claims by industrialists in favour of protection are simply self-interested attempts to consolidate established positions, with little evidence being offered to suggest that learning, for example, may be more important in their industry than in others.

If a respectable argument for encouragement of a particular industry has been established, then there are reasons to suppose that there are better ways to do this than with a tariff. We may think of a tariff as a production subsidy financed by a consumption tax, i.e. all users of the product pay more so that the price received by the producer can be raised above the price of the imported substitute. We can then ask whether it makes sense for the consumers of the product to be those who bear the burden of subsidy to the producer. It is more likely to be reasonable to spread the burden of finance across all taxpayers.

It seems that some more recent theories of international trade (without the competitive assumption) have provided arguments for protection, which are not present in the competitive models which yield very strong arguments in favour of free trade. Not all the theorists, however, would want to emphasise this point (see, for example, Dixit, 1984, and Helpman and Krugman, 1985). For example, as Dixit (1984, p. 14) puts it, there is the 'possibility that a partly countervailing duty may be desirable when a foreign country subsidises exports'. On the other hand, if oligopoly is associated with increasing returns to scale, then there are potential gains from specialisation which are not included in the standard model of gains from trade. The newer position seems well summarised by Krugman (1987): 'Its [free trade] status has shifted from optimum to reasonable rule of thumb. There is still a case for free trade as a good policy and as a useful target in the practical world of politics, but it can never again be asserted as the policy that economic theory tells us is always right.' Whilst those flying the protectionist flag might attempt to gain some support from the newer theories it would appear that the main argument for tariffs is that they are administratively easy ways of raising revenue. Experience has shown that special pleading by industry that learning-by-doing (or growing out of infancy) is of special importance in their case should be examined very carefully and treated with some scepticism. If tariffs are mainly for revenue purposes then they should be imposed to do least damage and thought should be given to the growth of other taxes which would eventually replace them.

The minimisation of damage done by revenue-oriented tariffs does not imply, however, uniformity of tariffs. There is no convincing theoretical argument behind this assertion, although one often hears it. One cannot, as we have seen, appeal to the desirability of uniform final goods taxes as support. As shown earlier there are strong arguments in favour of distributional considerations exerting an important influence on the taxes on final goods. Correspondingly a heavy tax on the importation of luxury cars would seem appropriate for most developing countries (where any costs associated with the possible (mistaken) encouragement of substitutes for Rolls-Royce cars are likely to be minimal). Even if we tried the line of argument which asserts the desirability of uniform final goods taxation we would have to recognise that uniform tariffs do not imply uniform effective taxes on final goods since tariffs on intermediates will accumulate in different ways into the prices of final goods. The argument for uniformity of tariffs would be administrative and political, and the plausibility of this line of argument is considered in section 3.4.

3.3.2 Domestic indirect taxes

Our next set of comparisons will be amongst domestic excises, sales taxes and the VAT. Excises on domestically produced goods distort production in an analogous manner to tariffs – this time in the opposite direction. When coupled with a tariff they have the effect of a sales tax if the good is for final consumption. Distortions arise, however, if the good concerned is also an input to production. Domestic excises, as with tariffs, may lead to unintended consequences. For example, in our calculation of effective taxes in India we found (see Ahmad and Stern, 1987a, and chapter 6 of this book) that some goods for which the government offered subsidies (e.g. *khadi* and handloom cloth) were in fact taxed if one took into account taxes on inputs, and the particular culprit was domestic excises. As with tariffs the main argument for domestic excises would appear to be administration. A relatively small number of large units producing basic commodities may be relatively easy to monitor. It is interesting to note that in India the revenue from domestic excises has overtaken that from tariffs as the productive base of the economy has expanded, following the stylised structure described by Hinrichs (1966). In the Indian case an important influence is also the federal structure. Excises on production are the preserve of the Centre whereas sales taxes are generally in the hands of the States.

The most attractive taxes from the point of view of theory are the final point sales tax and the value-added tax or VAT. The former has the advantage that it need involve only the final sale. Thus firms at each stage of the production and distribution chain are not brought in as is required with VAT. A disadvantage with this type of sales tax is that the final stage is difficult and costly to identify and this can lead to much evasion. However, many countries (for example, India) have had some success in levying a sales tax at the wholesale stage.

The value-added tax can take a number of forms but the general intention is to tax the value added by the enterprise, that is the difference between the value of sales and the value of purchased inputs. A common form for achieving this is to require a firm to remit to the tax authorities the tax collections on outputs less the taxes paid on inputs (usually it is required that the deductions be justified by receipts). The VAT has been introduced in a number of countries in recent years (Tanzi, 1987 noted twenty-two developing countries) stimulated in part perhaps by its extensive use in the European Community. It has the advantage of the inbuilt checking system whereby buyers have an incentive to reveal a purchase (in order to get credit for tax paid on inputs) thus discouraging concealment by a seller. Further it can be applied to services as well as goods since it does not require the specification of a unit of output (although a sales tax could be extended in this way too). It is also straightforward to rebate VAT on exports. A major disadvantage is that it involves everyone in the production and distribution chain thus imposing a substantial administrative cost both on the authorities and the enterprises.

One advantage that should *not* be claimed for the VAT is uniformity. There is nothing in the logic of a VAT to require uniformity and, as we have seen, neither does theory suggest that uniformity is a desirable property of an indirect tax system, except in rather special circumstances. The most persuasive arguments for uniformity are administrative – see section 3.4. However, a comprehensive single rate VAT would be almost impossible to administer in a developing country. The least differentiation in VAT that might be achieved is a standard rate, with exemption for agriculture, and a zero rate for exports.

This discussion therefore suggests a fairly clear strategy for indirect taxes. This consists of a replacement of trade taxes by taxes on final goods. This system of indirect taxes should be differentiated to take account of variations in the pattern of consumption across income groups, with such differentiation being less important the more successful is the income support system using direct transfers. Whilst this advice is useful as a description of a long-term goal, the strategy is not something that most developing countries could introduce very quickly. Administration is a central problem and many developing countries would have difficulty in levying taxes at the retail stage in anything like a comprehensive manner. This would appear to be true, for example, for Bangladesh. On the other hand, many other countries do levy taxes at the retail stage with some success. For example, in 1985, Turkey introduced a full-scale VAT including the retail stage which, with a standard rate of 12%, now raises around 3% of GDP. Thus the coverage is one quarter of GDP (with a notional legal coverage estimated around 50% of GDP). The non-uniform Mexican VAT was also introduced fairly successfully (see Gil Diaz, 1987), as is the sales tax in a number of Indian states.

The appropriate sequencing of an introduction of a consumption tax through to the final stage will depend on the circumstances of the country concerned. Most countries should be capable of handling the import and manufacturing stage and many could include a coverage at the wholesale level. Probably the majority could not go directly to the retail stage although one should not assume it is impossible without careful scrutiny. It is an advantage of the VAT that it can be introduced incrementally through the system, gradually increasing coverage and revenue. Thus if a stage is lost it does not imply that a good escapes tax altogether, whereas with a final-stage tax (such as the old UK purchase tax) all revenue is lost if evasion takes place at the final stage. So there is a great advantage of the VAT over other types of indirect taxation where introduction has to be gradual (see later chapters).

The basic theories of public finance do then provide help in judging the balance of taxes of different types. Further, if extended and used with enough data and assumptions they can be constructively applied to guide decisions on possible reforms. Explicit calculations comparing the impacts of different types of tax increases, domestic excises, tariffs, sales taxes and so on for India are provided in Ahmad and Stern (1987a), and for Pakistan in later chapters of this book.

3.4 Arguments concerning uniformity of indirect taxation

There are (at least) five groups of arguments which might suggest that indirect taxes should be at a uniform proportionate rate. The first is theoretical and concerns results which show that, under certain assumptions, uniform indirect taxation is an optimum solution in the sense of Pareto efficiency or a combination of equity and efficiency as reflected in a social welfare function. These arguments have been examined in sections 3.2 and 3.3. Related results characterise conditions under which movements towards or away from uniformity are welfare-improving. The second concerns our ignorance of the information on which theory suggests differential rates of tax should be based. The third group is administrative, where it is argued that uniform taxes are simpler to organise and collect, and provide less scope for evasion, than differentiated taxes. The fourth concerns the role of political and other influences, including unproductive or rent-seeking activities, where, it is suggested, the possibility of non-uniform taxes will lead to considerable opportunities for misuse of the tax system, including expenditure on lobbying by interested parties for special tax treatment. The fifth argues that it is wrong to discriminate between people (and thus goods) on the basis of their preferences. Most of the arguments in favour of uniformity have some serious content. Their proper evaluation, however, requires an understanding of the assumptions underlying the theoretical results, and this is what we have tried to provide above in sections 3.2 and 3.3. The remaining arguments concern mainly ignorance, administration and influence and we examine these in turn here.

It is commonplace to hear the claim that Ramsey taxation is all too difficult because we do not know the elasticities. Too often the claim not only is made in ignorance of what the Ramsey theory actually says but also leaves out the crucial basis for differentiation, which is excluded from the Ramsey model with its single consumer, that is, equity. Nevertheless the point that we are ignorant of elasticities is a serious one and has been stressed by Deaton (1981; also, particularly, 1987). He argues that we cannot expect to find solid evidence which would allow a convincing rejection of the hypothesis that goods are separable from labour or that, in the relevant sense, the Engel curves are sufficiently non-linear to suggest much departure from uniformity. By the relevant sense here we mean after allowing for differences across households other than in income. On the former point, for example, it is suggested, with some justification, that the kind of information on price variation and on individual household characteristics that is needed to identify cross-price elasticities is most unlikely to come together.

There are a number of reactions to this suggestion. The first and most compelling concerns income distribution and direct tax/transfer instruments. Whilst we may have limited knowledge of price elasticities, we do know that different goods are consumed by the rich and the poor. The poor in developing countries consume very few air conditioners and private cars, for example. We know further that the direct tax and transfer instruments are generally weak and far from universal. On this basis, and in accordance with the theory, there are therefore strong distributional grounds for higher taxes on goods consumed by the rich.

Second, it is not clear that ignorance implies uniformity. Our ignorance, one supposes, is such that there are a number of null hypotheses which we cannot convincingly reject and it is not clear that uniformity should occupy centre stage. Further there are some things on which our ignorance may not be overwhelming. We might, for example, be more happy with the hypothesis that the complementarity of tinned beans with leisure is less than that for golf clubs with leisure than we would with the null hypothesis that the two compensated cross-elasticities are equal. This, together with the distributional arguments, might help explain why in most countries the tax rate on food is less than that on golf clubs.

Administrative arguments do weigh against excessive differentiation. Where groups of goods are taxed at the same rate there is less need for accurate and detailed record-keeping. For developing countries in particular, this may be an important consideration. Differentiation makes presumptive methods (e.g. estimating sales) less easy to apply. Where new goods appear, then a general classification for tax purposes will be much easier to operate than a very detailed one. Notice, however, the kind of theory we have been discussing would, in any case, suggest similar rates of tax for goods which are close substitutes. If elasticities are a major element in the calculation then differential rates may have to be adapted to changes in tastes. Evasion may be easier with differential rates in that shopkeepers may be able to claim that the bulk of their sales are of goods classified under a category with a low tax rate.

These administrative considerations do provide powerful arguments against a myriad of different rates. They would not, however, provide convincing arguments against a VAT with, say, two rates supplemented with excises on easily identified goods such as tobacco, alcohol, private cars, air conditioners and the like.

Arguments concerning political influence and rent-seeking are less easy to evaluate. On the one hand it might be argued that differentiation gives governments tax handles which are too tempting. Thus they may be tempted to push up taxes on higher rated goods 'too far' or bring 'the wrong' goods into the higher rate category. Thus a selective indirect tax system, even if it can be justified on efficiency or equity grounds, might eventually lead to greater distortions because of the temptations it places before governments, compared with a broad-based system with uniform rates.

There may also be special pleading, lobbying and bribery or corruption by interested groups who attempt to have their goods taxed at special rates. It should be recognised, however, that in most of the models used above there is a competitive production sector and there are no pure profits or rents from monopoly positions associated with government regulation, quotas or licences. In such models there is therefore little scope for directly unproductive or rent-seeking activities. Thus, in these models, indirect taxation, uniform or differentiated, generates neither pure profits nor activities by firms which seek them. The absence of pure profits, whatever the rate structure of indirect taxation, points to an important difference between taxation measures and those based on firm-specific quotas. To the extent that this aspect of the model is a good description, rent-seeking arguments are less important for the discussion of indirect taxation than for other areas of government intervention.

One must not, however, take the models as literal descriptions of the world and it should be recognised that in the short run at least some industries can show pure profits. We would therefore expect to see, and we do, industry representatives or organisations lobbying governments for favourable treatment of their area of activity. It is unlikely, however, that the resources devoted to this industry-level lobbying would be very large (in relation to industry income, profits, etc.) since diminishing returns are likely to set in fairly quickly once the basic trade or industry associations are established and functioning (we return briefly to this issue in the concluding section). One must also ask about the marginal effect on lobbying activities of having differentiated as opposed to uniform indirect taxation. There will be exemptions, regulations and special excises in most systems so that the trade organisation is likely to be already in existence even with uniformity. If differentiated taxation is now allowed the additional resources devoted to trade lobbying may be small.

It would be very interesting to have empirical estimates of the quantity of resources devoted to lobbying in respect of the structure of indirect taxes (as opposed to lobbying in connection with regulations, licences, quotas, permissions and the like). These are rather difficult to come by but we would hazard the guess that they are small. One should ask 'Small in relation to what?' and we would suggest that a useful standard of comparison would be the collection costs of taxes. Each tax structure requires resources for its implementation and we could consider those resources which go into lobbying as part of the implicit cost associated with each type. We may take the revenue and collection costs from tobacco taxes in the UK as an example. The total revenue in 1986 was about £5 billion and if collection costs were, for example, $\frac{1}{2}\%$ (a low figure for most taxes and countries) our standard of comparison would be £25 million. This would be far more than the tobacco industry spends on lobbying against high tobacco taxes (as opposed, of course, to the advertising of individual brands, which is another matter). In this case, therefore, the resources spent on lobbying are unlikely to be crucial in determining whether a sharply differentiated tax on tobacco should be adopted.

'Political economy' considerations might also affect the balance of taxes between direct and indirect. Here it seems that the rich are likely to be more effective than the poor in manipulating the direct tax system to their advantage so that there is a general presumption that the direct tax and transfer system is unlikely to be fully optimal in the sense required for the theorems on uniform taxation. If this is the case then this aspect of political economy, together with concern for distribution, will point to differential taxation favouring goods consumed by poorer groups.

Finally we have the argument that it is wrong to distinguish between people on the grounds of preference either by types of good, or intensity of preference (or 'need') as measured by a low price elasticity. Notice that this argument makes sense only in a many-consumer economy because in a one-consumer model the Ramsey analysis is simply trying to make that consumer as well off as possible and any notion of discrimination across goods being wrong, *per se*, would have little force. It would appear, if it has content, to be an argument concerning discrimination between people. There we come back to the basic social cost–benefit calculus. Each individual is represented in the social welfare analysis embodied in the theory and has a given weight or way of entering the social welfare function. Those weights might be specified in many ways and would not generally imply uniformity except in the special conditions which are identified. The only recourse, if one is to justify this line of reasoning in favour of uniformity, is to assert that the government has no right to discriminate in taxation between those who like marmalade and those who like jam or that individuals have a right to an 'undistorted' choice between goods (goods themselves would, presumably, not have any rights to equality). In the end this boils down to simple assertion that differential taxation is wrong; this assertion appears to have little substance. For a more detailed discussion of the issues examined in this section see Stern (1990).

3.5 The general theory of reform and shadow prices

The reform analysis discussed in subsection 3.2.5 forms part of the more general theory of shadow prices. This has been examined at length in Drèze and Stern (1987) and a detailed discussion will not be provided in this book. Our aim here is to bring out the general principles and show how they provide a unifying framework for much of policy analysis. The treatment is based on Drèze and Stern (1987).

The government is concerned with the selection of certain policy variables, for example, taxes, quotas or rations. At the initial position some are chosen optimally (we call them endogenous) and the remainder are fixed at predetermined positions – the vector describing the former group is s and the latter group ω. The choice of the s for given ω may then be described by the solution of the problem:

$$\left.\begin{array}{c} \text{Maximise } V(s,\omega) \\ s \\ \text{subject to } E(s,\omega)=z \end{array}\right\} \tag{3.8}$$

where V is the social welfare function; E, net excess demands; z, public supply (many components of which may be zero). We suppose the problem has a solution. Broadly speaking we need to assume that the dimension of s is at least as great as that of z. When the two dimensions are exactly equal, then if the function $E(\ )$ is invertible, s will be defined as a function of z (and ω), and there will essentially be no choice. This situation, where the policy variables are fully determined and there is no scope for optimisation, is a special case of the model. The writing of equality in the constraint in (3.8) and the assumption that the dimension of s is at least as great as that of z are not strong assumptions but merely involve the assertion that there is a process by which equilibrium is established and by which goods are allocated in the economy (it may well be of the non-competitive variety with fixed prices, rationing and so on).

The Lagrangean for (3.8) is

$$L(s,\omega) = V(s,\omega) - v'[E(s,\omega) - z] \tag{3.9}$$

where v is the vector of shadow prices. The shadow price of a good is *defined* as the increase in the value of the social welfare function when an extra unit of public supplies becomes available, i.e., it is $\partial V^*/\partial z_i$, where $V^*(z,\omega)$ is the maximum V in the solution to (3.8). It is a standard result in optimisation theory that $\partial V^*/\partial z_i$ will be equal to the Lagrange multiplier in the optimisation problem (3.8) (whether or not the model is fully determined). The increment in social welfare from a given project dz (at constant ω but with s endogenous), from the definition of v, is $vd'z$. Hence the same shadow prices will be used both in the evaluation of projects and the evaluation of policy reform. Notice that the definition of the shadow prices here is precisely the familiar one of the opportunity costs of a good in terms of the objective (here V) and that the definition $\partial V^*/\partial z_i$ is logically prior to the Lagrangean, with equality to the Lagrange multiplier only if the constraint in (3.8) is written in the manner shown (there are, of course, many ways of writing it).

The first-order conditions for a maximum in (3.8) are

$$\frac{\partial V}{\partial s} - v'\frac{\partial E}{\partial s} = 0 \tag{3.10}$$

A reform is a change $d\omega$ in the variables ω which had previously been seen as predetermined. In order to satisfy the constraints we must have

$$\frac{\partial \mathbf{E}}{\partial \omega} d\omega + \frac{\partial \mathbf{E}}{\partial s} ds = 0 \qquad (3.11)$$

Using (3.10) and (3.11) we have

$$dV = \left(\frac{\partial V}{\partial \omega} - \mathbf{v}' \frac{\partial \mathbf{E}}{\partial \omega}\right) d\omega \qquad (3.12)$$

This is the general result on policy reform. It tells us that the welfare impact of a reform is given by the direct effect on social welfare less the cost of the extra net demands at shadow prices $\mathbf{v}' \, \partial \mathbf{E}/\partial \omega$. This is a unifying principle which underlies many discussions of policy change. It is at one level simple and obvious but it often seems to be imperfectly understood. An example will illustrate. Suppose we are considering introducing a pension for widows. The net benefit is the direct impact on the welfare of widows $(\partial V/\partial \omega_i)$ less the cost at shadow prices of the extra demands from the widows as a result of the income increase. No general equilibrium derivatives are involved. The general equilibrium repercussions involved in restoring equilibrium through the adjustment of s are fully captured in the shadow prices $\mathbf{v}$.

The model (3.8) and the derivation of (3.12) we have used make it very clear that the shadow prices will depend critically on how equilibrium is re-established after a change in z or ω, i.e. they will be different for different specifications of the endogenous variables s. For example we can think of a change in net demands of an imported good (whose world price is fixed) from a parameter change as being satisfied by extra imports with no price change or by rationed imports with an increase in the domestic price. In the former case it is the net imports that form part of s and in the latter case the price. The general equilibrium effect on social welfare will be different and thus, so too will be the shadow prices.

The marginal analysis of the preceding section can readily be seen as a special case of (3.12). The details are not provided here (see Stern, 1987) but one way of expressing the generalisation provided by (3.12) for the case where indirect taxes are to be reformed is through

$$\lambda_i^v = -\frac{\partial V}{\partial t_i} \bigg/ \frac{\partial R_v}{\partial t_i} \qquad (3.13)$$

where R_v is *shadow* revenue, i.e., government revenue where we treat $(\mathbf{g} - \mathbf{v})$ as shadow consumption taxes and $(\mathbf{v} - \mathbf{p})$ as shadow production taxes. This may be seen as follows. Let $\mathbf{Y}$ be the vector of net supplies from firms (negative entries are net factor demands) and X be the vector of net household demands (similarly negative entries represent supplies). Then $E = X - Y$. One can think of net imports as being the supply of a particular firm (and included in Y) which uses foreign exchange (identified as a separate good) to produce, that is buy, foreign goods (see Drèze and Stern, 1987). Then

$$-v'E = v'(Y - X) \tag{3.14}$$

$$= (v - p)'Y + (q - v)'X + p'Y - q'X. \tag{3.15}$$

But $p'Y - q'X$ is the profits of firms less the expenditure of households and may be seen as the direct tax revenue of the government (profits taxes less lump-sum transfers to households). Hence we can think of the right-hand side of (3.15) as shadow revenue, R_v, and write

$$-v'E = R_v \tag{3.16}$$

When $v = p$, shadow and producer prices coincide, and we are back with λ_i and (3.4). One can also write

$$dV = \left[\frac{\partial V}{\partial t} + \frac{\partial (t'X)}{\partial t} + (p - v)' \frac{\partial X}{\partial t} \right] dt \tag{3.17}$$

(where the derivatives are taken for constant p) so that in addition to the welfare and revenue effects (the first two terms on the r.h.s. of (3.17)) we have an additional shadow revenue term arising from the difference between shadow and producer prices.

There are many economies where shadow prices have been calculated. We have seen here that their use is not confined to project appraisal but applies also to the analysis of policy reform in general. Care should be taken, however, to ensure consistency of the models used in the reform discussion and those used to calculate shadow prices.

The shadow prices capture a great deal of information, essentially the full general equilibrium effects on welfare of a policy change. In principle they should be derived from a fully articulated general equilibrium model and one could argue that if such a model is available then welfare effects of policy changes can be calculated directly. However, in many cases the set of shadow prices will be a tool which is more flexible, reliable, less demanding and more easily understood than the full model. They provide sufficient statistics for policy from the full model and can be discussed directly. And one supposes that corresponding to any plausible set of shadow prices one could construct a general equilibrium model and welfare judgements which would be consistent with the shadow prices. Hence, for example, if one argued that population growth and better labour market policies were likely to bring about a substantial reduction in the shadow wage, one could then examine fairly rapidly the consequences for tax policy. On the other hand it may involve a great deal of effort to redesign a large model (if such already exists) to take account of the changed assumptions. At the same time one hopes that (or should try to check that) variations of assumptions in one area do not produce huge changes in the whole shadow price vector, otherwise the credibility of the approach would be undermined (although such a situation would be likely to make any approach perilous).

In practice shadow prices are generally calculated without a fully articulated general equilibrium model and using some fairly simple short-cuts. The hope is that the shadow prices thereby calculated may be fairly robust to changes in the implicit underlying model. The theory of shadow prices we have begun to describe above allows one to examine simple rules for the calculation of shadow prices and to investigate the circumstances under which such rules might be reliable. The best-known, and indeed the most robust of these rules is that for goods traded on world markets the shadow price should be the world or border price – f.o.b. for exports and c.i.f. for imports. This has been the basis of most of the widely used cost–benefit methods as recommended by national or international agencies – for example, Little and Mirrlees (1974) for the OECD; Dasgupta, Marglin and Sen (1972) for UNIDO; the recent British manual, Overseas Development Administration (1988); Squire and van der Tak (1975) for the World Bank. The other rules, for non-tradables and factors, are less robust, and rules for both tradables and other goods are discussed further in chapter 5 where we present the methods for calculating shadow prices used in our work.

3.6 Dynamic issues and problems for the theory

Discussions of the problems of developing countries often centre on growth and change, yet the theories we have examined so far focus on an apparently static trade-off between efficiency and equity. We ask in this section how the models can be adapted or reinterpreted to bring in dynamic aspects more explicitly and what different problems and issues arise when time, change and growth move to the centre of the stage.

We begin this analysis from a somewhat formal viewpoint, i.e. we ask how the standard models we have been analysing can be reinterpreted to give us immediately a dynamic theory of taxation. This will provide a benchmark so that a number of important issues can be seen as arising from the failure of the standard framework to allow for certain important dynamic problems. Whilst not all of the problems we shall indicate occur only in a dynamic context, they can take a more acute form. (For a more detailed discussion of some of the issues raised, see Newbery and Stern, 1987b.)

The familiar Arrow–Debreu model of general equilibrium which underlies the standard models presented in section 3.2 can be interpreted in the usual way as a full intertemporal model provided all goods are distinguished by their date of availability. Thus, if there are N (physically) different goods and T periods, there will be NT markets (a similar interpretation in terms of uncertainty and different states of nature is also possible). The standard results in welfare economics relating competitive equilibrium to Pareto efficiency then apply. One can extend this interpretation and these results to infinite horizons provided one adds an assumption about asymptotic behaviour to rule out 'over-saving'. Similarly the Diamond and Mirrlees taxation model can be applied to this framework too. Thus consumers maximise utility, defined over the indefinite future, with knowledge of future consumer prices and incomes and make commitments for supplies of services and purchases of goods. Producers choose intertemporal production to maximise the present value of profits at the producer prices which they face. The optimal taxes, which are the differences between consumer and producer prices, then define a tax system over the indefinite future. Interest rates are a central aspect of the intertemporal prices and the efficiency theorems imply that all producers should face the same interest rates. Profits taxation should apply to present values and not be based on period-by-period returns. Savings would, in general, be taxed (producer and consumer prices would differ) to raise revenue and improve the interpersonal distribution of income (which includes the distribution of income between individuals at different points of time).

The model is a useful point of reference but raises a number of basic difficulties for applied policy analysis for developing countries, many of which apply to analyses for developed countries too, and examples of which follow. First, many of the postulated markets do not exist. Second, it is difficult to separate savings and investment decisions (and thus consumer and producer intertemporal prices) for a large fraction of the private sector. For example, many or most business startups are financed out of individual savings (see Little, Mazumdar and Page, 1984). This problem arises in part from lack of markets but also has to do with the poor development of financial intermediaries, asymmetric perceptions or information (the bank may not share my view of my chances of success) and costs of enforcing arrangements in an informal sector. Third, the kind of dynamic optimisation by individuals and firms which is assumed is implausible since they may have only a hazy vision of the future and ill-formed and complex preferences over future outcomes. This is not to say that they are irrational but that the detailed dynamic optimisation model with unrestricted trading possibilities may not have an overwhelming claim as the appropriate representation of their behaviour. There is no doubt that all these problems arise in some shape or form in the static model but they are particularly pervasive and severe in the dynamic context. There has not, in our judgement, been great success in the literature in integrating these features into a dynamic tax analysis, but we shall discuss below some models which are specifically designed for a dynamic context.

Further, there are particular features and difficulties which arise when we move to dynamic problems. For example, there may be incentives to renege on previous commitments or announced policies, sometimes called 'dynamic inconsistency' (see below). Second, the open-endedness of the economy can lead to problems of dynamic inefficiency of the kind which do not arise in a static economy; for example, it is easy to write down growth problems where no optimum exists, essentially because there appear to be grounds in the model for postponing consumption indefinitely. Third, there are problems associated with how individuals are forced to observe budget constraints (there have to be mechanisms to prevent build-up of debt in circumstances where individuals can promise to pay later). Fourth, in models of overlapping generations, transfers between generations can produce types of inefficiency which do not arise in static problems; for example, if each generation is endowed with a chocolate then the first generation can be made better off by each generation passing a chocolate to its immediate antecedents – none of the others is worse off. One has to look carefully at how resources can be transferred. All these issues make the formal dynamic analysis of tax policy particularly problematic.

3.6.1 'Dynamic inconsistency' and tax amnesties

Of the problems special to dynamic economics perhaps the one which has received most attention in the policy literature is that of 'dynamic inconsistency'. The issue was raised by Kydland and Prescott (1977) and a clear description in the tax policy context is provided in Fischer (1980). The idea is that the future tax policy announced by the government last period will no longer be optimal when it comes to implementation this period, not because the future has developed in an unexpected way, but because the passage of time has now made certain disincentives irrelevant. Thus last period the government may have announced that capital taxation in the second (now current) period would be low in order to encourage accumulation. In the second period the government may then simply announce a capital levy. This is a lump-sum tax with no distortionary implications and, *ex post*, is the best way to raise second period revenue.

The two-period model makes the point starkly but the problem is clearly a general one. Further, individuals who realise that the government will want to depart from its announced policies may not believe the announcement. In this framework it is possible that governments may be able to do better if they can bind themselves not to change, for example in some constitutional manner.

Examples of the problem arise with amnesties for tax evaders. These are sometimes announced as one-off chances to 'come clean', with very lenient penalties if evasion is revealed before a certain date but very severe penalties if evasion is subsequently discovered. If the evader believes this, then he may be tempted to reveal, and the subsequent very severe penalties will become redundant and need not be used. However, if the taxpayers see this happen once they may be very tempted to evade subsequently in the hope of taking advantage of a future amnesty. This may also explain the behaviour of potential taxpayers in the Pakistan context.

3.6.2 'Savings and growth'

The discussion of practical policy towards taxation in developing countries has avoided the more esoteric modelling problems and has expressed the dynamic issues in terms of broader or more aggregated concepts such as savings, investment and growth. Much of the early post-war literature on development (see, for example, Lewis, 1954) placed the rate of growth at the centre of the stage and many authors have singled out government concern, and the perceived responsibility, for raising the rate of growth as a major distinguishing feature of public finance in developing countries (for example, Eshag, 1983; Goode, 1984; Prest, 1972). Developed countries may worry about the growth rate too but often greater emphasis is placed on the rate of technical progress than on savings and investment per se. And the experience of developing countries in the thirty years since Lewis was writing tells us that raising the savings rate is not necessarily a sufficient condition for rapid growth. For example, India raised her savings rate over a period of thirty years or so from 5–10% to 20–25%, a rate similar to that of most of the industrial market economies, yet saw little acceleration in economic growth. A number of other developing countries have had a similar experience in this respect.

If a growth objective is firmly adopted then a government should take careful account of the effects of its policies on saving and the level and productivity of investment. Policies for the encouragement of savings and investment include favourable tax treatment of saving, promotion of financial institutions and attention to the level and structure of interest rates. One would like to examine these policies in the consequentialist manner by first predicting their outcomes and then evaluating the changes. A major problem is that the relevant elasticities of response are very hard to judge. This applies to both savings and investment.

There has been considerable recent literature on modelling and estimating savings responses in developed countries. A useful survey is provided by King (1985) who argues that one often finds that life-cycle models are consistent with behaviour for 70–75% of the population but not for the remaining 25% or so, and one may suggest that for this minority credit constraints may be important. Whilst the data underlying these studies are very rich compared to those available for developing countries, the researchers have not found it easy to pick up the response of savings to post-tax returns, an aspect which is crucial for the design of tax policy.

The lessons for developing countries of these studies may be as follows. First, the minority of 25% in developed countries for whom life-cycle models are inappropriate may be much larger in developing countries where financial markets are less well-developed. Second, it is unlikely to be possible given current data to establish an interest elasticity of saving for developing countries. In the meantime policy has to be formulated and it seems sensible to avoid losing substantial amounts of tax revenue in schemes for the promotion of savings whose net effect is dubious or obscure. Further, one should try to avoid creating tax anomalies which may arise from special treatment of different kinds of savings since they can lose tax revenue and redistribute income in favour of the more rich and knowledgeable, and may have little further effect other than the rearrangement of some portfolios.

There have been a number of applied policy models focused on taxation and savings for developed countries but they will not be reviewed in detail here: for recent discussions see Chalmley (1983), Kotlikoff (1984), Newbery and Stern (1987b) and Auerbach and Kotlikoff (1987). In most of the models, however detailed, the interest elasticity is a crucial variable, yet it is one on which we have little to rely on in the way of estimates: see, for example, Gersovitz's chapter on savings in Chenery and Srinivasan (1989) or Giovannini (1985). The policy simulations have often been concerned with switches from income to consumption-based taxes and a central issue has been the effect on capital accumulation via saving.

3.6.3 The expenditure tax

The base of taxation has also been discussed in overlapping generations models which are in the same spirit as the Diamond–Mirrlees standard model of taxation in section 3.2 (see Atkinson and Sandmo, 1980, and

King, 1980). The relevant goods in the utility function are, for example, consumption in two periods and labour supply in one (if the second period is retirement). With separability of consumption from labour one can show (analogously to the results in the static model of section 3.2) that taxation of consumption in the two periods should be uniform and one can interpret this as a proportional expenditure tax in the two periods. However, with labour supply in more than one period, or without separability, the result does not hold and thus one can conclude that there is no strong theoretical argument for an expenditure tax. More recent advocacy of such taxes has been on practical grounds and, in particular, on the grounds that it removes the distinction between capital and income, a common basis of tax dodges and anomalies (see, for example, Meade, 1978 and Kay and King, 1986). These suggested practical advantages have not impressed themselves on many governments, at least not to the point of actually introducing such a tax. An unfortunate example, which still reinforces such hesitancy, was the Indian experience when, in the 1950s, an expenditure tax was introduced on the advice of Kaldor but, after raising negligible revenue and much protest, was very quickly withdrawn (see chapter 5).

The theoretical difficulties we have indicated together with the lack of empirical knowledge on the interest elasticity and tax responsiveness of savings and investment suggest that we should be cautious in drawing strong conclusions concerning dynamic tax policy. There are, nevertheless, a few guidelines one can offer and some cautionary tales. We saw, for example, that there is no convincing theoretical argument in favour of expenditure rather than income taxes although one should be aware of revenue losses associated with separate treatment of capital and income. On the investment side, promising areas for study of the dynamic effects of public policy concern more direct encouragement or the removal of hindrances (as opposed to tax concessions). Possibilities include the reform of financial markets to supply credit more easily, and relaxing constraints on investment associated with infrastructure such as water and electricity supplies. Thus there may well be substantial scope for promoting the profitability of investments in ways which do not involve big tax concessions. Arguments for tax concessions should be examined rather carefully to check that any claimed response is likely to be present. Otherwise the concessions may simply act as a transfer payment. It should be emphasised that there is no assertion here that we should assume from our lack of knowledge that savings and investment actually are inelastic. Our ignorance should make us cautious and we should not, therefore, tax investment heavily on the dubious grounds that we 'may as well assume' it is interest inelastic.

3.6.4 Public investment policy

Finally, a concern to promote savings and growth can be embodied in our appraisal of public investment policy. If it is thought appropriate, a premium on savings can be built into the shadow prices which are used to guide the selection of public projects so that we favour those which, *ceteris paribus*, generate more saving (see, for example, Little and Mirrlees, 1974, or Drèze and Stern, 1987). And the same shadow prices can be used to guide other policy appraisal such as tax and price reform. One should, however, first establish clearly that there *should be* a premium on savings – it is certainly not something which can be regarded as obvious.

3.7 The taxation of corporate and personal income

The analysis of this chapter has, to this point, been mainly concerned with indirect taxes, although in doing the analysis we have also had to discuss the personal income tax. We concentrate now on the taxation of corporations before returning briefly to the personal income tax.

3.7.1 The corporate income tax

In most developing countries the corporate income tax is much more important than the personal income tax. From the point of view of a theory which sees changes in welfare in terms of effects on households the corporate income tax has a limited role. In the class of models considered in section 3.2 the pure profits tax (where such can be identified) should in general be used where possible (assuming owners of firms do not have very high net social marginal utilities of income) but a corporate income tax does not otherwise appear in the models unless one considers it as, in part, a tax on entrepreneurial or capital services provided by households. However, in answering the question why there should be a corporate income tax within the type of theory we have been examining, one can point to four possible responses. First, it acts in part as a tax on monopoly rents or pure profits. Second, it provides a way of taxing foreign owners. Third, it may help in policies designed to promote savings or investment. Fourth, its removal would provide a windfall gain to those who are far from impoverished. All of these arguments apply to both developed and developing countries but they may well be stronger in the latter case. Hence the more prominent role of the corporate income tax, relative to the personal income tax, in developing countries is not without foundation in the principles we have been discussing. Perhaps the most important reason, however, for taxing corporations is as a means of collection of taxes on personal incomes. As we have already noted, this applies to foreign owners but it applies to domestic owners too where the system of domestic personal income taxation is weak and easily evaded, particularly by the owners of corporations who, we suppose, are not usually amongst the poorest of the population.

The form of the corporate income tax can vary greatly depending on its treatment of distributed and undistributed profits, depreciation allowances, inflation, interest payments, and so on. Profits can also be manipulated by multi-nationals through transfer-pricing, e.g. inflating the costs of certain inputs, or deflating output prices to depress measured profits in countries where profits taxation is high. These complications require careful scrutiny in the examination of policy for a particular country.

Theoretical and empirical research on the corporate income tax is even less easy to present in a coherent and integrated form than research on other taxes, partly because it sits somewhat unhappily in the economic theory of tax policy. Discussion has focused on a number of issues concerning the possible effects of the tax rather than on attempting to construct a theory of policy design. Further, the effects of the tax are rather difficult to quantify both theoretically and empirically. Thus concentration has often been on potential incentives and disincentives associated with different systems rather than the explicit modelling of the full effects of these incentives. Most of the work has been for developed countries although, as ever, the issues apply to developing countries too. However, in the latter case one suspects that the immediate problems are more in devising ways to actually collect revenue rather than in fine tuning. This should not, however, lead us to ignore the possible effects on the level and allocation of investment and saving. The revenue from the corporate income tax is likely to grow over time as more advanced sectors develop and it is important to have a sensible system in advance. It is surely possible to learn from the experience of developed countries; for example, from the UK where the corporate tax system has grown as a series of rather *ad hoc* responses to short-term pressures (see Kay and King, 1986).

We shall describe very briefly some of the prominent issues in the literature on the corporate income tax and then point to possible lessons for tax design. One of the major themes has been the different treatment of distributed and undistributed profits together with the returns to and choices between different forms of finance. With the *classical* system, for example, the corporate income tax applies (usually at a flat proportional rate) on all profits whether distributed or undistributed, together with a personal income tax on the dividends. Thus dividends are taxed at a higher rate than undistributed profits. In this sense there is a 'discrimination' in favour of retentions. Undistributed profits, it is true, may be taxed via a capital gains tax, if it exists, but this is usually at a lower rate than personal income taxes. Further, it is often haphazardly collected, raising very little revenue.

Under this classical system there is a bias in favour of loan finance rather than raising money from new share issues. Interest payments are deductible for corporate income tax purposes so that a project which yields a return above the rate of interest will generate a surplus for the shareholders if it is financed by a loan (assuming all costs are properly charged including depreciation). In this sense the corporate income tax treats loan-financed investment in a neutral way. On the other hand, a project financed out of a new share issue is financed by a promise to pay dividends (as opposed to interest). Dividends are not an allowable cost for corporate income tax purposes so that the required return on the company's investment now exceeds the rate of interest.

Finance out of retained profits is more complicated. If a firm retains profits rather than paying out dividends, then the shareholder forgoes the net-of-tax dividends. The company invests this amount gross-of-tax. If it retains the proceeds from the investment, then from the point of view of the net returns to the individual shareholder, these are taxed at the corporation tax rate plus the capital gains tax rate. If this latter combined rate exceeds the personal income tax rate then the required rate of return again exceeds the rate of interest. Thus, whether there is also a bias against retained earnings (relative to loan finance) depends on the personal tax position of the shareholders. If corporate taxes are collected more effectively than the personal income tax we would indeed expect this bias to be present.

The other major form of the corporate income tax in practice is the *imputation* system. Tax withheld on dividends is credited against the corporate tax at a rate known as the imputation rate. If the imputation rate is equal to the individual shareholder's personal marginal rate then that is the end of the matter. Otherwise there will be extra tax to pay by the individual if the imputation rate is lower than the marginal rate (and a refund if higher). This system reduces the bias in favour of loan versus equity finance but it is still present provided the imputation rate is lower than the corporate rate (if the former is 30% and the latter 50%, then £100 in gross dividends reduces corporate tax liability by £30, whereas £100 in interest reduces the liability by £50). The classical system operates in the US and several other developed and developing countries, whereas the imputation system applies in the UK and several Commonwealth countries.

The discussion makes it clear that the relation between the rate of return on an investment gross-of-tax and the return to savers will be a very intricate one depending on many things, including the form of finance, the corporate income tax system, the personal income tax system, the tax status of the saver, the tax treatment of the particular kind of asset, and so on. In these circumstances the task of describing the tax system in terms of the 'wedge' placed between the gross and net-of-tax rates of return is formidable, leaving aside any attempt to work out the allocative consequences of such wedges in terms of the response by individuals to the different incentives and the general equilibrium ramifications of these responses. For further discussion of the implications of different forms of corporation tax, along the lines presented above, see, for example, Kay and King (1986) and King (1977). Calculations of the different tax wedges for different forms of asset, sources of finance, and types of individual for the US, the UK, Sweden and West Germany are presented in King and Fullerton (1984). They show that within a country the range of tax wedges is very large. There are also considerable differences between countries in many important respects. For example, pre- and post-tax rates of return are on average very close (the average wedge is small) for the UK, and the latter is half the former, on average, for West Germany.

Notwithstanding the difficulties of even describing the system, there have been a number of calculations of the welfare losses associated with the tax wedges following the work of Harberger in 1962 (reprinted in Harberger, 1974); see, for example, McLure (1975) and Shoven and Whalley (1972). The assumptions involved are highly restrictive even for developed countries and, according to Goode (1984, p. 116), they have little influence or relevance for developing countries. It is nevertheless important to try to understand the likely important determinants of the incidence of the corporate income tax. This is often referred to as 'the shifting of the corporate income tax' although the term is ambiguous as it is sometimes taken to mean the effect on prices and sometimes the ultimate incidence in terms of its effect on households (see King, 1977, p. 248). In particular, Diamond (1970) has looked at the incidence of property taxes in a growth model. Perhaps the most important influence on incidence is the openness of the economy as Goode (1984), King (1977) and Gil Diaz (1987) all emphasise. Gil Diaz (1987) in particular provides a valuable practical example in his evaluation of Mexico's recent tax reform (1978–82) where he argues that post-tax rates of return in Mexico cannot fall below the pre-tax rates in the US for those Mexicans who cannot be prevented from having access to US investment opportunities. Hence taxes on capital income are borne in large part by those credit users without access to international markets.

Another interesting recent discussion of the role of corporate income tax has been provided by Gersovitz (1987), who examined the effects of such taxes on foreign private investment. These effects turn out to be very complex, depending on many factors, for example, the tax agreements and the treatment of host and home countries, the likelihood of expropriation and the potential for transfer pricing.

In such an intricate and rather messy problem one cannot expect to be able to provide a synthesis of the basic determinants of optimal policy in the manner attempted for indirect taxes. King's response (1977, p. 249) is to seek criteria of neutrality or to ask that the system be non-distortionary. Thus, for example, it is suggested that, unless there is special reason, it should not distinguish between different forms of finance or between different forms of assets. Possibilities are

(i)   a classical system without deductibility of interest payments, together with capital gains taxed at full personal rates;
(ii)   full integration of corporate and personal income taxation (with deductibility of interest);
(iii) a cash flow corporation tax (where the cash flow for tax purposes excludes financial transactions).

Space limitations prevent further detail here but it should be clear that the merits of any particular system will turn on the precise detail of the system and on what is practically possible in the country under study.

A corporate tax system which does not distort will, in general, act like a government shareholding in the firm, if losses are fully off-set, since the government takes a given fraction (the tax rate) of the gains and losses from any project. This implies a sharing of risks between public and private sector which may encourage risk-taking.

Special incentives for investment are very popular in developing countries. Amongst these, tax holidays are particularly popular (see, e.g., Shah and Toye, 1979). However, as Gersovitz (1987) points out, there are a number of problems and abuses which may lead simply to a loss of tax revenue without any corresponding increase in investment. And any tax bonus for investment should be very carefully justified. Are there externalities to investment which are not reflected in market prices? If so, perhaps taxation or subsidy policy should be focused directly on those prices which are supposed to be wrong. Is the proposed tax incentive compensating for some alleged disincentive elsewhere in the tax system of the kind we have been discussing? If so, then perhaps it is the disincentive which should be tackled directly. Or is it being argued that for reasons of inter-temporal allocation (e.g., future generations being under-represented) the tax wedge should be negative rather than positive? Again, the position is unclear. Too often, it is taken as obvious that special tax incentives for investment are needed. The evidence that they have much incentive effect is scanty and it is likely that revenue losses are substantial.

Our conclusions from the somewhat messy state of the subject are that the guiding principles should probably be simplicity, practicality and neutrality. Complex provisions without clear rationale should be discarded, particularly where they lose revenue. Special treatment for particular industries should be viewed with suspicion. Allowable deductions should be scrutinised very carefully. Finally we would suggest that the withholding of tax on dividends is likely to be a practical way of actually collecting the revenue.

3.7.2   Personal income taxation

As we have seen, the theory of the optimal personal income tax is rather better developed than that of the optimal corporate income tax. However, it probably has limited applicability to developing countries where the coverage of the income tax is usually very restricted. Nevertheless, like the corporate income tax, it has potential for the future and one should think ahead. Again it is sensible to focus on simplicity and practicality in designing policy.

One area where theory and practicality come together concerns transfers. The standard theory of welfare economics indicates that distributive objectives can be effectively pursued by direct transfers to the deserving. On practical grounds it is clear that the personal income tax is not a useful tool for protecting the poorest where they are outside the income tax system and devices such as the negative income tax are not relevant for them. How far it is a useful tool for redistribution by taxing the rich is largely a question of coverage and enforcement. Here, as broad a base as possible, together with moderate marginal rates, probably provides the best marriage between theoretical and administrative considerations. There is no general theoretical argument for anything other than a broad base. Permissible allowances should be confined to aspects of horizontal equity, principally concerned with family structure. There is no conceptual reason for excluding real capital gains or non-cash fringe benefits such as housing, cars and education. The major role of the capital gains tax is to protect the base for the income tax, rather than to generate revenues *per se*. A broad base for the income tax provides scope for lower rates and we find that calculations of optimal taxes in which redistribution and incentives are traded off do not provide arguments for very high rates, that is, above 65% or so (see, for example, Mirrlees, 1971, and Stern, 1976). It is often argued that very high rates encourage evasion so that theory and administration, in this case, point the same way. As with the taxation of dividends, the withholding of tax at source for all types of income is an important tool for collection.

The choice of exemption level for the personal income tax involves balancing redistribution, revenue and administration. A low exemption level is likely to bring more potential taxpayers into the tax net than can be dealt with by the revenue authorities. On the other hand, high exemption levels lose revenue and may be seen as unfair. There is no general rule, but often governments in developing countries seem to err on the side of generosity. This may be understandable where administrative resources are scarce but it may be desirable in some cases to let these exemption levels increase less fast than money GNP per capita so that over time a greater proportion of the population is brought into the income tax net. In this way one can provide for a growing role of the personal income tax.

We have seen in section 3.2 that theory has quite a lot to say about the optimal balance between income taxes and indirect taxes. The crucial elements are (i) the sources of differences between households, (ii) the structure of preferences, and (iii) the form of the available income tax. We saw, in particular, how one could check the requirement in this theory that an optimal uniform lump-sum transfer was in operation – one compares the social marginal cost of a rupee of revenue spent on such a transfer with the social marginal cost of raising it through indirect taxes. If the former is higher then indirect taxes should be increased to finance an increase in the transfer. In Ahmad and Stern (1987a) we carry out such a calculation for India and find that for most 'reasonable' value judgements the lump-sum transfer would appear to be too low. This is hardly surprising since the element of transfer for many of the very poor households would be negligible. We also carry out a comparison between the welfare costs of raising revenue from higher income taxpayers and from indirect taxes and find that the former is preferable under most value judgements.

There are, however, major problems with this type of calculation. First, one would normally be forced to leave out of account factor supply responses. These are imperfectly understood for developed countries notwithstanding the great amount of econometric work on rich data sets (see, for example, Hausman, 1981). There are few data sets in developing countries which would permit such exercises, and even those that exist are unlikely to provide answers. Second, it requires an assessment of the actual incidence of proposed changes in transfers or income taxes. If the food-ration system were to be expanded, would this really be a transfer to each household or would just a few benefit? If so, who? Similarly we have to ask about the pattern of extra payments if rates for upper income groups are changed. Third, one has to consider administration costs. It should be emphasised, however, that these are not problems special to the marginal or non-marginal techniques we have been examining. They would arise in any serious attempt to examine possible changes.

It is probably reasonable to suggest that the relatively small role for the income tax in developing countries can be attributed to costs of administration rather than judgements about items (i)–(iii) listed above. Nevertheless as the economy grows, the population becomes better educated, and accounting more widespread, one may suppose that the income tax will play an increasing role and one should think carefully how to structure the tax system to take advantage of the potential for growth. An advantage of the theory is that it points to tax tools and to comparisons which might otherwise be missed – for example the central role of lump-sum transfers, such as food rations, or taxes linked to household characteristics.

3.8 Alternative approaches

As we noted in our discussion of shadow prices in section 3.5, one of the sharpest contrasts between discussions of public economics for developed and for developing countries lies in the treatment of taxes and production. The concentration in the theory for developed countries has been on government revenue, on the allocation of consumption and on factor supply, issues which are within the spirit of the standard model of section 3.2. The assumption of fixed producer prices in that theory is common. On the other hand, in the study of developing countries great attention has been focused on the incentives facing producers in terms of the effects of government policies on the prices they face – these considerations lie at the heart of the discussions of shadow prices (see above, and chapter 4). Many have argued that the consequence of government policy in developing countries, particularly concerning taxes, has often been the wrong pattern of outputs, whereas in developed countries criticism is focused on the alleged curtailment of incentives for factor supply and on the distributive effects. In this section we discuss three methods, in addition to that using shadow prices which is adopted in this book, for bringing production distortions into the picture: the calculation of effective protection, the use of computable general equilibrium models, and consideration of marginal reform in general equilibrium models without the use of shadow prices.

Effective protection

The basic principles of the normative analysis of policy reform when shadow prices are not equal to producer prices were provided in section 3.5. One calculates the direct effect on households of a policy change and then adjusts this for the value at shadow prices of the net changes in excess demand associated with the direct effects in order to pick up the general equilibrium repercussions of the change. It is interesting to contrast this approach with discussions based on effective protection, a concept frequently used in discussions of tariffs and the pattern of production (see the *Journal of International Economics* symposium, 1983), where a number of aspects of effective protection are examined. The first point to note is that the rate of effective protection for an activity, defined as the value added at domestic prices in that activity less that at world prices (as a proportion of value added at world prices), is not a normative concept but an attempt to describe what happens to value added in different industries as a result of tariffs and quantitative restrictions. As a positive concept the rate of effective protection has important drawbacks since its satisfactory definition and predictive power depend crucially on the assumption of fixed coefficients for intermediate inputs. Without this assumption the value added per unit of output will be influenced by the combination of intermediate inputs involved and its role as an indicator of resource use will be confused. Further, 'it is possible that without this assumption the effective protection given to an activity rises, but this induces such strong substitution of intermediate inputs for primary ones, that the primary factor use in that industry actually falls' (Dixit and Norman, 1980, p. 163).

As a normative suggestion concerning resource movements the argument is unsatisfactory in further respects. First, it takes no account of possible divergences between market prices and social opportunity costs (or shadow prices) for non-traded and factor inputs. Once proper account is taken of the former we have essentially moved to the notion of domestic resource cost (or DRC), and the further step of treating the social opportunity cost of factors carefully takes us to a system of shadow prices. Second, the prescription of moving factors to less protected industries based on effective protection takes no account of the scale of movement. If coefficients for non-factor inputs are fixed it would appear to tell us to transfer an indefinite amount into the activity with the lowest effective protection rate. Third, one should ask the question as to why the protection is there in the first place. Whilst the arguments for protection are often spurious, one should not assume that they are always so.

Effective protection calculations are also often used in discussions of tariff reform in that it is suggested that tariffs should be adjusted to make lower the effective protection rates for industries with higher rates. Again this is unsatisfactory. There is nothing to suggest that uniform effective protection rates have any general optimality properties. As we argued in the previous section, in the absence of lump-sum taxes a government concerned with incentives and distribution should, in an open-economy competitive world, have taxes on final sales only, irrespective of origin. Thus there would be no tariffs or any other taxes affecting relative prices facing producers. Further, the taxes on final sales, that is those which create differences between producer and consumer prices, would not usually be uniform. One would require an articulated model with a careful statement concerning constraints on policies to justify any assertion that uniform effective rates of protection are optimal and it is very unclear how such an argument could be constructed.

The main advantage of calculations of effective rates of protection lies in reminding policy-makers that their actions affect not only output prices but also input costs and in making some of these effects explicit. As we have argued, however, they are unreliable guides to policy reform. The central notion in project appraisal is that of shadow prices and greater use of this concept outside the area of project appraisal could be valuable.

Computable general equilibrium models

The second alternative we shall consider is in sharp contrast to the effective protection analysis in that it works entirely with a fully articulated and detailed multi-sector general equilibrium model of the economy designed to predict explicitly the outcomes of non-marginal policy changes. These models are usually grouped under the heading of computable general equilibrium models (CGEs). It is unnecessary to review these in detail because there have already been excellent surveys: see, for instance, Shoven (1983), Shoven and Whalley (1984) and Robinson (1989). For a number of applications see, for example, Dervis, de Melo and Robinson (1982), or for a country case study (Mexico), Kehoe and Serra-Puche (1983). Typically production functions are constant elasticity of substitution (CES), factor markets are perfect and preferences are of a fairly standard type (often also CES). The free parameters in the model are chosen so that the national accounts structure fits for a particular base year. Policy variables are then changed and the new equilibrium is computed. Household utilities can be compared before and after the change to come to a judgement as to whether the change is beneficial.

This is not the place to discuss these models at length and we shall confine ourselves to some brief comments concerning their use in policy discussion. First, they require a very large number of parameters many or most of which are essentially imposed exogenously. Second, the scope for sensitivity analysis is rather narrow. For example, one can vary an elasticity of substitution fairly easily but it would generally require a great deal of work to change the structure of a market. Third, and related to the first two points, it is not easy to make an intuitive assessment of the role of crucial assumptions in determining the answers. Thus CGE models tend to be used as black boxes with few questions asked as to where answers are coming from. Fourth, the detail they provide on the consumption side is generally rather less than would be required in coming to a judgement about the different types of gainers and losers – typically there may be twenty or so household groups compared with a household survey of five or ten thousand households. One of the purposes of the analysis is to determine the characteristics of those who will be most affected and if the sub-groups are chosen in advance this kind of information can be obscured.

On the more positive side, the models are explicit and they do allow some flexibility. The greater detail in production may pick up important points which might be missed in a more aggregated framework. And the models allow estimation of changes in factor prices. However, some of the detail in the results is spurious in the sense that it is the consequence of fairly arbitrary assumptions, and the calculations for a particular industry would be unlikely to substitute for an industry study if some special sectors were at issue.

There are two main advantages of using the more aggregated comput-able applied models. First, in these smaller models it may be possible to gain a good intuitive understanding of how the model works. Second, they can allow optimisation. There are a number of recent examples of the study of models which allow the tracing of the effects of non-marginal changes in policy (e.g. Braverman, Hammer and Ahn, 1987). Heady and Mitra (1987) provide applied models of tax and investment policy which can be optimised numerically. They also show how the model's simple structure can be used to discuss the analytical framework before embarking on computations.

Marginal reforms without shadow prices

Similarly these less aggregated models can allow explicit analytical discussion of marginal changes in a manner which allows one both to see which are the important parameters and put in plausible parameter estimates (see, for example, Newbery, 1987a, on Korea). As in other models, however, it is crucial to define the way in which the public sector acts in the restoration of equilibrium after a policy change. The action of the public sector is often implicit and this can lead to considerable lack of clarity (see Newbery, 1987b, and for further discussion, chapter 5 below).

To conclude this section we should emphasise that each of the methods has its strengths and weaknesses. The shadow price approach we have adopted here has the advantage of being soundly based on a clear theory while allowing a number of short-cuts or rough and ready approximations (see chapter 5) using real data that permit practical implementation on a multi-sectoral scale. This approach also allows a broad class of sensitivity analyses and, as we shall see later, important parts, at least, of the calculations are fairly robust to changes in assumptions.

3.9 Some simple guiding principles

As a partial summary for this chapter we shall draw out some simple guiding principles from the analysis. We shall attempt to keep the statements short and direct, omitting the many qualifications which are necessary. We have discussed the relevant assumptions and the underlying logic in the preceding sections.

(i) Where possible lump-sum taxes and transfers, or close approximations, should be used to raise revenue and transfer resources. Possible examples are land taxes and subsidised rations. It is not easy to find other examples where the lump-sum taxation can be appropriately linked to a relevant criterion (particularly wealth or poverty) without the tax or transfer ceasing to be lump-sum. See section 3.2 for further discussion.

(ii) It can be very misleading to look at one set of tax tools in isolation from what is happening elsewhere in the tax system. For example, we should not allocate redistribution to the income tax and revenue raising to indirect taxes. Both taxes affect distribution, affect resource allocation *and* raise revenue. In particular, the desirability of the differentiation in commodity taxes on distributional grounds is closely related to other policies towards distribution. The stronger are the other tools the smaller is the redistributive role for commodity taxes. See section 3.2.

(iii) The focus of indirect taxation should be final consumption. This means that intermediate goods should not be taxed unless there is difficulty in taxing final goods or there are special distributional reasons for taxing these intermediates. This applies also to tariffs, which should be rebated on intermediate goods and linked to other taxes on final goods. They should be used for protection only when the case for supporting a particular domestic industry (and penalising other industries, particularly their users) is very strong and where other means of stimulating the industry are less satisfactory. It must be recognised that the elimination of tariffs except for protection is a long-term goal which for revenue reasons could not be achieved in the short or medium term in countries with very few tax handles. But it should be pursued in the sense that tariffs should be reduced as and when the revenue from final goods taxation can be built up. Again in the short term, it is generally preferable to replace quotas by tariffs so that the rent from the quota flows directly to the government rather than to those agents who allocate or receive the quota. See section 3.3.

(iv) Public-sector prices should be set according to the same principles as indirect taxes: price equal to marginal social cost for intermediate goods (except for the cases noted in (iii) above) and marginal social cost plus an element for taxation for final goods. See section 3.2.

(v) The appropriate microeconomic criterion for the expansion of industries is, for the public sector, profitability at shadow prices of the incremental output. Other criteria (such as effective protection rates or domestic resource costs) are reliable only where they coincide with shadow prices. Similarly a reform rule based on the other indicators, such as adjusting tariffs to move towards uniform effective protection, is incorrect. See sections 3.3, 3.4 and 3.5.

(vi) Where producer prices and shadow prices coincide (see section 3.2), indirect taxes should be guided by a trade-off between efficiency and equity in allocation across households, and, in the absence of well-functioning schemes for income support, there is no prescription for uniformity of the system of indirect taxation. For individual indirect tax instruments, considerations of administrative ease are likely to be important. Where producer prices are not equal to shadow prices then, to the simple efficiency–equity considerations, one must add an upward adjustment in the tax rate for goods with relative shadow prices which are higher than relative producer prices (see sections 3.3 and 3.5).

(vii) The main economic rationale, in principle, for the corporate income tax, as distinct from the personal income tax, lies in taxing foreign incomes and monopoly rents. Occasionally these elements will be of overriding importance but generally the primary focus of the corporate income tax should be as a means of collecting the personal income tax (see section 3.7). Thus an analysis of the tax should be closely integrated with the personal income tax. A structured framework for working out the benefits of corporate tax reform is not yet available and, at present, guiding principles should be simplicity, practicality and neutrality.

We have seen then that a little systematic theory can provide some helpful guidelines for the formulation of policy, and this, of course, is one of the central reasons for theorising about taxes. Whilst many of these principles, as one would hope, accord with common sense they are not necessarily immediately obvious. Indeed the analysis indicates the assumptions that lie behind the guidelines. These are generally rather strong and again the analysis is valuable in the sense that it focuses our attention on the judgements we have to make and the elements that require checking. A further upshot of our theoretical discussion is that we have, in the general theory of reform, a powerful apparatus for thinking about the many particular problems that will arise. And finally, this theory can provide a specific structure for detailed empirical enquiry, as we shall see in later chapters.

4　The taxation of agriculture: theoretical issues

4.1　Distinctive features for taxation

There are many reasons why the taxation of agriculture deserves special study in developing countries and cannot be treated as just another example of a production activity in the standard competitive model. First, it is of central importance in both employment and output, the contributions generally being in the ranges $\frac{1}{2}$–$\frac{3}{4}$ and $\frac{1}{4}$–$\frac{1}{2}$ respectively. It therefore plays a crucial role in development strategy and is of considerable political sensitivity. Second, there are strong limitations on the tax tools available to the government, in particular it is often impossible to tax transactions between producers and consumers, the difficulty arising both when the 'transaction' is within the household and when sales are between households or in informal markets. Third, the rural labour market and working arrangements, dominated by agriculture, interact directly and indirectly with labour markets throughout the economy with important repercussions for all households and production activities. Fourth, land is a crucial input, so that, in contrast to most other economic activities, the problems with taxing rents must play an important role. Fifth, the availability and distribution of food are often regarded as of special importance and all governments should take some responsibility for its price, quality and security.

The formal methods for the analysis of reform we have developed have been extended and illustrated in a number of cases (see parts 4 and 5 of Newbery and Stern, 1987a, for examples). The principles that emerge from the theories discussed in chapter 3, and which were emphasised at the end of that chapter, can guide the setting of policy for agriculture, as we shall see both in this chapter and in chapter 8 where we examine policies towards land taxation in Pakistan. This will, we trust, illustrate how principles derived from formal methods can be used to develop policies in situations where data are limited.

As for other industries, but particularly for agriculture, one should not take a narrow view of tax policy but should set it in the context of exchange rate and pricing policies, food policies, redistribution and income protection, and general development strategies. We begin in section 4.2 with some of these broader issues, including the balance of taxation between agriculture and industry. The central role of agriculture in a developing economy means that general equilibrium effects and the interactions between agricultural input, output and factor markets and the rest of the economy will exert a major influence on the way in which tax and other policy instruments function. We examine in section 4.3 how the structure of the economic models which bring in these effects will determine the predicted impact of different policy measures. As elsewhere the presence or absence of one kind of tax or policy will exert a crucial influence on the appropriate instruments and rates of other taxes. We examine in section 4.4 the important tax tools in the light of the issues and models discussed in sections 4.2 and 4.3. The political economy of agricultural taxation is discussed briefly in section 4.5. Concluding comments are offered in section 4.6.

Our discussion in this chapter will be fairly brief as we shall not be developing theoretical models in great detail. This should not be taken to imply that we think that agricultural issues are unimportant. The principles we have already set out have influenced our recommendations concerning the taxation of agriculture and we regard this sector as crucial in the reform of the fiscal systems of countries like Pakistan.

4.2 Agriculture and tax policy: some broader issues

Tax policy towards agriculture must be influenced by a view of the appropriate role of agriculture in the economy and of those who work there. This is much less true of other activities where some might argue that the activity *per se* has no special significance and all that matters is that, as far as production goes, tax policy should avoid creating distortions between one activity and another, or at least confine itself to correcting distortions. Profitability at the 'undistorted' prices, so the argument runs, then becomes the key to which sectors should be viable. The argument, however, suffers from a lack of clarity as to the meaning of 'undistorted' prices. The selection of appropriate prices for agriculture is itself a problem which should be examined directly. Such an examination should take explicit account of the welfare of people who work there since it is particularly difficult to transfer to another sector. It would not generally be the case that the optimal prices for agricultural goods equal shadow prices.

In the medium term it is possible, and may be desirable, to close down factories making motor cycles, automobiles or steel if the market or economic analysis suggests that they are not viable. The workers involved can be diverted, via the market or a plan, to more productive industries. Tax or subsidy policies towards motor cycles or steel do not affect the incomes of unskilled workers, engineers and so on in the economy (except in the short term for those who work in the particular industry) to anything like the same extent as policies towards agriculture affect the incomes of agriculturalists.

Much of early development economics, however, concentrated less on the welfare of agriculturalists than on the contribution that agriculture might make in helping the growth of other sectors. This concerned particularly the provision of finance, labour and food. Thus the taxation of agriculture (either directly or by the manipulation of prices) is seen as a source of investible surplus in many models, including those of writers on the early stages of growth in the Soviet Union, nineteenth-century Japan and on early post-war development economics (Preobrazhensky, 1926; Fei and Ranis, 1964; Nurkse, 1953). This was closely linked to a view that the marginal productivity of labour in agriculture was very low so that labour could be withdrawn to work on an industrial project without it being necessary to reduce consumption (see Nurkse, 1953). Whether or not the marginal product was seen to be low, a decreasing share of labour in agriculture and an increasing share in industry was a central feature of the dual economy models following the Lewis (1954) article.

The view of agriculture as facilitating the growth of other sectors was not confined to finance and labour but included the provision of food to the growing industrial workforce, and the problem of the 'marketed surplus' was emphasised. Early analyses of policy models of the marketed surplus include Hornby (1968), Dixit (1971), Newbery (1974) and Dixit and Stern (1974). The importance of food production in the growth strategy is strongly influenced by whether or not the economy is open (see Newbery, 1987b, and Sah and Stiglitz, 1987, for recent analyses; see also below).

The provision of finance and labour for growth appears to militate in favour of heavy taxation of agriculture. This, of course, begs the questions of how fast growth should be, the extent to which it should be outside agriculture, and the problem of the marketed surplus. There does often seem to be an assumption by some that agriculture should be heavily taxed. The appropriate distribution of the tax burden between agriculture and industry has become a controversial question to which we shall return, although we note immediately that questions of fair or unfair burdens should ultimately be related to individuals (now and in the future) rather than sectors. Before one comes to a judgement on the appropriateness or otherwise of burdens, however, one should try to discover just how much agriculture really is taxed and this can be a complicated question. In many countries, including those of the sub-continent, it is common to hear the claim that agriculture is untaxed, on the grounds that direct taxes on land and agricultural income are either negligible in their collections or non-existent. But this is to ignore the crucial questions of prices paid for inputs and prices received for outputs and the way in which these are influenced by government policy directly or indirectly, for example, via the exchange rate.

One way in which agriculture is taxed is through import tariffs and quotas which restrict imports and therefore raise the exchange rate. This lowers the domestic price for potential exports. Since many of the exports of developing countries come from agriculture this has the effect of lowering the domestic price for agricultural outputs and in this sense is like a tax on those outputs. The estimation of the extent to which the exchange rate is raised by import tariffs and restrictions is not easy but the effects are unlikely to be small relative to the tariffs or tariff equivalents. For example, in theory an export subsidy, together with a tariff on imports, would be equivalent to a devaluation. For this equivalence to hold, the export subsidy would be at the same rate as the import tariff. The import tax cum export subsidy which is equivalent to an exchange rate adjustment would raise no revenue. This indicates also that the costs of carrying through fully compensating export subsidies are likely to be prohibitive for most developing countries. And such a tariff cum subsidy system would be pointless – one might as well simply adjust the exchange rate.

A second way that agriculture can be taxed arises through controlled buying prices for output. This can take the form of a requisition price (e.g. wheat in India) at which a farmer must sell to the authorities. If this is below world market prices (adjusted to domestic currency through an appropri-ately calculated exchange rate) then this amounts to a proportional output tax. A similar effect from the viewpoint of the farmer arises from subsidised imports (e.g. wheat in Pakistan) which has the effect of subsidising consumers and taxing producers. In the former case if the requisitioned quantities are less than the total produced by a farmer then the system acts like a lump-sum rather than a proportional tax. It is possible, therefore, for such a system to be made progressive although a land tax might be a simpler and less costly way of carrying through such taxation. Outputs of exportable commodities may be taxed via an export tax (e.g. rice in Thailand and, in recent years, cotton in Pakistan). In many African countries (e.g. Côte d'Ivoire) exports are taxed via marketing boards which are monopsonistic purchasers of cash crops such as cocoa and buy from farmers at prices well below those of the world market.

Third, one must consider prices paid for inputs in calculating any overall level of tax on agriculture. Here the situation is commonly one of subsidy with apparently low prices, in relation to marginal cost, for fertilisers, electricity and water. Even here one has to be careful, particularly for fertiliser and electricity, to check on the taxation of fuel inputs such as natural gas, oil and coal.

Fourth, those earning agricultural incomes pay indirect taxes on their consumption and investment purchases just like any other buyers of goods. And fifth, one must acknowledge the presence of taxes which are fairly direct in nature in the form of land revenue charges and, in Pakistan, *ushr* (see chapter 8).

It can be seen that the calculation of the tax burden on agriculture and its comparison with other sectors raises very difficult conceptual issues and would be very problematic to carry through. This is not something we have attempted in our applied work. It does seem, however, that the existing and somewhat roundabout ways of taxing agriculture, principally through the exchange rate and output prices, which dominate in most developing countries, are likely to be less satisfactory than more direct methods such as land taxes. The indirect ways do, however, have the political advantage that they are more easily concealed and do not involve the direct handing over of money by farmers. Their apparent attraction to governments (by revealed preference) relative to land taxes may have much to do with this particular aspect.

Finally, before turning to more detailed modelling questions and taxes in sections 4.3 and 4.4, we comment briefly on discussions of what *should* be the balance between taxation of industry and agriculture. The terms of trade between agriculture and industry and the allocation of resources between agricultural and non-agricultural sectors has long been a central topic in discussions of development (see, for example, the early Indian Five-Year Plans; Dixit, 1973, and Lipton, 1977). We examine briefly here the implications of some of the issues raised for the analysis of tax policy. There are a number of arguments which have been advanced for turning the terms of trade against agriculture. Given that the discussion is often in terms of a single price and we are looking at the agricultural sector as a whole the discussion is at a fairly aggregated level. First, it may be suggested that aggregate agricultural supply is relatively inelastic so that a tax on agricultural output may only be 'mildly' distortionary. Second, one might argue that investible surplus should be extracted from agriculture to finance growth elsewhere. Third, it might be argued that food producers are relatively well off, whereas consumers, rural or urban, are not. We examine these suggestions briefly.

Given that food is such a high proportion of output and budgets, it may well be necessary to spread the tax net to include it if sufficient revenue is to be raised. It may also be true that it will be difficult to separate consumer and producer prices. Standard deadweight loss arguments in an open economy framework suggest that taxes should be higher on food (relative to other things) the lower are the supply and demand elasticities. The size of supply elasticities is then an important element in the analysis. The magnitude of the aggregate elasticity is an empirical issue. A recent survey by Binswanger *et al.* (1985) has suggested rather low aggregate own-price elasticities (between 0.1 and 0.3). Individual crop elasticities will, of course, be higher (see, for example, Askari and Cummings, 1976, and Timmer, Falcon and Pearson, 1983). The argument may have some content but would have to be set out rather carefully and, of course, begs the distributional questions.

The second argument which concentrates on dynamic aspects is less well-founded. The allocation of investment is related to but distinct from its source of finance. If the marginal investment has high social productivity in a certain sector this does not tell us whether the revenue should come from that sector or some other. And there should be no presumption that investment in agriculture is less productive than elsewhere; often the opposite will be true (see, for example, Schultz, 1978).

The third suggestion relates to the incidence of taxes. It is not obviously correct that food producers are relatively well off, and incidence may not only be on landowners or producers. As we shall see in the next section, incidence is sensitive to a number of questions concerning the structure of the labour market (e.g., what happens to agricultural workers and the rural and urban wage) and the government's ability to control prices in different sectors of the economy.

Overall we would suggest that there are no strong and general arguments one way or another. The appropriate terms of trade and their control by government policy would depend on the structure of the economy, the country's position in world markets, investment possibilities, the distribution of income for consumers and producers, and the availability of tax tools in a particular context. And it should be remembered that agriculture versus industry may not be a very useful way of putting any question. Welfare does not reside in industries or sectors but in households or, more particularly, individuals. We should be asking about the distribution and incentive effects of combinations of taxes and of investment policies in different parts of agriculture and industry rather than focusing on an ill-defined balance between the two.

4.3 Models, instruments and incidence

The combination of tax tools available and the workings of the different markets in which they operate exert a crucial influence on the effects of any particular tax tool, how it should be used and the rate at which it should be set. We shall not go into different possible models in great detail but concentrate on identifying the important assumptions and issues in building models for the analysis of tax design and reform for agriculture. Given that, in many developing countries, the state to a large extent influences incentives and incomes in agriculture by administered prices, rather than with tools which are formally called taxes, we must include price regulation within our discussion of agricultural taxation. We begin with a discussion of the combination of taxes and prices which influence incomes and outputs in peasant agriculture; second, we examine different possible methods of taxing or controlling the prices of traded goods; third, we look at non-traded goods; fourth, we examine the importance of labour market mechanisms; and fifth, we discuss the role of market imperfections in the analysis of tax issues.

In many countries the prices of important agricultural commodities are controlled, taxed or subsidised. These include purely cash crops such as cotton, or in West Africa, cocoa, as well as crops which are used both for food and cash such as wheat and rice. Where a crop is used purely for subsistence then it will not be possible to tax the output directly. Of course, whether or not a crop is sold by a farmer depends on prices and is determined within the system and there are very few crops which are not bought and sold by someone. Nevertheless in certain areas there are some crops, such as coarse grains, which are bought and sold in rural communities somewhat less than others and for administrative reasons it may not be worthwhile trying to control these rural output prices. The presence of such crops is, however, important for tax and price analysis because it is in the substitution amongst cash crops and between cash and subsistence crops that one can expect higher price elasticities, and thus revenue and efficiency effects, to emerge.

The effects of different taxes and combinations of taxes may be examined by looking at the household budget constraint and the revenue from agricultural activities. Let x, y and z be the outputs of cash crops, cash–food crops, and subsistence crops respectively. We are to think of x-crops as being non-consumable, y-crops as being both sold and eaten, and z-crops as being eaten and not sold (where we assume that the relevant range of prices and incomes is such that z-crops are neither bought nor sold). Let consumption of cash–food crops be c, of non-agricultural goods be m, and labour supply off and on the farm be l_0 and l_1 respectively. Suppose that the minimum cost of buying inputs to produce x, y and z using l_1 and land A is $C(x, y, z; l_1, A, \mathbf{p})$ when purchased input prices are $\mathbf{p}$. Prices of the x, y and m goods are p_x, p_y and p_m.

The budget constraint for monetary transactions is then

$$p_m m = p_x x + p_y (y - c) - C + w l_0 \qquad (4.1)$$

and one may think of the household as choosing x, y, z, c, m, l_0 and l_1 together with productive inputs (embodied in C) to maximise $u(c, z, m, l)$, where $l \equiv l_0 + l_1$, subject to (4.1). The rent from the land, R, may be defined as

$$R \equiv (p_x x + p_y y + \rho z) - C(x, y, z; l_1, A, \mathbf{p}) - w l_1 \qquad (4.2)$$

where

$$\rho \equiv \frac{1}{\lambda} \frac{\partial u}{\partial z} = \frac{\partial C}{\partial z} \qquad (4.3)$$

i.e., the value of the non-marketed subsistence good will be equal to its marginal cost (λ is the Lagrange multiplier on (4.1)), where the choice variables take their optimal values (we are assuming that purchased inputs for z are used here). One could in principle drop z and l_1 from the model and include w as an entry in $\mathbf{p}$, thus leaving the optimal choice of within farm allocation implicit. With this definition of the rent the budget constraint may be written

$$p_y c + p_m m + \rho z - w(l_0 + l_1) = R \qquad (4.4)$$

Or writing T for total time availability and L for leisure, $T - (l_0 + l_1)$, we have

$$p_y c + p_m m + \rho z + w L = R + w T \qquad (4.5)$$

We are now in a position to see the effects of different taxes. A lump-sum tax linked to total spending power would have as its basis $R + wT$ – the returns from the land and labour endowments. This is known as 'full income' in the literature on labour economics and we have some rather basic problems in measuring it. Not only is T, and often w, unobservable but we have, in calculating R, to impute the value of subsistence crops ρz and subtract the value of the on-farm family labour. The analysis does, however, indicate the appropriate concept of rent for the purpose of vertical equity (i.e. considerations of distribution across households) based on spending power.

We can also look at taxes on inputs and outputs and examine their distortionary effects relative to a tax on spending power. From (4.5) we can see that raising all prices, p_x, p_y, p_z, $\mathbf{p}$ and w, by the same factor has no effect on the budget constraint and welfare, since equation (4.1), or its alternative (4.5), is homogeneous degree 1 in prices. Generally, where households consume goods which they produce on the farm (we include labour as a consumption good at this point – own on-farm labour enters the utility function) it will not be possible to mimic a lump-sum tax by manipulating prices. This is possible, however, if those goods which enter production do not enter consumption. Then lowering the price of all outputs produced and all of the inputs used will have the effect of a proportional reduction in the rent – in (4.2) one can exclude y and z from the model and think of l_1 as a factor which is bought in and distinct from household labour. In that case we have

$$R = p_x x - \mathbf{p} \cdot \mathbf{v} \qquad (4.6)$$

where we now include l_1 within $\mathbf{v}$, the vector of purchased inputs, and it is clear that deflating p_x and $\mathbf{p}$ by a multiple $(1 - \tau)$ simply reduces R by that factor. Notice this is an output tax and an input *subsidy* applying to all inputs. More generally the goods y, z and l_1 enter both production and consumption so that output or input taxes or pricing policies affecting the right-hand side of the budget constraint (4.5) will also affect the left-hand side.

A tax on marketed surplus would have as its base $p_x x + p_y(y - c)$. If there were no purchased inputs ($C = 0$) and no off-farm labour sales ($l_0 = 0$) this would have (see (4.1)) the same effect as a tax on non-agricultural goods (where C and l_0 are not zero then inputs become relatively more expensive and off-farm labour more attractive). The non-agricultural goods are generally taxed anyway so in this sense a tax on marketed surplus adds little. If, however, the government wishes to tax agriculturalists more than others (we assume everyone pays the same price for m-goods) a tax on marketed surplus would be one way of doing this. Some might argue that the absence of an income tax on agriculture (either *de facto* or *de jure*) justifies on equity grounds such further taxation, but this particular argument is less persuasive where the income tax on non-agriculture sectors is weak too. Notice that the tax on marketed surplus changes the relative price of m and y in consumption but not of x and y in production (if it is at a uniform rate on x and y). The relative price of z is changed for both production and consumption.

A tax on gross output has as its base $(p_x x + p_y y + \rho z)$. This leaves the relative prices of x, y, z in production unchanged but lowers them relative to labour and purchased inputs. There is then a disincentive effect, although we cannot say whether it will increase or reduce output (there is an income effect which, as in the simple labour supply model, works in the direction of increasing output). The relative prices of m and c in consumption are unaltered (c can still be bought and sold at p_c) but that of z is raised in terms of purchased inputs so there would be some substitution towards purchased consumption (although the income effect would work to reduce it).

It can be seen, therefore, that for neither the tax on marketed surplus nor that on gross output can neutrality be claimed. The tax on gross output does provide an extra degree of freedom, when combined with a tax on non-agricultural goods, in the case where the tax on marketed surplus is similar to a tax on non-agricultural purchases. This can be seen by rewriting (4.1) in the special case where C and l_0 are zero as

$$p_m m + p_y c = p_x x + p_y y \tag{4.7}$$

Lowering the price of x and y in production through the output tax is equivalent to increasing the price of m and c in consumption. Given that the price of m can be affected directly by taxation of non-agricultural goods the extra degree of freedom lies in the ability to tax food.

The prices of inputs such as electricity, fertiliser, water, fuel oil and seed are also under strong government influence. These prices affect both incentives to use the inputs and spending power through the cost of production, C. In the preceding chapter we looked at the theory of pricing when producers and consumers can be separated in the sense of facing different price vectors. Under special conditions we saw that inputs should not be taxed and that efficiency of the productive sector taken as a whole was desirable. Examination of the special conditions led to the suggestion that deviations of price from marginal social cost for inputs could be justified where the output could not be taxed and/or there were important income distribution considerations. It is clear that both these arguments are likely to apply in agriculture. Taxing or subsidising inputs provides an indirect way of taxing or subsidising the outputs.

One often does hear the argument that input subsidies are desirable for the promotion of agriculture. To the extent that agricultural outputs are taxed by exchange rate overvaluation (arising from protective tariffs on, say, manufacturing) then this argument may have some force, but a more direct way to overcome the problem would be with trade policy rather than input pricing. And generally any subsidy is only on the purchased inputs and not on labour used. This may imply some damaging distributional effects in the sense that substitution towards the other inputs lowers the real agricultural wage, or the price of agricultural labour, which is the main source of income for many of the landless, although it is conceivable that greater intensification of agriculture could compensate for this substitution amongst inputs. The simplest and probably the best solution would be to reduce both protection and the input subsidies. In this way it is likely that resource allocation would be improved without any clearly damaging distributional effects or net revenue loss.

If different inputs are to be treated differently for tax, subsidy or pricing purposes, it should be on the basis of the differential taxation of the outputs to which they correspond most closely and their differential use by different agriculturalists. Of course, if all factor markets are perfect and there is no uncertainty (or if we include insurance markets) then the intensity of factor use would be identical across all land. In that case there would be no reason to differentiate amongst inputs and all should be taxed or subsidised at the same rate (as has been argued by Sah and Stiglitz, 1987). In the real world, however, we know that there can be very large differences in agricultural techniques so that, on average, tractors would be more intensively used by richer farmers than animal power. For this reason there may be an argument for taxing tractors or subsidising bullocks (this latter does occur, for example, through special credit schemes in India for subsidising the purchase of animals). One would also want to look closely into the various reasons for differential use of inputs across farmers and we return to this issue briefly below.

We have to this point in our discussion of tax and pricing policy for agriculture assumed that prices are linear, i.e. there is no variation in price according to quantity purchased. Where goods are resaleable then varying the price paid per unit can be difficult since agents can arbitrage by transacting amongst themselves. There are, however, some examples in agriculture where non-linear pricing may be possible. For example, one can stipulate that a producer sells a given quantity of wheat to the government and is then free to sell any remainder on the open market. This has been a feature of the contract-responsibility system in Chinese agriculture and of grain requisition systems in India. This acts like a lump-sum tax equal to the requisition quantity times the difference between market price and requisition price. This avoids incentive problems and can be made progressive. Where a rent or land tax is not possible then this system may provide an alternative which looks somewhat like it. However, it is hard to provide administrative reasons why the two-tier price system in a progressive form (e.g. linked to land owned) should be feasible, whereas a land tax should not be.

Thus far we have been focusing on the effects of different taxes on the agriculturalist. We now turn to how different possible ways of taxing agriculture may affect the rest of the economy. We begin with traded goods such as rice or wheat, and suppose, initially, that it is not possible to have different prices for producers and consumers (apart from selling and transport costs). Let us suppose, for example, that the good (rice, say) is imported (without quantity restrictions and from a competitive world market) and subsidised. This will act as a tax on producers, as well as a subsidy to the domestic price (the domestic price is the world price less the subsidy). This means that the (marginal) incidence of the subsidy is as an imposition on producers related to their production and as a benefit to consumers related to their consumption. The policy analysis of the subsidy must therefore take account of the welfare weights on incomes of both consumers and producers. The revenue cost will be given by net imports in equilibrium (times the subsidy) and this will depend on net supply elasticities of producers and demand elasticities of consumers. We can think of the subsidy to the consumers being financed in part by the tax on producers and partly by the government subsidy payments. Similarly an import tariff may be seen as a subsidy to producers financed by a tax on consumers with the government now receiving revenue equal to the tariff times imports. Again an export tax can be seen in the same manner – it is a tax on producers and a subsidy to consumers, with the government making positive revenue (and correspondingly with an export subsidy). As we saw in the preceding section, however, the effects of these taxes are somewhat more complicated than this simple description would make them appear. An import tariff, for example, pushes up the exchange rate and penalises exporters.

Taxation of imports and exports is generally the easiest way to tax traded agricultural outputs. In some cases, however, particularly for certain export crops, it will be possible to set up marketing boards which are sufficiently dominant in the market to set the price. This has been common in West Africa, for example, with cocoa. In this case the difference between the purchase price (plus selling and transport costs) and the export price goes as profit to the marketing board and is equivalent to a tax.

The taxation of non-traded agricultural commodities is less straightforward as this involves the measurement of output or sales. For vegetables, for example, which may be grown in small quantities on a large number of plots this would be extremely difficult. It may be possible to set up marketing boards or buying agencies of sufficient dominance to keep the price to growers lower than prices in urban areas. The enforcement of this would require prevention of sales directly to urban consumers. Governments do occasionally attempt to control the movement of food in this way. The Korean government seems to be able to separate urban and rural grain prices (see Braverman *et al.*, 1987, and Newbery, 1987a). It is more common to control the price of non-traded inputs into agriculture such as electricity or water, the pricing principles for which have been discussed.

Taxes on agriculture would in general affect the wages and real incomes of both urban and rural workers. They will affect different kinds of workers in different ways. If the price to producers of food is lowered then the agricultural labourer will be worse off to the extent that the real wage in agriculture would be expected to fall – for example, less inputs complementary with labour may be used thus lowering the marginal product. This is an argument sometimes used against food aid. Further, any reduction in agricultural wages may also have an effect on urban wages although urban workers would benefit from the reduction in food prices. And a reduction in urban wages might increase investible surpluses. So one has to ask, for example, whether urban and rural labour and food markets can be separated and whether food is imported (lower prices then implying an import subsidy) or produced domestically. A number of models can be constructed and we shall not go into details, but it should be clear that the consequences flowing through the labour market may be of importance for the income of the poor, for profits and for government revenue.

Finally, on judging incidence one must remember the very broad range of production techniques one finds within agriculture, indeed within a single village. Thus some farmers will use electrically powered tube-wells, others bullock-driven Persian wheels, while some land will not be irrigated at all. Some will use a combination of chemical fertilisers, some farmyard manure and others no fertiliser at all. Cropping patterns and thus input choice will vary considerably. The reasons for these differences may be many; for example, differences in knowledge, attitude to risk, access to credit, influence over government suppliers, position and quality of land. Many although not all of these involve market imperfections. One cannot assume that techniques are homogeneous and thus the pricing and taxing of inputs should take account of these differences in practices amongst peasant householders and other producers. Such differences would not matter for the consideration of incidence if they were uncorrelated with social marginal utilities of income. *Prima facie* this is unlikely and should at least be investigated. For further discussion of some of these issues see part V of Newbery and Stern (1987a).

4.4   The use of individual tax instruments

We have so far in this chapter discussed broad issues and the structure of models concerning the taxation of agriculture. We shall now examine where these issues and models and the economic principles of chapter 3 leave the arguments for different forms of taxation in agriculture. As we have emphasised throughout, the appropriate policy for any particular tax instrument will depend on the availability and levels of other taxes and policies.

4.4.1 The land tax

An obvious and important example is the *land tax*. Land, it is claimed, is in inelastic supply (we return to this below) and its distribution is unequal. From the viewpoint of both efficiency and equity it would seem the natural base for taxation and has been seen as such by economists from David Ricardo and Henry George. Historically (see, for example, Bird, 1974) the land tax seems to have been of substantial or dominant importance in many countries (for example in India under Moghul and British rule; see chapters 2 and 8). Now, however, land taxes seem to be a negligible source of revenue. Land taxation requires careful land records but this is not in principle difficult compared to measuring the base for other taxes, since landowners have a strong incentive to establish the legal title to their lands, an aspect which has no strong analogy in other taxes. One can adjust for the quality of the land by basing the tax on its presumptive value. The tax can be made progressive by taxing only holdings above a certain level.

One economic reservation concerning land taxation is whether land really is in inelastic supply. In some African countries uncleared land may be in plentiful supply and in most countries there are major investments in land through irrigation and water control, fencing, wind-breaks, terracing and so on. Land taxation based on quality constitutes, in part, taxation of land improvement activities and to this extent it is not a lump-sum tax and does have efficiency effects. Some, although probably not all, of this reservation could be met by valuation rules. For example, they could be based on soil quality, rainfall and access to canal irrigation, which would, to a large extent, be outside the control of the farmer. There is probably no hard evidence on the possible magnitude of these disincentive effects, and they would surely be different for different countries and regions. We would be prepared, however, to hazard the guess that they may be small relative to disincentive effects from other taxes, not least because major land improvement often involves access to credit which may be allocated in a non-competitive market so that the improvement decision may be infra-marginal.

A second consideration pointing away from sole reliance on a fixed payment such as land tax concerns risk. A tax based on output allows the government to share in some of the agricultural risk and one can show that a small move in the direction of an output tax (preserving revenue) and away from a pure land tax would improve efficiency (Hoff, 1989). However, output taxes have severe measurement problems and it may not be desirable to institute a small one, given the administrative costs. Neverthe-less the presence of *ushr* (in principle an output tax above an exemption level) may serve a purpose in this risk-sharing respect.

A land tax may provide a revenue base for local governments which gives them some independence from central government. It may also be easier for local governments with special knowledge to administer such taxes. It appears common for land and residential property taxes to be locally administered. A land tax, however, is not the only form that can be locally administered.

The decline in land taxation may be associated, in part, with the success of the rich and powerful in opposing it (see Bird, 1974, and Wald, 1959). And where it is tried, resistance to proper valuation and collection can be fierce and effective. Apart from possible disincentives to the improvement of land, this resistance to legislation or effective implementation seems the crucial argument against land taxation. There are two possible reactions. One can either advise governments to attempt to find ways of overcoming this resistance or take the absence of land taxation as a constraint and devise other taxes. The former course can be perilous for the government, possibly also for the economist, and may damage credibility as an adviser. We shall discuss some of the alternatives, but, the possible political difficulties notwithstanding, one should not remove land taxation from the agenda without careful discussion and thought concerning the circumstances in the particular country under examination. The alternatives are generally, from the economic viewpoint, less satisfactory. Their attraction to governments is that they may be less visible.

4.4.2   Taxation of inputs and outputs

We saw in the preceding section that it would not, in general, be possible for taxes on inputs and outputs to substitute for a land tax. Only where produced goods were not consumed (thereby excluding the important case of family labour) and prices of all outputs and inputs were reduced in the same proportion could output/input taxes be equivalent to a proportional tax on land. This would involve an output tax and an input subsidy, including hired labour. Where hired labour was not also subsidised an attempt at such a system would shift incentives towards non-labour inputs.

The tax on gross output has a general disincentive effect on production (abstracting from any income effect on labour supply) and makes subsistence goods relatively more expensive than purchased goods. Thus it hits harder those who purchase less, although this possibly regressive effect could be mitigated by an exemption level. A tax on marketed surplus does not affect the relative producer and consumer price for the cash-food good or for the subsistence good and acts in a similar manner to a tax on non-agricultural consumer goods. As such it may add little to such taxation although it does allow an extra tax on agriculturalists for such goods if that were to be desired. Compulsory procurement of a fixed quantity at a price below the market price acts like a lump-sum tax (this is not the system in Pakistan).

4.4.3 Water and electricity

Water and electricity are important examples of publicly provided services to agriculture. The basic tax and pricing principles discussed in chapter 2 would seem to suggest prices at least as high as marginal cost, for reasons of revenue and of distribution. Similar second-best analysis can be applied to the other main inputs, fertilisers and draught power. Bullock power, however, would not easily be taxed, and such a tax is likely to be undesirable for distributional reasons (at least relative to a tax on tractors) since it is the richer farmers who own the tractors; however, poorer farmers may rent their use, so the issue is not clear-cut. One would also want to take into account the extent to which governments wished to encourage technical change based on water and/or electricity. If there were benefits which were underestimated by households or considered too risky then there might be an argument for subsidy. Insofar as the underestimation of benefits is based on ignorance and will diminish over time then this element of subsidy should be gradually removed. It is unlikely, however, that adequate insurance for risk in agriculture will emerge quickly and it is possible that some subsidy might be justified on these grounds. The argument would have to be developed rather carefully and in our judgement it is far from obvious that subsidies are the best vehicle for dealing with promoting insurance markets.

4.4.4 Agricultural income tax

An agricultural income tax is, in principle, equivalent to a tax on income from land and household labour and so is close to being a desirable base. However, to avoid disincentive effects on labour supply it should in principle be based on earning power rather than earnings (this is not a base one could ever expect to achieve). A major problem concerns the definition and measurement of the value of inputs and outputs, particularly where there are a vast number of small producers and limited resources available to the tax authorities. A partial solution would be to use *forfaits* or taxes on presumptive income, and a land tax is an example. A challenge of an assessment of *forfait* should then require production of accounts. An alternative would be to have an output levy, with some standard adjustment for inputs. This could be made progressive and would reduce administration costs if it were limited to larger farmers.

4.4.5   Trade taxes

In practice certain crops are often singled out for special treatment. Often these are export crops such as cocoa in Ghana or cotton in Pakistan. And in many cases such taxation occurs through marketing boards. Given that supply elasticities for individual crops (see section 4.2) are likely to be much higher than for agriculture as a whole, considerable distortions are possible through substitution between taxed and untaxed crops. Smuggling can also become a major problem. Generally the arguments for such taxes are administrative rather than economic since it is generally one group which is subsidising another (e.g. consumers when there is an import tariff) and there is often no special reason for this type of transfer or for the production inefficiencies generated.

4.5   The political economy of agricultural taxation

What determines the degree of opposition to different taxes and the success or failure of that opposition? These are difficult questions but ones which the analysis of taxation cannot ignore. They must affect our economic analysis in a number of ways. First, we must be aware of political and administrative constraints which influence what is feasible. Second, we should discuss how far different forms of taxation are open to manipulation or abuse. Third, our analysis should bring out who gains and who loses from the different measures under discussion. Fourth, we would highlight the existence and meaning of obscure or hidden forms of taxation, both because these may be attractive to politicians and, as alternatives to more explicit taxation, they will have their own costs which should be identified. Careful economic analysis can contribute substantially to these issues, particularly the third and fourth.

The third is essentially the question of incidence. One cannot work out who gains and who loses without a model (whether implicit or explicit) which includes differences between households. This is crucial not only to the well-motivated commentator who wants to balance gains and losses for different groups, but also for the identification of potential opposition. Such analysis can also help either to mobilise or mollify opposition since it is not always easy for the lay person to work out or understand the workings of the economy. In other words it should inform and influence the political debate. Incidence analysis, as such, should not be treated as a special subject within public economics. It is essentially what public economics is about.

The fourth issue is central for the political economy of agricultural taxation. Two of the most important forms of concealed taxation of agriculture are exchange rate overvaluation and direct price control of output. Both involve taxation of agriculture and subsidy for industry. The government can also gain revenue from both (where the exchange rate overvaluation comes via protective tariffs on industry and where output prices are held below world prices). Another important form of concealed taxation is inflation, although this impinges less strongly on rural households if they hold less money.

The attractiveness to politicians of hidden taxation would be less worrying from the economic viewpoint if it were true that it was the concealed taxes which were also those suggested by economic analysis. Unfortunately it seems for agriculture, and often elsewhere, that the best taxes from the economic arguments are the *most* visible. This is particularly true of the land tax. Such a tax would generally involve a payment directly by the landowner, in contrast to exchange rate overvaluation or the discrepancy between world and domestic prices for a marketing board which are much less visible taxes on the price paid for output. It seems generally true that indirect taxes have a political advantage over direct taxes in this respect and, further, that withholding taxes are less politically sensitive than those which involve an actual payment by a taxpayer to the government.

The political economy arguments suggest that land taxes are unlikely to be adopted and alternative less efficient taxes will be chosen. It is also probable that an attempt to claim a fraction of output from farmers as a gross output tax would run into severe political problems. Certainly the responsibility of collecting taxes from a powerful landlord would not be easy to discharge conscientiously, particularly where substantial rewards would be offered to look the other way. It is perhaps not surprising that cautious or insecure governments look for revenue from agriculture from export taxes, import tariffs cum exchange rate overvaluation, marketing boards and the like. It may be that earmarking of land tax collections for local spending might exert local pressure on the rich to pay more but too much should not be expected from this source.

4.6 Concluding comments

In addition to our warning concerning the importance of seeing the system as a whole, our brief discussion of agriculture has led us to a number of specific conclusions. Some of these are reflected in our discussion of individual taxes in section 4.4. In concluding this chapter we shall emphasise the following.

The principles of analysis and methods developed here (see chapter 3) do provide us with guidance for the taxation of agriculture both in terms of general principles and particular applied methods. Examples include the pricing of inputs, the combination of efficiency and equity arguments in the land tax and the marginal approach to applied reform analysis.

From the point of view of both distribution and efficiency the arguments for basing agricultural taxation on land are strong. As a base it is easier to measure than others, such as output or income, and as such the administrative problems would, in principle, probably be less than other forms of agricultural taxation. There is no doubt, however, that the tax would raise real political difficulties and it has been fiercely and successfully opposed around the world.

The political economy arguments suggest that governments are more likely to go for less visible taxes, those that involve manipulating prices paid by farmers, rather than taking cash or produce from them. This involves particularly indirect taxation of goods bought by consumers in rural areas, exchange rate overvaluation, export taxes, marketing boards and the like. These are generally poor substitutes for a land tax.

The pricing of inputs to agriculture should be based on social marginal cost. Arguments for pricing below this level could include the encouragement of learning new techniques, the desire to boost incomes of particular groups (and the absence of other methods of doing so), and the provision of partial compensation for low output prices.

Taxes on gross output or marketed surplus may have a general disincentive effect (always remembering that income effects could increase output) and make purchased goods relatively cheaper than home-produced goods. They can, however, make some contribution to risk-sharing. Both the tax on gross output and on marketed surplus would be difficult to administer – the base is very hard to measure – except for the latter in the case where there is a dominant marketing board.

The general conclusion on the basis of the economic arguments would be a system based on world prices for outputs, social marginal costs for inputs and land taxation. Distributional considerations could be brought in through an exemption level for the land tax. There are also a number of possible methods for direct help to the landless, such as public works schemes, preferential hiring and so on, together with programmes such as preferential credit for small farmers. It is, however, a crucial part of the logic of this combination that revenue-raising comes from land taxation. Where governments rule this out, and their political concerns are understandable, then less satisfactory measures will be adopted. Which of them are used will depend on the blend of political, administrative and economic arguments. If taxes which involve the collection of revenue from agricultural house-holds (land, income or output) are ruled out then all that is left are those which operate through prices. Similar methods to those developed in this book can be applied directly to the analysis of the reform of these prices (see, for example, Braverman *et al.*, 1987, Heady and Mitra, 1987, and Newbery, 1987a).

Of all the taxes which do involve collection from households we would argue that the land tax is both the most satisfactory economically and the easiest to administer (although for related reasons it is the most fiercely resisted politically). We return to this issue when we offer some proposals in chapter 8.

5   Applying the theory

5.1 Theory and data

One of the main purposes of the theory developed in chapter 3 was to derive some basic principles for the design and reform of taxes. A further objective, however, was to produce models and methods which could provide an organising framework for the applied analysis of possible reforms. In this chapter we show how the ideas presented in chapter 3 can be translated into such a framework. Our concentration is on reform starting from a given initial position. Nowhere in this chapter or book do we make any attempt to calculate optimal taxes. We shall discuss the data requirements, how the data should be used and problems that arise from tax measures and economic structures which are more complicated than those that are handled in the earlier theory.

The simple theory of reform set out in section 3.2 described the marginal effects of reforming indirect taxes where it could be assumed that producer prices reflect social opportunity costs or shadow prices. In these circumstances the improving directions of tax reform could be identified using the marginal social cost of public funds from each tax instrument. If the marginal social cost of raising a rupee via instrument i is lower than for instrument j then we improve welfare at constant revenue by raising more on the margin from instrument i and less from instrument j. If, on the other hand, social marginal costs of goods are not well reflected by producer prices then the constancy of revenue does not properly capture the general equilibrium constraints of the system and the criterion for finding improving methods must be modified. As we showed in section 3.5 an appropriate guide is the relative marginal social cost of raising a unit of shadow revenue (correctly defined) using the different tax instruments. Alternatively, one can compare the direct benefit of a measure, e.g. a tax increase or a new pension to a certain group, with the cost at shadow prices of meeting the extra demands which are associated with the tax or pension change. The reform is beneficial if the former exceeds the latter.

We can examine the data requirements for the reform analysis if we set out these expressions explicitly. We begin with the simple case of section 3.2 where producer prices coincide with shadow prices. The social marginal cost, λ_i, of public funds generated via an increase in the ith tax was defined by equation (3.5) as

$$\lambda_i = \frac{\sum_h \beta^h x_i^h}{X_i + \mathbf{t}' \dfrac{\partial \mathbf{X}}{\partial q_i}} \tag{3.5}$$

where x_i^h is the consumption of the ith good by household h and $\mathbf{X} = \sum_h \mathbf{x}^h$ is the vector of total demands. The information required to calculate λ_i involves the welfare weights β^h, the consumption of households x_i^h, the taxes $\mathbf{t}$, and the aggregate demand responses $\partial \mathbf{X}/\partial q_i$. The first of these, the β^h, are essentially value judgements although there are technical issues involved in their formulation and scaling. Both ethical and technical issues concerning welfare weights are discussed in section 5.4. In section 5.2 we examine the problem of calculating tax rates on final goods when a large part of indirect taxation falls on intermediate goods through tariffs and excise taxes. We call the tax element in the price of final goods the effective tax. The use of household survey data for information on expenditure patterns is the subject of section 5.3.

Where we do not make the assumption that shadow and producer prices coincide then we have to make explicit calculations of shadow prices. The method adopted here will be that proposed by Little and Mirrlees (1974). This is described briefly in section 5.5 – its main data requirements are an input–output table (as for effective taxes) and information on tariffs and taxes. In section 5.6 we assemble the elements and show how the approach can be used to examine various different types of taxes, for example, excise versus sales or domestic versus imports. We also indicate how administrative costs can be brought into the analysis. Section 5.7 outlines briefly a method for assessing non-marginal reforms. In section 5.8 we offer some concluding comments. The calculations of effective taxes and shadow prices are presented in chapter 6 and of directions of reform in chapter 7.

Finally in this section, we note the difference between our reform approach here and its data requirements and those which would be required for the calculation of optimal taxes. The reform analysis involves consumption data for households which describe the *existing* situation, and *aggregate* demand derivatives, also at the existing position. Similarly the effective tax calculations are based on the existing production structure. The optimal tax calculations on the other hand require us to describe demand and production over the *full* range of prices, so that the optimal state of affairs can be selected. Thus the data demands are much more formidable and we could have very little confidence in our results. This is one of the central reasons why we do not attempt any calculation of optimal tax rates.

5.2 Effective taxes

Many taxes in the sub-continent fall on inputs, particularly import duties and excise taxes. We want to trace the effects of these taxes through to final goods so that we can calculate how demand adjustments in response to tax changes will affect tax collections. This will involve us in modelling price determination to see how taxes feed through the system.

We start with very simple models and then consider some complications. Our objective is to produce a set of taxes $\mathbf{t}^e$, which we call effective taxes, so that an increase in the effective tax corresponds to an increase in the price of the final good. Further, if we use $\mathbf{t}^e$ as the tax vector in the denominator of (3.5) (which is $\partial R/\partial t_i$; see chapter 3), then this denominator should give us the effect on tax revenue of a marginal increase in the effective tax (using X_i and $\partial X_i/\partial q_j$ from information on consumer demand and demand responses). Our definition of the effective tax t_i^e is the amount by which government revenue would increase if there were a unit increase in final demand for the good: if the final demand vector is $\mathbf{Z}$ then $t_i^e \equiv \partial R/\partial Z_i$. This is a partial derivative in the sense that other final demands are held constant and we ignore any changes in factor uses and factor prices. Some care is necessary here and the usefulness of the concept is limited to certain models. We return to this issue in section 5.8 (see also section 3.3). We have two motivations for introducing the effective tax. The first is to put into practice the reform analysis described in chapter 3. This requires us to calculate the effects of tax changes on revenue and this requires in turn consumer demand information which is in terms of final goods. The second is as a useful summary statistic for a complicated tax system. In other words it describes for the government the upshot for final goods of its many different tax measures.

We begin this section with the simple, static closed-economy Leontief model, and we then consider in turn an open economy, dynamic aspects, flexible coefficients and multiple factors. We subsequently turn to capital and some dynamic issues and, finally, we consider shifting assumptions.

Closed economy; fixed coefficients; one factor

All purchasers of a good pay a price inclusive of tax. The purchasers' price vector $\mathbf{q}$ is defined as the price paid by consumers and is also that paid by producers for the purchase of inputs. The producers' price vector $\mathbf{p}$ represents the price received by producers for sales. We consider the simple input–output model of production with fixed input–output matrix A, gross output vector $\mathbf{Y}$, and net output vector $\mathbf{Z}$. Then inputs are $A\mathbf{Y}$, and

$$\mathbf{Z} = \mathbf{Y} - A\mathbf{Y} = (I - A)\mathbf{Y} \tag{5.1}$$

Competitive pricing conditions for this model are

$$\mathbf{p}' = \mathbf{q}'A + \mathbf{v}' \tag{5.2}$$

where primes denote row vectors and $\mathbf{v}$ is the vector of per unit value added by industry (which we assume for the moment to be fixed – we can think of it as the vector of labour requirements × the wage). If $\mathbf{t}$ is the tax vector, then

$$\mathbf{q} = \mathbf{p} + \mathbf{t} \tag{5.3}$$

and from equations (5.2) and (5.3) we have

$$\mathbf{q}' = \mathbf{t}'(I - A)^{-1} + \mathbf{v}'(I - A)^{-1} \tag{5.4}$$

In this model the effective tax vector $\mathbf{t}^e$ is

$$\mathbf{t}^{e'} = \mathbf{t}'(I - A)^{-1} \tag{5.5}$$

The per unit resource cost vector which we call the 'basic' price vector, $\mathbf{p}^b$, is

$$\mathbf{p}^{b'} = \mathbf{v}'(I - A)^{-1} \tag{5.6}$$

and is equal to prices in the absence of taxes. Government revenue, R, is $\mathbf{t}'\mathbf{Y}$, which is the same as $\mathbf{t}^{e'}\mathbf{Z}$ so that $\mathbf{t}'(I - A)^{-1}$ conforms with our definition of $\partial R / \partial \mathbf{Z}$. It is easy to check, using the definitions and methods of section 3.4, that the shadow price vector in this model is proportional to $\mathbf{p}^b$.

We may also define $\mathbf{t}^{\mathrm{diff}}$, where

$$\mathbf{t}^{\mathrm{diff}} = \mathbf{t}^e - \mathbf{t} \tag{5.7}$$

which measures the difference between the effective tax, $\mathbf{t}^e$, and the nominal tax, $\mathbf{t}$. Thus $\mathbf{t}^{\mathrm{diff}}$ tells us the extent to which inputs are taxed. The overall level of taxation of inputs in the economy is given by $\mathbf{t}^{\mathrm{diff}}$ times the final demand vector $\mathbf{Z}$, or

$$\begin{aligned}
\mathbf{t}^{\mathrm{diff}'}\mathbf{Z} &= \mathbf{t}^{\mathrm{diff}'}(I - A)\mathbf{Y} \\
&= \mathbf{t}^{e'}(I - A)\mathbf{Y} - \mathbf{t}'(I - A)\mathbf{Y} \\
&= \mathbf{t}'(I - A)^{-1}(I - A)\mathbf{Y} - \mathbf{t}'\mathbf{Y} + \mathbf{t}'A\mathbf{Y} \\
&= \mathbf{t}'A\mathbf{Y} \tag{5.8}
\end{aligned}$$

Alternatively, we can see this last measure of the taxation of inputs as simply a decomposition of the total tax payment

$$t'Y = t'(I - A)Y + t'AY$$

$$= t'Z + t'AY \qquad (5.9)$$

into a tax on final demand, $t'Z$, and a tax on intermediate goods, $t'AY$.

Although t^{diff} measures the extent to which inputs are taxed in the above model, it does not indicate any costs associated with distortions of choice of technique resulting from the taxation of inputs, because all coefficients are fixed. And changes in factor price and pure profits have been assumed away, because we have a single factor and zero profits. The relaxation of some of these assumptions is discussed below. Here we concentrate on the effect of taxation on the composition of inputs and relax only the assumption of fixed coefficients (thus retaining a single factor and zero profits).

Closed economy; flexible coefficients; one factor

We assume as before that each industry has a single output (no joint production). We may then write $c_i(\mathbf{q}, w)$ as the minimum factor cost of producing good i when input prices are $\mathbf{q}$ and the single factor has price w. If we choose the single factor as numeraire, we may write the vector of costs as a function $\mathbf{c}(\mathbf{q})$ of $\mathbf{q}$ only. The most efficient way of producing each good can be defined simply in terms of the technique requiring the minimum quantity of the factor directly and indirectly in production. These minimum unit costs, γ, as is well known (for example, Bliss, 1975, chapter 11), are the prices of the non-substitution theorem satisfying

$$\gamma = \mathbf{c}(\gamma) \qquad (5.10)$$

so that

$$\gamma' = \mathbf{v}'(\gamma)[I - A(\gamma)]^{-1} \qquad (5.11)$$

where $\mathbf{v}(\gamma)$ is the vector of factor requirements per unit of output for each industry and $A(\gamma)$ the input–output matrix at prices γ. Notice that $\mathbf{v}$ and A now depend on prices, whereas they were previously fixed, and that

$$[A(\mathbf{q})]_{ij} = \frac{\partial c_i}{\partial q_i} \qquad (5.12)$$

from the standard properties of the cost function.

Where we have taxation of sales, producers receive a price $\mathbf{p}$ but pay $\mathbf{q}$ for inputs. Thus in equilibrium, if we generalise equation (5.12) above,

$$\mathbf{p} = \mathbf{c}(\mathbf{q}) \qquad (5.13)$$

The difference between prices with and without taxation is $(\mathbf{q}-\gamma)$, which may be written, by means of equations (5.3), (5.10) and (5.13), as

$$\mathbf{q}-\gamma = \mathbf{c}(\mathbf{q})-\mathbf{c}(\gamma)+\mathbf{t}$$

$$\geqslant A'(\mathbf{q})(\mathbf{q}-\gamma)+\mathbf{t} \qquad (5.14)$$

using the concavity of the cost function and equation (5.12). Thus

$$\mathbf{q}'-\gamma' \geqslant \mathbf{t}'[I-A(\mathbf{q})]^{-1} \qquad (5.15)$$

because $[I-A(\mathbf{q})]^{-1}$ is assumed to be a non-negative matrix. The implication of equation (5.15) is that the effective tax calculated in our empirical work, which is based on the input–output matrix as measured at the ruling prices, *underestimates* the price-raising effect of the taxes. The reason is that the fixed coefficients assumption ignores the rise in price associated with the reorganisation of inputs from those associated with $A(\gamma)$, which minimise resource costs, to $A(\mathbf{q})$.

It remains true, however, that the effect on revenue of a shift in final demand is still $\mathbf{t}'(I-A)^{-1}$ so that this expression still gives us the effective tax. And again it is easy to check that $\mathbf{v}'(I-A)^{-1}$, which we have called $\mathbf{p}^{b'}$, the basic price vector, continues to measure the shadow price. It is also straightforward to see from (5.3), (5.12) and (5.13) that

$$\frac{\partial \mathbf{q}'}{\partial \mathbf{t}} = (I-A)^{-1} \qquad (5.16)$$

Hence a change in the tax rate $\Delta\mathbf{t}$ corresponds to a change in consumer prices $(I-A)^{-1}\Delta\mathbf{t}$. This means that we carry out our analysis of marginal tax reform entirely in the space of effective taxes since changes in nominal taxes $\mathbf{t}$ can be translated into effective taxes, which reflect both price changes for consumers and revenue changes for the government. And shadow prices are simply the consumer prices less the effective taxes, i.e. $\mathbf{v}'(\mathbf{q})[I-A(\mathbf{q})]^{-1}$ as before. The difference between this case and the previous one for marginal reform analysis is simply that $A(\mathbf{q})$ now depends on prices.

Open economy; fixed coefficients; one factor

So far we have considered the case of a closed economy. Let us now allow for imports. Superscripts m and d refer to imported and domestic goods respectively. Unless otherwise stated, all imports are assumed to be complementary; that is, production of good j at unit level requires a_{ij}^d of good i produced domestically and a_{ij}^m of imported good i. The assumption is relaxed below, where we show that the analysis of price effects is correct for marginal changes even where we allow some substitutability. Restrictive import policies may imply that complementarity has to be established before imports are allowed. In the absence of taxes the competitive pricing conditions for domestically produced goods become

$$\mathbf{q}' = \mathbf{q}'A^d + \mathbf{v}' \qquad (5.17)$$

where A^d is a matrix of input–output coefficients for domestic flows. The foreign exchange costs ($\mathbf{p}^{m'}A^m$ if $\mathbf{p}^m$ are import prices) of imported inputs have been included in the vector of value added, $\mathbf{v}$, and there are assumed to be no import quotas for these inputs. If we allow for the imposition of excise taxes on domestic production $\mathbf{t}^d$, and for import duties $\mathbf{t}^m$ (both expressed per unit), the pricing equation becomes

$$\mathbf{q}' = \mathbf{t}^{d'}(\mathbf{I} - A^d)^{-1} + \mathbf{t}^{m'}A^m(I - A^d)^{-1} + \mathbf{v}'(I - A^d)^{-1} \qquad (5.18)$$

where A^m is the matrix with the ijth element a_{ij}^m. Thus the effective taxes, $\mathbf{t}^{e'}$, are given by

$$\mathbf{t}^{e'} = \mathbf{t}^{d'}(I - A^d)^{-1} + \mathbf{t}^{m'}A^m(I - A^d)^{-1} \qquad (5.19)$$

In this formulation the contribution of excise taxes, which fall only on domestic production, to effective taxes is given by $\mathbf{t}^{d'}(I - A^d)^{-1}$ and that of import duties $\mathbf{t}^{m'}A^m(I - A^d)^{-1}$. Note that in this model the tax effects are additive (the imported and domestic inputs are different goods, and we cannot add A^d and A^m to get an aggregate input–output matrix). The effects of sales taxes levied on total commodity flows, regardless of the origin of the commodity, may also be given by equation (5.19) because we can see these (sales taxes) as affecting prices of domestically produced goods in part through imported inputs and in part through domestic inputs.

We have confined attention here to the effect of taxes on the prices of domestically produced goods in a fixed-coefficients linear model with only one domestic factor and a fixed exchange rate (domestic factors and foreign inputs are added to form $\mathbf{v}$ using a relative price, the exchange rate, which we assume is constant). More general models are discussed below.

Tariffs come into the picture not only through their effects on the cost of production of imported inputs but also through the prices of and tax revenue from consumption goods. Where imported consumption goods are different from domestic, and consumption imports are freely permitted, then the list of relevant taxes in the space of final demands is the effective taxes for domestically produced goods together with tariffs for imported consumption goods. If imports of consumer goods are banned then all that matters for revenue are the domestically produced goods, and the effective taxes capture the relevant information. Where imported consumer goods are freely permitted and competitive with domestically produced goods, then we can treat the effective tax as falling on both parts of consumption if the tariff is equal to the effective tax (in this sense the tariff is not protective but simply compensates for domestic taxation). In this case an increase in effective tax would be coupled with an increase in the tariff. Finally where consumer imports are competitive with domestically produced goods, but subject to quota, then effective taxes on domestic goods and changes in total consumption may capture the relevant information. A rise in the price of a domestic good through taxation would raise the price of the goods imported under quota, but the government would capture this revenue for itself only if it increased the tariff on the imports along with the effective tax.

If not, then the change in revenue $\partial R/\partial t_i^e$ is $X_i^d + \sum_j t_j^e \partial X_j/\partial q_i$, rather than

$X_i + \sum_j t_j^e \partial X_j/\partial q_i$, where X_i^d is consumption from domestic sources. (Note that in this case changes in X_i are the same as changes in X_i^d.) In our applied work we do not have information on the proportions of consumption coming from domestic production and from imports. We shall therefore assume, using one of the approaches described, that effective taxes can be used to measure revenue changes. Given that import controls in the subcontinent for consumer goods have been very strong, the versions of the argument involving these controls may be most appropriate.

Open economy; flexible coefficients; several factors

We have so far considered models for all of which there is just one factor. We have examined the closed economy case with and without flexible coefficients and the open economy case with fixed coefficients. For all of these the effective tax was an appropriate tool for the reform analysis. It is straightforward to show using similar methods that it can be extended to the case of flexible coefficients and an open economy. Important difficulties arise, however, with more than one factor. The last case we shall examine has an open economy, flexible coefficients and more than one factor.

The buyer's price is the producer price plus the tax. Then

$$\mathbf{q}^m = \mathbf{p}^* + \mathbf{t}^m \tag{5.20}$$

and

$$\mathbf{q}^d = \mathbf{p}^d + \mathbf{t}^d \tag{5.21}$$

where $\mathbf{p}^*$ is the (exogenous) world price vector for imports and $\mathbf{t}^m$ and $\mathbf{t}^d$ are taxes on imports and domestically produced goods respectively.

$$\mathbf{q}^d = \mathbf{c}^d(\mathbf{q}^d, \mathbf{q}^m, \mathbf{w}) + \mathbf{t}^d \tag{5.22}$$

and

$$\frac{\partial q_j^d}{\partial t_i^d} = \sum_l \frac{\partial c_j^d}{\partial q_l^d} \frac{\partial q_l^d}{\partial t_i^d} + \sum_f \frac{\partial c_j^d}{\partial w_f} \frac{\partial w_f}{\partial t_i^d} + \delta_{ij} \tag{5.23}$$

$$\frac{\partial q_j^d}{\partial t_k^m} = \sum_r \frac{\partial c_j^d}{\partial q_r^d} \frac{\partial q_r^d}{\partial t_k^m} + \sum_f \frac{\partial c_j^d}{\partial w_f} \frac{\partial w_f}{\partial t_k^m} + \frac{\partial c_i^d}{\partial q_k^m} \tag{5.24}$$

where w_k is the price of the kth factor (we abstract here from the taxation of factors), and δ_{ij} is the Kronecker delta.

On writing

$$\Delta^d = \left(\frac{\partial q_l^d}{\partial t_i^d} \right) \tag{5.25}$$

and

$$\Delta^m = \left(\frac{\partial q_r^d}{\partial t_k^m} \right) \tag{5.26}$$

we have

$$\Delta^d = \Delta^d A^d + W^d B + I \tag{5.27}$$

and

$$\Delta^m = \Delta^m A^d + W^m B + A^m \tag{5.28}$$

where A^d is the domestic input–output matrix $(\partial c_j^d / \partial q_l^d)$ giving the coefficients of domestic goods into domestic production, A^m is the coefficient matrix giving imported inputs into domestic production $(\partial c_i^d / \partial q_k^m)$, B is the coefficient matrix giving factor inputs into domestic production, W^d is the matrix of factor price responses to the taxation of domestic inputs, and W^m is the corresponding matrix for taxes on imported goods. Finally, we have

$$\Delta^d = (I - A^d)^{-1} + W^d B (I - A^d)^{-1} \tag{5.29}$$

and

$$\Delta^m = A^m (I - A^d)^{-1} + W^m B (I - A^d)^{-1}. \tag{5.30}$$

The first terms on the right-hand side of these two equations represent the marginal versions of equation (5.19) (which used fixed coefficients) for the case of flexible coefficients. Thus if we confine ourselves to marginal changes, we do not have to insist that imported inputs are strict complements in domestic production.

The second terms in the equations give us the effect on commodity prices of changes in factor prices resulting from the tax change. In the non-substitution theorem, there is only one factor, and if this is the numeraire, the price change is zero. Thus our previous reform analysis applies to flexible coefficients with only one factor, and with more than one factor we have to examine $WB(I-A)^{-1}$. Note, however, that the effect is additive, so that direct examination of $(I-A)^{-1}$ does give us an important part of the effect on prices of a tax change. To this should be added any effect on goods prices through the change in factor prices. In principle, W^d and W^m cannot be calculated without a full model of the economy. We cannot tell, for example, how the relative prices of land and labour will change without knowing whether the demand changes brought about by taxes will lead to a greater emphasis on land or on labour-intensive commodities.

The analysis also allows us to characterise the effects of factor taxes, e.g. on labour or land. In equation (5.22) we can change $\mathbf{w}$ to $\mathbf{w} + \mathbf{t}^f$ where $\mathbf{t}^f$ is the vector of per unit factor taxes. If we write Δ^f as $(\partial q_j^d / \partial t_k^f)$ then the effect of an increase in factor taxes on the prices of domestically produced goods is given by $(B + W^f)(I - A^d)^{-1}$ where W^f is the matrix of factor price changes which result from changes in factor taxes.

Capital goods

So far we have assumed a static model. Much of the input taxation, however, arises through the taxation of capital goods. In principle, we would need a fully articulated dynamic model to determine the effect of taxes imposed in one period on prices in all other periods. To keep things simple, we may attempt to capture the effects of taxes on capital goods by including a term in equation (5.2) that is $r\mathbf{p}'K$, where K is a capital stock matrix and r a rate of interest – thus we charge an implicit rental for the equipment. This formulation would be correct in steady state and we hope an adequate approximation out of steady state. In equations (5.4) to (5.6) we would therefore simply replace A by $(A + rK)$.

To give an aggregative indication of the orders of magnitude involved, suppose that the real rate of interest is 5% and the capital–output ratio is 5. Then capital represents 25% of cost, and an effective tax rate of 20% on capital goods will contribute 5% to effective tax rates. Given effective rates of 10% or so, this contribution is not small. It is clear that the theoretical and empirical aspects of the dynamic effects of taxes on prices deserve further research.

Shifting

In the first group of models examined above, taxes are shifted entirely in the sense that profits are unchanged (at zero with constant returns and perfect competition). Thus we took the price, w, of the single factor to be unchanged. The rise in prices from the taxes, of course, means that the real wage and household welfare fall but this was presented in terms of a rise in output prices. In this sense we have 100% shifting. Where imported goods were introduced we considered them first only as complementary inputs into production. Imported consumption goods were discussed less formally.

With several factors the question of incidence and shifting enters through changing factor prices as well as through output prices, although the matrix of factor price changes was not calculated explicitly. It would be determined in the structure of the general equilibrium and would require full details of the demand side of the economy. One can, however, point to some models of special interest. Where a good is freely traded on the world market under a fixed tariff then a change in the tax on domestic production of that good will not change its market price. The import tax will fall on factor prices. If the good is produced using perfectly mobile factors, then, under constant returns and perfect competition, factor prices and technical coefficients will change so that the domestic production breaks even or, if this is not possible, the good is no longer produced. If a factor is specific to the industry then it is likely to bear the brunt of the tax increase. Examples of this case are contained in Hughes (1987).

We can also consider the consequences of dropping the assumptions of constant returns and perfect competition. The main issues can be illustrated in a partial equilibrium analysis. The traditional analysis of tax shifting in the ordinary supply–demand diagram with perfect competition, but without constant returns, gives (for small taxes) a proportion $\eta/(\varepsilon+\eta)$ shifted to consumers, and $\varepsilon/(\varepsilon+\eta)$ to producers, where ε is the elasticity of demand and η is the elasticity of supply (see, for example, Stern, 1987). In this sense shifting lies between 0 and 100%, and 100% shifting to consumers occurs only where the elasticity of supply is infinite (or there are constant returns to scale).

If on the other hand we drop the assumption of perfect competition in the partial equilibrium model, then a very broad range of outcomes is possible. For example, in the monopoly case the price increase as a result of a tax is $1/(1-\varepsilon^{-1})$ which is greater than one (since ε must be bigger than one for equilibrium). Similarly in oligopoly and imperfect competition models (see Stern, 1987) shifting can be above or below 100%. Generally then the assumption of 100% shifting of indirect taxes is not a polar case if one widens the perspective beyond perfect competition.

We have been examining in this subsection how far it is legitimate to translate our analysis from nominal taxes to effective taxes. We want to capture the effects of changes in taxes both on prices and on government revenue. Our immediate motivation for doing this was to link our analysis to consumer demand which is in terms of final goods, the link being necessary to calculate changes in government revenue. We have seen that flexible coefficients are not an obstacle to such a translation. The open economy can also be introduced and we can characterise the different contributions to effective taxes of domestic taxes and those which enter through trade. One must recognise that the concept of effective taxes is one applying here *only* to domestically produced goods. Problems arise with more than one factor, however, since nominal taxes can shift relative factor prices in a manner not easily captured by effective taxes, and these factor price changes will contribute to changes in the prices of final goods. Nevertheless, in this case too, effective taxes can tell an important part of the marginal story with price effects, operating through relative factor prices, being additional to those operating through the taxation of inputs.

The effective taxes will be important ingredients for our marginal reform calculations in that they tell us the effects on government revenue of output increases in domestic production. They are also of substantial interest in their own right as descriptions of the tax system. Governments will often find it difficult to judge the consequences of taxes in a complicated production and fiscal structure. In this context the t^e will be a very useful summary statistic of the fiscal system that itself may well influence policy directly if it reveals, for example, that the government is, in fact, taxing heavily goods that it meant to subsidise or to tax only lightly.

5.3   Household demands

If a household is consuming 5 kg of oranges and the price per kilogram goes up by one penny then it is, in money terms, five pence worse off. A more formal way of saying this is that the price derivative of the indirect utility function is (minus) the marginal utility of income times the quantity, or that the price derivative of the expenditure function is the quantity. This simple idea lay behind our characterisation of the term $\partial V / \partial t_i$, or the welfare impact on households from a tax increase, as $-\sum_h \beta^h x_i^h$ where β^h are the welfare weights and x_i^h the consumer demands. The welfare weights are discussed in section 5.4 and in this section we concentrate on the money measures of losses to households and problems of measurement of household demands and responses. We shall be interested in describing the distribution of gains and losses across household types, i.e. in the identification of gainers and losers, as well as the aggregate measures such as $\sum_h \beta^h x_i^h$ or the distributional characteristics $\sum_h \beta^h x_i^h / X^i$.

Since the gains and losses from marginal changes are based on actual household consumption, it would seem that we can perform this part of the reform calculation without recourse to a demand system. A demand system will, however, be necessary for the calculation of revenue effects $(\partial R/\partial t_i)$, although in this case it is aggregate price responses $(\partial X/\partial q_i)$ which are required rather than individual demand responses. And we would continue to use X_i, the measured consumption. We shall, however, need to consider a demand system at the level of individual households for two reasons. First, if we wish to consider non-marginal changes in price, then we shall need a version of consumer surplus or equivalent variation (using the indirect utility or expenditure functions) which incorporates a demand response (we return to the issue of non-marginal reforms in section 5.7). Second, it must be recognised that the data come from a household survey which is a sample, and not the whole population, and which will be subject to sampling errors, measurement errors and so on. We discuss these two reasons in turn.

The money impact of a price change from $(\mathbf{q}^0$ to $\mathbf{q}^1)$ on a household may be measured by the equivalent variation (EV), i.e. the money loss (in the absence of the price increase) which would give an equivalent loss of utility to that resulting from the price change. This is

$$EV \equiv E(\mathbf{q}^1, u^1) - E(\mathbf{q}^0, u^1) \qquad (5.31)$$

where $E(\mathbf{q}, u)$ is the expenditure function. A second-order approximation is

$$EV = (\mathbf{q}^1 - \mathbf{q}^0)'\mathbf{x}^0 + \tfrac{1}{2}(\mathbf{q}^1 - \mathbf{q}^0)'S(\mathbf{q}^1 - \mathbf{q}^0) \qquad (5.32)$$

where S is the Slutsky matrix $(\partial^2 E/\partial q_i \partial q_j)$ and we have used the property that the derivative of the expenditure function is the compensated demand $(\mathbf{x}^0 = \partial E/\partial \mathbf{q}^0)$. For a single price change we may write, where the ith price increases by Δq_i,

$$EV = \Delta q_i x_i \left(1 - \tfrac{1}{2}\varepsilon \frac{\Delta q_i}{q_i}\right) \qquad (5.33)$$

where ε is $-(q/x)(\partial x/\partial q)$, the compensated elasticity measured as a positive number.

From (5.32) and (5.33) we see that, whilst the level of demand is a first-order approximation of the money loss per unit price change, it is an over-statement of the loss since the consumption bundle is reorganised to substitute away from a good whose price has increased. The degree of over-statement is higher the higher is the (compensated) elasticity of demand, as we see from (5.33).

When a change in many prices is being considered then it will generally be convenient to use an explicit functional form for E. To illustrate we have the linear expenditure system

$$E(\mathbf{q}, u) = (M - \mathbf{q} \cdot \mathbf{a}) \Pi \mathbf{q}_i^{\alpha_i} \qquad (5.34)$$

where M is household income, $\mathbf{a}$ is the vector of 'minimum requirements' and α_i is the marginal budget share of good i. Household characteristics can enter via $\mathbf{a}$ or α_i or both. From one point of view, 5.34 works with the fitted rather than the actual values for a household, which will be inaccurate to the extent that the household demands are badly fitted. On the other hand if we divide through by $E(\mathbf{q}, u^1)$, (5.31) gives EV/E, an index of price change (see, for example, Deaton and Muellbauer, 1980a and 1980b) which may be applied to household income. Aggregating across goods one might hope that the price index would not be too misleading. Nevertheless it must be acknowledged that cross-section fits to consumption patterns are generally rather weak (an R^2 of 0.2 would often be considered rather good) so that the error in representing the welfare outcome (in money terms) of the price change for a single sample household might be quite large.

This takes us to the second set of reasons for being interested in a fitted demand system, which concerns the random term in a fitted equation. There are many interpretations of a random term, including, for example, specific household variation (known to the household but not to the observer), measurement error, variation in mood, optimisation error by the household, and misspecification by the modeller. Let us suppose that we have a demand system

$$x_i^h = F(\mathbf{q}, \mathbf{z}^h) + \eta^h \qquad (5.35)$$

where $\mathbf{z}^h$ is a vector of household characteristics and η^h is a random term. For any given $\mathbf{z}^h$ there will be just one η^h in the sample but the model takes it that η^h was just one drawing from an underlying distribution representing the full population. From this point of view we may be interested in the average of x_i^h conditional on $\mathbf{z}^h$ (the conditional expectation) as representing the money loss averaged for the assumed population of people with characteristics $\mathbf{z}^h$. The overall distribution of money losses in the population (as opposed to the sample) is given by the joint distribution of $(\mathbf{z}, \eta)$.

The distributional characteristic $\left(\sum_h \beta^h x_i^h / X_i \right)$ would then be measured by the integral of βx_i across the population divided by total consumption (assuming this last term can be accurately measured). We would expect β to depend on $\mathbf{z}$ which would include income, household structure and the like. We have not attempted to provide a full treatment of the distributional characteristic and the distributional effects of taxation along these lines and it would involve considerable further research to be carried out carefully.

Notice that we are thinking of the random term here as representing genuine variation within the population. If it is simply measurement error, for example, we would not want to attach welfare significance to it in our distributional calculations.

The considerations we have been discussing warn us that we should not attach a great deal of significance to sub-samples of just a few households. On the other hand, household surveys generally contain several thousand observations, and averages for sub-samples of a hundred or so may be sufficient to average out a large part of the sampling variation, and provide reasonably accurate measures of the effects of tax reform on that sub-sample. Also, detailed survey information at the level of the household would be required to allow the researcher to make the choice of the appropriate sub-sample for distributional analysis. The distributional characteristic calculated for the sample is itself an average and may have some robustness to the different treatments of the problems we have been discussing.

We have in our work focused on sample values in forming distributional characteristics. As we have noted, the distributional characteristic is an average. Further, the choice of functional form for demand analysis is not something we can make with any confidence and we wish to minimise its effects on the results. Given the weak fits one must expect in cross-section analysis, it is possible that its influence on the distributional characteristic would be large. By using actual sample values we have avoided this problem and this part of the analysis is, at least, robust to the choice of functional form. This is an important issue in tax design as we have seen in chapter 3 (see also Deaton, 1987, and Stern, 1987, for further discussion). We cannot avoid, however, the influence of functional form in estimating revenue effects, although, as we have noted, these enter only through aggregate demand elasticities.

5.4   The choice of welfare weights

Policy choices generally involve implicit or explicit trade-offs of gains or losses to different groups. Tax policy is no exception and we have treated this problem in two ways. The first is to exhibit the gains and losses for different groups. This allows the commentator to make his or her own judgement (see chapter 7), or to suggest how interest groups might be expected to behave. The second is to make the judgements explicit and introduce the welfare weights β (see chapter 7). In this section we examine how the βs might be discussed and selected.

The most direct way to investigate views on distribution is to ask questions about hypothetical transfers between people in different circumstances for very simple models. If, for example, we are prepared to transfer one unit of income from a richer household to a poorer one, in a state of affairs where there are no off-setting effects such as incentive problems, revenue changes and the like, then we can say that the welfare weight β decreases with household income or wealth. We would also be interested in how quickly β decreases with (say) income. Suppose, for illustration, we choose a functional form, where I is income,

$$\beta(I) = kI^{-\varepsilon} \qquad (5.36)$$

Then

$$\frac{\beta(I_A)}{\beta(I_B)} = \left(\frac{I_B}{I_A}\right)^{\varepsilon} \qquad (5.37)$$

This says that if household A has twice as much income as household B then the social marginal utility of income, or welfare weight, for B is 2^{ε} times that of A. For $\varepsilon = \frac{1}{2}, 1, 2$, we have 2^{ε} as 1.414, 2, 4. For $\varepsilon = 1$ we would be saying that we would be prepared to take one unit from A and give it to B even if half of it were lost *en route*. We would hope that the answers we get in this very simple framework where the questions we ask are fairly easy to understand would provide guidance for our distributional values in more complex problems.

The assumptions made for a simple model bring out a number of difficulties. We can ask whether we would use income, expenditure, wealth or some other measure as a base. Probably wealth is the most natural, as a measure of lifetime spending power, but it is usually unavailable. One can ask also which concept of income is appropriate. These are questions to which the answers will be determined mainly by which data are available. It will also be important to consider household size and structure since a large household with a given income would usually be judged to be worse off than a smaller one with the same income. We may wish to consider β as depending on other household characteristics, or parameters facing the household, such as education, wages or prices. If households are not free to choose work hours then we may wish also to include time worked. We should also consider functional form. The example given in (5.36) and (5.37) has relative welfare weights depending only on relative income. This does not allow any notion of a basic minimum to enter the welfare analysis and one may wish to adjust the functional form for this. There are, of course, great problems in deciding what is meant by a basic minimum but, nevertheless, the isoelastic form (5.36) is just one of the possibilities. In this book we shall keep things simple and β will generally be a function only of household real expenditure per capita and we shall use the isoelastic form (5.36).

The simple model of our thought experiment, based around (5.36) and (5.37), had no incentive problems or taxes. We inferred values from policy judgements in the least complex framework that we could postulate. This was a prototype of the 'inverse optimum problem' which has been studied in more complicated models: we write down a model of the government's perception of its policy problem, optimal savings or optimal taxation for example, and ask of a given savings rate or tax rate, 'What welfare judgements would have led to the selection of that tax rate as optimal?' An early survey of the possibilities is contained in Stern (1977). More recently we have linked the inverse optimum problem to our analysis of marginal tax reform (Ahmad and Stern, 1984). We describe this briefly.

As we saw in chapter 3, the problem of choosing optimal indirect tax rates in a model where shadow prices are proportional to producer prices can be written

$$\text{Maximise } V(\mathbf{t}) \text{ subject to } R(\mathbf{t}) \equiv \mathbf{t}'\mathbf{X} \geqslant \bar{R} \qquad (5.38)$$

where $\mathbf{t}$ is the tax vector, $\mathbf{X}$ the aggregate demand vector, and producer prices are treated as fixed. Taking λ as the Lagrange multiplier on the revenue constraint the first-order conditions may be written

$$\sum_h \frac{\beta^h}{\lambda} x_i^h = r_i \qquad (5.39)$$

where β^h is the welfare weight on household h, x_i^h is the consumption by household h of the ith good and r_i is $\partial R/\partial t_i$. Generally the optimisation problem is to solve (5.39) and $\mathbf{t}'\mathbf{X} = \bar{R}$ for the optimal $\mathbf{t}$ (and λ).

The inverse optimum problem can be stated as follows: *given* an initial position x_i^h, and taxes and revenue responses ($\partial R/\partial t_i$), is there a set of welfare weights on households, β^h, with respect to which that state of affairs would be judged optimal? Writing (5.39) in matrix form

$$\boldsymbol{\beta}'C = \mathbf{r}' \qquad (5.40)$$

where $\boldsymbol{\beta}'$ is (β^h), $\mathbf{r}'$ is (r_i) and C is the $H \times n$ consumption matrix with hth element x_i^h, we try to solve for $\boldsymbol{\beta}$. Our ability to solve this problem will generally depend on the relation between H and n. Equation (5.40) is only n equations; hence if there are many more households than goods we would expect to find many solutions. And if there are less households than goods we are likely to find no solutions.

We are also interested in whether or not there are solutions with non-negative β^h and here the Minkowski–Farkas lemma gives us an interesting link with the reform problem. The problem of finding a Pareto improving tax reform is to solve the problem of finding a change in taxes $d\mathbf{t}$ such that

$$C\,d\mathbf{t} \leqslant \mathbf{0} \quad \text{and} \quad \mathbf{r}'d\mathbf{t} > 0 \qquad (5.41)$$

The former says that each household is no worse off (the condition for this, for household h, is simply $-x^{h'}dt \geqslant 0$) and the second is that dt does not lose revenue. The Minkowski–Farkas lemma then says that *either* there exists a solution to (5.40) with non-negative welfare weights *or* there exists a dt satisfying (5.41). In other words either a solution to the inverse optimum exists, with non-negative welfare weights, or a Pareto improving tax reform is possible. The either/or is strict in the sense that one and only one of the situations applies.

In our analysis of the Indian economy using data for the 1970s and a demand system with nine goods and twenty-eight household groups (fourteen urban and fourteen rural), we found that Pareto improving tax reforms were indeed possible. Thus there would be no solution with non-negative welfare weights to the inverse optimum problem. This result, however, would be unlikely to survive a large increase in the number of household groups. In this case (5.40) is just nine equations and the number of variables (β^h) is equal to the number of households. As h is increased we would eventually expect to find non-negative welfare weights.

The inverse optimum problem was formulated in terms of finding the β^h but it can also be expressed in other ways. For example, one could ask, for given β^h and C, what revenue responses, r_i, the government must have in mind if it believes the existing system of indirect taxes to be optimal. We shall not take the inverse optimum problem further here; for more extensive discussion, see Ahmad and Stern (1984).

The interest in welfare weighting should be seen not only in its link with Pareto improvements but also as a commentary on government policies. One interpretation is as an attempt to discover the government's values so that they can be used in another problem. A different one would be as a criticism of the tax system. Thus we could argue that indirect taxes were poorly set because they could only be construed as desirable with respect to a very peculiar set of values. This argument would not be assuming that the government has these peculiar values and has chosen optimally: rather, we would be arguing that whatever process produced these taxes has led to an unsatisfactory outcome in the sense that the implicit values which would be necessary (for that outcome to be deliberately selected) would be peculiar or unattractive.

The final aspect of the welfare weights we shall consider concerns their normalisation. From one point of view the normalisation of the β^h is unimportant since it simply represents a scaling of the social welfare function $V(\ )$. It can, however, be useful in interpreting the βs to have some simple comparisons embodied in the units. One could, for example, normalise the βs so that the average is 1. Alternatively one could choose a household income level, e.g. at some poverty line, for β^h to be unity. A third possibility could be to work in terms of an average of net marginal utilities of income, adjusting β for the tax payments of households in the case where shadow and producer prices are proportional, or the value at shadow prices of the commodity bundle consumed out of marginal income, where producer and shadow prices are not proportional (see chapter 3, and Newbery, 1987a). This last method would take as a unit of value the net social worth of a unit of income distributed equally within the population. These are all methods of interest but we have chosen for the most part to take the welfare weight at a given level of income (per capita) to be unity. This is, of the three, the most clearly understood since the other two depend both on the distribution of income and on shadow prices and cannot really be understood without reference to them.

5.5   Calculating shadow prices

We saw in chapter 3 that knowledge of the social opportunity costs of changed demands on the economic system will in general be required to implement the analysis of reform. This is explicit in the methods we are adopting here but it is clear that it is implicit in any method of reform analysis, since any change will involve alterations in net demands, which must form part of the evaluation. We also saw that, in principle, the shadow prices take into account the full general equilibrium consequences of an extra unit of demand on the system including the effects of changes in government actions, which must form a specific part of the story. In practice, however, one must take short-cuts and the method we shall adopt here is that proposed by Little and Mirrlees (1974) and which is based mainly on information about production. We shall first describe the basic elements of their system and then discuss its suitability for the reform analysis. Calculations of the shadow price systems for Pakistan, together with the shadow prices themselves, are provided in the next chapter.

There are three main ingredients:
(i) Relative shadow prices should be equal to relative world prices for traded goods.
(ii) For non-traded goods the shadow price is the marginal cost of production evaluated at shadow prices.
(iii) Careful account should be taken of how the project changes incomes and we should weight the incomes which accrue to different groups in different ways.

We examine the arguments in favour of these three elements and how they can be put to practice.

5.5.1 Traded goods

The arguments for using world prices take a number of forms but are essentially similar. The idea is that the world prices represent the net benefits on the margin associated with an adjustment to production or consumption of a traded good. If, for example, a good is traded at fixed prices then the net effect of an expansion in production is not to change prices and the welfare of households directly but simply to save imports or increase exports. All that matters therefore is the foreign exchange earnings or savings. These foreign exchange earnings may have a different value from that given by the official exchange rate but the *relative* values of traded goods are given by their relative world prices. A formal presentation of this argument is provided in Drèze and Stern (1987) using the methods of section 3.5.

Another form of the argument is to point to the desirability of public sector production efficiency (see section 3.2). Given that the public sector should be efficient, the marginal rates of transformation between a pair of goods should be the same wherever those goods are transformed one into the other. Foreign trade is an activity open to the government for transforming one good into another and the marginal rates of transformation in that activity are equal to the relative world prices. These should therefore be the marginal rates of transformation elsewhere and thus the relative shadow prices to be used for evaluating projects.

These arguments tell us that many of the prices to be used in cost–benefit analysis may be found *without* working out the consequences of a project in a detailed model. This is a very valuable result since it tells us that these shadow prices will be appropriate for many different models – hence they are robust and we avoid difficult and dubious modelling work.

There are, however, difficulties. First, we must decide on which goods will be or should be traded; second, the level of trade may affect world prices (particularly for a large country like India); third, world prices for some goods may be volatile and difficult to forecast; and, fourth, there may be some varieties of a good which are traded and some which are not. This makes classification and the calculation of prices problematic. We discuss these difficulties briefly.

The first of these problems is the most basic from the conceptual point of view. It reminds us very forcefully that the shadow prices which should be used depend on the policies which are chosen by the government (see section 3.5). For example, if the government places a quota on the imports of certain goods it means that extra supplies must come domestically and the goods should be classified as non-traded. On the other hand the

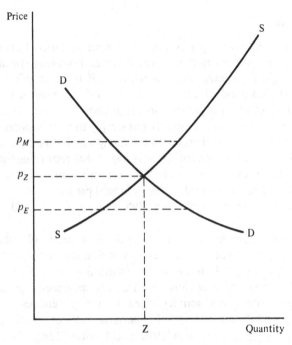

Fig. 5.1 The classification of tradables and non-tradables: $P_M > P_Z > P_E$ implies that the good is a non-tradable.

analysts working on project appraisal and trade policy together may discuss the appropriate trade policy and, after seeing the effect of the quota on project selection, they may propose removing the quota. Hence the appropriate classification will depend on the influence of the policy analysts. For a country with a growing domestic industry which is currently importing but hopes to eventually export, the good could be an importable in the first few years, then a non-tradable, then an exportable. We can illustrate the process of change through the familiar partial equilibrium diagram (figure 5.1).

Generally the import price is higher than the export price ($p_M > p_E$). The curve SS is domestic supply and DD domestic demand and Z is the point of intersection, at price p_Z. Then if $p_M > p_Z > p_E$ the good is a non-tradable. If $p_Z > p_M$ it is an importable and if $p_E > p_Z$ it is an exportable.

The use of shadow prices to guide investment decisions will lead to an industrial structure which itself will change shadow prices. This link between prices and quantities should be familiar and is not really disturbing – prices and quantities should both come from the same analysis or model. The discussion tells us that the classification of goods as traded or non-traded is not a straightforward matter and we shall in our calculations (see chapter 6) consider a number of possibilities.

The second difficulty is that extra exports may depress world prices. Here the marginal revenue becomes relevant. If the good is produced only in the public sector the appropriate shadow price for such a tradable is marginal revenue. Where the good is produced also in the private sector (which is not insulated from the price fall) then there should be an adjustment for the effect on private-sector profits. A similar analysis applies when extra imports raise the price – we should consider the marginal cost.

Uncertainty about the levels of world prices raises the two distinct, but related, questions of forecasting and the handling of risk. For the former, one can simply say that one has to try as best one can to construct a forecast of the distribution of the price or, at least, its mean. The correct measure of the value of an extra unit depends on how risk is handled. If risk can be costlessly spread from year to year then the correct measure is the mean (we are ignoring the problem of price being greater than marginal revenue which we discussed above). It may, however, be the case that insurance and capital markets are not perfect so that years of low prices cause special hardship. If this is a problem then the correct value will be lower than the mean price. We shall not consider the question of uncertainty further in our analysis in this book.

The final difficulty concerns calculation more than concepts. It may be that some varieties of rice or machine tools are exported and some are not. However, most of our statistics would treat rice or machine tools as a group. With better statistics we could subdivide rice or machine tools into different varieties but such data may not be available. In these circumstances we may have to choose to classify a good as tradable or non-tradable or deal with some kind of weighted average (e.g., if an extra unit is produced then half is imported and half releases the resources which would have been required for domestic production elsewhere). We have not pursued this kind of refinement.

5.5.2 Non-traded goods

We now turn to non-traded goods. The Little–Mirrlees rule is that the shadow price is the marginal cost of production at shadow prices. Let us write ω_j for the shadow value of domestic factors used directly in the production of good j and μ_j for the shadow value of the tradable inputs which are direct inputs into good j. Then, for the m non-tradable goods, indexed by $j = 1, 2, \ldots, m$, we have

$$v_j = \sum_{k=1}^{m} v_k a_{kj} + \omega_j + \mu_j \qquad (5.42)$$

where v_j is the shadow price of non-tradable good j and a_{kj} is the marginal amount of good k required for the production of a unit of good j. In matrix notation we have

$$\mathbf{v}' = \mathbf{v}'A + \boldsymbol{\omega}' + \boldsymbol{\mu}' \tag{5.43}$$

and

$$\mathbf{v}' = (\boldsymbol{\omega}' + \boldsymbol{\mu}')(I - A)^{-1} \tag{5.44}$$

where a prime denotes a row vector and A the matrix (a_{kj}). We should note two aspects of the formula (5.44). First, the method indicates that we should use the marginal requirements (a_{kj}) but in practice all we have are the average (per unit) requirements from the input–output tables. Second, the theory requires us to know the shadow values $\boldsymbol{\omega}$ of the domestic factors used in production. We now turn to this issue.

5.5.3 Factors

Labour

When we employ labour on a project it is diverted from another activity where it was producing and consuming. In considering its opportunity cost we must examine how its withdrawal from other activities will affect output and incomes elsewhere. The basic principles are those embodied in the theory described in chapter 3 but we shall begin with a very simple one-good model which focuses on the income of the government, the worker and those involved in his previous occupation. We shall then consider more than one good and the complications arising from differences between relative market and relative shadow prices. Suppose that we employ (in a public-sector company) a labourer at a wage c and that the labourer was earning m (his marginal product) in the previous occupation. Then the consequence of the extra employment is that the labourer has an extra income $(c - m)$ and the public sector loses the wage it has paid c (note that the productivity of the worker in the public-sector company is a separate issue – it will be compared, in appraising a project, with the shadow wage which we are trying to calculate). Then the social cost of employing the labourer, or the *shadow wage rate* (SWR) is given by

$$\text{SWR} = c - \lambda(c - m) \tag{5.45a}$$

where λ here is the value of the extra income to the labourer as seen by the government, and government income is the numeraire. Notice that where income to different groups has different values then we should specify a numeraire group and the government is a convenient entity to use. We have also assumed here that previous earnings m were equal to the marginal product elsewhere, say, in the rural sector. If, on the other hand, the labourer was earning an amount a, but had a marginal product of $m(<a)$ then the earnings of the people with whom he used to work (the family farm or the work unit) will increase by $(a-m)$ and his increase will be $(c-a)$, so the total increase will still be $(c-m)$. If more (or less) than one person leaves the rural sector as a result of extra employment then the SWR becomes

$$\text{SWR} = c - \lambda(c - \sigma m) \qquad (5.45b)$$

where σ is the number leaving the rural sector.

It is clear that the shadow wage will depend on the functioning of the labour market. To illustrate this, and for its own interest, we consider a simple model of migration following that of Todaro (1969). Suppose that the urban wage is c and the rural wage is m. Let the total employment in urban areas be E and the number in the urban areas seeking jobs be S. The number of urban unemployed is therefore $U = S - E$. Let us suppose also that work in the rural areas is guaranteed for those who want it. The central hypothesis in the model is that a worker will leave the rural area to seek work in the town if the expected wage in the town, pc, exceeds the wage in the country, m, where p is the perceived probability of finding employment. The equilibrium level of unemployment is given by

$$\left.\begin{array}{l} pc = m \\[2mm] p = \dfrac{E}{E+U} \end{array}\right\} \quad \text{so that } U = \left(\frac{c}{m} - 1\right)E \qquad (5.46a)$$

since Todaro also supposes that the perceived probability of finding employment is given by the number of jobs divided by the total number of job seekers S. We wish to calculate $dS/dE(=\sigma)$.

The effects of an extra job in the town on the number of unemployed and the number leaving the rural areas are

$$\frac{dU}{dE} = \left(\frac{c}{m} - 1\right); \frac{dS}{dE} = \frac{c}{m} \qquad (5.46b)$$

Suppose, for example, c/m is 2. If an extra job is created then 2 people will leave the rural areas since if the number were less than 2 the expected probability of finding a job would rise above $\frac{1}{2}$ and further migrants would have an incentive to move. So in this model an increase in urban employment *increases* urban unemployment. The model can be modified in a number of ways to introduce, for example, risk aversion, intertemporal aspects (you may have to wait for a job), priority hiring (so that some applications have a better chance of finding a job than others), more than one urban sector (for example an informal or traditional urban sector which allows some further job seeking), or different support schemes (for example from relatives) whilst a job is being sought. Many of these ideas will reduce the level of unemployment as predicted by the model. We can now see how this will affect the shadow wage rate we have been calculating. Where more than one person leaves the countryside following extra employment then the loss of output from one more urban job is $m(dS/dE)$, or c, in the Todaro model. In this case the SWR is equal to c, the actual wage payment.

Notice that we shall have the shadow wage equal to the actual wage payment only if $\lambda = 0$ or $c = m(dS/dE)$. The former case is where the government attaches no value to extra income for the workers; for example the government may think it has overwhelmingly important other uses for further funds. The second arises where the wage payment is equal to the marginal product elsewhere and there is no unemployment (as in the Todaro example above). This is the perfectly functioning labour market where the move does not provide the worker with any extra income. We can now see that there is a wide class of possibilities for the shadow wage depending on, for example, the structure of the labour market, priority on government expenditure, or the marginal product elsewhere. And one could add more complications such as price effects on food.

We now consider a second aspect of the shadow wage which is that the shadow prices for the marginal product elsewhere (m) may not be equal to market prices and the value of c at market prices will not be the same as its value at shadow prices. Hence we need to convert c and m into shadow prices. To do this we multiply by a *standard conversion factor* or SCF. This converts market prices into shadow prices for a bundle of goods. The make-up of the bundle depends on the problem under discussion. For m we would want a bundle relevant to the quantities that the worker would have produced if he had been working elsewhere. For c we need a bundle corresponding to the consumption of the worker. We call the ratio of shadow price to market price the *accounting ratio*, and the SCF is an appropriate weighted average of the accounting ratios.

To calculate the SCF and the other shadow prices we need a unit of account and in the Little–Mirrlees method we use foreign exchange; more specifically we have foreign exchange in the hands of the government since we have already specified the government as the numeraire group in the economy. If the SCF to be applied to m is 0.75, this says that the shadow prices of goods which would have been produced by the worker elsewhere are 75% of the market price, i.e. for traded goods (if these are what would have been produced) the market price is four-thirds of the world price. Then the reciprocal of the shadow wage is like a shadow exchange rate. Suppose for example that there were a tariff of 33% on a good. If the worker would have produced a unit of that good then employing the worker on our project means one more import elsewhere. The market price, however, overstates the cost of the import since one-quarter of the market price is tax. Hence if the wage is equal to the marginal product at market prices then the marginal product as shadow prices is three-quarters of the wage and the SCF is 0.75.

Capital

Typically the data on cost of production will include some element of profit or payment to capital. We may interpret this as partly rental for capital services, partly depreciation and partly pure profit. The rental for capital services, and depreciation, should be treated just like other inputs – we decide how much is tradable, how much is non-tradable and apply the appropriate accounting ratios. Pure profit does not involve direct resource inputs but is an income increase for the capitalist. We therefore subtract as a cost $(1-\lambda)$ times pure profit where λ is the welfare weight on capitalist income. This is equivalent to counting a unit increase in capitalists' income as contributing λ to social welfare. If $\lambda=1$ (for a public-sector firm) then we do not subtract anything (a unit of surplus committed to the public firm involves no cost). Notice that we also have to multiply by an SCF representing an average of the accounting ratios for the consumption bundle of the capitalist.

Discounting

We weight the benefits B_t for each year by factors μ_t, which we call the discount factors, to construct a *net present value* (NPV) of the project

$$\text{NPV} = B_0 + \mu_1 B_1 + \mu_2 B_2 + \dots + \mu_t B_t + \dots \qquad (5.47)$$

The *discount factors* are therefore the values seen from the present (time 0), i.e. the present value of a unit of the numeraire in the relevant period. Thus μ_t is the value, in terms of a unit of the numeraire at time 0, of a unit of the numeraire at time t.

The discount rate r_t is the rate of fall of the discount factor, i.e. it measures how much less a unit of the numeraire is worth next year relative to this year. So,

$$r_t \equiv \frac{\mu_t - \mu_{t+1}}{\mu_{t+1}} \quad \text{or} \quad \mu_{t+1} \equiv \frac{\mu_t}{1+r_t} \qquad (5.48)$$

Thus

$$\mu_{t+1} = \frac{1}{(1+r_t)(1+r_{t-1})\dots(1+r_1)(1+r_0)} \qquad (5.49)$$

since $\mu_0 = 1$. If the discount rate is constant then $\mu_{t+1} = 1/(1+r)^{t+1}$ where r is the common value. It is usual to assume that the discount rate *is* constant, but there is nothing in the theory to suggest that this is true. Here the numeraire is foreign exchange in the hands of the government. We have to judge how fast this value is falling. If the government is borrowing then the value of one unit this year is at least $(1+r)$ times the value of a unit next year if r is the government borrowing rate on world capital markets. If the government has selected optimally from its sources of finance then the discount rate will actually be equal to r.

5.5.4   Summary

We have now set out the central elements of the method we shall use to calculate shadow prices. At a number of points we saw that there were various possible assumptions that might be made and a number of possible methods for specifying key parameters. These include in particular the classification of traded goods and non-traded goods, the shadow wage, the standard conversion factor and the treatment of profit income. Accordingly we shall allow for a number of different possibilities when we calculate systems of shadow prices.

Criticisms of the particular method focus on its emphasis on world prices. It is seen as part of the 'neoclassical resurgence' and as part of the attempt to persuade developing countries to pursue more open policies. Some people have reservations about that general direction. Nevertheless the theoretical arguments indicate that the use of world prices for traded goods is correct as a measure of opportunity costs for traded goods in a wide class of circumstances. Where an economy is not very open then the attractive simplicity of the method, it has been argued, is not in reality available. Most goods will have to be treated as non-traded so that the rule for non-traded goods should come under close scrutiny. Thus, we have to ask whether the extra output will in fact come from extra production. If it does not then the method becomes complicated. It is here that the method plumps for simplicity. To decide on the origin of an extra unit of a non-traded good (production or consumption or some combination) poses very difficult problems of modelling and estimation. The Little–Mirrlees method avoids these difficulties by basing its calculations on the production side and input–output information. As we have emphasised, the problems of the appropriate treatment of traded and non-traded goods have led us to consider a number of possibilities for classification in our applied work.

5.6 Using the notion of the marginal cost of funds

A central concept in the theory of reform we have presented was the idea of the marginal cost of funds from different sources. We wish to calculate this marginal cost for the different sources and direct the raising of marginal revenue to lower cost sources, or existing revenue from a higher to a lower cost source. In this section we discuss methods, and their associated difficulties, for calculating these marginal costs for the different types of taxes one finds in the sub-continent. We shall also consider costs of administration. For ease of reference we repeat equation (3.5) for the social marginal cost of public funds generated via an increase in the ith tax

$$\lambda_i = \frac{\sum_h \beta^h x_i^h}{X_i + \sum_j t_j^e \frac{\partial X_j}{\partial q_i}} \tag{3.5}$$

where we have put the superscript e on taxes to remind us that these are taxes on final goods. A useful reformulation is

$$\lambda_i = \frac{\sum_h \beta^h q_i x_i^h}{q_i X_i + \sum_j (t_j^e/q_j) q_j X_j \varepsilon_{ji}} \tag{5.50}$$

where ε_{ji} is $(q_i/X_j)(\partial X_j/\partial q_i)$, the uncompensated elasticity of good j with respect to the ith price. This is a convenient form to apply to the data because $q_i x_i^h$ represents expenditure by the hth household on the ith good, and consumer demand information often comes in the form of the ε_{ji}. Notice that t_j^e/q_j is simply the effective tax as a proportion of the market price; expressing taxes in this way allows us to calculate on the consumption side using expenditures and elasticities. We assume in this section, unless otherwise indicated, that producer prices are proportional to shadow prices.

As we saw in chapter 3, it is interesting and important to compare the social marginal cost λ_i from raising revenue by indirect taxation of the good i (for each i) with the social marginal cost λ^{PT} of raising revenue by a poll tax. This is given by

$$\lambda^{PT} = \frac{1}{1 - \bar{\delta}} \tag{5.51}$$

where

$$H\bar{\delta} = \Sigma \, \delta^h \tag{5.52}$$

and

$$\delta^h = \mathbf{t}' \frac{\partial \mathbf{x}^h}{\partial m^h} \tag{5.53}$$

where δ^h is the indirect tax revenue following from a marginal increase in lump-sum income or the marginal propensity to spend on indirect taxes out of lump-sum income (m^h), and we have used $\bar{\beta} = 1$. The cost $(-\Delta V)$ to households of a unit increase in a poll tax is $H\bar{\beta}$ and the extra revenue is $H - H\bar{\delta}$, because the loss in indirect tax payments must be subtracted from the revenue H. The ratio $(-\Delta V/\Delta R)$ is λ^{PT} and yields equation (5.51). If $\lambda_i < \lambda^{PT}$, then we would want to increase the ith tax to finance a reduction in the poll tax, or an increase in the poll transfer.

5.6.1 Different tax instruments

There will often be more than one type of indirect tax instrument and each of them will feed into the final price of a good and raised revenue. Examples might be domestic sales taxes on the one hand (which we call group S) or customs duties on the other (which we call group C). A government may be considering the option of raising all taxes in group S or raising all those in C and would like advice on the relative merits. It may also be of importance to know the effect on the revenue collected under one group of a tax increase on the other. This would be of particular importance where the authorities in charge of the different groups were separate entities in important respects. For example, in India the Centre is responsible for customs and the States for sales taxes.

Where the taxes accrue on inputs and both sets of taxes can impinge on the same good we cannot simply focus on one group of goods corresponding to C and one to S. Because we shall be speaking of effective taxes much of the time, this problem is pervasive. We shall write the two effective tax vectors arising from group C and group S as $\mathbf{t}^{eC}$ and $\mathbf{t}^{eS}$. With our assumptions on the production structure, the vector of total effective taxes, $\mathbf{t}^e$, is $\mathbf{t}^{eC} + \mathbf{t}^{eS}$, and we can examine marginal reforms by specifying an increase in S and C taxes as involving an increase $\Delta \mathbf{t}^{eS}$ and $\Delta \mathbf{t}^{eC}$ respectively. The $\Delta \mathbf{t}^{eS}$ and $\Delta \mathbf{t}^{eC}$ may be chosen in a number of ways, which we shall discuss below. The marginal loss from raising one rupee in S taxes then is

$$\lambda^S = \frac{\sum_h \sum_i \beta^h x_i^h \Delta t_i^{eS}}{\sum_i \left(X_i + \Sigma t_j^e \frac{\partial X_j}{\partial t_i^e} \right) \Delta t_i^{eS}} \tag{5.54}$$

(with a similar expression for λ^C). This expression may be written as a weighted average of the λ_i using weights θ_i^S that sum to one:

$$\lambda^S = \sum_i \theta_i^S \lambda_i \tag{5.55}$$

where

$$\theta_i^S = \frac{\Delta t_i^{eS}\left(X_i + \sum_j t_j^e \frac{\partial X_j}{\partial t_i^e}\right)}{\sum_i \left(X_i + \sum_j t_j^e \frac{\partial X_j}{\partial t_i^e}\right)\Delta t_i^{eS}} \tag{5.56}$$

This has the natural interpretation of being the proportion of the extra rupee arising from the increase in taxes on the ith good. From equations (5.55) and (5.56), it is clear that only the relative values of the components of t_i^{eS} come into the calculation of λ^S.

We may now compare λ^C and λ^S, which correspond to different options for raising revenue. $\Delta \mathbf{t}^{eC}$ and $\Delta \mathbf{t}^{eS}$ may be specified in a number of ways. For example, we could increase all import tariffs by one percentage point – that is, from $\mathbf{t}^m$ to $(\mathbf{t}^m \times 1.01)$ – and calculate the effect on $\mathbf{t}^{eC}$; or we could do the same thing for sales taxes. Some examples appear below.

We could also consider separate budget constraints for the two sources. To ease notation, we drop the superscript e here and concentrate only on effective taxes, or taxes on final goods. It may help to define issues if we deal first with the optimisation problem and then with that of reform.

We write the optimisation problem as

$$\text{Maximise } V(\mathbf{t}^C + \mathbf{t}^S)$$
$$\mathbf{t}^C, \mathbf{t}^S$$

subject to

$$\begin{aligned} \mathbf{t}^{C'}\mathbf{X} &\geqslant R^C \\ \mathbf{t}^{S'}\mathbf{X} &\geqslant R^S \end{aligned} \tag{5.57}$$

where R^C and R^S are the revenue requirements for group C and group S. Demands $\mathbf{X}$ and social welfare V are functions of the consumer price vector given by the sum of producer prices (assumed fixed) and $(\mathbf{t}^C + \mathbf{t}^S)$. Thus the taxes from the two sources are additive. Taking Lagrange multipliers for the two constraints, we have as first-order conditions

$$\frac{\partial V}{\partial t_i^C} + \lambda^C \frac{\partial}{\partial t_i^C}(\mathbf{t}^{C'}\mathbf{X}) + \lambda^S \frac{\partial}{\partial t_i^C}(\mathbf{t}^{S'}\mathbf{X}) = 0 \tag{5.58}$$

$$\frac{\partial V}{\partial t_i^S} + \lambda^C \frac{\partial}{\partial t_i^S}(\mathbf{t}^{C'}\mathbf{X}) + \lambda^S \frac{\partial}{\partial t_i^S}(\mathbf{t}^{S'}\mathbf{X}) = 0 \tag{5.59}$$

Given that the derivatives of V with respect to t_i^C and t_i^S are equal (and similarly for $\mathbf{X}$), we have, on subtracting equation (5.59) from equation (5.58),

$$\lambda^C = \lambda^S \tag{5.60}$$

This expression tells us that, at the optimum, the marginal cost of the two sources should be the same even though there are two budget constraints. This situation is intuitively obvious, because we can consider the standard problem with one budget constraint, $R^C + R^S$, and one overall tax vector, $\mathbf{t}$, solve this, and then divide the optimal tax vector $\mathbf{t}$ into portions $\mathbf{t}^C$ and $\mathbf{t}^S$, a procedure that yields R^C and R^S as required.

Away from the optimum, we cannot suppose that λ^C and λ^S are equal. If there are separate budget constraints, we should consider the effect of raising a unit of S-revenue on the C-revenue. Thus we can calculate

$$-\frac{\Delta R^C}{\Delta R^S} \equiv \mu_S^C \tag{5.61}$$

The number μ_S^C tells us the loss in C-revenue group if S taxes are increased by an amount sufficient to raise one rupee. As before in our discussion of (5.55) and (5.56), we may consider the extra revenue being raised through some vector $\Delta \mathbf{t}^S$. Then

$$\mu_S^C = \frac{-\sum_i \mathbf{t}^{C'} \dfrac{\partial \mathbf{X}}{\partial t_i} \Delta t_i^S}{\sum_i \left(X_i + \mathbf{t}^{S'} \dfrac{\partial \mathbf{X}}{\partial t_i} \right) \Delta t_i^S} \tag{5.62}$$

and we can compare μ_S^C and μ_C^S.

5.6.2   Comparing alternative sources of revenue

A comparison of different sources of extra revenue would involve a number of issues or criteria, for example (1) the marginal social loss to households; (2) shadow costs of incremental net demands where producer and shadow prices differ; (3) relations between different groups of taxes or jurisdictions; (4) administration and evasion; and (5) political acceptability and pressures. We focus first on comparisons of λ.

We derived λ_i for the taxation of good i, λ^{PT} for a poll tax, λ^C for C-taxes and λ^S for S-taxes. A comparison between taxes on the basis of λ would in general involve the suggestion that, other things being equal, we would shift from sources with high λ or high social losses from the marginal rupee to sources with low λ. Thus if λ_i for good i is greater than λ_j then we would

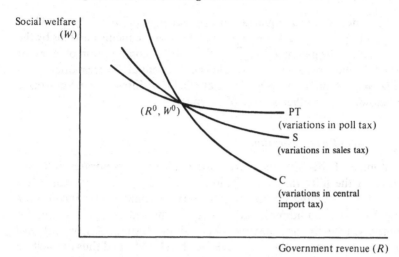

Fig. 5.2 The choice among taxes with different marginal social costs (*Source*: Ahmad and Stern, 1984).

want to shift on the margin from commodity i to commodity j. If λ^{PT} is lower than all the λ_i, we would want to shift from indirect taxation to a poll tax or if λ^C is bigger than λ^S, then the marginal rupee using the S-group taxes causes less social loss than that from the C group.

The use of λ for different instruments involves considering the rate of change of household welfare and social welfare with respect to government revenue. The idea may therefore be illustrated graphically by plotting social welfare, W, against R (figure 5.2). In the figure we have drawn three curves passing through the point (R^0, W^0) – the status quo described by the existing tax structure and associated level of social welfare W^0 and government revenue R^0. The curve labelled PT shows the relationship between W and R if all movement from R^0 is through a poll tax with other taxes constant; that labelled S shows movement in welfare if all taxes except S-taxes are held constant, and, similarly, C is for movement in C-taxes. The gradients of the curves are $-\lambda^{PT}$, $-\lambda^S$ and $-\lambda^C$ respectively. As we have drawn it we have $\lambda^{PT} < \lambda^S < \lambda^C$.

The best the government can do, for movements from R^0, using a single instrument is to follow the highest curve, that is, to maximise welfare at each level of R. Thus, in figure 5.2, for increases in government revenue we would follow the PT curve, that is, we would increase revenue through poll taxation, and for decreases in revenue we would follow the C curve. The rule is: for increases in R, raise the taxes that do least marginal damage, and for reductions in R lower the taxes that do greatest marginal damage.

If the values of λ are unequal (as above), we can improve W at given R^0 by raising a marginal rupee through poll taxation and reducing customs by the same amount; the gain is $\lambda^C - \lambda^{PT}$. At the optimal combination of taxes for given R^0, the three curves would be tangential, corresponding to $\lambda^{PT} = \lambda^S = \lambda^C$. Similar analyses can be applied if we introduce income taxes (see below) or any other source of revenue.

5.6.3   Costs of administration

An estimate of the administrative costs could be incorporated into our analysis in the following way. Suppose that raising an extra rupee via income tax (including effects on other tax revenues of the income tax change) involves an administrative cost θ^T. The superscript T stands for income tax. Then to raise one rupee net of administrative costs, we will have to have an increment in the gross revenue of $1/(1 - \theta^T)$, and thus the welfare cost to the households will be $\lambda^T/(1 - \theta^T)$. Similarly, the welfare cost of an extra rupee *net*, via the taxation of good i will be $[\lambda_i/(1 - \theta_i)]$, where θ_i is the administrative cost of a rupee via the ith good. Then a reform that raises one rupee net via the income tax and loses one rupee net via taxation of the ith good is beneficial if

$$\frac{\lambda^T}{(1 - \theta^T)} < \frac{\lambda_i}{(1 - \theta_i)} \tag{5.63}$$

where we have assumed that administrative savings of θ_i arise if the tax is reduced.

Our empirical analysis deals entirely with actual collections, and in this sense evasion is taken into account. Furthermore, our analysis of marginal reforms is in terms of an extra rupee actually collected from consumers rather than in terms of some notional expected revenue. The effective taxes reflect revenue collections and not simply the rate structures of the various constituent taxes. Thus, in cases where there is significant evasion or inefficiency of collection, effective taxes can be increased through better enforcement without changing statutory rates.

5.6.4   The theory of income tax reform

The analysis of the reform of the income tax can in principle proceed in the same way as the analysis of the reform of indirect taxes which was summarised in (5.50). We review the analysis only briefly here as it has not been a central feature of our work. For a given marginal reform of the income tax, we consider the effects on revenue ΔR and on social welfare ΔV, aggregating across households using welfare weights. As before, a beneficial reform is available if $\Delta V > 0$ and $\Delta R > 0$. Where extra revenue involves a loss in social welfare, we calculated $\lambda = -\Delta V / \Delta R$ as the social loss per marginal rupee of revenue associated with the reform. A beneficial reform at constant revenue is then achieved by switching a marginal rupee from a source with a higher social loss to one with a lower social loss.

In the absence of estimates of factor supply responses to tax changes one might start by assuming that pre-tax incomes are unchanged, although this is unsatisfactory and we discuss ways in which the results might be affected by relaxing this assumption. A reform of the income tax system will then imply changes of Δm^h in post-tax incomes, m^h.

Suppose for the moment that all individuals face the same consumer prices, $\mathbf{q}$, that the indirect utility function of household h is $v^h(\mathbf{q}, m^h)$, and that purchases are $x^h(\mathbf{q}, m^h)$. We express social welfare through a Bergson–Samuelson social welfare function $W(v', \dots, v^H)$, where $V(\mathbf{q}, \mathrm{m}^1, m^2, \dots, m^H) = W(v^1(\mathbf{q}, \mathrm{m}^1), \dots, v^H(\mathbf{q}, \mathrm{m}^H))$. An income tax reform represented by $(\Delta m^1, \dots, \Delta m^H)$, then yields a change in social welfare

$$\Delta W = \sum_h \beta^h \Delta m^h \tag{5.64}$$

where $\beta^h = \partial W / \partial m^h$ and is the social marginal utility of income for household h.

The change in government revenue ΔR from household h involves $-\Delta m^h$ as a transfer, but in addition we must take into account the change in indirect tax revenue from the adjustment in purchases consequent on Δm^h. Suppose the vector of per unit tax rates is $\mathbf{t}$ (the same for all households). The change in indirect tax payments by households is then

$$\sum_h \mathbf{t}' \frac{\partial \mathbf{x}^h}{\partial m^h} \Delta m^h \tag{5.65}$$

Thus

$$\Delta R = -\sum_h \Delta m^h + \sum_h \mathbf{t}' \frac{\partial \mathbf{x}^h}{\partial m^h} \Delta m^h \tag{5.66}$$

The quantitites ΔW and ΔR give us the marginal social loss and the marginal tax revenue from the reform associated with $(\Delta m^1, \Delta m^2, \dots, \Delta m^H)$ and defined by the income tax change under consideration. A number of possibilities may be considered. For comparisons with other possible reforms, it is convenient to define the marginal loss per rupee raised by an income tax reform as

$$\lambda^T = \frac{-\Delta W}{\Delta R} \tag{5.67}$$

The β^h, or welfare weights, are, as above, value judgements, specified exogenously, and we experiment with a number of possibilities. The $\partial x^h/\partial m^h$ would be based on the demand studies. In using the demand information, it is helpful to rewrite the second term in ΔR (see (5.65)) using

$$\delta^h \equiv t' \frac{\partial x^h}{\partial m^h} = \sum_i \frac{t_i}{q_i} \frac{\partial(q_i x_i^h)}{\partial m^h} \tag{5.68}$$

Thus we use the marginal budget share $\partial(q_i x_i^h)/\partial m^h$ and the proportion of tax in price t_i/q_i. The quantity δ^h is itself a feature of the hth household and the tax system that is useful to policy-makers: it is the marginal propensity to pay indirect taxes by household h (see (5.53)).

There are a number of possible income tax reforms one could consider. We give just one example. For a marginal change in the exemption limit, we may suppose that the effect applies to one household type only. In this case we label λ^T as λ^h to remind us that the change applies only to h, and we have

$$\lambda^h = \frac{\beta^h}{1 - \delta^h} \tag{5.69}$$

Again λ^h (like δ^h) is an interesting feature of household h, whether or not the household is at the exemption limit, because it tells us, for fixed gross incomes, the impact on welfare from reducing government revenue by one rupee in the form of transfers to household h. The transfer $1/(1 - \delta^h)$ would be more than one rupee because the government recoups δ^h per rupee transferred via indirect tax revenue. The net change in government revenue is

$$-\frac{1}{1 - \delta^h} + \frac{\delta^h}{1 - \delta^h} = -1 \tag{5.70}$$

We have so far supposed that pre-tax incomes are fixed. The analysis for the case of variable labour supply is broadly similar to that for indirect taxes but, for data reasons, we are unable to put this analysis into practice for the sub-continent, as estimates of a commodity demand and labour supply system would be required, and we know of no such information.

The modification in the analysis of marginal reform comes in the prediction of the effects on revenue of a tax change. The effects on household welfare of a marginal change are given simply by the change in pre-tax income at zero supply response, just as the marginal effects on household welfare of price changes are given by the consumptions of the goods whose prices have changed, and we do not need estimates of household responses. If factor supplies are reduced as the result of an income tax increase, then the increase in revenue ΔR as described above has been overestimated, and the marginal damage $-\Delta W/\Delta R$ per rupee of revenue has been underestimated. We may therefore focus a discussion of the effects of incentives in this analysis by asking how much extra revenue will be raised by the tax increase.

In the applied work for Pakistan presented in the next chapter we have focused on λ_i and λ_i^y, i.e. social marginal costs corresponding to particular goods with and without the assumption that market prices are equal to shadow prices. However, in our work on India (see, for example, Ahmad and Stern, 1987a) we put the other social marginal costs into practice. And we hope it is useful to have the formulae assembled for others who may wish to apply these ideas.

5.7 Non-marginal reforms

The marginal approach we have adopted is robust in a number of respects (as we saw in chapter 3). It is fairly economical on assumptions and data in that it leans heavily on the result that the extent of current purchases of a good reflects the cost to a household of a price increase resulting from a tax change. Thus behavioural responses arise only in predicting the change in revenue.

These advantages flow from the consideration only of marginal reforms, but therein lies the disadvantage. The approach in its simple form rules out the analysis of substantial changes. It is highly complementary to non-marginal analysis in a number of ways. First, it allows greater detail in that consumption and production responses are required only locally and not in a tax environment that is very different from the current one. Second, much, but not all, of the data for the non-marginal analysis could be collected simultaneously. Third, we can use a marginal analysis to check on a non-marginal one, not only in terms of possible directions of reform at the beginning and end of the change, but also to provide extra, supplementary detail. Thus we would like to see the two approaches carried out simultaneously and have illustrated this plan of action in our analysis of the possible introduction of a VAT in Pakistan, which is described in Ahmad and Ludlow (1989) and in later chapters.

An alternative view of the marginal approach could refer to the problem of collecting extra revenue using existing tax tools as opposed to a non-marginal problem of replacing the existing system with entirely different instruments. Strictly speaking, the distinctions between existing and new instruments, on the one hand, and marginal and non-marginal analyses, on the other, are not the same, but the dividing lines will often be similar.

We shall outline briefly a method for assessing some non-marginal reforms. For substantial reforms, we can no longer work with the differentials of welfare and revenue, and we must compare welfare and revenue before and after reform. The same kind of approach, however, continues to apply. If we write $\mathbf{q}^1$ and $\mathbf{q}^0$ for the post- and pre-reform prices, $\mathbf{t}^{e^1}$ and $\mathbf{t}^{e^0}$ for the effective tax rates, and similarly W^1 and W^0 and R^1 and R^0 for post- and pre-reform social welfare and revenue respectively, we are looking for changes from $\mathbf{t}^{e^0}$ to $\mathbf{t}^{e^1}$ that yield $W^1 > W^0$ and $R^1 \geqslant R^0$. We shall assume here that there are fixed basic prices, $\mathbf{p}^b$, so that $\mathbf{q}^i = \mathbf{p}^b + \mathbf{t}^{e^i}$, for $i = 0, 1$. The calculation of W^1 now involves a full specification of the social welfare function $W(u^1, \ldots, u^H)$ and the individual utility functions, u^h, or the indirect utility functions, v^h, and we can no longer work simply with the β^h evaluated at the initial position. These functions in turn will yield the demand functions $\mathbf{x}^h(\mathbf{q}, m^h)$ and thus $\mathbf{X}^1$, which is required for the calculation of R^1.

An analysis might then proceed as follows: we first find a $\mathbf{q}^1$ that satisfies $R^1 \geqslant R^0$. We might, for example, be interested in equal revenue reforms and could then solve $R^1 = R^0$. Thus we could express the reform in terms that involve one degree of freedom, which is then settled by the equal revenue condition. We might, for example, consider an increase in certain taxes and a reduction in one particular tax, or we could consider changing all taxes and distributing the extra revenue as a uniform lump-sum handout. More generally, however, we would simply want to establish what happens to government revenue and, if necessary, to demonstrate that $R^1 \geqslant R^0$.

As before (see section 5.3) we can drop any reference to the social welfare function and calculate v^{h^1} and v^{h^0} for each household and thus determine who gains and who loses. A natural way of expressing $v^{h^1} - v^{h^0}$, or the utility increase for household h, is using the equivalent variation EV_{01}^h defined in the standard way by the implicit equation

$$v^{h^1} = v^h(\mathbf{q}^0, m^{h^0} + EV_{01}^h) \qquad (5.71)$$

EV_{01}^h is simply the amount of money we would have to give to household h, if the original prices were ruling, to allow it to reach the post-reform utility level (see (5.31)). If we define EV_{01}^h explicitly using the expenditure function $E^h(\mathbf{q}, u^h)$, as in (5.31),

$$EV_{01}^h = E^h(\mathbf{q}^0, v^{h^1}) - m^{h^0}. \qquad (5.72)$$

Thus EV_{01}^h is a money measure of the benefit of the reform to household h; it is positive for a utility increase and negative for a decrease (see section 5.3 for further discussion). Notice that the identification of who gains and who loses, and by how much, would be a vital ingredient not only to a welfare analysis but also to one concerned with political economy, since the losers, if they understand the reform, would be likely to oppose it and the gainers to support it.

We must emphasise that the data requirements and assumptions for non-marginal reforms are much more stringent than for marginal reforms. The utility function and related demand function must be specified for each household, and we cannot simply use the existing consumer expenditure and aggregate demand functions as before. In the marginal case, we may be able to provide a reasonable guess at the aggregate functions without specifying in detail the constituent elements from different households. Similarly, for aggregating utility changes, we need the social welfare *function*, W and not simply the marginal social welfare weights, β^h, although, if real income changes are not large, the β^h may not vary a great deal with the price and income changes under consideration. Examples of the use of household data sets and non-marginal methods to identify gainers and losers from reforms are Atkinson, Stern and Gomulka (1980), Atkinson and Sutherland (1988) and King (1983).

5.8 Concluding comments

We have shown in this chapter that the theoretical ideas developed in chapter 3 can be cast in a form that allows them to structure and guide applied work. In some ways our approach may have looked overly technical or spuriously precise for applied analysis which will always have to be rough-and-ready. We have, however, simply been concerned with issues which should be central to the work of any tax adviser – revenue, distribution and production. For the analysis of the revenue effects of a marginal change we must consider aggregate demand derivatives and effective taxes, and for distribution we have to consider the pattern of consumption of households. Most of the analysis was concerned with nothing more sophisticated than this.

The simple approach using revenue and distribution is valid only where producer prices reflect social opportunity costs, i.e. shadow prices. Where they do not we should move away from effective taxes and work with shadow prices. They become part of the theory of marginal reform, as we showed in chapter 3, in that we replace the revenue cost of a tax change by the shadow cost of the net extra demands. This shadow cost can be alternatively expressed in terms of a shadow revenue. The impact on consumers is calculated as before using data on the distribution of consumption. The effective taxes are strictly speaking irrelevant where shadow and producer prices are not proportional, but as we saw in chapter 3 the social marginal cost of funds using shadow prices can be decomposed into constituent elements where we look first at marginal revenue and then at the effects associated with the discrepancy between producer and shadow prices. Effective taxes may also be useful for the policy-maker as simple summary statistics which may help in tracking the workings of a complex tax system which has effects throughout the production process.

The shadow prices themselves are, in principle, rather sophisticated instruments capturing the social opportunity costs which are the outcome of a full general equilibrium system embodying the behaviour of all the agents including the government. We have chosen to work with a relatively simple system, that of Little and Mirrlees (1974), which cuts through many of the complications by using two rules: world prices for traded goods and social marginal costs of production for non-traded. The first of these is generally robust in that it is correct in a wide range of circumstances. The second is less so, but has the great advantage that it allows an analysis based largely on the structure of production and suppresses or conceals the demand side.

The marginal analysis of reform using a fully explicit general equilibrium system in place of shadow prices is possible (see, for example, Newbery, 1987a). It does, however, require a considerable array of assumptions concerning important parameters. It also requires great care in specifying government behaviour and in treating the general equilibrium constraints which cannot be captured simply in terms of revenue. The use of revenue as the basic constraint involves the assumption of the proportionality of shadow and producer prices – a very important condition which is often overlooked.

Nevertheless governments may find it easier to focus on the revenue effects of a tax change rather than the marginal cost of extra demands at shadow prices (or shadow revenue). Even though the concept of social opportunity cost or shadow price should be central it is often subject to some scepticism, and given the assumptions required in the calculation of some shadow prices, one should not be overly assertive about the accuracy of calculations. Accordingly, in our applied work, we shall experiment with a number of sets of shadow prices. And we shall give some prominence to calculations which avoid explicit estimation of a new system of shadow prices by making the assumption that they are proportional to producer prices, or consumer prices less effective taxes.

Finally there are many practical features which require further work which we have avoided or where our analysis has been superficial. We have already emphasised that our tools for empirical work have been fashioned more for industry than agriculture and devoted chapter 4 to considering the special problems that arise for the latter. However, it is time to put the tools to use in our applied analysis.

6   Effective taxes and shadow prices in Pakistan

6.1   Introduction

As we have seen, indirect taxes in Pakistan form the major source of tax revenue. Within indirect taxes, customs duties and excises are predominant and these, to a large extent, fall on intermediate goods. In chapters 3 and 5 we introduced a number of analytical concepts and methods for the analysis of the reform of indirect taxes, and the purpose of this chapter is to begin the task of putting them to use to help identify beneficial directions of reform for Pakistan. In particular we showed how taxation which falls on intermediate goods can be translated, using the concept of 'effective taxes', into taxation on final goods thus facilitating the analysis of distributional and revenue effects of reform. We showed, further, how the concept of the social marginal cost of funds from different sources could be used to characterise beneficial directions of reform in the case where producer prices reflect social opportunity costs. We also showed how this concept might be extended, using shadow prices, to the case where producer prices diverge from social opportunity costs. Effective-tax calculations are presented in section 6.2 and shadow prices in section 6.3. These raw materials will be used in the analysis of the social marginal cost of funds in the next chapter. In addition to their usefulness for this type of calculation, estimates of effective taxes and economy-wide shadow prices are of interest in their own right, in understanding both the effect of the tax and tariff system on prices and revenue, and the distortions to which they contribute.

We shall provide substantial detail on the methods we have used not only so that they can be subject to proper scrutiny but also because we wish to put the reader in a position to embark on corresponding calculations for different contexts or countries. The reader who does not wish to work through these details can in most cases go directly to the main tables of effective taxes, shadow prices, social marginal costs of funds, etc., and be able to follow without difficulty the discussion based on these tables.

6.2   Effective taxes

In a world where there are many types of taxes and their effects may be complex, one may wish to find simple ways of summarising the tax system. We shall do this for indirect taxes by asking, for each domestically produced good, how much government revenue would increase if net output went up by one unit (as we saw in chapter 5, this concept is a partial equilibrium one and needs to be formulated rather carefully). We call the answer to this question 'the effective tax'. We have already seen that under certain assumptions we can interpret the calculation of the effective tax as a decomposition of the market price of a good into a portion (the effective tax) going to the government and a portion which is payment to domestic factors and to foreigners (see equation 5.18). It should be clear from the definition of the effective tax that we are referring to domestic production. Further, the answer to our question will depend on the conditions under which production takes place and the way in which prices are formed.

We use here the model developed in section 5.2 which has a fixed coefficient technology in which domestic inputs and complementary imported inputs combine with labour to produce output under competitive conditions. This led us to the expression (5.19) for effective taxes which is repeated here for convenience. Notice that we are now writing e as a subscript for ease of notation, since in this chapter we are looking at different contributions to effective taxes, each of which will have its own index which we will write as a superscript.

$$t_e' = t^{d'}(I - A^d)^{-1} + t^{m'}A^m(I - A^d)^{-1} \qquad (5.19)$$

As we pointed out in section 5.2 the model can be considered as incorporating 100% forward shifting of taxes. We pointed out that shifting under conditions of oligopoly or monopolistic competition could quite possibly exceed 100% so that this feature of the model might be considered an intermediate rather than a polar assumption. For empirical observations from Pakistan see Radhu (1965), Irfan (1974), Naqvi (1975) and Jeetun (1980). The evidence is somewhat less than conclusive on this point.

We have implicitly been ignoring the income tax in our discussion of the effective tax. Thus the effective tax here is the change in indirect tax revenue arising from the output change.

Finally, up to this point we have not taken into account the taxation of goods which arises through the capital stocks required in their production. In a steady-state model framework the formula (5.19) can be modified in a straightforward way by replacing A^d by $(A^d + rK^d)$ and A^m by $(A^m + rK^m)$ where K^d is the matrix of stocks of domestic goods required as capital for the production of domestic goods, K^m the matrix of stocks of imported capital goods for domestic production, and r a real rate of interest. The steady-state assumption is necessary since otherwise we would have to consider carefully the time pattern of accumulation, taxes and rates of interest in the determination of prices. Whilst it is unsatisfactory in some respects, it is the simplest way of introducing capital into the analysis. Depreciation is discussed in the next subsection where we describe calculations around the K-matrices.

6.2.1 Data

Major data requirements for estimating effective taxes include information on revenue collections for the main indirect taxes, classified by commodities, and tables of input–output coefficients for absorptions of domestic and imported goods and services. At the time of our fieldwork, the table for 1976 was the latest available. The study of distribution requires data on household consumption for different households and this was available from the Micro-Nutrient Survey (MNS) for the year 1975–6 (see Government of Pakistan, 1976). We discuss this survey in greater detail in chapter 7, where the directions of reform are analysed. Hence 1976 was the principal year chosen for carrying out the calculations which illustrate our methods.

Data on federal tax collections for the year 1975–6 have been obtained mainly from the Pakistan Ministry of Finance (Government of Pakistan, Ministry of Finance, *Economic Memorandum to the Budget*, 1976). The major domestic tax is the excise duty, which realised a gross revenue of Rs 4596 million. Tax revenues collected across commodities, taken from the Ministry of Finance, were mapped to an eighty-seven-good classification chosen to match a revised input–output table for 1975–6. Dividing revenues for each good by flows of the good we derive the implicit rate of tax which we call the *nominal* rate. This way of calculating nominal rates, since we deal with actual revenue collections, circumvents the problem of evasion associated with the use of announced statutory rates. Moreover, there may be a multiplicity of announced tax rates for the commodities at the level of aggregation of most input–output tables. Actual collections thus provide a weighted average of the implicit tax rates for any given commodity group. The commodity collections of revenue for each of the major indirect taxes for 1976 are presented in table 6.1. Some excisable goods are also subject to a sales tax, which applies to imports as well as to domestically produced goods. Of the total revenue collection of Rs 300 million from the sales tax on domestic goods, we have been able to allocate Rs 245 million to the eighty-seven commodity groups (the remaining Rs 55 million are not included in this calculation). The revenue breakdowns by commodity allocations are also presented in table 6.1. In addition there were, in

Table 6.1. *Revenue collections, 1975–6*

	Excise	Surcharge	Sales (D)	Subsidies	Imports	Sales (M)
			(Rs million)			
1 Wheat	0.00	0.00	0.00	−1 209.28	0.00	0.00
2 Rice	0.00	0.00	0.00	0.00	0.00	0.00
3 Cotton	0.00	0.00	0.00	0.00	0.00	0.00
4 Sugar cane	0.00	0.00	0.00	0.00	0.00	0.00
5 Tobacco growing	88.80	0.00	0.00	0.00	5.90	0.00
6 Oilseeds	0.00	0.00	0.00	0.00	9.02	10.29
7 Pulses	0.00	0.00	0.00	0.00	0.00	0.00
8 Other crops	0.00	0.00	0.00	0.00	195.78	13.50
9 Livestock	0.00	0.00	0.00	0.00	0.00	0.00
10 Fishing	0.00	0.00	0.00	0.00	0.00	0.00
11 Forestry	0.00	0.00	0.00	0.00	0.00	0.00
12 Mining and quarrying	22.90	0.00	0.00	0.00	88.90	21.67
13 Grain milling	0.00	0.00	0.00	0.00	0.00	0.00
14 Rice milling and husking	0.00	0.00	0.00	0.00	0.00	0.00
15 Edible oils	588.60	0.00	0.00	0.00	11.50	0.00
16 Sugar refining	670.00	0.00	0.00	0.00	1.90	0.00
17 Gur and *khandsari*	0.00	0.00	0.00	0.00	0.00	0.00
18 Tea blending	59.70	0.00	0.00	0.00	59.00	0.00
19 Fish and preparations	0.00	0.00	0.00	0.00	0.00	0.00
20 Confectionery and bakery	0.00	0.00	14.58	0.00	0.00	0.00
21 Other food industries	4.01	0.00	0.00	0.00	7.70	13.90
22 Beverages	40.40	0.00	6.37	0.00	9.40	0.00
23 Cigarettes and tobacco products (LS)	1 189.90	0.00	0.00	0.00	0.00	0.00
24 Bidis (i.e. tobacco, SS)	0.00	0.00	0.00	0.00	0.00	0.00
25 Cotton yarn	83.60	0.00	0.00	0.00	0.23	0.00
26 Cotton ginning	0.00	0.00	0.00	0.00	10.68	0.00
27 Cotton textiles (LS)	52.10	0.00	0.00	0.00	0.69	0.00
28 Cotton textiles (SS)	0.00	0.00	0.00	0.00	0.00	0.00
29 Silk and synthetic textiles	117.60	0.00	0.00	0.00	4.20	0.00
30 Woollen textiles and hosiery	38.10	0.00	0.00	0.00	41.00	1.41
31 Threadballs and other textiles	0.00	0.00	0.00	0.00	525.50	10.52
32 Carpets and rugs	0.00	0.00	0.00	0.00	1.30	0.00
33 Made-up garments	0.00	0.00	0.00	0.00	0.00	0.00
34 Footwear (non-rubber)	0.00	0.00	4.93	0.00	0.00	0.00
35 Wood, cork and furniture	0.00	0.00	0.00	0.00	0.00	2.44

Table 6.1. (*cont.*)

	Excise	Surcharge	Sales (D)	Subsidies	Imports	Sales (M)
36 Paper and products	11.00	0.00	28.00	0.00	86.90	31.06
37 Printing and publishing	0.00	0.00	0.00	0.00	0.00	3.62
38 Leather and products	17.80	0.00	0.00	0.00	1.80	0.00
39 Rubber footwear	0.00	0.00	0.00	0.00	0.00	0.00
40 Rubber products	30.90	0.00	48.93	0.00	97.70	23.82
41 Pharmaceuticals	0.00	0.00	0.00	0.00	2.40	0.00
42 Fertiliser	0.00	321.47	0.00	−606.50	0.00	0.00
43 Perfumes and cosmetics	31.60	0.00	0.00	0.00	23.50	1.82
44 Paints and varnishes	58.90	0.00	0.00	0.00	87.90	9.09
45 Soaps and detergents	60.10	0.00	0.00	0.00	0.00	0.00
46 Chemicals	40.10	0.00	29.08	0.00	185.50	27.96
47 Plastic products	14.20	0.00	29.90	0.00	0.00	25.46
48 Petroleum products	1 073.70	163.25	0.00	0.00	320.00	0.00
49 Cement	132.70	0.16	0.00	0.00	0.00	0.00
50 Glass and products	8.60	0.00	10.80	0.00	61.30	17.03
51 Non-metallic mineral products	0.00	0.00	10.77	0.00	0.00	0.00
52 Basic metals	0.00	0.00	0.00	0.00	545.60	106.47
53 Metal products	28.80	0.00	30.10	0.00	46.30	12.73
54 Iron and steel remoulding	0.00	0.00	0.00	0.00	0.00	0.00
55 Agricultural machinery	0.00	0.00	0.00	−24.38	0.00	0.00
56 Other non-electrical machinery	0.00	0.00	0.00	0.00	431.10	95.45
57 Electrical machinery	0.00	0.00	0.00	0.00	303.90	72.46
58 Bicycles	0.00	0.00	0.00	0.00	0.00	0.00
59 Transport (LS)	0.00	0.00	4.01	0.00	513.30	166.20
60 Shipbuilding	0.00	0.00	0.00	0.00	0.00	0.00
61 Transport equipment (SS)	0.00	0.00	0.00	0.00	0.00	0.00
62 Office equipment	0.00	0.00	0.00	0.00	0.00	0.00
63 Sports goods	0.00	0.00	0.00	0.00	2.80	0.00
64 Surgical instruments	0.00	0.00	0.00	0.00	0.00	0.00
65 Other large-scale manufacturing	90.00	0.00	24.07	0.00	65.60	25.33
66 Other small-scale manufacturing	0.00	0.00	0.00	0.00	0.00	0.00
67 Low-cost residential buildings	0.00	0.00	0.00	0.00	0.00	0.00
68 Luxurious residential buildings	0.00	0.00	0.00	0.00	0.00	0.00

158   Effective taxes and shadow prices in Pakistan

Table 6.1. (*cont.*)

	Excise	Surcharge	Sales (D)	Subsidies	Imports	Sales (M)
69 Rural buildings	0.00	0.00	0.00	0.00	0.00	0.00
70 Factory buildings	0.00	0.00	0.00	0.00	0.00	0.00
71 Public buildings	0.00	0.00	0.00	0.00	0.00	0.00
72 Roads	0.00	0.00	0.00	0.00	0.00	0.00
73 Infrastructure	0.00	0.00	0.00	0.00	0.00	0.00
74 Ownership of dwellings	0.00	0.00	0.00	0.00	0.00	0.00
75 Electricity	0.00	0.00	0.00	0.00	0.00	0.00
76 Gas	0.00	321.00	3.20	0.00	0.00	0.00
77 Wholesale and retail trade	0.00	0.00	0.00	0.00	0.00	0.00
78 Road transport	0.00	0.00	0.00	0.00	0.00	0.00
79 Rail transport	0.00	0.00	0.00	0.00	0.00	0.00
80 Air transport	0.00	0.00	0.00	0.00	0.00	0.00
81 Water transport	0.00	0.00	0.00	0.00	0.00	0.00
82 Television	0.00	0.00	0.00	0.00	0.00	0.00
83 Radio	0.00	0.00	0.00	0.00	0.00	0.00
84 Phone, telegraph and post	0.00	0.00	0.00	0.00	0.00	0.00
85 Banking and insurance	10.70	0.00	0.00	0.00	0.00	0.00
86 Government	0.00	0.00	0.00	0.00	0.00	0.00
87 Other services	32.00	0.00	0.00	0.00	0.00	0.00

Notes: (i) Sales (D) are sales tax collections on domestically produced goods and Sales (M) refers to sales tax collections on imports. The surcharges are levelled on domestic production. Subsidies include, for 'wheat', Rs 961 million on imported wheat, Rs 222 million on domestic wheat and Rs 26 million on wheat seeds.
(ii) LS denotes 'large-scale' and SS denotes 'small-scale'.
(iii) Subsidies are entered as negative taxes.
Source: Ahmad and Stern (1986), pp. 67–70. Based on Government of Pakistan, Ministry of Finance, *Economic Memorandum to the Budget*, 1976.

1975–6, production surcharges on specific locally produced goods. We have allocated the Budget estimates for surcharges (Rs 805 million) to petroleum, natural gas and fertilisers.

The major federal government subsidies have been allocated to the imported and domestically produced goods according to the eighty-seven-commodity classification. The largest subsidy was on wheat, Rs 961 million being incurred on imported wheat and Rs 222 million on domestic production. These subsidies form part of the current expenditures. There was also a subsidy of Rs 26.48 million on wheat seeds shown under Non-Development Capital Expenditure. The other major subsidy is on fertilisers, which is treated as a development expenditure in the government accounts. Expenditures on plant protection have not been allocated. We have also not included provincial government subsidies.

Losses of public-sector enterprises might be treated as implicit subsidies on the goods produced, but these have not been included in our analysis. And their inclusion poses the problem of distinguishing between a subsidy on the output, on the one hand, and special privileges, subsidised inefficiency and protected jobs and incomes for those involved in the production process, on the other.

The rate implicit in the revenue collections is treated as an average for the sector concerned. To the extent that the revenue collections are net of refunds, particularly in the case of sales tax, the implicit rate will not overstate the tax attributable to a commodity. Another advantage of using revenue collections is that these incorporate the result of the tax collection effort, given administrative considerations and evasion, in a way that announced or statutory rates do not. However, it is important to keep in mind the level of aggregation of the analysis dictated by the classification of the input–output table. For very detailed sectoral work, one would in principle use estimates from the more aggregative calculations for broad categories of inputs but go into closer detail of the tax treatment for the output and for particularly important inputs.

Of the main trade taxes, export duties do not affect the calculation of effective taxes, since exports are assumed not to enter into the domestic production circuit (they are omitted from table 6.1). However, if world prices are fixed, then export taxes would be shifted backwards on to factors of production. During our reference period, export duties in Pakistan were relatively small. Revenue collections from exports are shown in table 6.8 below.

On imported goods, the main taxes are import duties and sales taxes. The import duties realised a sum of Rs 4430 million in 1975–6. Of this we have been able to allocate all except Rs 600 million to our commodity groups. The 'missing' import tax collection might bias our implicit import duties downwards for some commodity groups. The sales tax on imports yielded a revenue of Rs 850 million in 1975–6. Again, we have been able to allocate only Rs 700 million of this revenue to our commodity groups. The commodity-wise allocations for import duties and sales taxes on imports are also presented in table 6.1.

The input–output matrix used in this paper is a revised version of the PIDE table for 1975–6 (see Pakistan Institute of Development Economics, 1985). This was an 118-sector matrix of domestic and import flows at purchaser prices. Thus we have estimates for both imported and domestic coefficient matrices, A^m and A^d. The 118-sector input–output table has been merged to 87 sectors. This reclassification has been governed, as mentioned above, by a need to match as closely as possible the tax revenue categories and input–output sectors. A consequence of this is to limit the groups of commodities that might be classified as tradables and non-tradables, an issue which arises in the calculation of shadow prices.

The final data set required is an estimate of a capital stock matrix, K. From the data available to us (Government of Pakistan, Federal Bureau of Statistics, *National Accounts Statistics*, 1982 and 1983) we have been able to put together an estimate for this under some admittedly crude assumptions. Assuming that all assets depreciate by a fraction β per year and that a fraction α of the current investment I (expressed as a matrix) is used for replacement, then $K = (\alpha/\beta)I$ and $rK = r(\alpha/\beta)I$. Of course we have to count not only the interest on capital but also the resources, αI, used for replacement assuming that these are not captured in the input–output matrix. Hence we must augment A by $[r(\alpha/\beta) + \alpha]$ times the investment matrix. In the absence of good information on α and β, we have taken this factor to be unity and simply augmented A by the investment matrix. One example consistent with this assumption would be $r = \beta$ and $\alpha = \frac{1}{2}$. The investment matrix is constructed by taking the investment for each sector and allocating it across the various investment sectors using the proportions given by the national accounts. The resulting matrix is, in turn, divided into assets which are imported and those which have been domestically produced, using the proportions of the absorption of imports and domestic goods in 1975–6.

6.2.2 The effective-tax calculations

The effective-tax estimates for 1975–6 may be decomposed into the component domestic and imported sources as shown in (5.19), where the first element on the right-hand side is the vector of effective taxes, $\mathbf{t}_e^d$, arising from domestic sources, and the second element represents $\mathbf{t}_e^m$ or the vector of effective taxes arising from inputs of imported goods into domestic production. These are modified when we take into account the tax element in price attributable to the taxation of capital assets. The resulting components of effective taxes, including this last effect, are

$$\bar{\mathbf{t}}_e^{d'} = \mathbf{t}^{d'}[I - \hat{A}^d]^{-1} \tag{6.1}$$

and

$$\bar{\mathbf{t}}_e^{m'} = \mathbf{t}^{m'}(\hat{A}^m)[I - \hat{A}^d]^{-1} \tag{6.2}$$

where $\hat{A}^m$ is the matrix of imported good requirements (for domestic good production) modified by the capital inputs as described above, and similarly $\hat{A}^d$ is the capital-augmented domestic good matrix. We define $\bar{\mathbf{t}}_e^{m'}$

Table 6.2. *Effective taxes on imports into domestic production*

	t_e^m	$\bar{t}_e^m$
1 Wheat	0.0038	0.0078
2 Rice	0.0084	0.0137
3 Cotton	0.0034	0.0079
4 Sugar cane	0.0023	0.0063
5 Tobacco growing	0.0020	0.0051
6 Oilseeds	0.0020	0.0057
7 Pulses	0.0061	0.0118
8 Other crops	0.0024	0.0046
9 Livestock	0.0025	0.0054
10 Fishing	0.0027	0.0042
11 Forestry	0.0017	0.0039
12 Mining and quarrying	0.0097	0.0148
13 Grain milling	−0.0503	−0.0413
14 Rice milling and husking	0.0137	0.0259
15 Edible oils	0.0086	0.0200
16 Sugar refining	0.0028	0.0110
17 Gur and *khandsari*	0.0026	0.0099
18 Tea blending	0.0239	0.0332
19 Fish and preparations	0.0076	0.0144
20 Confectionery and bakery	0.0103	0.0209
21 Other food industries	0.0064	0.0180
22 Beverages	0.0246	0.0339
23 Cigarettes and tobacco products (LS)	0.0056	0.0124
24 Bidis (i.e. tobacco, SS)	0.0070	0.0109
25 Cotton yarn	0.0227	0.0370
26 Cotton ginning	0.0049	0.0150
27 Cotton textiles (LS)	0.0204	0.0357
28 Cotton textiles (SS)	0.0145	0.0254
29 Silk and synthetic textiles	0.0522	0.0613
30 Woollen textiles and hosiery	0.0317	0.0451
31 Threadballs and other textiles	0.0183	0.0365
32 Carpets and rugs	0.0433	0.0530
33 Made-up garments	0.1182	0.1283
34 Footwear (non-rubber)	0.0238	0.0326
35 Wood, cork and furniture	0.0095	0.0210
36 Paper and products	0.0096	0.0261
37 Printing and publishing	0.0186	0.0317
38 Leather and products	0.0059	0.0123
39 Rubber footwear	0.0847	0.0923
40 Rubber products	0.0296	0.0415
41 Pharmaceuticals	0.1276	0.1379
42 Fertiliser	0.0146	0.0364
43 Perfumes and cosmetics	0.0493	0.0596
44 Paints and varnishes	0.0612	0.0735
45 Soaps and detergents	0.0099	0.0208

Table 6.2. (*cont.*)

	t_e^m	$\bar{t}_e^m$
46 Chemicals	0.0155	0.0335
47 Plastic products	0.0127	0.0265
48 Petroleum products	0.0218	0.0298
49 Cement	0.0157	0.0460
50 Glass and products	0.0726	0.0939
51 Non-metallic mineral products	0.0166	0.0291
52 Basic metals	0.0339	0.0519
53 Metal products	0.0544	0.0640
54 Iron and steel remoulding	0.0085	0.0135
55 Agricultural machinery	0.0878	0.0981
56 Other non-electrical machinery	0.0406	0.0556
57 Electrical machinery	0.0702	0.0817
58 Bicycles	0.0368	0.0512
59 Transport (LS)	0.0820	0.0940
60 Shipbuilding	0.0402	0.0498
61 Transport equipment (SS)	0.0090	0.0211
62 Office equipment	0.0707	0.0823
63 Sports goods	0.0425	0.0507
64 Surgical instruments	0.0153	0.0249
65 Other large-scale manufacturing	0.0140	0.0264
66 Other small-scale manufacturing	0.0310	0.0415
67 Low-cost residential buildings	0.0145	0.0236
68 Luxurious residential buildings	0.0285	0.0377
69 Rural buildings	0.0050	0.0101
70 Factory buildings	0.0344	0.0434
71 Public buildings	0.0344	0.0405
72 Roads	0.0036	0.0072
73 Infrastructure	0.0337	0.0630
74 Ownership of dwellings	0.0024	0.0122
75 Electricity	0.0040	0.0854
76 Gas	0.0024	0.0796
77 Wholesale and retail trade	0.0010	0.0066
78 Road transport	0.0472	0.0512
79 Rail transport	0.0167	0.0383
80 Air transport	0.0183	0.0243
81 Water transport	0.0059	0.0094
82 Television	0.0392	0.0459
83 Radio	0.0107	0.0178
84 Phone, telegraph and post	0.0049	0.0188
85 Banking and insurance	0.0081	0.0145
86 Government	0.0049	0.0229
87 Other services	0.0012	0.0069

Table 6.2. (*cont.*)

Notes: (i)

$$t_e^{m'} = t^{m'} A^m (I - A^d)^{-1}$$
$$\bar{t}_e^{m'} = t^{m'} \hat{A}^m (I - \hat{A}^d)^{-1}$$

where t^m includes import duties, sales taxes and subsidies on imported goods. $\hat{A}^m$ and $\hat{A}^d$ represent the matrix of imported good requirements (for domestic good production) modified by capital inputs, and the capital-augmented domestic good matrix respectively.

(ii) LS denotes 'large-scale' and SS denotes 'small-scale'.

Source: Ahmad and Stern (1986), pp. 57–9.

and $\bar{t}_e^{d'}$ to be the effective taxes on domestic goods arising from import taxation and domestic taxation respectively. The total effective tax including the effects arising from assets is

$$\bar{t}_e = \bar{t}_e^d + \bar{t}_e^m \qquad (6.3)$$

In table 6.2 we present an estimate of that part of the effective tax, t_e^m and $\bar{t}_e^m$, which arises from the taxation of imported inputs into domestic production. The taxes included in the estimation of t^m in (6.2) are the import duty, the sales tax, and the subsidy on imported wheat discussed above. As is evident from the table, all domestic commodities are affected by the taxation of inputs, although the effect on agricultural products is quite small – in most cases well under 1% of the purchaser price. Note, however, that on manufactured items the effective tax is higher at around 1–3%. There is an effective subsidy of 5% on 'grain milling', which is reduced to 4% if the taxation of imported capital stock is taken into account. Other consumer items such as textiles display a much higher effective import tax, generally between 3 and 5% (with 'rubber footwear' at 9%). The production of domestic intermediate goods and durable items shows a yet higher effective rate arising from import taxation – in the 5 to 10% range. Pharmaceuticals have the highest effective tax rate arising through import taxation at 13%. The taxation arising through imported capital goods ($\bar{t}_e^m - t_e^m$) adds less than 2% to the purchaser price of most items – the exceptions are 'electricity' and 'gas' (both around 8%). However, the taxation of imported capital goods forms a significant contribution to the value of $\bar{t}_e^m$ for most goods, contributing, for example, around half of $\bar{t}_e^m$ for the agricultural sector as a whole, and two-thirds for 'cement'.

That part of the taxation which arises through domestic intermediate inputs is also of interest (table 6.3) and this is measured by the divergence $\bar{t}_{\text{diff}}^d$ between the 'domestic' effective tax $\bar{t}_e^d$ and the nominal tax on domestic production, t^d. Whilst $\bar{t}_{\text{diff}}^d$ is less than 1% for agricultural commodities (1)–

Table 6.3. *Domestic effective taxes*

		t_e^d	$\bar{t}_e^d$	$\bar{t}_{\text{diff}}^d$
1	Wheat	−0.0217	−0.0214	−0.0013
2	Rice	0.0085	0.0096	0.0096
3	Cotton	0.0014	0.0020	0.0020
4	Sugar cane	0.0027	0.0031	0.0031
5	Tobacco growing	0.1934	0.1933	0.0052
6	Oilseeds	0.0043	0.0043	0.0043
7	Pulses	0.0083	0.0086	0.0086
8	Other crops	0.0016	0.0025	0.0025
9	Livestock	0.0001	−0.0003	0.0003
10	Fishing	0.0054	0.0063	0.0063
11	Forestry	0.0023	0.0041	0.0041
12	Mining and quarrying	0.0271	0.0294	0.0165
13	Grain milling	−0.0106	−0.0067	−0.0067
14	Rice milling and husking	0.0128	0.0188	0.0188
15	Edible oils	0.1142	0.1187	0.0264
16	Sugar refining	0.2721	0.2761	0.0080
17	Gur and *khandsari*	0.0029	0.0061	0.0061
18	Tea blending	0.0774	0.0792	0.0097
19	Fish and preparations	0.0071	0.0112	0.0112
20	Confectionery and bakery	0.1590	0.1644	0.0593
21	Other food industries	0.0205	0.0250	0.0224
22	Beverages	0.1273	0.1325	0.0566
23	Cigarettes and tobacco products (LS)	0.7613	0.7649	0.0445
24	Bidis (i.e. tobacco, SS)	0.0523	0.0542	0.0542
25	Cotton yarn	0.0424	0.0498	0.0218
26	Cotton ginning	0.0050	0.0092	0.0092
27	Cotton textiles (LS)	0.0509	0.0592	0.0370
28	Cotton textiles (SS)	0.0283	0.0343	0.0343
29	Silk and synthetic textiles	0.1273	0.1330	0.0537
30	Woollen textiles and hosiery	0.1057	0.1116	0.0285
31	Threadballs and other textiles	0.0353	0.0425	0.0425
32	Carpets and rugs	0.0332	0.0382	0.0382
33	Made-up garments	0.0148	0.0205	0.0205
34	Footwear (non-rubber)	0.0362	0.0407	0.0264
35	Wood, cork and furniture	0.0245	0.0286	0.0286
36	Paper and products	0.1163	0.1231	0.0587
37	Printing and publishing	0.0419	0.0482	0.0482
38	Leather and products	0.0174	0.0197	0.0090
39	Rubber footwear	0.0101	0.0145	0.0145
40	Rubber products	0.3341	0.3375	0.0273
41	Pharmaceuticals	0.0268	0.0309	0.0309
42	Fertiliser	−0.1992	−0.1884	0.0787
43	Perfumes and cosmetics	0.3894	0.3934	0.0492
44	Paints and varnishes	0.3239	0.3266	0.0389

Table 6.3. (*cont.*)

	t_e^d	$\bar{t}_e^d$	$\bar{t}_{\text{diff}}^d$
45 Soaps and detergents	0.1605	0.1661	0.0452
46 Chemicals	0.0972	0.1041	0.0515
47 Plastic products	0.3689	0.3717	0.0815
48 Petroleum products	0.3188	0.3207	0.0092
49 Cement	0.2066	0.2250	0.1045
50 Glass and products	0.2964	0.3056	0.0989
51 Non-metallic mineral products	0.0607	0.0670	0.0632
52 Basic metals	0.0183	0.0243	0.0243
53 Metal products	0.0852	0.0880	0.0150
54 Iron and steel remoulding	0.0183	0.0214	0.0214
55 Agricultural machinery	−0.0713	−0.0692	0.0092
56 Other non-electrical machinery	0.0235	0.0269	0.0269
57 Electrical machinery	0.0120	0.0143	0.0143
58 Bicycles	0.0433	0.0487	0.0487
59 Transport (LS)	0.0160	0.0186	0.0153
60 Shipbuilding	0.0122	0.0156	0.0156
61 Transport equipment (SS)	0.0146	0.0202	0.0202
62 Office equipment	0.0140	0.0168	0.0168
63 Sports goods	0.0120	0.0162	0.0162
64 Surgical instruments	0.0253	0.0296	0.0296
65 Other large-scale manufacturing	0.5041	0.5073	0.0364
66 Other small-scale manufacturing	0.0496	0.0538	0.0538
67 Low-cost residential buildings	0.0519	0.0572	0.0572
68 Luxurious residential buildings	0.0523	0.0577	0.0577
69 Rural buildings	0.0241	0.0271	0.0271
70 Factory buildings	0.0542	0.0594	0.0594
71 Public buildings	0.0320	0.0358	0.0358
72 Roads	0.0194	0.0215	0.0215
73 Infrastructure	0.0425	0.0631	0.0631
74 Ownership of dwellings	0.0108	0.0226	0.0226
75 Electricity	0.0775	0.1306	0.1306
76 Gas	0.4134	0.4641	0.0618
77 Wholesale and retail trade	0.0019	0.0055	0.0055
78 Road transport	0.0296	0.0323	0.0323
79 Rail transport	0.0581	0.0725	0.0725
80 Air transport	0.0692	0.0730	0.0730
81 Water transport	0.0020	0.0043	0.0043
82 Television	0.0204	0.0240	0.0240
83 Radio	0.0116	0.0164	0.0164
84 Phone, telegraph and post	0.0055	0.0157	0.0157
85 Banking and insurance	0.0254	0.0293	0.0268
86 Government	0.0092	0.0227	0.0227
87 Other services	0.0045	0.0089	0.0058

Table 6.3. (cont.)

Notes (i)

$$t_e^d = t^{d'}(I - A^d)^{-1}$$
$$\bar{t}_e^d = t^{d'}(I - \hat{A}^d)^{-1}$$
$$\bar{t}_{\text{diff}}^d = \bar{t}_e^d - t^d$$

where t^d includes excises, surcharges, sales taxes on domestically produced goods and services and $\hat{A}^d$ is the capital-augmented domestic good matrix.

(ii) LS denotes 'large-scale' and SS denotes 'small-scale'.

Source: Ahmad and Stern (1986), pp. 61–2.

(8), it represents around 5% of the purchaser price of manufactured food items, beverages and tobacco. For most textile items, $\bar{t}_{\text{diff}}^d$ is between 3 and 5%, and is generally higher for intermediate goods, buildings and infrastructure at between 5 and 10%. In the case of 'electricity', which had no nominal tax in 1975–6, the domestic effective tax was as much as 13% of the purchaser price, $\bar{t}_{\text{diff}}^d$ coinciding with $\bar{t}_e^d$ in this case.

The overall effective tax, from both domestic and imported sources, is shown in table 6.4. In column 1 we present the nominal tax on domestic production, t^d. The effective taxes with and without the effects of the taxation of the capital stock, $\bar{t}_e$ and t_e, are given in columns 3 and 2 respectively. As in the previous cases, all commodity groups are affected by the structure of indirect taxes, even though only thirty-five out of the total eighty-seven domestic commodity groups are actually subject to a nominal tax. In some cases the effective tax is quite high, as for 'tobacco products', for which the effective tax as a proportion of the purchaser price is around 78%. High effective taxes may reflect high nominal taxes, and tobacco is a case in point. It is the difference between effective and nominal taxes, $\bar{t}_{\text{diff}}$, which reflects taxation arising through other commodities and assets, and which may sometimes be an unintended consequence of government policy. In the case of 'tobacco products', $\bar{t}_{\text{diff}}$ is actually only 5.7% and nominal tax accounts for the bulk of the high effective tax. In general, for agricultural commodities, $\bar{t}_{\text{diff}}$ is quite low – less than 2% of the purchaser price. It may be noted, however, that the effective subsidy on wheat is only two-thirds of the nominal subsidy.

Most manufactured food items have a value of $\bar{t}_{\text{diff}}$ ranging from 4% in the case of 'tea' to over 9% for 'beverages'. Clothing items are also considerably affected by the direct and indirect taxation of inputs, $\bar{t}_{\text{diff}}$ varying from 6% for 'cotton yarn', to 11.5% for 'silk and synthetics' and to almost 15% of the purchaser price of 'made-up garments'. Other consumer items such as footwear and paper fall in the same range. Intermediate goods

Table 6.4. *Total effective taxes, 1975–6*

	t^d	t_e	$\bar{t}_e$	$\bar{t}_{\mathrm{diff}}$	$\bar{t}_e - t_e$
1 Wheat	−0.0200	−0.0179	−0.0136	0.0065	0.0043
2 Rice	0.0000	0.0168	0.0233	0.0233	0.0065
3 Cotton	0.0000	0.0048	0.0099	0.0099	0.0051
4 Sugar cane	0.0000	0.0050	0.0094	0.0094	0.0044
5 Tobacco growing	0.1882	0.1953	0.1984	0.0103	0.0031
6 Oilseeds	0.0000	0.0063	0.0100	0.0100	0.0036
7 Pulses	0.0000	0.0144	0.0205	0.0205	0.0060
8 Other crops	0.0000	0.0040	0.0071	0.0071	0.0031
9 Livestock	0.0000	0.0026	0.0052	0.0052	0.0026
10 Fishing	0.0000	0.0081	0.0106	0.0106	0.0025
11 Forestry	0.0000	0.0040	0.0080	0.0080	0.0040
12 Mining and quarrying	0.0129	0.0367	0.0442	0.0314	0.0075
13 Grain milling	0.0000	−0.0609	−0.0480	−0.0480	0.0129
14 Rice milling and husking	0.0000	0.0265	0.0448	0.0448	0.0183
15 Edible oils	0.0923	0.1228	0.1388	0.0465	0.0160
16 Sugar refining	0.2681	0.2749	0.2871	0.0190	0.0122
17 Gur and *khandsari*	0.0000	0.0055	0.0159	0.0159	0.0105
18 Tea blending	0.0695	0.1013	0.1123	0.0428	0.0110
19 Fish and preparations	0.0000	0.0147	0.0256	0.0256	0.0109
20 Confectionery and bakery	0.1052	0.1693	0.1854	0.0802	0.0160
21 Other food industries	0.0026	0.0270	0.0430	0.0404	0.0160
22 Beverages	0.0759	0.1519	0.1665	0.0906	0.0146
23 Cigarettes and tobacco products (LS)	0.7204	0.7669	0.7773	0.0569	0.0104
24 Bidis (i.e. tobacoo, SS)	0.0000	0.0593	0.0652	0.0652	0.0059
25 Cotton yarn	0.0280	0.0651	0.0868	0.0588	0.0217
26 Cotton ginning	0.0000	0.0099	0.0241	0.0241	0.0143
27 Cotton textiles (LS)	0.0222	0.0714	0.0949	0.0727	0.0235
28 Cotton textiles (SS)	0.0000	0.0427	0.0596	0.0596	0.0169
29 Silk and synthetic textiles	0.0793	0.1795	0.1943	0.1150	0.0148
30 Woollen textiles and hosiery	0.0831	0.1374	0.1567	0.0736	0.0193
31 Threadballs and other textiles	0.0000	0.0536	0.0790	0.0790	0.0254
32 Carpets and rugs	0.0000	0.0764	0.0912	0.0912	0.0147
33 Made-up garments	0.0000	0.1330	0.1487	0.1487	0.0157
34 Footwear (non-rubber)	0.0143	0.0601	0.0733	0.0590	0.0132
35 Wood, cork and furniture	0.0000	0.0340	0.0496	0.0496	0.0156
36 Paper and products	0.0644	0.1259	0.1492	0.0848	0.0233
37 Printing and publishing	0.0000	0.0605	0.0799	0.0799	0.0194
38 Leather and products	0.0107	0.0233	0.0319	0.0213	0.0087

Table 6.4. (*cont.*)

	t^d	t_e	$\bar{t}_e$	$\bar{t}_{\text{diff}}$	$\bar{t}_e - t_e$
39 Rubber and footwear	0.0000	0.0948	0.1068	0.1068	0.0120
40 Rubber products	0.3102	0.3637	0.3789	0.0687	0.0152
41 Pharmaceuticals	0.0000	0.1544	0.1688	0.1688	0.0144
42 Fertiliser	−0.2670	−0.1846	−0.1519	0.1151	0.0327
43 Perfumes and cosmetics	0.3442	0.4387	0.4531	0.1088	0.0144
44 Paints and varnishes	0.2877	0.3851	0.4001	0.1124	0.0150
45 Soaps and detergents	0.1209	0.1704	0.1868	0.0659	0.0164
46 Chemicals	0.0527	0.1127	0.1376	0.0849	0.0249
47 Plastic products	0.2902	0.3816	0.3982	0.1080	0.0166
48 Petroleum products	0.3115	0.3407	0.3505	0.0390	0.0098
49 Cement	0.1204	0.2223	0.2710	0.1505	0.0487
50 Glass and products	0.2067	0.3690	0.3995	0.1927	0.0304
51 Non-metallic mineral products	0.0038	0.0773	0.0961	0.0923	0.0189
52 Basic metals	0.0000	0.0523	0.0762	0.0762	0.0240
53 Metal products	0.0730	0.1396	0.1519	0.0790	0.0124
54 Iron and steel remoulding	0.0000	0.0268	0.0349	0.0349	0.0081
55 Agricultural machinery	−0.0785	0.0166	0.0289	0.1074	0.0123
56 Other non-electrical machinery	0.0000	0.0641	0.0824	0.0824	0.0183
57 Electrical machinery	0.0000	0.0821	0.0961	0.0961	0.0139
58 Bicycles	0.0000	0.0800	0.1000	0.1000	0.0199
59 Transport (LS)	0.0032	0.0979	0.1125	0.1093	0.0146
60 Shipbuilding	0.0000	0.0524	0.0654	0.0654	0.0130
61 Transport equipment (SS)	0.0000	0.0236	0.0413	0.0413	0.0177
62 Office equipment	0.0000	0.0847	0.0991	0.0991	0.0144
63 Sports goods	0.0000	0.0545	0.0669	0.0669	0.0124
64 Surgical instruments	0.0000	0.0406	0.0545	0.0545	0.0139
65 Other large-scale manufacturing	0.4709	0.5182	0.5337	0.0629	0.0156
66 Other small-scale manufacturing	0.0000	0.0806	0.0954	0.0954	0.0148
67 Low-cost residential buildings	0.0000	0.0664	0.0808	0.0808	0.0144
68 Luxurious residential buildings	0.0000	0.0808	0.0954	0.0954	0.0146
69 Rural buildings	0.0000	0.0291	0.0372	0.0372	0.0081
70 Factory buildings	0.0000	0.0887	0.1028	0.1028	0.0141
71 Public buildings	0.0000	0.0664	0.0763	0.0763	0.0099
72 Roads	0.0000	0.0230	0.0287	0.0287	0.0057
73 Infrastructure	0.0000	0.0762	0.1262	0.1262	0.0499
74 Ownership of dwellings	0.0000	0.0131	0.0348	0.0348	0.0217
75 Electricity	0.0000	0.0815	0.2160	0.2160	0.1344

Table 6.4. (*cont.*)

	t^d	t_e	$\bar{t}_e$	$\bar{t}_{\text{diff}}$	$\bar{t}_e - t_e$
76 Gas	0.4023	0.4158	0.5437	0.1414	0.1279
77 Wholesale and retail trade	0.0000	0.0029	0.0120	0.0120	0.0092
78 Road transport	0.0000	0.0768	0.0836	0.0836	0.0068
79 Rail transport	0.0000	0.0748	0.1108	0.1108	0.0360
80 Air transport	0.0000	0.0875	0.0973	0.0973	0.0098
81 Water transport	0.0000	0.0079	0.0137	0.0137	0.0058
82 Television	0.0000	0.0596	0.0699	0.0699	0.0102
83 Radio	0.0000	0.0233	0.0342	0.0342	0.0120
84 Phone, telegraph and post	0.0000	0.0105	0.0345	0.0345	0.0240
85 Banking and insurance	0.0025	0.0335	0.0438	0.0413	0.0103
86 Government	0.0000	0.1414	0.0455	0.0455	0.0314
87 Other services	0.0030	0.0058	0.0157	0.0127	0.0100

Notes:

$$t'_e = t_e^{d'} + t_e^{m'}$$
$$\bar{t}_e = \bar{t}_e^{d'} + \bar{t}_e^{m'}$$
$$\bar{t}_{\text{diff}} = \bar{t}_e - t^d$$

See also notes to tables 6.2 and 6.3.
Source: Ahmad and Stern (1986), pp. 63–5.

generally show a substantial effect from the direct and indirect taxation of inputs and the range is on average between 10 and 20% of the purchaser price. For instance $\bar{t}_{\text{diff}}$ for 'electricity' is over 21%. In the case of 'fertilisers' a $\bar{t}_{\text{diff}}$ of 12% implies that the effective subsidy is 43% lower than the nominal subsidy.

The inclusion of the taxation of capital stock has had a small, though substantial impact on purchaser prices. For agricultural commodities $\bar{t}_e - t_e$ is less than 1% of the purchaser price, although this constitutes over half of $\bar{t}_{\text{diff}}$ for 'wheat' and 'cotton'. For most other goods, $\bar{t}_e - t_e$ lies between 1 and 2% of the purchaser price, and exceeds 2% for several highly capital-intensive sectors such as 'large-scale cotton textiles', 'fertilisers', 'chemicals', 'cement', and 'basic metals'.

We saw in chapter 2 that a programme of export compensatory rebates was in operation during the early 1980s. A comparison of these rebates (see table 2.18), say for 1984–5, with the effective taxes, would (on the assumption that the 'cascading' effects of indirect taxes, a function of the production structure, would not have changed drastically) provide an indication of whether the rebates were in the correct 'ball park'. A comparison with $\bar{t}_{\text{diff}}$ in table 6.4, suggests that only in the cases of plastics, engineering goods and synthetic textiles, were the rebates justified. In many cases, e.g. 'poultry', 'leather goods', and 'surgical instruments', the rebates were not justified in terms of a compensation for taxes on inputs and thus acted like a pure export subsidy.

We have seen that the 'effective tax' differs greatly from the nominal tax implicit in revenue collections. This exercise may be of use to policy-makers in helping them understand the effects of a complex system, particularly when some of these may be unintended consequences of tax policy. An example where such calculations could be of direct benefit is in the setting of appropriate levels of export subsidies. Effective taxes could be used to provide a quantification of the direct and indirect taxation involved in the domestic production of goods for export. Under GATT rules these taxes could be rebated. Schemes such as zero-rating of exports under a VAT embody the repayment of taxes paid on inputs as part of their structure.

6.3   A system of economy-wide shadow prices for Pakistan

In this section we provide a consistent set of economy-wide shadow prices for Pakistan. It is based on our work jointly with David Coady (see Ahmad, Coady and Stern, 1988). Since shadow prices embody the full effects on social welfare of the extra supply of a good, their calculation requires a model of the economy. Data limitations usually dictate that such a model be rather simple and essentially based on input–output information. The information base also largely dictates the level of aggregation we can adopt, i.e. that of the input–output table, and the estimates here use the same set of data as in section 6.2. The shadow prices will be useful in the analysis of policy at the sectoral level and for tax reforms designed to shift taxes from one class of goods to another. They will also be of value for broad classes of inputs in the analysis of particular investment projects. We shall comment briefly on the implications of the shadow prices for the social value of expanding output in different sectors, i.e. on which sectors should be encouraged and which discouraged. We use the Little–Mirrlees methods, described in section 5.5, and the basic equations are summarised in table 6.5.

6.3.1   Data and some key parameters

Our calculations are based on the 87-sector input–output table derived from the 1975–6 PIDE 118-sector matrix, the table used for the effective tax

Table 6.5. *Shadow prices of non-traded and imported goods*

	Non-traded	Traded	Factors
Non-traded	$p_1^N = p_1^N a_{11} + \ldots + p_r^N a_{r1} + \ldots + p_n^N a_{n1} + p_i^a a_{i1} + \ldots + p_j^a a_{j1} + \ldots + p_k^a a_{k1} + p_f a_{f1}$		
	$p_r^N = p_1^N a_{1_r} + \ldots + p_r^N a_{rr} + \ldots + p_n^N a_{nr} + p_i^a a_{ir} + \ldots + p_j^a a_{jr} + \ldots + p_k^a a_{kr} + p_f a_{f_r}$		
	$p_n^N = p_1^N a_{1_n} + \ldots + p_r^N a_{rn} + \ldots + p_n^N a_{nn} + p_i^a a_{in} + \ldots + p_j^a a_{jn} + \ldots + p_k^a a_{kn} + p^f a_{f_n}$		
Imported	$p_i^a = \quad \ldots 0 \ldots + p_r^N a_{ri} +$	$\ldots 0 \ldots$	$+ p_i^{cif}$

Notes: p_i^a = Shadow price of imported (i to j) and exported ($j+1$ to k) goods.

p_f = Shadow price of factors (exogenously determined). In this model there is only a single factor but there may be more.

p_i^{cif} = Border price (i.e. c.i.f.) of imported goods.

p_i^N = Shadow price of non-traded goods ($i+1, \ldots, r, \ldots, n$).

a_{ij} = Input–output coefficients – ith input per unit production of jth good.

p_r^N = Shadow price for trade and transport (denoted r), a non-traded good.

The shadow prices of exported goods coincide with their f.o.b. prices in this model.

Source: Ahmad, Coady and Stern (1988), p. 12.

calculations. The 87 sectors must be classified into traded and non-traded activities. This classification is based on an assumed response of supply to marginal demand changes. If a change in demand leads to a change in imports (exports) then the good is treated as imported (exported) at the margin. If the change leads to an adjustment in home production then the good is treated as non-traded. As explained in chapter 5 it is assumed that, for non-traded goods, a marginal extra demand is produced, rather than diverted from another consumption source. This assumption would not be required if other sources had equal opportunity cost to that of extra production, as would be the case where certain policies were chosen optimally.

One can make different sets of plausible assumptions concerning these adjustments to extra demand and they are, in part, dependent on government policy. Accordingly we work with three rather different classifications. In case A we have fifty-two traded goods and thirty-five non-traded, and this has the maximum number of traded sectors (see table 6.6). In case B, there are thirty-nine non-traded goods, with (1) 'wheat', (8) 'other crops', (9) 'livestock' and (12) 'mining and quarrying' being reclassified as non-traded. In going from case A to case C we have reclassified fourteen sectors as non-traded to allow for binding quotas, giving forty-nine non-traded sectors in all. These categories include: (16) 'sugar refining', (18) 'tea blending', (29) 'silk and synthetic textiles', (30) 'woollen textiles', (35) 'wood, cork and furniture', (36) 'paper and

Table 6.6 *Non-traded sectors*

Case A	Case B	Case C
04 Sugar cane	01 Wheat	04 Sugar cane
07 Pulses	04 Sugar cane	07 Pulses
11 Forestry	07 Pulses	11 Forestry
13 Grain milling	08 Other crops	13 Grain milling
14 Rice milling and husking	09 Livestock	14 Rice milling and husking
17 Gur and *khandsari*	11 Forestry	16 Sugar refining
20 Confectionery and bakery	12 Mining and quarrying	17 Gur and *khandsari*
24 Bidis (i.e. tobacco, SS)	13 Grain milling	18 Tea blending
26 Cotton ginning	14 Rice milling and husking	20 Confectionery and bakery
37 Printing and publishing	17 Gur and *khandsari*	24 Bidis (i.e. tobacco, SS)
54 Iron and steel remoulding	20 Confectionery and bakery	26 Cotton ginning
58 Bicycles	24 Bidis (i.e. tobacco, SS)	29 Silk and synthetic textiles
60 Shipbuilding	26 Cotton ginning	30 Woollen textiles and hosiery
66 Other small-scale manufacturing	37 Printing and publishing	35 Wood, cork and furniture
67 Low-cost residential buildings	54 Iron and steel remoulding	36 Paper and products
68 Luxurious residential buildings	58 Bicycles	37 Printing and publishing
69 Rural buildings	60 Shipbuilding	40 Rubber products
70 Factory buildings	66 Other small-scale manufacturing	41 Pharmaceuticals
71 Public buildings	67 Low-cost residential buildings	43 Perfumes and cosmetics
72 Roads	68 Luxurious residential buildings	46 Chemicals
73 Infrastructure	69 Rural buildings	48 Petroleum products
74 Ownership of dwellings	70 Factory buildings	54 Iron and steel remoulding
75 Electricity	71 Public buildings	58 Bicycles
76 Gas	72 Roads	59 Transport (LS)
77 Wholesale and retail trade	73 Infrastructure	60 Shipbuilding
78 Road transport	74 Ownership of dwellings	61 Transport equipment (SS)
79 Rail transport	75 Electricity	62 Office equipment

80 Air transport
81 Water transport
82 Television
83 Radio
84 Phone, telegraph and post
85 Banking and insurance
86 Government
87 Other services

(35 non-traded sectors)

76 Gas
77 Wholesale and retail trade
78 Road transport
79 Rail transport
80 Air transport
81 Water transport
82 Television
83 Radio
84 Phone, telegraph and post
85 Banking and insurance
86 Government
87 Other services

(39 non-traded sectors)

66 Other small-scale manufacturing
67 Low-cost residential buildings
68 Luxurious residential buildings
69 Rural buildings
70 Factory buildings
71 Public buildings
72 Roads
73 Infrastructure
74 Ownership of dwellings
75 Electricity
76 Gas
77 Wholesale and retail trade
78 Road transport
79 Rail transport
80 Air transport
81 Water transport
82 Television
83 Radio
84 Phone, telegraph and post
85 Banking and insurance
86 Government
87 Other services

(49 non-traded sectors)

Notes: (i) 87 sectors in all.
(ii) For a more detailed classification of sectors into non-traded, imported and exported, see table 7.1.
(iii) LS denotes 'large-scale' and SS denotes 'small-scale'.
Source: Ahmad, Coady and Stern (1988), pp. 15–16.

products', (40) 'rubber products', (41) 'pharmaceuticals', (43) 'perfumes and cosmetics', (46) 'chemicals', (48) 'petroleum products', (59) 'transport (large-scale)', (61) 'transport equipment (small-scale)' and (62) 'office equipment'. We have based this reclassification on PIDE (1983, vol. I, p. 97) in which implicit nominal protection rates, using market prices, are compared with explicit nominal protection rates, which use published tariff rates. When the former exceed the latter (i.e. the premium over the world price exceeds the published tariff) then quotas are taken as binding. Whilst the PIDE study was conducted for the year 1981, we have made the supposition that the results give appropriate guidance for the earlier period (and quotas in 1975–6 would seem to have been at least as prevalent as in 1981). Case B may be considered as the central case.

In practice, within an input–output category, there may be several commodities which are non-traded, or which have associated quotas, and others which are clearly traded. At the level of disaggregation available to us many sectors are both traded and non-traded, and we have tried to use informed judgement on the basis of data relating to imports and exports. The broad indicators resulting from this study would be an important input into more disaggregated analyses, in which commodities may be more adequately identified as tradable or non-tradable, but in which economy-wide parameters are difficult to determine.

Once we have assembled information on inputs, outputs and taxes, and classified sectors into tradables and non-tradables, we can apply the method described in section 5.5. We consider shadow prices for expo-rtables, importables, factors and non-traded goods in that order.

We express a shadow price in terms of its 'accounting ratio' (or AR) which is the shadow price divided by the market price. The values used in the input–output table are at purchaser prices. For exported goods, these are taken as equivalent to f.o.b. values and the accounting ratios are 1 for goods which do not have export taxes. The commodities which had export taxes in 1975–6 were rice, raw cotton, leather and cotton waste. Table 6.7 gives details of export taxes, f.o.b. export values (see Government of Pakistan, Federal Bureau of Statistics, *National Accounts Statistics*, 1983) and the accounting ratios. The ARs are derived as a proportion of f.o.b. to purchaser price valuations, where the latter are f.o.b. prices less the export tax. The revised PIDE input–output table presents gross absorptions at purchaser prices. In the case of imports, subtracting taxes and trade and transport margins from purchaser prices we derive the c.i.f. values. The accounting ratios for importables are presented in table 6.8.

The calculation of shadow prices requires estimates of the breakdown of the payments to different factor inputs, since, in general, these factors will have different accounting ratios. Such a breakdown is not available in the

Table 6.7. *Accounting ratios for exports*

	Value of exports	Export tax	Accounting ratio
	(Rs million)		
Rice	2 479.1	241.2	1.1078
Cotton (raw)	980.5	330.0	1.5073
Leather	595.5	80.0	1.1551
Cotton waste	1 422.3	10.0	1.0071

Source: Ahmad, Coady and Stern (1988), p. 33.

Table 6.8. *Value of imports and c.i.f. values*

	c.i.f. values	Value at purchaser price	p_i^{cif}
	Rs '000s)		
01 Wheat	2 992 595.1	2 296 062.0	1.3034
02 Rice	37.2	49.0	0.7584
03 Cotton	0.0	0.0	0.8177
04 Sugar cane	0.0	0.0	0.8174
05 Tobacco growing	17 468.4	26 574.0	0.6573
06 Oilseeds	50 504.7	78 225.0	0.6456
07 Pulses	0.0	0.0	0.8824
08 Other crops	271 515.1	546 751.0	0.4966
09 Livestock	4 834.7	5 124.0	0.9435
10 Fishing	0.0	0.0	0.8726
11 Forestry	93 190.4	115 446.0	0.8072
12 Mining and quarrying	3 461 943.7	3 973 445.0	0.8713
13 Grain milling	0.0	0.0	0.9503
14 Rice milling and husking	0.0	0.0	0.8058
15 Edible oils	1 825 805.5	2 061 018.0	0.8859
16 Sugar refining	3 437.8	6 014.0	0.5716
17 Gur and *khandsari*	0.0	0.0	0.8862
18 Tea blending	1 583 598.4	1 724 178.0	0.9185
19 Fish and preparations	1 276.9	1 495.0	0.8541
20 Confectionery and bakery	136.7	176.0	0.7767
21 Other food industries	594 552.6	797 763.0	0.7453
22 Beverages	251.5	12 416.0	0.0203
23 Cigarettes and tobacco products (LS)	16 817.6	19 060.0	0.8824
24 Bidis (i.e. tobacco, SS)	0.0	0.0	0.8816
25 Cotton yarn	40 636.9	65 113.0	0.6241
26 Cotton ginning	45 977.3	79 329.0	0.5796
27 Cotton textiles (LS)	187 028.0	301 963.0	0.6194

Table 6.8. (*cont.*)

		c.i.f. values	Value at purchaser price	p_i^{cif}
28	Cotton textiles (SS)	0.0	0.0	0.8776
29	Silk and synthetic textiles	53 605.5	129 254.0	0.4147
30	Woollen textiles and hosiery	50 225.0	114 019.0	0.4405
31	Threadballs and other textiles	934 925.4	1 751 184.0	0.5339
32	Carpets and rugs	12 806.3	14 593.0	0.8776
33	Made-up garments	5 877.0	6 018.0	0.9766
34	Footwear (non-rubber)	584.6	620.0	0.9430
35	Wood, cork and furniture	181 627.0	184 483.0	0.9845
36	Paper and products	281 851.7	492 313.0	0.5725
37	Printing and publishing	23 073.7	33 270.0	0.6935
38	Leather and products	87 441.8	91 476.0	0.9559
39	Rubber footwear	4.0	5.0	0.8051
40	Rubber products	256 594.5	469 707.0	0.5463
41	Pharmaceuticals	383 390.9	441 392.0	0.8686
42	Fertiliser	681 405.3	890 057.0	0.7656
43	Perfumes and cosmetics	3 758.2	32 167.0	0.1168
44	Paints and varnishes	13 628.3	19 632.0	0.6942
45	Soaps and detergents	17 098.2	19 544.0	0.8749
46	Chemicals	1 255 973.2	1 678 039.0	0.7485
47	Plastic products	239 096.9	281 362.0	0.8498
48	Petroleum products	4 642 386.5	5 782 756.0	0.8028
49	Cement	0.0	0.0	0.8474
50	Glass and products	51 507.4	166 658.0	0.3091
51	Non-metal mineral products	189 059.5	218 654.0	0.8647
52	Basic metals	1 317 511.0	2 167 368.0	0.6079
53	Metal products	691 465.4	905 562.0	0.7636
54	Iron and steel remoulding	0.0	0.0	0.7833
55	Agricultural machinery	661 498.4	746 050.0	0.8867
56	Other non-electric machinery	2 287 805.2	2 964 953.0	0.7716
57	Electric machinery	1 517 298.1	2 025 417.0	0.7491
58	Bicycles	23 533.1	26 066.0	0.9028
59	Transport (LS)	1 345 314.0	2 270 005.0	0.5926
60	Shipbuilding	130 580.2	144 635.0	0.9028
61	Transport equipment (SS)	0.0	0.0	0.9631
62	Office equipment	104 441.9	116 757.0	0.8945
63	Sports goods	6 595.3	9 727.0	0.6780
64	Surgical instruments	21 946.7	25 247.0	0.8693
65	Other large-scale manufacturing	325 253.9	473 515.0	0.6869
66	Other small-scale manufacturing	0.0	0.0	0.9307
67	Low-cost residential buildings	0.0	0.0	1.0000
68	Luxurious residential buildings	0.0	0.0	1.0000

Table 6.8. (*cont.*)

	c.i.f. values	Value at purchaser price	p_i^{cif}
69 Rural buildings	0.0	0.0	1.0000
70 Factory buildings	0.0	0.0	1.0000
71 Public buildings	0.0	0.0	1.0000
72 Roads	0.0	0.0	1.0000
73 Infrastructure	0.0	0.0	1.0000
74 Ownership of dwellings	0.0	0.0	1.0000
75 Electricity	0.0	0.0	1.0000
76 Gas	0.0	0.0	0.9967
77 Wholesale and retail trade	0.0	0.0	0.9804
78 Road transport	0.0	0.0	1.0000
79 Rail transport	0.0	0.0	1.0000
80 Air transport	0.0	0.0	1.0000
81 Water transport	0.0	0.0	1.0000
82 Television	0.0	0.0	0.9731
83 Radio	0.0	0.0	0.9694
84 Phone, telegraph and post	0.0	0.0	0.9632
85 Banking and insurance	0.0	0.0	0.9792
86 Government	0.0	0.0	0.9875
87 Other services	0.0	0.0	0.9809

Notes: (i) The third column is the second divided by the first and represents p_i^{cif}, the value of a unit of the importable at c.i.f. prices. Recall that units of goods are chosen so that purchaser prices are unity. To get from p_i^{cif} to shadow prices we must add trade and transport margins evaluated at shadow prices.

(ii) LS denotes 'large-scale' and SS denotes 'small-scale'.
Source: Ahmad, Coady and Stern (1988), pp. 36–7.

input–output matrix. Employment costs for large-scale manufacturing were taken from estimates calculated from the Census of Manufacturing Industry (CMI) for the 118-sector classification. However, since the value-added figures for the input–output study were lower than those for large-scale manufacturing from the CMI, the employment costs have been adjusted downwards (by a factor of 0.66) to match the input–output estimates. We have assumed other employment costs as follows: 0.5 of value added in agriculture and small-scale industries, and 0.6 of value added in construction and services. For agriculture, we have taken land opportunity costs at market prices as 0.3 of value added. For capital coefficients we have used a rental charge based on a rate of interest of 10%. The residual of value added after these elements have been deducted is 'pure profit'. It is sometimes positive and sometimes negative. Given that it is an item derived as a residual after many assumptions it is not likely to be accurate. We have ignored it in the calculation of shadow prices, which essentially involves treating it as a transfer payment with no social cost. The breakdown of value added into the above components is given in table 6.9.

To calculate the accounting ratios for non-traded activities we need those for traded goods (these have been discussed above) and for the disaggregated value-added terms. For land, we assume throughout an accounting ratio of 0.9. This is based on a rough average of accounting ratios for agricultural goods since one can regard the marginal product of land as being in terms of a bundle of agricultural goods. For the employment accounting ratio, we experiment with values including 0.9, 0.75 and 0.5. We refer to these ratios as the *wage conversion factors* (WCF). It should be noted that there may be several models which could yield an AR for employment (or shadow wage) equivalent to say 0.75. However, we may regard variations in the AR for employment as corresponding to different assumptions concerning the Pakistan labour market, with higher shadow prices associated with tighter markets or greater social costs of employment. These different assumptions could include, for instance, models which incorporate the migration of Pakistani workers to the Middle East and others which do not. Lower ARs would correspond to cases where one assumes a relative abundance of labour. The numbers used also cover a range that has been generated by detailed studies; see, for example, Squire, Little and Durdag (1979) and Khan (1974). The reason that 0.9 is the maximum AR for labour (or WCF) we have used is that the shadow price is (see chapter 5.5) the SCF times $[c - \lambda(c-m)]$, the expression for the Little–Mirrlees shadow wage, where λ is the value of extra income to the factor in terms of government revenue, c is the factor's payment and m, earnings foregone elsewhere (assumed equal to the factor's marginal product). Given the high tariffs in Pakistan, 0.9 would be a high estimate for the SCF corresponding to labour's marginal product, and this in turn would be multiplied by a factor less than one, corresponding to the ratio $[c - \lambda(c-m)]/c$, to get to the WCF.

In a similar manner, an AR for assets may be generated by different combinations of the accounting rate of interest (r), the capital matrix, and the shadow price of capital goods. We refer to this AR as the *asset conversion factor*, or ACF. We have taken values of 0.75, 0.5 and 0.25 to provide a wide range of alternatives. For example, if 10% is thought to be reasonable for r and our estimate of the capital coefficient matrix is satisfactory (see Ahmad and Stern, 1986, and section 6.2 above) then the appropriate AR is that corresponding to capital goods (so that the shadow cost of equipment is r times its value at market prices times the AR). In this

Table 6.9. *Breakdown of value added*

	Labour	Capital	Residual	Value added
01 Wheat	0.5000	0.0358	0.1642	0.5625
02 Rice	0.5000	0.0428	0.1572	0.4712
03 Cotton	0.5000	0.0350	0.1650	0.5758
04 Sugar cane	0.5000	0.0305	0.1695	0.6616
05 Tobacco growing	0.5000	0.0273	0.1727	0.7391
06 Oilseeds	0.5000	0.0335	0.1665	0.6012
07 Pulses	0.5000	0.0855	0.1145	0.2357
08 Other crops	0.5000	0.0324	0.1676	0.6228
09 Livestock	0.5000	0.0355	0.1645	0.5684
10 Fishing	0.5000	0.0234	0.1766	0.8609
11 Forestry	0.5000	0.0255	0.1745	0.7904
12 Mining and quarrying	0.5000	0.0628	0.1372	0.6378
13 Grain milling	0.4428	1.2166	−0.6594	0.0756
14 Rice milling and husking	0.4959	0.9162	−0.4121	0.1004
15 Edible oils	0.3458	1.1611	−0.5068	0.0792
16 Sugar refining	0.2541	0.5838	0.1621	0.1575
17 Gur and *khandsari*	0.5000	0.1902	0.3098	0.0871
18 Tea blending	0.3248	0.5291	0.1461	0.1738
19 Fish and preparations	0.2547	0.6296	0.1157	0.1460
20 Confectionery and bakery	0.2972	0.5097	0.1930	0.1804
21 Other food industries	0.4090	0.2659	0.3252	0.3459
22 Beverages	0.4851	0.2685	0.2464	0.3425
23 Cigarettes and tobacco products	0.2012	0.6661	0.1327	0.1380
24 Bidis (i.e. tobacco, SS)	0.5000	0.0502	0.4498	0.3297
25 Cotton yarn	0.3673	0.3674	0.2653	0.2503
26 Cotton ginning	0.1514	1.0495	−0.2009	0.0876
27 Cotton textiles (LS)	0.7376	0.4386	−0.1762	0.2097
28 Cotton textiles (SS)	0.5000	0.0728	0.4272	0.2275
29 Silk and synthetic textiles	0.5535	0.6343	−0.1878	0.1450
30 Woollen textiles and hosiery	0.4635	0.4329	0.1036	0.2124
31 Threadballs and other textiles	0.3622	0.3905	0.2472	0.2355
32 Carpets and rugs	0.4369	0.2897	0.2734	0.3174
33 Made-up garments	0.2789	0.2444	0.4768	0.3763
34 Footwear (non-rubber)	0.4960	0.2504	0.2536	0.3672
35 Wood, cork and furniture	0.4706	0.2399	0.2895	0.3833
36 Paper and products	0.3063	0.3217	0.3720	0.2858
37 Printing and publishing	0.3104	0.3373	0.3523	0.2726
38 Leather and products	0.1682	0.4590	0.3729	0.2004
39 Rubber footwear	0.4913	0.9115	−0.4027	0.1009
40 Rubber products	0.2833	0.5707	0.1460	0.1611
41 Pharmaceuticals	0.2785	0.8719	−0.1503	0.1055

Table 6.9. (*cont.*)

	Labour	Capital	Residual	Value added
42 Fertiliser	0.1746	0.2818	0.5436	0.3263
43 Perfumes and cosmetics	1.1219	0.6254	−0.7473	0.1470
44 Paints and varnishes	0.1111	2.2353	−1.3464	0.0411
45 Soaps and detergents	0.3283	0.7046	−0.0329	0.1305
46 Chemicals	0.3218	0.2898	0.3884	0.3173
47 Plastic products	0.4445	0.2399	0.3156	0.3834
48 Petroleum products	0.1743	0.6105	0.2152	0.1506
49 Cement	0.4311	0.4403	0.1286	0.2089
50 Glass and products	1.7755	0.7902	−1.5657	0.1164
51 Non-metal mineral products	0.5023	0.3403	0.1574	0.2702
52 Basic metals	0.3557	0.5126	0.1316	0.1794
53 Metal products	0.6196	0.2177	0.1627	0.4224
54 Iron and steel remoulding	0.5000	0.0347	0.4653	0.4772
55 Agricultural machinery	0.4263	0.9338	−0.3601	0.0985
56 Other non-electric machinery	0.2393	0.2637	0.4970	0.3488
57 Electric machinery	0.4483	0.5949	−0.0432	0.1546
58 Bicycles	0.2897	0.4623	0.2479	0.1989
59 Transport (LS)	0.2627	0.3957	0.3417	0.2324
60 Shipbuilding	0.3321	0.2010	0.4669	0.4575
61 Transport equipment (SS)	0.5000	0.2343	0.2657	0.3925
62 Office equipment	1.0701	1.8286	−1.8987	0.0503
63 Sports goods	0.2196	0.2442	0.5362	0.3766
64 Surgical instruments	0.3305	0.1742	0.4953	0.5278
65 Other large-scale manufacturing	0.1679	0.1634	0.6687	0.5629
66 Other small-scale manufacturing	0.5000	0.0479	0.4521	0.3459
67 Low-cost residential buildings	0.6000	0.0108	0.3892	0.4366
68 Luxurious residential buildings	0.6000	0.0118	0.3882	0.3997
69 Rural buildings	0.6000	0.0094	0.3906	0.5000
70 Factory buildings	0.6000	0.0116	0.3884	0.4036
71 Public buildings	0.6000	0.0110	0.3890	0.4258
72 Roads	0.6000	0.0085	0.3915	0.5549
73 Infrastructure	0.6000	1.2007	−0.8007	0.4165
74 Ownership of dwellings	0.6000	0.2556	0.1444	0.8997
75 Electricity	0.6000	1.8999	−1.4999	0.7671
76 Gas	0.6000	1.7862	−1.3862	0.8159
77 Wholesale and retail trade	0.6000	0.1134	0.2866	0.9449

Table 6.9. (*cont.*)

	Labour	Capital	Residual	Value added
78 Road transport	0.6000	0.1825	0.2175	0.3157
79 Rail transport	0.6000	0.7169	−0.3169	0.5510
80 Air transport	0.6000	0.1408	0.2592	0.4092
81 Water transport	0.6000	0.0703	0.3297	0.8198
82 Television	0.6000	0.1076	0.2924	0.5354
83 Radio	0.6000	0.0751	0.3249	0.7669
84 Phone, telegraph and post	0.6000	0.3891	0.0109	0.8055
85 Banking and insurance	0.6000	0.0376	0.3624	0.7285
86 Government	0.6000	0.5082	−0.1082	0.5342
87 Other services	0.6000	0.1119	0.2881	0.9581

Notes: (i) The figures for labour, capital and the residual are proportions of value-added while those for value added are proportions of gross output value.
(ii) For agricultural goods land is regarded as contributing 0.5 of value added.
(iii) LS denotes 'large-scale' and SS denotes 'small-scale'.
Source: Ahmad, Coady and Stern (1988), pp. 38–9.

case 0.75 might be plausible. Alternatively if 10% is thought to be too high for a *real* accounting rate of interest (and historically this might be so) then a lower AR might be more appropriate. Given the uncertainty concerning the estimates (particularly of *r* and the capital matrix) we have chosen the broad range.

6.3.2 Shadow price estimates for Pakistan

Estimates for shadow prices for Pakistan based on the three cases described above are discussed further in this section. The accounting ratios for non-traded goods corresponding to each combination of the ARs for labour and assets are presented for cases A, B and C in table 6.10(a–c). Recall that we value the residual profit/loss at zero, thus treating it as a transfer payment with no social cost. Therefore, *ceteris paribus*, one would expect non-traded activities which exhibit high positive residuals to have relatively low ARs and those which have high negative residuals to have relatively high ARs (because the social input costs are high relative to the value of output). As one can see from table 6.10 this holds true for most non-traded ARs. Some ARs are, however, greatly affected by the ARs of major inputs. These effects can be seen by examining table 6.10c. The results discussed are for case C with an employment AR of 0.9 and asset AR of 0.75. For example, sector (1) 'wheat' has a high AR of 1.30 and this gives (13) 'grain milling' a high AR of

Table 6.10. *Non-traded accounting ratios for various values of ACF and WCF*
(a) Case A (ACF = 0.75)

	WCF		
	0.9	0.75	0.5
04 Sugar cane	0.7532	0.6833	0.5669
07 Pulses	0.8870	0.8511	0.7913
11 Forestry	0.7239	0.6479	0.5211
13 Grain milling	1.3168	1.3003	1.2728
14 Rice milling and husking	1.0503	1.0310	0.9989
17 Gur and *khandsari*	0.7272	0.6549	0.5344
20 Confectionery and bakery	0.7554	0.7221	0.6666
24 Bidis (i.e. tobacco, SS)	0.6028	0.5456	0.4504
26 Cotton ginning	1.3572	1.3478	1.3322
37 Printing and publishing	0.6540	0.6114	0.5404
54 Iron and steel remoulding	0.5907	0.5189	0.3992
58 Bicycles	0.7707	0.7474	0.7086
60 Shipbuilding	0.8575	0.8179	0.7520
66 Other small-scale manufacturing	0.6075	0.5664	0.4979
67 Low-cost residential buildings	0.7586	0.7114	0.6327
68 Luxurious residential buildings	0.7361	0.6869	0.6050
69 Rural buildings	0.7175	0.6585	0.5601
70 Factory buildings	0.7349	0.6883	0.6106
71 Public buildings	0.7219	0.6695	0.5824
72 Roads	0.7321	0.6793	0.5913
73 Infrastructure	1.1055	1.0556	0.9725
74 Ownership of dwellings	0.7329	0.6476	0.5054
75 Electricity	1.7579	1.6825	1.5568
76 Gas	1.7071	1.6311	1.5044
77 Wholesale and retail trade	0.6330	0.5441	0.3960
78 Road transport	0.7499	0.7046	0.6290
79 Rail transport	0.9674	0.9114	0.8183
80 Air transport	0.7170	0.6567	0.5563
81 Water transport	0.6352	0.5527	0.4151
82 Television	0.7527	0.6955	0.6003
83 Radio	0.6769	0.5954	0.4595
84 Phone, telegraph and post	0.8203	0.7375	0.5996
85 Banking and insurance	0.6528	0.5719	0.4369
86 Government	0.8379	0.7582	0.6253
87 Other services	0.6330	0.5444	0.3967

(b) Case B (ACF = 0.75)

	WCF		
	0.9	0.75	0.5
01 Wheat	0.7578	0.6875	0.5703
04 Sugar cane	0.7401	0.6663	0.5432
07 Pulses	0.7731	0.7035	0.5876
08 Other crops	0.7438	0.6704	0.5480
09 Livestock	0.7474	0.6743	0.5523
11 Forestry	0.7239	0.6478	0.5210
12 Mining and quarrying	0.7557	0.6863	0.5706
13 Grain milling	0.8100	0.7413	0.6269
14 Rice milling and husking	1.0511	1.0315	0.9988
17 Gur and *khandsari*	0.7176	0.6423	0.5168
20 Confectionery and bakery	0.7068	0.6675	0.6021
24 Bidis (i.e. tobacco, SS)	0.6017	0.5442	0.4484
26 Cotton ginning	1.3573	1.3478	1.3321
37 Printing and publishing	0.6541	0.6114	0.5402
54 Iron and steel remoulding	0.5907	0.5185	0.3981
58 Bicycles	0.7710	0.7474	0.7081
60 Shipbuilding	0.8576	0.8178	0.7514
66 Other small-scale manufacturing	0.6113	0.5684	0.4969
67 Low-cost residential buildings	0.7465	0.6952	0.6096
68 Luxurious residential buildings	0.7267	0.6743	0.5869
69 Rural buildings	0.6899	0.6216	0.5077
70 Factory buildings	0.7277	0.6786	0.5967
71 Public buildings	0.7160	0.6615	0.5708
72 Roads	0.7172	0.6594	0.5630
73 Infrastructure	1.0986	1.0463	0.9591
74 Ownership of dwellings	0.7314	0.6456	0.5026
75 Electricity	1.7565	1.6806	1.5541
76 Gas	1.6796	1.5945	1.4527
77 Wholesale and retail trade	0.6330	0.5441	0.3958
78 Road transport	0.7548	0.7076	0.6288
79 Rail transport	0.9589	0.9000	0.8020
80 Air transport	0.7173	0.6569	0.5562
81 Water transport	0.6353	0.5527	0.4150
82 Television	0.7524	0.6951	0.5995
83 Radio	0.6769	0.5953	0.4592
84 Phone, telegraph and post	0.8202	0.7374	0.5993
85 Banking and insurance	0.6523	0.5711	0.4357
86 Government	0.8398	0.7593	0.6250
87 Other services	0.6329	0.5443	0.3966

(c) Case C (ACF = 0.75)

	WCF		
	0.9	0.75	0.5
04 Sugar cane	0.7524	0.6821	0.5648
07 Pulses	0.8860	0.8495	0.7886
11 Forestry	0.7238	0.6476	0.5207
13 Grain milling	1.3165	1.2992	1.2705
14 Rice milling and husking	1.0494	1.0287	0.9943
16 Sugar refining	0.5332	0.4865	0.4085
17 Gur and *khandsari*	0.7366	0.6538	0.5325
18 Tea blending	0.5438	0.4972	0.4195
20 Confectionery and bakery	0.7293	0.6871	0.6166
24 Bidis (i.e. tobacco, SS)	0.6013	0.5432	0.4463
26 Cotton ginning	1.3570	1.3473	1.3312
29 Silk and synthetic textiles	0.7748	0.7251	0.6423
30 Woollen textiles and hosiery	0.8307	0.7892	0.7199
35 Wood, cork and furniture	0.6681	0.6091	0.5106
36 Paper and products	0.6163	0.5613	0.4696
37 Printing and publishing	0.6225	0.5652	0.4696
40 Rubber products	0.7472	0.7035	0.6308
41 Pharmaceuticals	0.6248	0.5806	0.5070
43 Perfumes and cosmetics	0.6289	0.5765	0.4891
46 Chemicals	0.6426	0.5984	0.5248
48 Petroleum products	0.8731	0.8496	0.8106
54 Iron and steel remoulding	0.5900	0.5170	0.3954
58 Bicycles	0.7721	0.7447	0.6990
59 Transport (LS)	0.7440	0.7209	0.6824
60 Shipbuilding	0.8568	0.8164	0.7489
61 Transport equipment (SS)	0.6863	0.6284	0.5319
62 Office equipment	0.6852	0.6441	0.5755
66 Other small-scale manufacturing	0.6006	0.5563	0.4824
67 Low-cost residential buildings	0.7585	0.7110	0.6319
68 Luxurious residential buildings	0.7360	0.6866	0.6043
69 Rural buildings	0.7174	0.6582	0.5594
70 Factory buildings	0.7348	0.6880	0.6099
71 Public buildings	0.7217	0.6691	0.5814
72 Roads	0.7320	0.6789	0.5904
73 Infrastructure	1.1042	1.0540	0.9702
74 Ownership of dwellings	0.7329	0.6475	0.5053
75 Electricity	1.7528	1.6752	1.5459
76 Gas	1.7067	1.6305	1.5034
77 Wholesale and retail trade	0.6329	0.5438	0.3954
78 Road transport	0.7485	0.6956	0.6074
79 Rail transport	0.9625	0.9043	0.8074
80 Air transport	0.7106	0.6476	0.5426
81 Water transport	0.6351	0.5524	0.4146

Table 6.10(c) (cont.)

	WCF		
	0.9	0.75	0.5
82 Television	0.7287	0.6682	0.5672
83 Radio	0.6773	0.5945	0.4565
84 Phone, telegraph and post	0.8189	0.7355	0.5965
85 Banking and insurance	0.6504	0.5681	0.4310
86 Government	0.8369	0.7566	0.6227
87 Other services	0.6324	0.5435	0.3953

Note: LS denotes 'large-scale' and SS denotes 'small-scale'.
Source: Ahmad, Coady and Stern (1985), p. 51 (part b); Ahmad, Coady and Stern (1988), p. 40 (part a) and p. 19 (part c).

1.32 (grain milling also has a negative residual). Also sectors (2) 'rice' and (3) 'cotton' have high ARs of 1.11 and 1.51 respectively, and these give (14) 'rice milling' and (26) 'cotton ginning' high ARs of 1.05 and 1.36 respectively. The high ARs of (73) 'infrastructure', (75) 'electricity', (76) 'gas' and (79) 'rail transport' are due to high negative residuals which in turn are caused by high capital service coefficients (thus charging appropriately for capital inputs implies a high social cost of production relative to the market value of output). Also notice that activities with high labour coefficients are most sensitive to the wage conversion factor chosen – for example, (77) 'wholesale and retail trade'. Similarly, those which have high capital coefficients are most sensitive to the asset conversion factor chosen, e.g. (73) 'infrastructure', (74) 'ownership of dwellings', (75) 'electricity' and (76) 'gas'.

   One minus the accounting ratio for a sector can be interpreted as a shadow subsidy on output in that sector since it measures the extent to which producers are paid more than the shadow price of their product. As such it provides a direct commentary on the incentives which have been provided. Another commentary on sectoral priorities and incentives is provided by the analysis in terms of social profitability (described below) which involves an examination of the social profitability of expanding exports (at the margin) or of expanding domestic production of importables (at the margin). A more complete analysis, integrating the shadow prices with a reform analysis incorporating the effects on households in different circumstances, is presented in chapter 7, along the lines of Drèze and Stern (1988) and Ahmad and Stern (1986).

The inputs and outputs of each sector are evaluated at shadow prices to derive shadow profits or losses. However, for non-traded goods the method will automatically involve zero net profits at shadow prices since the shadow price is the shadow marginal cost which we have assumed equal to shadow average cost. The classification into traded and non-traded is therefore crucial in interpreting results on social profitability. Recall that there are three cases: (A) with 52 traded sectors, (B) with 48 traded sectors, and (C) with 38 traded sectors. In practice, given the level of aggregation, one might expect to find within any one sector commodities or sub-sectors which may be traded, or 'intrinsically' non-traded (e.g. because of high transport costs), or non-traded at the margin given the existence of quotas. Consequently, this analysis should be seen only as suggestive of sectoral social profitability, rather than a detailed commentary on specific industries.

In table 6.11 we present the social profitability (shadow profit or loss as a proportion of the shadow value of output) for case A (corresponding to the definition of 52 traded goods sectors). We have chosen the smallest number of non-traded sectors here since such sectors break even at shadow prices by definition. In each table we present the sensitivity of the social profitability to ARs for labour ranging from 0.9 to 0.5 for given ARs for assets, ranging from 0.75, in table 6.11a, to values 0.5 and 0.25, in tables 6.11b and 6.11c, respectively.

Given that there is zero net shadow profit for non-tradables by definition, the policy interest in the calculations for these sectors lies in examining the shadow marginal cost. For example, we could ask whether there would be any benefit in the relaxation of import quotas in a sector (if this is the reason why it is non-traded) by comparing the shadow price with the import price. If there appear to be particularly beneficial domestic uses of the non-traded output we could try to calculate a shadow value of these uses (for example, extra electricity supply). If the shadow value of the use exceeds the shadow marginal cost, then one might argue that the output should be expanded and directed towards the beneficial use.

One expects that activities whose outputs have relatively low ARs will exhibit negative social profitability. Focusing on case A with a conversion factor for labour of 0.9 and for capital of 0.75, our results suggest (broadly speaking) that sectors with an AR less than 0.75 tend to fall into this category. This implies that the average AR applied to all input costs is around the value of 0.75. So an AR for output of 0.75 is a rough threshold: sectors with an AR below this value generally exhibit a negative social profitability. However, there are important exceptions. For instance, sector (16) 'sugar refining' has an AR less than the mean (at 0.64) and yet it exhibits a social profit. This is due to the large indirect tax element (0.25)

Table 6.11. *Social profitability for various values of ACF and WCF (Case A)*
(a) ACF = 0.75

	WCF		
	0.9	0.75	0.5
01 Wheat	0.3973	0.4332	0.4939
02 Rice	0.2657	0.3152	0.3977
03 Cotton	0.4717	0.5124	0.5801
04 Sugar cane	0.0000	0.0000	0.0000
05 Tobacco growing	−0.0181	0.0606	0.1965
06 Oilseeds	−0.1176	−0.0510	0.0638
07 Pulses	0.0000	0.0000	0.0000
08 Other crops	−0.3336	−0.2515	−0.1082
09 Livestock	0.2368	0.2869	0.3712
10 Fishing	0.2657	0.3394	0.4623
11 Forestry	0.0000	0.0000	0.0000
12 Mining and quarrying	0.1968	0.2641	0.3790
13 Grain milling	0.0000	0.0000	0.0000
14 Rice milling and husking	0.0000	0.0000	0.0000
15 Edible oils	0.0666	0.0803	0.1036
16 Sugar refining	0.1708	0.2313	0.3362
17 Gur and *khandsari*	0.0000	0.0000	0.0000
18 Tea blending	0.1618	0.1773	0.2033
19 Fish and preparations	0.1054	0.1264	0.1613
20 Confectionery and bakery	0.0000	0.0000	0.0000
21 Other food industries	0.2645	0.3103	0.3866
22 Beverages	−2.1608	−2.2111	−2.3274
23 Cigarettes and tobacco products (LS)	0.6453	0.6622	0.6903
24 Bidis (i.e. tobacco, SS)	0.0000	0.0000	0.0000
25 Cotton yarn	−0.0525	−0.0251	0.0206
26 Cotton ginning	0.0000	0.0000	0.0000
27 Cotton textiles (LS)	−0.0271	0.0086	0.0681
28 Cotton textiles (SS)	0.1638	0.1928	0.2411
29 Silk and synthetic textiles	−0.4236	−0.3903	−0.3308
30 Woollen textiles and hosiery	−0.4459	−0.4183	−0.3686
31 Threadballs and other textiles	−0.2281	−0.2003	−0.1511
32 Carpets and rugs	0.3532	0.3867	0.4426
33 Made-up garments	0.2594	0.2829	0.3221
34 Footwear (non-rubber)	0.1547	0.1907	0.2506
35 Wood, cork and furniture	0.3007	0.3557	0.4474
36 Paper and products	0.0647	0.1052	0.1772
37 Printing and publishing	0.0000	0.0000	0.0000
38 Leather and products	0.2827	0.2945	0.3143
39 Rubber footwear	0.2422	0.2886	0.3660
40 Rubber products	−0.1118	−0.0760	−0.0121
41 Pharmaceuticals	0.2421	0.2621	0.2963
42 Fertiliser	0.1646	0.1943	0.2458
43 Perfumes and cosmetics	−2.7978	−2.7328	−2.6100

Table 6.11(a). (cont.)

	WCF		
	0.9	0.75	0.5
44 Paints and varnishes	0.1342	0.1479	0.1716
45 Soaps and detergents	0.1637	0.1817	0.2128
46 Chemicals	0.1864	0.2216	0.2823
47 Plastic products	0.2721	0.3175	0.3951
48 Petroleum products	0.0315	0.0449	0.0680
49 Cement	0.1731	0.2169	0.2900
50 Glass and products	−1.3082	−1.2110	−1.0391
51 Non-metallic mineral products	0.1220	0.1500	0.1977
52 Basic metals	0.0264	0.0571	0.1111
53 Metal products	0.1609	0.2205	0.3239
54 Iron and steel remoulding	0.0000	0.0000	0.0000
55 Agricultural machinery	0.1278	0.1442	0.1720
56 Other non-electric machinery	0.2173	0.2476	0.2989
57 Electric machinery	0.0873	0.1101	0.1487
58 Bicycles	0.0000	0.0000	0.0000
59 Transport (LS)	−0.0893	−0.0681	−0.0320
60 Shipbuilding	0.0000	0.0000	0.0000
61 Transport equipment (SS)	0.1852	0.2191	0.2761
62 Office equipment	0.2185	0.2405	0.2779
63 Sports goods	0.2630	0.2887	0.3316
64 Surgical instruments	0.4064	0.4519	0.5278
65 Other large-scale manufacturing	0.5094	0.5394	0.5894
66 Other small-scale manufacturing	0.0000	0.0000	0.0000
67 Low-cost residential buildings	0.0000	0.0000	0.0000
68 Luxurious residential buildings	0.0000	0.0000	0.0000
69 Rural buildings	0.0000	0.0000	0.0000
70 Factory buildings	0.0000	0.0000	0.0000
71 Public buildings	0.0000	0.0000	0.0000
72 Roads	0.0000	0.0000	0.0000
73 Infrastructure	0.0000	0.0000	0.0000
74 Ownership of dwellings	0.0000	0.0000	0.0000
75 Electricity	0.0000	0.0000	0.0000
76 Gas	0.0000	0.0000	0.0000
77 Wholesale and retail trade	0.0000	0.0000	0.0000
78 Road transport	0.0000	0.0000	0.0000
79 Rail transport	0.0000	0.0000	0.0000
80 Air transport	0.0000	0.0000	0.0000
81 Water transport	0.0000	0.0000	0.0000
82 Television	0.0000	0.0000	0.0000
83 Radio	0.0000	0.0000	0.0000
84 Phone, telegraph and post	0.0000	0.0000	0.0000
85 Banking and insurance	0.0000	0.0000	0.0000
86 Government	0.0000	0.0000	0.0000
87 Other services	0.0000	0.0000	0.0000

(b) ACF = 0.5

	WCF		
	0.9	0.75	0.5
01 Wheat	0.4048	0.4407	0.5017
02 Rice	0.2828	0.3323	0.4148
03 Cotton	0.4816	0.5222	0.5899
04 Sugar cane	0.0000	0.0000	0.0000
05 Tobacco growing	−0.0094	0.0698	0.2065
06 Oilseeds	−0.1061	−0.0390	0.0766
07 Pulses	0.0000	0.0000	0.0000
08 Other crops	−0.3219	−0.2391	−0.0946
09 Livestock	0.2444	0.2946	0.3791
10 Fishing	0.2749	0.3487	0.4715
11 Forestry	0.0000	0.0000	0.0000
12 Mining and quarrying	0.2177	0.2854	0.4011
13 Grain milling	0.0000	0.0000	0.0000
14 Rice milling and husking	0.0000	0.0000	0.0000
15 Edible oils	0.1017	0.1158	0.1398
16 Sugar refining	0.2193	0.2808	0.3876
17 Gur and *khandsari*	0.0000	0.0000	0.0000
18 Tea blending	0.1892	0.2048	0.2311
19 Fish and preparations	0.1373	0.1582	0.1931
20 Confectionery and bakery	0.0000	0.0000	0.0000
21 Other food industries	0.3032	0.3490	0.4253
22 Beverages	−2.0775	−2.1201	−2.2203
23 Cigarettes and tobacco products (LS)	0.6740	0.6908	0.7189
24 Bidis (i.e. tobacco, SS)	0.0000	0.0000	0.0000
25 Cotton yarn	−0.0009	0.0265	0.0722
26 Cotton ginning	0.0000	0.0000	0.0000
27 Cotton textiles (LS)	0.0207	0.0564	0.1160
28 Cotton textiles (SS)	0.1755	0.2045	0.2528
29 Silk and synthetic textiles	−0.3598	−0.3246	−0.2616
30 Woollen textiles and hosiery	−0.3958	−0.3665	−0.3136
31 Threadballs and other textiles	−0.1749	−0.1457	−0.0941
32 Carpets and rugs	0.3827	0.4162	0.4721
33 Made-up garments	0.2865	0.3100	0.3493
34 Footwear (non-rubber)	0.1820	0.2180	0.2779
35 Wood, cork and furniture	0.3325	0.3876	0.4793
36 Paper and products	0.1289	0.1712	0.2466
37 Printing and publishing	0.0000	0.0000	0.0000
38 Leather and products	0.3069	0.3188	0.3385
39 Rubber footwear	0.2802	0.3267	0.4041
40 Rubber products	−0.0610	−0.0235	0.0432
41 Pharmaceuticals	0.2750	0.2954	0.3305
42 Fertiliser	0.2494	0.2807	0.3352
43 Perfumes and cosmetics	−2.6910	−2.6198	−2.4852
44 Paints and varnishes	0.1697	0.1839	0.2086
45 Soaps and detergents	0.1952	0.2137	0.2455

Table 6.11(b). (cont.)

	WCF		
	0.9	0.75	0.5
46 Chemicals	0.2482	0.2844	0.3468
47 Plastic products	0.3061	0.3520	0.4304
48 Petroleum products	0.0628	0.0767	0.1006
49 Cement	0.2833	0.3271	0.4002
50 Glass and products	−1.1403	−1.0384	−0.8582
51 Non-metallic mineral products	0.1508	0.1792	0.2273
52 Basic metals	0.0768	0.1088	0.1651
53 Metal products	0.1959	0.2564	0.3614
54 Iron and steel remoulding	0.0000	0.0000	0.0000
55 Agricultural machinery	0.1569	0.1735	0.2018
56 Other non-electric machinery	0.2567	0.2873	0.3393
57 Electric machinery	0.1221	0.1453	0.1845
58 Bicycles	0.0000	0.0000	0.0000
59 Transport (LS)	−0.0507	−0.0290	0.0080
60 Shipbuilding	0.0000	0.0000	0.0000
61 Transport equipment (SS)	0.2104	0.2445	0.3017
62 Office equipment	0.2541	0.2765	0.3146
63 Sports goods	0.2925	0.3183	0.3612
64 Surgical instruments	0.4397	0.4852	0.5611
65 Other large-scale manufacturing	0.5397	0.5697	0.6197
66 Other small-scale manufacturing	0.0000	0.0000	0.0000
67 Low-cost residential buildings	0.0000	0.0000	0.0000
68 Luxurious residential buildings	0.0000	0.0000	0.0000
69 Rural buildings	0.0000	0.0000	0.0000
70 Factory buildings	0.0000	0.0000	0.0000
71 Public buildings	0.0000	0.0000	0.0000
72 Roads	0.0000	0.0000	0.0000
73 Infrastructure	0.0000	0.0000	0.0000
74 Ownership of dwellings	0.0000	0.0000	0.0000
75 Electricity	0.0000	0.0000	0.0000
76 Gas	0.0000	0.0000	0.0000
77 Wholesale and retail trade	0.0000	0.0000	0.0000
78 Road transport	0.0000	0.0000	0.0000
79 Rail transport	0.0000	0.0000	0.0000
80 Air transport	0.0000	0.0000	0.0000
81 Water transport	0.0000	0.0000	0.0000
82 Television	0.0000	0.0000	0.0000
83 Radio	0.0000	0.0000	0.0000
84 Phone, telegraph and post	0.0000	0.0000	0.0000
85 Banking and insurance	0.0000	0.0000	0.0000
86 Government	0.0000	0.0000	0.0000
87 Other services	0.0000	0.0000	0.0000

(c) ACF = 0.25

	WCF		
	0.9	0.75	0.5
01 Wheat	0.4122	0.4483	0.5095
02 Rice	0.2998	0.3493	0.4318
03 Cotton	0.4915	0.5321	0.5998
04 Sugar cane	0.0000	0.0000	0.0000
05 Tobacco growing	−0.0006	0.0790	0.2167
06 Oilseeds	−0.0944	−0.0269	0.0895
07 Pulses	0.0000	0.0000	0.0000
08 Other crops	−0.3101	−0.2266	−0.0808
09 Livestock	0.2520	0.3023	0.3870
10 Fishing	0.2842	0.3579	0.4808
11 Forestry	0.0000	0.0000	0.0000
12 Mining and quarrying	0.2387	0.3069	0.4234
13 Grain milling	0.0000	0.0000	0.0000
14 Rice milling and husking	0.0000	0.0000	0.0000
15 Edible oils	0.1371	0.1515	0.1762
16 Sugar refining	0.2682	0.3308	0.4395
17 Gur and *khandsari*	0.0000	0.0000	0.0000
18 Tea blending	0.2166	0.2324	0.2589
19 Fish and preparations	0.1691	0.1900	0.2250
20 Confectionery and bakery	0.0000	0.0000	0.0000
21 Other food industries	0.3418	0.3876	0.4639
22 Beverages	−1.9866	−2.0197	−2.0990
23 Cigarettes and tobacco products (LS)	0.7026	0.7195	0.7476
24 Bidis (i.e. tobacco, SS)	0.0000	0.0000	0.0000
25 Cotton yarn	0.0507	0.0781	0.1238
26 Cotton ginning	0.0000	0.0000	0.0000
27 Cotton textiles (LS)	0.0685	0.1043	0.1638
28 Cotton textiles (SS)	0.1872	0.2162	0.2645
29 Silk and synthetic textiles	−0.2949	−0.2576	−0.1910
30 Woollen textiles and hosiery	−0.3448	−0.3136	−0.2575
31 Threadballs and other textiles	−0.1208	−0.0902	−0.0361
32 Carpets and rugs	0.4122	0.4457	0.5016
33 Made-up garments	0.3136	0.3372	0.3764
34 Footwear (non-rubber)	0.2093	0.2453	0.3052
35 Wood, cork and furniture	0.3644	0.4194	0.5112
36 Paper and products	0.1941	0.2384	0.3173
37 Printing and publishing	0.0000	0.0000	0.0000
38 Leather and products	0.3311	0.3430	0.3627
39 Rubber footwear	0.3183	0.3648	0.4422
40 Rubber products	−0.0092	0.0299	0.0997
41 Pharmaceuticals	0.3082	0.3291	0.3649
42 Fertiliser	0.3361	0.3692	0.4268
43 Perfumes and cosmetics	−2.5805	−2.5028	−2.3555
44 Paints and varnishes	0.2056	0.2204	0.2460

Table 6.11(c). (cont.)

	WCF		
	0.9	0.75	0.5
45 Soaps and detergents	0.2270	0.2460	0.2785
46 Chemicals	0.3107	0.3478	0.4118
47 Plastic products	0.3404	0.3868	0.4660
48 Petroleum products	0.0944	0.1087	0.1334
49 Cement	0.3935	0.4373	0.5104
50 Glass and products	−0.9693	−0.8626	−0.6738
51 Non-metal mineral products	0.1798	0.2085	0.2572
52 Basic metals	0.1280	0.1613	0.2200
53 Metal products	0.2314	0.2928	0.3994
54 Iron and steel remoulding	0.0000	0.0000	0.0000
55 Agricultural machinery	0.1862	0.2031	0.2317
56 Other non-electric machinery	0.2964	0.3273	0.3799
57 Electric machinery	0.1573	0.1808	0.2206
58 Bicycles	0.0000	0.0000	0.0000
59 Transport (LS)	−0.0115	0.0108	0.0487
60 Shipbuilding	0.0000	0.0000	0.0000
61 Transport equipment (SS)	0.2357	0.2698	0.3272
62 Office equipment	0.2900	0.3127	0.3515
63 Sports goods	0.3221	0.3478	0.3907
64 Surgical instruments	0.4730	0.5185	0.5944
65 Other large-scale manufacturing	0.5700	0.6000	0.6500
66 Other small-scale manufacturing	0.0000	0.0000	0.0000
67 Low-cost residential buildings	0.0000	0.0000	0.0000
68 Luxurious residential buildings	0.0000	0.0000	0.0000
69 Rural buildings	0.0000	0.0000	0.0000
70 Factory buildings	0.0000	0.0000	0.0000
71 Public buildings	0.0000	0.0000	0.0000
72 Roads	0.0000	0.0000	0.0000
73 Infrastructure	0.0000	0.0000	0.0000
74 Ownership of dwellings	0.0000	0.0000	0.0000
75 Electricity	0.0000	0.0000	0.0000
76 Gas	0.0000	0.0000	0.0000
77 Wholesale and retail trade	0.0000	0.0000	0.0000
78 Road transport	0.0000	0.0000	0.0000
79 Rail transport	0.0000	0.0000	0.0000
80 Air transport	0.0000	0.0000	0.0000
81 Water transport	0.0000	0.0000	0.0000
82 Television	0.0000	0.0000	0.0000
83 Radio	0.0000	0.0000	0.0000
84 Phone, telegraph and post	0.0000	0.0000	0.0000
85 Banking and insurance	0.0000	0.0000	0.0000
86 Government	0.0000	0.0000	0.0000
87 Other services	0.0000	0.0000	0.0000

Table 6.11. (*cont.*)

Notes: (i) The social profitability is defined as the difference between the shadow value of outputs and the shadow value of inputs, as a proportion of the shadow value of output.
(ii) The social profitability for non-tradables is identically zero.
(iii) LS denotes 'large-scale' and SS denotes 'small-scale'.
Source: Ahmad, Coady and Stern (1988), pp. 24–5 (part *a*), pp. 26–7 (part *b*), pp. 28–9 (part *c*).

which must be subtracted from costs to get shadow prices. Also sector (15) 'edible oils' has a low social profit even though it has a relatively high AR of 0.95. This reflects the high AR of its major input sector (26) 'cotton ginning'. Sector (19) 'fish and preparations' exhibits a lower social profit than might be expected from its relatively high AR. This arises from the large input of sector (10) 'fishing' which also has a high AR. Sector (22) 'beverages' has a very low AR of 0.17 (due to high import tariffs) and this leads to a high social loss despite the fact that it has a relatively high indirect tax coefficient. Sector (43) 'perfumes and cosmetics', with a low AR of 0.18, makes a large social loss despite a high indirect tax coefficient. This low AR arises from high tariffs and the analysis indicates that the domestic industry survives behind this tariff wall. However, sector (44) 'paints and varnishes' has a relatively high indirect tax coefficient, and this contributes to a return greater than might be expected from its AR.

From table 6.11 one can see that some sectors have negative social profitability across all our combinations of WCF and ACF. These include (08) 'other crops'; (22) 'beverages'; (29) 'silk and synthetic textiles'; (30) 'woollen textiles and hosiery'; (31) 'threadballs and other textiles'; and (43) 'perfumes and cosmetics'. Other sectors which have negative social profits at high WCF–ACF combinations switch to a positive social profit as we reduce the CFs. These include (05) 'tobacco growing'; (06) 'oilseeds'; (25) 'cotton yarn'; (27) 'cotton textiles (LS)'; (40) 'rubber products'; (50) 'glass and products'; and (59) 'transport (LS)'. Thus if low levels of CFs (in the spectrum we have chosen) are ascribed then the activities in the latter list appear attractive; but, even at the lowest levels we have considered, the former activities do not.

One can analyse the effect on social profitability in going from case A to case B, i.e. considering fewer sectors to be tradable. Since agricultural ARs fall, this leads to an increase in the social return of other sectors which use these as inputs (in case A the high ARs are the result of low domestic prices relative to world prices). The social profitability of sector (38) 'leather and products' increases, reflecting the fall in the AR of (9) 'livestock' which is its

Table 6.12. *Change in social profitability for selected manufacturing sectors on decreasing the number of tradable sectors* (A *to* C)

	Change in social profitability	Input sector (sign of AR change)
22 Beverages	+0.106	16 Sugar refining (−)
32 Carpets and rugs	−0.060	30 Woollen textiles (+)
44 Paints and varnishes	+0.106	46 Chemicals (−)
50 Glass and products	+0.070	46 Chemicals (−)

Note: Social profitability is defined as the difference between the shadow value of output and the shadow value of inputs, as a proportion of the shadow value of output.
Source: Ahmad, Coady and Stern (1988), p. 30.

major input. The same is true for (48) 'petroleum products' due to the reclassification of (12) 'mining and quarrying'. Other changes are relatively insignificant.

Moving from case A to case C, when more sectors are treated as non-traded, the social profitability for those manufacturing activities reclassified as non-traded go to zero by definition. There is no effect of any significance on the social profitability of the agricultural sectors reflecting the fact that manufactures, on the whole, are not important inputs into agricultural activities. However, some manufacturing activities, whose classification between traded and non-traded does not change, exhibit changes in social profitability due to the reclassification of inputs. Table 6.12 above presents these changes. (These results are for a WCF of 0.9 and an ACF of 0.75.)

It is also interesting to compare the social profitability presented above with commercial profitability as reflected by the residual. Again we concentrate on case A for WCF of 0.9 and ACF of 0.75. Notice that the residual is calculated as value added less assumed wage and asset costs. The results in table 6.13 suggest that there is a substantial difference between social and commercial profitability and that these differences vary across sectors. However, as we have seen above, the social profitability of some sectors is not sensitive to the CFs chosen.

For the results presented above we have valued the residual at zero thus treating it as a transfer with no social cost. The analysis was repeated with the residual valued at 0.8. This may be interpreted as assuming that profits have a social value of only 0.2 so that the transfer of a unit from public funds

Table 6.13. *Social profitability and commercial profitability*

	Social profitability	Commercial profitability
5 Tobacco growing	−0.02	+0.13
6 Oilseeds	−0.12	+0.10
8 Other crops	−0.33	+0.10
15 Edible oils	+0.07	−0.04
22 Beverages	−2.16	+0.08
25 Cotton yarn	−0.05	+0.07
30 Woollen textiles	−0.23	+0.02
39 Rubber footwear	+0.24	−0.04
40 Rubber products	−0.11	+0.02
41 Pharmaceuticals	+0.24	−0.02
44 Paints and varnishes	+0.13	−0.05
45 Soaps and detergents	+0.16	−0.01
55 Agricultural machinery	+0.13	−0.03
57 Electrical machinery	+0.09	−0.01
59 Transport (LS)	−0.09	+0.08
62 Office equipment	+0.22	−0.09

Note: LS denotes 'large-scale'.
Source: Ahmad, Coady and Stern (1988), p. 31.

to private profit has social cost of 0.8. The social profitability of only three sectors exhibit sign changes: (27) 'cotton textiles (LS)' from −0.03 to +0.02; (36) 'paper and products' from +0.06 to −0.03; and (48) 'petroleum products' from +0.03 to −0.01. The sign of the social profitability of most of the sectors does not seem to be sensitive to the valuation of the residual.

Despite the broad range of the sensitivity tests, there are a number of reforms suggested by the analysis that would appear desirable under most of the configurations considered. Thus on the basis of these calculations one might recommend, for instance, that the 'fertiliser' sector be expanded (although this may be sensitive to more precise analysis of the social value of important inputs such as natural gas, and negative externalities on the environment have not been considered). The social profitabilities indicate the following general directions for industrial and commercial policy. In general, the agricultural sectors are socially profitable, especially sectors (1) 'wheat' and (3) 'cotton'. Given stable world prices, domestic policy should be directed towards increased production in these areas. Although (8) 'other crops' is socially unprofitable throughout, one must be careful in deriving policy conclusions given the level of aggregation of this sector, since individual crops within the classification may be socially profitable. For the most part, manufacturing activities proved socially profitable, especially those classified as exported on the margin, e.g. (64) 'surgical instruments' and (63) 'sports goods'. This may well have implications for future industrialisation policy, which may need to be more export-oriented in comparison to the import-substitution policies to date. A method of mitigating the effects of high import duties is to allow for rebating of the tax element on inputs, and this might be achieved for instance through a value-added tax (see chapter 7).

Traditional sectors such as cotton textiles and carpets and rugs also exhibit relatively high social returns, reflecting Pakistan's current comparative advantage. Carpets and rugs are, in particular, fairly labour intensive. Sectors such as (29) 'silk and synthetic textiles' and (30) 'woollen textiles' were socially unprofitable during the late 1970s and 'perfumes and cosmetics' and 'beverages' do not appear to be sectors that should be encouraged. It is interesting to note that excises on beverages were increased substantially during the 1980s.

Notwithstanding the social profitability of 'traditional' sectors, our estimates also point to basic and heavy industry as desirable activities across a wide range of possible valuations of labour and assets, and one would identify the cement, basic metals and machinery sectors as examples of non-traditional activities that are socially profitable, and that should be encouraged.

As we have emphasised above, the economy-wide shadow prices are at the broad sectoral level, but can feed into more detailed analyses of industries within a given sector; or at the project level. Other extensions should include an examination of the stability of the shadow prices, since policies and the international economic environment are both subject to many vagaries. We use the shadow prices to assess the welfare consequences of policy changes in the analysis of the reform in chapter 7.

6.4   Concluding comments

We have presented in this chapter the calculation of two basic policy tools in the analysis of tax reform: effective taxes and shadow prices. This, we hope, has served a number of purposes. First, we have shown how the theories and methods presented in chapters 3 and 5 can be directly applied. In other words we provide worked examples which may be useful to others who may wish to make similar calculations. Second, we have seen which are the important assumptions, the data difficulties and the key determinants of results. Finally, we have used the calculations to comment on tax policy, effective taxes bringing out the effects of a complicated mixture of taxes, and on sectoral policy where shadow prices can be employed to characterise socially profitable activities. In the next chapter we shall put these calculations to work in the analysis of tax reform.

7   The reform of indirect taxes in Pakistan

7.1 Introduction

In this chapter we put the theory and calculations to work in the analysis of indirect taxation in two ways. First, we look at possible directions for reform using the marginal methods developed in earlier chapters and taking account, through shadow prices, of distortions in the production sector. Second, we examine more substantial, non-marginal, reforms of indirect taxation looking in detail at their effect on households in different circumstances. The cost of the greater detail and of the non-marginal form of analysis is that we do not simultaneously analyse the production distortions. A judgement as to what are the appropriate policy moves must come from a combination of the different pieces of applied analysis, the theory of design and judgements of administrative and political difficulties. We comment further on policy choice when we consider a medium-term fiscal plan in chapter 10.

The information and calculations required to put the theory of marginal reform described in chapters 3 and 5 into practice include consumption data by household, demand responses and a set of shadow prices (for the case where producer prices are assumed to be distorted) or a description of the existing tax system which allows one to identify the tax element in the final price of a good, i.e. the effective tax (for the case where producer prices are assumed not to be distorted). The calculations of effective taxes and shadow prices were presented in chapter 6. Our particular task in section 7.2 is to compare an application of the theory which assumes producer prices are proportional to shadow prices, with one which acknowledges that there may be a number of distortions to producer prices and which takes account of the fact that an equal revenue adjustment may shift demands towards goods with high social costs. We shall see that the results can look very different. The analysis is based largely on data from 1976 – the input–output information, consumer expenditures and demand responses relate to that year. This section is based on Ahmad and Stern (1990).

Section 7.3 considers non-marginal changes and discusses the introduction of a new tax instrument, the value-added tax (VAT), examining the effects of alternative proposals on households in different circumstances. While these proposals are couched in terms of a VAT and a set of excises, the suggested rate structure could, in principle, have been achieved with a combination of existing tax instruments. For this analysis we utilise a much more recent data set, the 1984–5 Household Income and Expenditure Survey, which is used to assess the effects of different policy packages. The section is based on Ahmad and Ludlow (1989). The final section contains further comments on the results.

7.2 The reform of existing taxes

The theory of reform has been set out in some detail in earlier chapters, and here we concentrate on the examination of appropriate directions of change from the status quo for Pakistan, using information from 1976. We provide first in subsection 7.2.1 a brief review and assembly of the theory. In subsection 7.2.2 we examine the basic data inputs required for the analysis and in subsection 7.2.3, we present directions for reform. Finally, in subsection 7.2.4 we highlight some of the important lessons for tax policy emerging from our analysis.

7.2.1 Theory

We recall here the concepts of shadow revenue, social marginal cost of revenue and social marginal cost of shadow revenue. A general analysis of the conditions for a marginal reform to increase welfare was provided in chapter 3 and in particular is summarised in the equation

$$dV = \left(\frac{\partial V}{\partial \omega} - \mathbf{v}' \frac{\partial \mathbf{E}}{\partial \omega} \right) d\omega. \tag{3.12}$$

To recapitulate, social welfare V is a function of predetermined variables ω and endogenous variables $\mathbf{s}$ which are chosen to maximise $V(\mathbf{s}, \omega)$ subject to the scarcity constraints $\mathbf{E}(\mathbf{s}, \omega) = \mathbf{z}$, where $\mathbf{z}$ is the vector of public supplies and $\mathbf{E}$ is the vector of excess demands arising from $(\mathbf{s}, \omega)$. The shadow prices, $\mathbf{v}$, the marginal social values of extra public supplies, are shown to be equal to the Lagrange multipliers on the scarcity constraints.

We showed that $-\mathbf{v}'\mathbf{E}$ could be reformulated as the shadow government revenue, R_v, where, for example, shadow consumer taxes were defined as $(\mathbf{q} - \mathbf{v})$. Shadow revenue is equal to government revenue when shadow prices $\mathbf{v}$ are equal to producer prices. When we consider the indirect taxes $\mathbf{t}$ as the predetermined variables then $d\mathbf{t}$ represents a marginal reform in indirect taxes. Based on (3.12) and the interpretation of $-v'E$ as shadow revenue we defined

$$\lambda_i^v = -\frac{\partial V}{\partial t_i} \bigg/ \frac{\partial R_v}{\partial t_i} \qquad (3.13)$$

as the marginal cost of shadow revenue from taxing good i. This is a generalisation of the marginal social cost of revenue

$$\lambda_i = -\frac{\partial V}{\partial t_i} \bigg/ \frac{\partial R}{\partial t_i} \qquad (3.4)$$

When shadow prices are equal to producer prices then a welfare improving change is provided by a constant revenue shift from taxation of good i to good j when

$$\lambda_i > \lambda_j \qquad (7.1)$$

Constant revenue correctly captures the general equilibrium, or scarcity, constraints, however, only where producer and shadow prices are equal (or rather proportional). When they are unequal the condition corresponding to (7.1) which correctly identifies the improving marginal reforms is

$$\lambda_i^v > \lambda_j^v \qquad (7.2)$$

If this holds then a switch from taxation of i to j which holds shadow revenue constant will improve welfare. The preservation of shadow revenue is here equivalent to the satisfaction of the scarcity or general equilibrium constraints.

For the reform of indirect taxes we have

$$\frac{\partial V}{\partial t_i} = -\sum_h \beta^h x_i^h \qquad (7.3)$$

$$\frac{\partial R_v}{\partial t_i} = -\sum_j v_j \frac{\partial X_j}{\partial t_i} \qquad (7.4)$$

$$\frac{\partial R}{\partial t_i} = X_i + \sum_j t_j \frac{\partial X_j}{\partial t_i} \qquad (7.5)$$

where β^h is the social marginal utility of income to household h, x_i^h is the demand by household h for good i and $X_i = \sum_h x_i^h$.

In this section we contrast the directions of reform which result from an analysis where we assume producer prices are equal to shadow prices with those which follow from suggesting that relative shadow and producer prices differ. We shall do this by comparing the rankings of λ_i and λ_i^v.

7.2.2   *Effective taxes, shadow prices and household behaviour*

The data requirements to calibrate (7.3), (7.4) and (7.5), and thus to identify λ_i^y and λ_i, and improving directions of reform, include tax collections by commodity group and input–output information to calculate effective taxes and shadow prices, estimates of aggregate demand responses and information on household expenditures (for the welfare weights β^h see chapter 5). The empirical analysis is based on data from Pakistan for the mid-1970s and the calculations of tax collections, effective taxes and shadow prices were described in chapter 6.

The 1976 Micro-Nutrient Survey (MNS) was a one-off survey of 1105 households conducted for the Planning Commission (see Government of Pakistan, 1976). It contains information on household consumption and production for both rural and urban households and also their sources of income. The consumption levels used here were taken from this survey, which was also used to estimate demand responses using an extended linear expenditure system with cross-section data (for a description of the method see Ahmad, Ludlow and Stern, 1988). We use the level of aggregation of the MNS (thirteen commodities) for the empirical analysis. The demand system was estimated separately for urban and rural households, and household characteristics were included as influences on consumption of different goods. The rankings of λ_i and λ_i^y, presented in table 7.3b and table 7.4b below, were fairly insensitive to the precise specification we used and note that it is only *aggregate* demand responses which enter the analysis. We use actual demands by households to represent the x_i^h.

The effective taxes, taken from chapter 6 for the eighty-seven sectors, are merged (see table 7.1 for procedures) to correspond to the thirteen-good classification of the estimated demand derivatives and are presented in table 7.2. The data available do not permit a separation of consumption into domestic and imported elements. We are supposing in using the effective taxes that the effective tax on domestic production also represents the tax associated with an imported good, or alternatively that marginal consumption falls on domestically produced goods.

The shadow price estimates, described in chapter 6, are based on the same eighty-seven sector input–output table, and correspond to the same year as the household data (see Ahmad, Coady and Stern, 1988). A Little–Mirrlees method of calculation was used, with goods being classified as importable, exportable or non-traded at the margin. The classification depends, in part, on government policy since a quota on a good that can be imported would imply that the good should be treated as non-traded. Moreover, given the level of aggregation of the input–output categories, there may be a combination of traded and non-traded goods within a given

Table 7.1. *Commodity classifications and shadow prices*

87-sector I–O categories	Shadow price cases A	B	C	13-sector mapping
01 Wheat	M	N	M	1
02 Rice	X	X	X	2
03 Cotton	X	X	X	–
04 Sugar cane	N	N	N	8
05 Tobacco	M	M	M	13
06 Oilseeds	M	M	M	7
07 Pulses	N	N	N	3
08 Other crops	M	N	M	6, 12
09 Livestock	M	N	M	4, 5
10 Fishing	X	X	X	4
11 Forestry	N	N	N	10
12 Mining and quarrying	M	N	M	10
13 Grain milling	N	N	N	1
14 Rice milling and husking	N	N	N	2
15 Edible oils	M	M	M	7
16 Sugar	M	M	N	8
17 Gur and *khandsari*	N	N	N	12
18 Tea blending	M	M	N	9
19 Fish and preparations	X	X	X	4
20 Confectionery and bakery	N	N	N	12
21 Other food industries	X	M	X	12
22 Beverages	M	M	M	12
23 Cigarettes and tobacco products (LS)	X	X	X	13
24 Bidis (i.e. tobacco, SS)	N	N	N	13
25 Cotton yarn	X	X	X	11
26 Cotton ginning	N	N	N	11
27 Cotton textiles (LS)	X	X	X	11
28 Cotton textiles (SS)	X	X	X	11
29 Silk and synthetic textiles	M	M	N	11
30 Woollen textiles and hosiery	M	M	N	11
31 Threadballs and other textiles	M	M	M	11
32 Carpets and rugs	X	X	X	10
33 Made-up garments	X	X	X	11
34 Footwear (non-rubber)	X	X	X	11
35 Wood, cork and furniture	M	M	N	10
36 Paper and products	M	M	N	13
37 Printing and publishing	N	N	N	13
38 Leather and products	X	X	X	11
39 Rubber footwear	X	X	X	11
40 Rubber products	M	M	N	13
41 Pharmaceuticals	M	M	N	13
42 Fertiliser	M	M	M	–
43 Perfumes and cosmetics	M	M	N	13
44 Paints and varnishes	M	M	M	–

Table 7.1. (*cont.*)

87-sector I–O categories	Shadow price cases			13-sector mapping
	A	B	C	
45 Soaps and detergents	M	M	M	13
46 Chemicals	M	M	N	10
47 Plastic products	M	M	M	10
48 Petroleum products	M	M	N	10
49 Cement	X	X	X	–
50 Glass and products	M	M	M	10
51 Non-metallic mineral products	M	M	M	13
52 Basic metals	M	M	M	–
53 Metal products	M	M	M	13
54 Iron and steel remoulding	N	N	N	–
55 Agricultural machinery	M	M	M	–
56 Other non-electric machinery	M	M	M	13
57 Electrical machinery	M	M	M	13
58 Bicycles	N	N	N	13
59 Transport (LS)	M	M	N	13
60 Shipbuilding	N	N	N	–
61 Transport equipment (SS)	M	M	N	13
62 Office equipment	M	M	N	13
63 Sports goods	X	X	X	13
64 Surgical instruments	X	X	X	13
65 Other large-scale manufacturing	X	X	X	13
66 Other small-scale manufacturing	N	N	N	13
67 Low-cost residential buildings	N	N	N	–
68 Luxurious residential buildings	N	N	N	–
69 Rural buildings	N	N	N	–
70 Factory buildings	N	N	N	–
71 Public buildings	N	N	N	–
72 Roads	N	N	N	–
73 Infrastructure	N	N	N	–
74 Ownership of dwellings	N	N	N	10
75 Electricity	N	N	N	10
76 Gas	N	N	N	10
77 Wholesale and retail trade	N	N	N	13
78 Road transport	N	N	N	13
79 Rail transport	N	N	N	13
80 Air transport	N	N	N	13
81 Water transport	N	N	N	13
82 Television	N	N	N	13
83 Radio	N	N	N	13
84 Phone, telegraph and post	N	N	N	13
85 Banking and insurance	N	N	N	13
86 Government	N	N	N	13
87 Other services	N	N	N	13

Table 7.1. (*cont.*)

Notes: (i) The table shows the classifications of goods for the calculation of shadow prices (M is importable, X exportable and N non-traded) and the translation of the eighty-seven input–output categories to the thirteen categories for which demand responses have been estimated.

(ii) Where more than one input–output category corresponds to a given sector from the thirteen-commodities list, accounting ratios have been merged using eighty-seven-sector consumption weights.

(iii) The thirteen-commodities list is: (1) Wheat; (2) Rice; (3) Pulses; (4) Meat, fish and eggs; (5) Milk and products; (6) Vegetables, fruits and spices; (7) Edible oils; (8) Sugar; (9) Tea; (10) Housing, fuel and light; (11) Clothing; (12) Other foods; and (13) Other non-food.

(iv) A dash (–) indicates that the sector in question does not enter into final consumption.

(v) LS denotes 'large-scale', SS 'small-scale' and I–O 'input–output'.

Source: Ahmad, Coady and Stern (1988). See also chapter 6 of this volume.

Table 7.2. *Accounting ratios, shadow consumption taxes and effective taxes*

(*a*) Accounting ratios

	Case B				Case A	Case C
WCF	0.9		0.75		0.9	0.9
ACF	0.75	0.5	0.75	0.5	0.75	0.75
1 Wheat	0.795	0.761	0.726	0.692	1.336	1.335
2 Rice	1.059	1.028	1.042	1.011	1.058	1.058
3 Pulses	0.773	0.751	0.704	0.682	0.887	0.886
4 Meat, fish and eggs	0.758	0.746	0.687	0.676	0.983	0.983
5 Milk and products	0.747	0.735	0.674	0.662	0.982	0.982
6 Vegetables, fruits and spices	0.744	0.730	0.670	0.657	0.576	0.576
7 Edible oils	0.949	0.946	0.940	0.937	0.949	0.949
8 Sugar	0.696	0.686	0.652	0.642	0.703	0.652
9 Tea	0.949	0.948	0.945	0.944	0.949	0.544
10 Housing, fuel and light	0.827	0.777	0.767	0.718	0.852	0.818
11 Clothing	1.003	0.996	0.998	0.991	1.003	1.047
12 Other foods	0.738	0.725	0.677	0.664	0.644	0.644
13 Other non-food	0.760	0.722	0.702	0.664	0.759	0.749

Note: Accounting ratios are defined as shadow prices divided by consumer prices. WCF and ACF represent the wage and asset conversion factors used in calculating the shadow prices. See table 7.1 for a sectoral classification for cases A, B and C.

(b) Shadow consumption taxes and effective taxes

	Case B				Case A	Case C	
WCF	0.9		0.75		0.9	0.9	
ACF	0.75	0.5	0.75	0.5	0.75	0.75	Effective taxes
1 Wheat	0.205	0.239	0.274	0.308	−0.336	−0.335	−0.038
2 Rice	−0.059	−0.028	−0.042	−0.011	−0.058	−0.058	0.042
3 Pulses	0.227	0.249	0.296	0.318	0.113	0.114	0.020
4 Meat, fish and eggs	0.242	0.254	0.313	0.324	0.017	0.017	0.006
5 Milk and products	0.253	0.265	0.326	0.338	0.018	0.018	0.005
6 Vegetables, fruits and spices	0.256	0.270	0.330	0.343	0.424	0.424	0.007
7 Edible oils	0.051	0.054	0.060	0.063	0.051	0.456	0.135
8 Sugar	0.304	0.314	0.348	0.358	0.297	0.348	0.137
9 Tea	0.051	0.052	0.055	0.056	0.051	0.456	0.112
10 Housing, fuel and light	0.173	0.223	0.233	0.282	0.148	0.182	0.103
11 Clothing	−0.003	0.004	0.002	0.009	−0.003	−0.047	0.081
12 Other foods	0.262	0.275	0.323	0.336	0.356	0.356	0.021
13 Other non-food	0.240	0.278	0.298	0.336	0.241	0.251	0.085

Note: Shadow consumption taxes $(q-v)$ are the differences between consumer prices and shadow prices (see chapter 5) expressed as a proportion of consumer prices (here taken to be one), and are presented in the first six columns of numbers.

sector. Thus, to introduce sensitivity with respect to different assumptions about policy, as well as to allow different possible interpretations, we present shadow prices for three cases (see table 7.1): case C has the maximum set of sectors classified as non-traded (forty-nine); case A the fewest number of sectors classified as non-traded (thirty-five); and case B, an intermediate with thirty-nine non-traded sectors. In this chapter we present results mostly based on case B and refer only occasionally to the results from cases A and C.

In estimating shadow prices of non-tradables, we require shadow valuations for factors, in addition to the shadow prices of tradables based on border-price valuations. The input–output table indicates only total value added in an industry and does not separate it into components. Using a variety of extraneous information we constructed a breakdown into payments to labour, land (where relevant), assets and a residual. The payments to labour were weighted by a wage conversion factor (WCF) and those for assets by an asset conversion factor (ACF). In chapter 6 we assumed a plausible range for the valuation of factors: 0.9, 0.75 and 0.5 for labour; and 0.75, 0.5 and 0.25 for assets; this provided a wide range of alternatives corresponding to a number of models which could be used to describe the markets for labour and capital goods in Pakistan. There were, thus, nine sets of shadow prices per case. Here we consider only four – WCF (0.9, 0.75) and ACF (0.75, 0.5). The lower range for the ACF (as compared with WCF) is used since capital goods are subject to particularly heavy taxation in Pakistan. The conversion factor for land is 0.9 throughout. The numeraire for the evaluation of shadow prices, following Little and Mirrlees, is foreign exchange in the hands of the government.

The shadow prices are presented, together with the effective taxes, for the thirteen-good classification in table 7.2. They are expressed in terms of accounting ratios which are shadow prices divided by market prices. Units of quantities are chosen so that consumer prices are one. One way of focusing on the source of differences between social marginal costs of shadow revenue, λ_i^γ, and social marginal costs of actual revenue, λ_i, is to compare the effective taxes used in the calculations of λ_i, and the shadow consumption taxes. Both are presented in table 7.2 and we can see that they are very different.

The examples of wheat and rice are instructive. Wheat is subsidised and this is reflected in the negative effective tax for wheat (table 7.2b). However, in case B wheat is treated as a non-traded good (during the latter half of the 1970s there were some years of exports and some of imports) so that the shadow producer taxes on its inputs become translated into a shadow tax on wheat (table 7.2b). This does not apply in cases A and C where wheat is treated as an importable (and with a domestic price held substantially below the world price). Rice on the other hand has an effective tax (table 7.2b) of 4.2% based on taxes on its inputs (it is not subsidised). It is, however, subject to an export tax which makes the domestic price lower than the world price and so gives an accounting ratio (shadow price divided by consumer price) less than one and a shadow consumer subsidy. The export tax is ignored in the effective tax case since those calculations are based on a simple model where goods are non-traded, there are fixed coefficients and only one factor. This yields mark-up pricing and shadow prices equal to market producer prices. The model may be satisfactory for some simple revenue calculations which focus on non-traded goods and for indicating some of the cascading effects of input taxes. It is not appropriate where trade, trade distortions and factor market distortions are central issues. It is precisely for this reason that we use a different model as a basis for the shadow price calculations and wish to compare the results with those of the simpler model.

The model for the shadow price calculations is, as in Little and Mirrlees

(1974), not fully articulated. It is based on the two simple rules for traded and non-traded goods which we have stated. This raises the standard, but subtle, problem involved in most uses of shadow prices. If shadow prices are, indeed, solved out from the fully articulated model then they are redundant – one simply recomputes the equilibrium in the model with the reform and compares the welfare level with and without. This indicates that we have to think of shadow prices in a different way than as somewhat useless additions to a computable general equilibrium model. They are summary statistics from a model which is not fully articulated but which usually contains levels of detail which are not feasible in a fully computable model. The more practical methods (such as that of Little and Mirrlees used here) look for rules (such as world prices for traded goods) which are applicable in a large class of models.

The summary statistics (the shadow prices) are much fewer in number than the parameters of a fully articulated computable general equilibrium (CGE) model and there would usually, therefore, be many possible models consistent with a given set of shadow prices. This allows them to be used much more subtly than a CGE model. For example, we can suppose that the labour market functions in some changed way and guess that the main effect would be to give a lower shadow wage rate. Such thought experiments will often be impractical if CGEs are the only tools available. Here we use shadow prices in this spirit. This is the same approach as used in project evaluation and we have simply transferred it to tax reform.

7.2.3 Directions of reform

Where shadow prices are proportional to producer prices, improving directions of reform may be characterised through the effects of tax changes on households and on government revenue. We defined λ_i as the marginal cost of government revenue in terms of social welfare (see equations (3.4), (7.3) and (7.5) above), and appropriate directions of reform arise from a switch in taxation from a good with a higher λ_i to one with a lower λ_i. The data requirements have been discussed in the previous section. However, we need to specify the welfare weights, β^h, and this can be done in a number of ways, as described in chapter 5. We characterise the distributional judgements lying behind the welfare weights through an elasticity ε which, following fairly standard practice, we call an inequality aversion parameter. We write

$$\beta^h = (\hat{I}/I^h)^\varepsilon \qquad (7.6)$$

where $\hat{I}$ is the lowest income and ε is the elasticity of the marginal utility of income. For example choosing an ε of 1 would place equal weights on income increments regardless to whom they occur, an ε of 2 would place a weight of $\frac{1}{4}$ on an income to someone with twice the income of the worst off. One may think of $\varepsilon = 5$ as placing a very high weight on the lowest incomes and thus approaching the Rawlsian maxi-min criterion of maximising the income of the worst off.

Notice that the scaling of the β^h is irrelevant to the ranking of the λ_i. When we work with shadow prices and R_v and use government revenue as numeraire, then our normalisation involves the assumption that a unit of government revenue is equal in value to a unit of income for the poorest household.

Directions of reform: using λ_i

The social marginal costs of government revenue from the ith commodity, λ_i, corresponding to various levels of inequality aversion for the thirteen commodity groups are presented in table 7.3a, with the ranks in table 7.3b. Commodities ranked higher are preferred to commodities ranked lower as candidates for additional taxation. The determination of the ranks may be understood using the interpretation of λ_i as the ratio of the distributional characteristic $\sum_h \beta^h x_i^h / X_i$ and a tax elasticity term $[t_i/t_i X_i][\partial(\mathbf{t'X})/\partial t_i]$. At low levels of inequality aversion, specifically $\varepsilon = 0$, commodities such as wheat and pulses are relatively attractive candidates as sources of extra revenue, ranking 10 and 8 respectively. The distributional characteristic is 1 for all goods and λ_i is determined only by the tax elasticity. However, even with moderate inequality aversion, $\varepsilon = 1$, the rankings change dramatically, with wheat at rank 1 (the least attractive candidate for additional taxation) and pulses at rank 3; and for $\varepsilon \geqslant 2$, these two commodities rank 1 and 2 respectively. On the other hand, a commodity such as 'housing, fuel and light', which ranks fairly low (2) as a choice for marginal taxation at $\varepsilon = 0$, appears increasingly attractive as inequality aversion increases, and ranks 10th for $\varepsilon = 5$.

The changing pattern of ranks for λ_i for different values of ε is reflected in table 7A.1a, which presents Spearman rank correlation coefficients. (Tables numbered, for example, 7A.1 are to be found in the appendix to this chapter.) We observe that the λ_i for $\varepsilon = 0$ are only weakly correlated with those for $\varepsilon \geqslant 1$. However, once inequality aversion is above the (moderate) level $\varepsilon = 0.5$, say, the ranks of λ_i are strongly correlated – the rank correlation for pairs of ε each above 0.5 are all above 0.8. And the rank correlation coefficient for the λ_i for moderate inequality aversion, $\varepsilon = 1$, and those for $\varepsilon = 5$, is as high as 0.96. This is an indication of the predominant role played by the distributional characteristic in determining the λ_i. Thus,

Table 7.3. *Social marginal costs of revenue, λ_i, with effective taxes*

(a) λ_i

	ε				
	0	0.5	1.0	2.0	5.0
1 Wheat	1.036	0.765	0.585	0.374	0.162
2 Rice	1.050	0.737	0.535	0.312	0.111
3 Pulses	1.047	0.762	0.576	0.362	0.154
4 Meat, fish and eggs	0.999	0.655	0.446	0.232	0.068
5 Milk and products	1.023	0.705	0.502	0.281	0.090
6 Vegetables, fruits and spices	1.012	0.690	0.490	0.276	0.096
7 Edible oils	1.122	0.786	0.572	0.335	0.123
8 Sugar	1.103	0.776	0.564	0.329	0.116
9 Tea	1.094	0.781	0.578	0.351	0.138
10 Housing, fuel and light	1.109	0.750	0.527	0.289	0.093
11 Clothing	1.078	0.736	0.521	0.290	0.098
12 Other foods	1.037	0.726	0.527	0.308	0.113
13 Other non-food	1.099	0.718	0.487	0.251	0.073

Note: λ_i represents the marginal social cost of a unit of government revenue from the ith good, and ε is an inequality aversion parameter. See text (equations (3.4), (7.3) and (7.5)) for definitions. See equation (7.6) for a definition of ε.

(b) Ranks for λ_i

	ε				
	0	0.5	1.0	2.0	5.0
1 Wheat	10	4	1	1	1
2 Rice	7	7	6	6	7
3 Pulses	8	5	3	2	2
4 Meat, fish and eggs	13	13	13	13	13
5 Milk and products	11	11	10	10	11
6 Vegetables, fruits and spices	12	12	11	11	9
7 Edible oils	1	1	4	4	4
8 Sugar	3	3	5	5	5
9 Tea	5	2	2	3	3
10 Housing, fuel and light	2	6	8	9	10
11 Clothing	6	8	9	8	8
12 Other foods	9	9	7	7	6
13 Other non-food	4	10	12	12	12

Note: Ranking number 1 represents the lowest priority as a source of extra taxation – see table 7.3a.

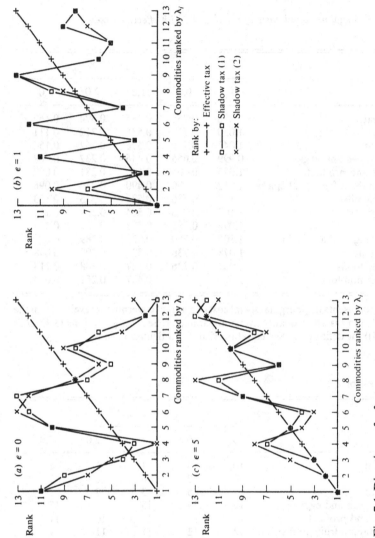

Rank by:
+————+ Effective tax
□————□ Shadow tax (1)
×————× Shadow tax (2)

Fig. 7.1 Directions of reform.
Note: See text and Appendix 7A.1 for detailed explanatory notes for this figure.

in determining the appropriate directions for reform, the precise specification of the inequality aversion parameter is less important than broad indications as to whether the policy-makers are (i) not at all concerned with distributional aspects in their decision-making, (ii) only moderately influenced, or (iii) primarily concerned with the welfare of the poor. The dominant role of the distributional characteristic is reassuring from one point of view since empirically we can be much more sure of the distribution of consumption than of the tax elasticity. On the other hand there is likely to be some disagreement over distributional values.

Directions of reform: using λ^v

Where shadow prices are not proportional to producer prices, directions of reform are evaluated here keeping shadow revenue, rather than actual revenue, constant. The λ^v for a commodity encapsulates the general equilibrium ramifications of tax changes including the effects of shifts in demand towards goods with high or low shadow prices – see equations (3.13), (7.3) and (7.4) for definitions. The λ^v's for the two sets of shadow price vectors, corresponding to (WCF, ACF) combinations (0.9, 0.75) and (0.75, 0.5), are presented in table 7.4a. Ranks for each set and level of inequality aversion are shown in table 7.4b and it is clear that the ranks differ strongly between λ_i and λ_i^v (cf. table 7.3b).

The rankings of the λ_i^v are determined by the interplay of three aspects – the distributional characteristics, the demand responses, and the shadow prices. This interplay is illustrated in figures 7.1(a–c). On the horizontal axis we have plotted the commodities ranked with respect to the λ_i for $\varepsilon=0$ (figure 7.1a), $\varepsilon=1$ (figure 7.1b) and $\varepsilon=5$ (figure 7.1c). The rank by λ_i^v is plotted on the vertical axis. Hence the 45-degree line represents the case where shadow prices are proportional to producer prices. From figure 7.1a we see that when distribution is not an issue ($\varepsilon=0$) the ranking by λ_i^v bears little relation to the ranking by λ_i. This reflects the sharp differences in effective taxes and shadow taxes that we saw in table 7.2b. On the other hand as the aversion to inequality increases, the ranking by λ_i^v gets closer to the 45-degree line – see figures 7.1b and 7.1c. Even for very high inequality aversion (figure 7.1c), however, the difference in ranking for λ_i and λ_i^v does not disappear. The figures (and tables) illustrate that the differences between λ_i and λ_i^v are substantially greater than those associated with the differences amongst the λ_i^v for different shadow price systems.

From table 7.4b the ranks of the λ_i^v suggest that, as with the λ_i, items of

Table 7.4. *The social marginal cost of shadow revenue*
(a) λ_i^y

	0	0.5	1.0	2.0	5.0
			ε		
	WCF = 0.9, ACF = 0.75				
1 Wheat	1.236	0.913	0.698	0.446	0.194
2 Rice	1.045	0.733	0.533	0.310	0.111
3 Pulses	1.248	0.909	0.686	0.431	0.183
4 Meat, fish and eggs	1.333	0.874	0.595	0.309	0.091
5 Milk and products	1.297	0.894	0.636	0.356	0.114
6 Vegetables, fruits and spices	1.332	0.908	0.644	0.363	0.127
7 Edible oils	1.106	0.776	0.564	0.331	0.122
8 Sugar	1.317	0.927	0.674	0.393	0.139
9 Tea	1.127	0.804	0.596	0.361	0.142
10 Housing, fuel and light	1.211	0.819	0.575	0.316	0.102
11 Clothing	1.064	0.726	0.514	0.286	0.097
12 Other foods	1.298	0.908	0.659	0.385	0.141
13 Other non-food	1.330	0.869	0.589	0.304	0.088
	WCF = 0.75, ACF = 0.5				
1 Wheat	1.370	1.012	0.773	0.495	0.214
2 Rice	1.112	0.780	0.567	0.330	0.118
3 Pulses	1.382	1.007	0.760	0.478	0.203
4 Meat, fish and eggs	1.499	0.983	0.669	0.348	0.102
5 Milk and products	1.449	0.998	0.711	0.397	0.127
6 Vegetables, fruits and spices	1.502	1.025	0.727	0.410	0.143
7 Edible oils	1.147	0.804	0.585	0.343	0.126
8 Sugar	1.439	1.012	0.736	0.429	0.151
9 Tea	1.175	0.838	0.621	0.377	0.148
10 Housing, fuel and light	1.389	0.939	0.660	0.362	0.117
11 Clothing	1.101	0.751	0.531	0.296	0.100
12 Other foods	1.434	1.004	0.729	0.426	0.156
13 Other non-food	1.532	1.001	0.679	0.350	0.101

Note: The social marginal cost of shadow revenue, λ^y, is defined in equations (3.13), (7.3) and (7.4). The index of 'aversion to inequality', ε, is presented in equation (7.6). The conversion factors WCF and ACF are used in the calculation of shadow prices; see chapter 6 of this volume.

(b) Ranks for λ_i^y

			ε		
	0	0.5	1.0	2.0	5.0
WCF = 0.9, ACF = 0.75					
1 Wheat	8	2	1	1	1
2 Rice	13	12	12	10	9
3 Pulses	7	3	2	2	2
4 Meat, fish and eggs	1	7	8	11	12
5 Milk and products	6	6	6	7	8
6 Vegetables, fruits and spices	2	5	5	5	6
7 Edible oils	11	11	11	8	7
8 Sugar	4	1	3	3	5
9 Tea	10	10	7	6	3
10 Housing, fuel and light	9	9	10	9	10
11 Clothing	12	13	13	13	11
12 Other foods	5	4	4	4	4
13 Other non-food	3	8	9	12	13
WCF = 0.75, ACF = 0.5					
1 Wheat	9	3	1	1	1
2 Rice	12	12	12	12	9
3 Pulses	8	4	2	2	2
4 Meat, fish and eggs	3	8	8	10	11
5 Milk and products	4	7	6	6	7
6 Vegetables, fruits and spices	2	1	5	5	6
7 Edible oils	11	11	11	11	8
8 Sugar	5	2	3	3	4
9 Tea	10	10	10	7	5
10 Housing, fuel and light	7	9	9	8	10
11 Clothing	13	13	13	13	13
12 Other foods	6	5	4	4	3
13 Other non-food	1	6	7	9	12

Note: Ranking number 1 represents the lowest priority as a source of extra taxation
– see table 7.4a.

general consumption which also form a large proportion of the consumption of the poor, such as 'wheat' and 'pulses' (ranking 8 or 9 for 'wheat', and 7 or 8 for 'pulses', for $\varepsilon = 0$), are attractive candidates for additional taxation only at low levels of inequality aversion. However, for $\varepsilon \geqslant 0$, 'wheat' ranks 1 and 'pulses' 2 for both shadow price combinations considered here, indicating that these commodities are the last ones that should be considered when extra revenue is required, and there is some concern for the poor. Hence the distributional characteristic continues to play a major role in determining the rankings of directions of reform for $\varepsilon \geqslant 1$.

The differences in rankings between λ_i and λ_i^v for given ε arise from the effects of switches of demand from and to goods with high and low shadow taxes. The switches in rank between λ_i and λ_i^v revealed in tables 7.3b and 7.4b (see also table 7A.1b) may be understood using the shadow taxes shown in table 7.2. The case of 'meat, fish and eggs' is instructive, since this sector has the highest own-price elasticity (-1.11) and a low distributional characteristic. For the (WCF, ACF) combination (0.9, 0.75) this sector switches from the lowest ranking λ^v at $\varepsilon = 0$, to the highest at $\varepsilon = 5$. Thus, at low levels of inequality aversion, the high price elasticity makes this an undesirable candidate for additional taxation. At higher levels of inequality aversion, the effects of the distributional characteristic predominate. A similar, though less marked, contrast is seen for this sector for the (WCF, ACF) combination (0.75, 0.5). Note that, with respect to the λ_i's (table 7.3b), this sector ranks 13, or as the most desirable item for additional taxation (for all $\varepsilon = 0, \ldots, 5$). The effective tax here is very low (see table 7.2b) so that the large price elasticity does not, in this case, lead to worries about revenue loss from increased taxation. The shadow tax on the other hand is substantial, hence shadow revenue losses are significant, giving the low rank for λ_i^v when $\varepsilon = 0$. If the government's preferences are such that $\varepsilon = 0$, then ignoring effects operating through shadow taxes would yield misleading results. The aggregate price elasticities are presented in table 7A.2.

The example of rice also illustrates the role of the differences between effective taxes and shadow prices in generating the differences between λ_i and λ_i^v. For $\varepsilon = 1$ (WCF, ACF $= 0.75$, 0.5), for example, the rank changes from 6 to 12 as we introduce shadow taxes. Thus it becomes one of the top two candidates for extra taxation. The reason is that it has a high shadow price (and a low shadow tax) so that we want to discourage domestic consumption of this valuable commodity. The reason its shadow price is high (relative to the market price) in this system of shadow prices is that it is an exportable. Similar results apply for edible oils (rank changes from 4 to 11 as we introduce shadow taxes) and clothing (9 to 13) and tea (2 to 10).

7.2.4 Lessons

Policy suggestions which arise from the rankings should not be taken too literally. There are five main ingredients for the calculations: consumption patterns, demand responses, effective taxes, shadow prices and welfare weights. They can only be specified after many assumptions and the data themselves are not necessarily reliable. Further, much important detail has been omitted. We have not explored in this chapter sensitivity to the assumptions involved in all the major ingredients. We have focused here on the role of shadow prices and distributional values. Elsewhere (Ahmad and Stern, 1984, 1986 and 1987a), we have provided some discussion of the robustness of the results to other elements in the analysis. It would be interesting in further work to treat the lack of certainty about the parameters and model in a more formal way which would lead to probabilistic statements about policy. This, however, would be a major (though important and interesting) exercise which would take us beyond the scope of this book.

We have seen that each of the ingredients plays an important role in the evaluation of overall directions for reform. Other things being equal we are less likely to want to increase taxes on a good the more it is consumed by the poor, the less responsive is revenue to the tax increase, and the lower its shadow price. Ignoring any of these elements can produce misleading results. The distributional aspects have appeared to be of particular importance in our calculations provided there is some reasonable concern with inequality. The principal purpose of this section, however, has been to bring out the role of the divergence between market and shadow prices, and we have seen that the effect on the rankings of goods as candidates for extra taxation may be strong. Goods with high shadow prices are valuable and the tax system should take this into account in discouraging their consumption. These are all important lessons which should be integrated with the other basic considerations, including administration, evasion and political acceptability, in designing and assessing practical packages for tax and price reform.

7.3 Value-added taxation

With a narrow indirect-tax base, Pakistan has come to rely increasingly on revenue from customs duties combined with excises on domestic production to meet continuing demands for additional resources. A consequence of this tax structure is a dependence on high rates of tax or duty on a limited set of commodities. As we saw in chapter 2, this limitation of the availability of tax instruments is not uncommon in developing countries, and in the Pakistan case reflects a structure of taxation essentially inherited from pre-independence days. Despite frequent rate changes the tax structure has scarcely evolved, particularly in terms of coverage and new instruments.

One response to these difficulties and problems is to examine a new form of indirect taxation to replace the existing system. A method which has been used with considerable success in some developing countries in response to these kinds of difficulties is the value-added tax or VAT. Some of its main advantages were discussed in subsection 3.3.2. The introduction of a VAT in practice involves many difficult decisions including the definition of base and coverage, rate structures, specification of administrative authorities and procedures and the transition from the existing system to a new one. Our principal concern here is with investigating the distributional conse-quences of different rate structures. We shall, however, consider important administrative issues in designing those rate structures, particularly in terms of exemptions for those sectors where it would be impractical to try to levy a VAT. The detail of the administrative problems is not our central concern here. We comment briefly in subsection 7.3.4 and return to some administrative issues in section 9.5.

Administrators of the VAT would much prefer a single uniform rate. Attempts have sometimes been made to use theory to support this position (see sections 3.2 and 3.4 for a review) but this approach has failed to provide plausible support principally because all the arguments involve assuming a fairly powerful system of direct taxation which, *inter alia*, can and does provide direct transfers to all households. This assumption is highly inappropriate for most developing countries on administrative grounds. Uniformity is simply impractical since a number of agricultural sectors cannot be covered in this way. At the same time a highly differentiated system would pose real administrative difficulties.

The key question on rates becomes the extent to which distributional considerations can effectively be built into a system with rather few different rates. There is considerable value in adding a few excises to the indirect tax armoury. Accordingly our main concern here is to investigate the distributional consequences of simple variants of the combination of VAT and specific excises on final goods.

The details of the distributional calculations are presented in subsection 7.3.5. We use an extensive and fairly recent household survey (1984–5) to look at the distributional impacts for households in different positions. The remainder of this section is devoted to a brief discussion of some problems of design and administration.

7.3.1 Design

Value added is the difference between the value of a firm's sales and the value of purchased inputs used in producing the goods sold. It is thus equivalent to the wage and salary bill, interest payments and gross profits of the firm. Under the most common version, a liable firm adds VAT at a given percentage rate to its sales and deducts certified payments of VAT on its purchases before paying the net amount to the authorities. The effect, in principle, is to avoid the taxation of inputs so that the base of taxation is final goods – consumers cannot reclaim VAT which they pay. In practice the base has to be treated carefully, taking into account desired definitions of final goods and the degree of coverage of the VAT amongst firms. Thus the VAT involves firms right through the production chain although its base is only on final goods. This has disadvantages and advantages in that, on the one hand, more firms are involved, creating extra work, while, on the other, they are required to keep accounts which may be useful for other purposes. Generally VAT is paid on imports but not on exports.

There are three major types of VAT with respect to the treatment of investment. The 'consumption' type VAT permits the full deduction of VAT paid on investment goods during the tax year from the tax liability, treating investment as analogous to current inputs. This type of VAT is in use in Europe. Another method allows the deduction of VAT associated with permitted depreciation in the current period: this VAT is of the 'net-income' variety. The base in this case is consumption plus net investment. A third method is to disallow any deductions for investment or depreciation, making the base 'gross-income'. The 'consumption' type VAT would be the most appropriate for Pakistan if it replaces the present sales taxes, imports and selective excises that fall on intermediate goods. The net income variety would be very difficult to administer in that it involves more information than simply sales and purchases.

Uniformity/rate structures

It is often assumed that a VAT involves a uniform proportional tax, i.e. a single rate, and it is often argued that this 'neutrality' is an advantage. However, the VAT is not necessarily a single rate tax, and many countries have operated the VAT with multiple tiers (Tait, 1988). While excessive differentiation is likely to lead to considerable administrative difficulty, a system with zero rating (e.g. for exports, so that taxes on inputs can be reclaimed), exemptions for the agricultural sector (no contact with VAT authorities is necessary), a standard rate and, possibly, a 'luxury rate', together with excises, may be sufficient to meet both administrative and distributional concerns. Such a structure may be much easier to administer than the present state of affairs with its complex system of specific and *ad valorem* rates with extreme differentiation by commodity type.

We saw in section 7.2 above that commodities such as wheat, pulses, tea and sugar (the former two commodities bearing little tax) are poor candidates for additional taxation if distributional considerations are taken seriously. While the definition of goods to be taxed at the higher rate may be difficult in some instances (see, for example, Bird, 1987), and obvious candidates such as cosmetics and tobacco products may be consumed by the poor, a more detailed examination of the distributional characteristics of these goods is quite often useful, since we have seen that this plays a central role in identifying the potential directions of reform. For instance, in Pakistan, the tobacco products consumed by the poor are mainly *bidis*, which bear little tax, and which are different from processed cigarettes (which are highly taxed). A VAT, with selective excises, could achieve considerable differentiation, with particular final goods such as cigarettes (which also raise much of the existing excise revenue) being taxed heavily on distributional, revenue, externality and paternalistic grounds (if smoking is considered harmful to health). In the final analysis, what is important is the structure of the overall indirect tax system, and an examination would include a joint evaluation of the VAT and excises.

7.3.2   Trade policy

Imports should be subject to VAT at the same rate as equivalent domestic goods. The revenue authorities would still collect much of the yields from imports at ports of entry, but the cascading effects of taxation of imported inputs would be avoided. Additional import duties on particular goods may be justifiable if either a case can be made for special protection of certain domestic manufacturers (see chapter 6) or it is judged that particular types of consumption should be heavily taxed (for reasons of distribution and revenue or because they are held to be socially unattractive). Note that the arguments do not necessarily overlap – a 300% import duty on Mercedes Benz and BMW cars cannot be seen as protecting the domestic production of the people's car (even if the design is that of the Suzuki).

7.3.3   Alternatives

A value-added tax, even if it extends to the retail stage, is preferable to a retail sales tax, since the former is not collected at one stage and there may be less incentive to evade. If there is evasion at the retail stage, as may be likely in the initial period given the Pakistan context, only the tax on the retailers' margin would be lost and not the whole tax. A retail sales tax is subject to the possibility of evasion without the assurance of prior collections.

Since the VAT is not so closely linked to particular goods or to specific rates, it embodies many dynamic advantages that are lacking in the present system of a combination of specific and *ad valorem* taxes. With a VAT, revenues would respond automatically to changes in activity. Thus the government would not need to make frequent changes in rate structure to maintain revenues in the face of increasing incomes. Moreover, if a change is desired then an across-the-board modification can be achieved reasonably quickly.

7.3.4 Administration

The experience of many developing countries, such as Turkey, suggests that it is possible to introduce the VAT within eighteen months or so of legislation (although there have been problems since introduction as avenues for avoidance and evasion became clearer over time), and if there is sufficient publicity the period may be shorter. The Mexican VAT transition period was around one year. There was no loss of revenue from indirect taxes during the transition period and a sharp increase in corporate income tax collections reflected 'better compliance' (Gil Diaz, 1987). None the less, for some countries there are important decisions to be made in terms of initial coverage, subsequent extensions and enforcement. Given that the VAT encourages systematic record-keeping, considerable work is required to prepare the administrative machinery to utilise and digest this information. To some extent, the Pakistan Central Board of Revenue already requires the production of detailed accounts in cases where, say, the income or excise tax liability of firms is in question. A VAT would make it easier for the administration, and would also protect 'honest producers' from potential harassment by the revenue authorities by making assessments much more standard (with receipts for inputs and outputs).

Note that a potential advantage of the information flows generated with the operation of a VAT is that it becomes easier to check on the evasion of income tax. However, the costs of administering such a checking system would need to be considered relative to the capabilities of the income tax department. To take full advantage of the potential of a VAT, there may have to be closer cooperation between the income tax and commodity tax administrations than is commonly the case in countries such as Pakistan. It should be stressed that a VAT is not evasion-proof, and that any system will require a modicum of administrative capability.

7.3.5   *Distributional consequences of reform*

In this section we examine alternative tax packages by identifying potential gainers and losers (the analysis is based on Ahmad and Ludlow, 1989). A method of arriving at an alternative tax package is to assume that the domestic effective taxes are being replaced by a combination of excises on particular goods and the VAT at various rates, with exemption for the agricultural sector. We have selected a number of packages for close attention, the choice being influenced in large part by the analysis of directions of reform in section 7.2. Our choice of rate structure in the packages is intended to embody moves in the directions indicated in that analysis. We found that considerations of distribution were the major element in the determination of the results of section 7.2 and have therefore designed zero rates or exemptions, standard rates, higher rates and supplementary excises with this in mind. Given that administrative reasons constrain agriculture to be exempt it is fortunate that these commodities also generally had low priority for extra taxation in the analysis of marginal reform. Meat, however, was consistently an item for which there were low marginal social costs of taxation at higher levels of inequality aversion, and in the experiments described below, we examine the possibility of an excise on this item (although administrative difficulties might be formidable). In attempting to match administrative convenience with the directions of reform, we allow for two rates of VAT, in some cases, with higher rates roughly corresponding to those items identified as being desirable candidates for additional taxation. The distributional characteristics for the twenty-one commodity groups of the survey used here (the Household Income and Expenditure Survey, HIES, 1984–5) are provided in table 7.5. The reform packages are described in tables 7.6 and 7.7. The set of reforms described in table 7.6 is intended to raise approximately the same revenue as at present. These may be expressed as (i) a standard rate VAT for all goods subject to the tax, (ii) a reduced rate of VAT on specific groups of items combined with a standard rate on remaining items, and (iii) combinations of the two with additional excises on items which one might wish to tax, as indicated by the analysis of section 7.2. We consider also (see table 7.7) a class of reforms designed to provide a substantial increase in revenue. Gainers and losers are characterised with respect to both 'first round' effects (i.e. as if demands were unchanged) and using equivalent variations (see chapter 5).

Data

This analysis of the effects of a tax reform on households is based on HIES 1984–5, with 16 575 households. This survey is carried out periodically by

Table 7.5. *Distributional characteristics for commodities (1984–5)*

(a) Distributional characteristics

		0	0.5	1.0	2.0	5.0
				ε		
1	Wheat	1	0.565	0.355	0.177	0.064
2	Rice	1	0.516	0.299	0.130	0.036
3	Pulses	1	0.527	0.313	0.144	0.047
4	Maize	1	0.515	0.296	0.124	0.031
5	Meat	1	0.442	0.228	0.085	0.019
6	Milk	1	0.497	0.280	0.118	0.032
7	Vegetables, fruits and spices	1	0.489	0.276	0.118	0.034
8	Edible oils	1	0.526	0.313	0.146	0.049
9	Sugar	1	0.504	0.287	0.122	0.033
10	Gur	1	0.595	0.386	0.199	0.074
11	Confectionery	1	0.405	0.194	0.065	0.013
12	Tea	1	0.496	0.281	0.120	0.034
13	Beverages	1	0.345	0.141	0.035	0.003
14	Cigarettes	1	0.452	0.237	0.090	0.020
15	Bidis	1	0.505	0.289	0.125	0.036
16	Housing, fuel and light	1	0.446	0.236	0.095	0.026
17	Clothing	1	0.488	0.276	0.119	0.035
18	Hygiene and medicine	1	0.466	0.254	0.104	0.029
19	Recreation and transport	1	0.366	0.164	0.052	0.010
20	Other foods	1	0.395	0.189	0.066	0.014
21	Other non-food	1	0.390	0.185	0.064	0.014

(b) Ranging of distributional characteristics

		0	0.5	1.0	2.0	5.0
				ε		
1	Wheat	1	2	2	2	2
2	Rice	1	5	5	5	6
3	Pulses	1	3	4	4	4
4	Maize	1	6	6	7	12
5	Meat	1	16	16	16	16
6	Milk	1	9	10	12	11
7	Vegetables, fruits and spices	1	11	12	11	8
8	Edible oils	1	4	3	3	3
9	Sugar	1	8	8	8	10
10	Gur	1	1	1	1	1
11	Confectionery	1	17	17	18	19
12	Tea	1	10	9	9	9

Table 7.5. (b) (cont.)

	0	0.5	1.0	2.0	5.0
			ε		
13 Beverages	1	21	21	21	21
14 Cigarettes	1	14	14	15	15
15 Bidis	1	7	7	6	5
16 Housing, fuel and light	1	15	15	14	14
17 Clothing	1	12	11	10	7
18 Hygiene and medicine	1	13	13	13	13
19 Recreation and transport	1	20	20	20	20
20 Other foods	1	18	18	17	18
21 Other non-food	1	19	19	19	17

Note: The distributional characteristic (see equation 3.7) has been estimated using the 1984–5 Household Income and Expenditure Survey for Pakistan.

Table 7.6. *Effective taxes and possible reforms*

	Effective tax %	Reform					
		I	Ia	II	IIa	III	IIIa
		%					
1 Wheat	0.0	0.0	0.0	0.0	0.0	0.0	0.0
2 Rice	2.3	2.3	2.3	2.3	2.3	2.3	2.3
3 Pulses	2.0	0.0	0.0	0.0	0.0	0.0	0.0
4 Maize	0.7	0.0	0.0	0.0	0.0	0.0	0.0
5 Meat	0.5	0.0	0.0	5.0	5.0	5.0	5.0
6 Milk	0.5	0.0	0.0	0.0	0.0	5.0	5.0
7 Vegetables, fruits and spices	0.7	0.0	0.0	0.0	0.0	0.0	0.0
8 Edible oils	13.9	14.1	10.8	13.5	10.3	13.1	9.9
9 Sugar	28.7	14.1	10.8	13.5	10.3	13.1	9.9
10 Gur	1.6	1.6	1.6	1.6	1.6	1.6	1.6
11 Confectionery	18.5	14.1	16.7	13.5	16.1	13.1	15.5
12 Tea	11.0	14.1	16.7	13.5	16.1	13.1	15.5
13 Beverages	17.0	14.1	16.7	13.5	16.1	13.1	15.5
14 Cigarettes	77.0	77.0	77.0	77.0	77.0	77.0	77.0
15 Bidis	6.0	6.0	6.0	6.0	6.0	6.0	6.0
16 Housing, fuel and light	10.0	14.1	10.8	13.5	10.3	13.1	9.9
17 Clothing	9.0	14.1	16.7	13.5	16.1	13.1	15.5
18 Hygiene and medicine	25.0	14.1	10.8	13.5	10.3	13.1	9.9
19 Recreation and transport	9.0	14.1	16.7	13.5	16.1	13.1	15.5

Table 7.6. (*cont.*)

	Effective tax %	Reform					
		I	Ia	II	IIa	III	IIIa
		%					
20 Other foods	3.0	3.0	3.0	5.0	5.0	5.0	5.0
21 Other non-food	15.0	14.1	16.7	13.5	16.1	13.1	15.5
Gainers ($n = 16\,575$)		60.87	62.76	61.86	62.95	54.59	61.57

Notes: (i) I to IIIa are reforms which are 'approximately revenue neutral' – see text.
(ii) The effective taxes reflect the tax element in the price of the twenty-one commodity groups, and the proposed tax vectors are shown for reforms I–IIIa. The last row indicates the proportion of households that gain from the reform.

Table 7.7. *Effective taxes and additional revenue reforms*

	Effective tax %	Reform						
		IV	V	VI	VII	VIII	IX	X
		%						
1 Wheat	0.0	0.0	0.0	0.0	0.0	0.0	0.0	0.0
2 Rice	2.3	2.3	2.3	2.3	2.3	2.3	0.0	0.0
3 Pulses	2.0	0.0	0.0	0.0	0.0	0.0	0.0	0.0
4 Maize	0.7	0.0	0.0	0.0	0.0	0.0	0.0	0.0
5 Meat	0.5	0.0	5.0	5.0	5.0	5.0	5.0	5.0
6 Milk	0.5	0.0	5.0	5.0	5.0	0.0	5.0	0.0
7 Vegetables, fruits and spices	0.7	0.0	0.0	0.0	0.0	0.0	0.0	0.0
8 Edible oils	13.9	10.0	10.0	15.0	5.0	5.0	5.0	15.0
9 Sugar	28.7	20.0	15.0	15.0	20.0	20.0	20.0	20.0
10 Gur	1.6	1.6	1.6	1.6	1.6	1.6	0.0	1.6
11 Confectionery	18.5	20.0	15.0	20.0	20.0	20.0	20.0	20.0
12 Tea	11.0	10.0	15.0	15.0	5.0	5.0	10.0	5.0
13 Beverages	17.0	20.0	15.0	20.0	20.0	20.0	20.0	20.0
14 Cigarettes	77.0	77.0	77.0	77.0	77.0	77.0	77.0	77.0
15 Bidis	6.0	6.0	10.0	6.0	6.0	6.0	6.0	15.0
16 Housing, fuel and light	10.0	10.0	15.0	15.0	5.0	5.0	10.0	5.0
17 Clothing	9.0	10.0	15.0	15.0	20.0	20.0	20.0	20.0
18 Hygiene and medicine	25.0	20.0	15.0	15.0	20.0	20.0	20.0	20.0
19 Recreation and transport	9.0	20.0	15.0	15.0	20.0	20.0	20.0	20.0

Table 7.7. (*cont.*)

	Effective tax %	Reform						
		IV	V	VI	VII	VIII	IX	X
					%			
20 Other foods	3.0	3.0	5.0	5.0	5.0	5.0	5.0	5.0
21 Other non-food	15.0	20.0	15.0	15.0	20.0	20.0	20.0	20.0
Gainers (*n* = 16 575)		50.7	17.2	9.5	23.3	34.1	7.3	16.3
Additional revenue 'first-round effects' – (as a percentage of existing revenue)		6.6	9.8	12.2	13.1	10.2	19.8	14.5

Note: Reforms IV–X reflect a set of proposed tax rates that would replace the existing 'effective tax' vector. The gainers represent the proportion of households benefiting from the reform. The estimates of additional revenue are based on the assumption of unchanged consumption, and are therefore only representative of 'first-round' effects. For revenue estimates taking into account demand responses, see table 7.8.

the Federal Bureau of Statistics. It contains information on household income and consumption patterns for several thousand rural and urban households. Note that for convenience of presentation the results are grouped in terms of half-deciles of households ranked by per capita expenditure, although the analysis of gainers and losers is conducted for each individual household.

For the description of the existing tax system we draw on calculations of 'effective taxes' at the level of eighty-seven sectors. This method incorporates problems such as evasion and the multiplicity of announced rates for various commodity groups, in that the analysis uses actual collections rather than announced rates. The eighty-seven sector effective taxes were merged to twenty-one broad commodity groups to match categories that we were able to identify in the consumer expenditure data in the 1984–5 HIES. In the absence of an input–output table for 1984–5, and since our estimates for effective taxes are for 1975–6, we update these on the assumptions (a) that the Leontief inverse would not have greatly changed over the period to 1984–5; and (b) that administration and/or enforcement were similar in the two years, so that nominal rates (collections as a proportion of the base) could be adjusted by a factor proportional to the change in announced rates. The resulting effective taxes are shown in tables 7.6 and 7.7.

For the equivalent variations we use the Stone–Geary utility function, and these have been estimated using the extended LES method (ELES), for five per capita expenditure groups in urban areas (i.e. five different sets of parameters for urban areas) and for a similar number for rural areas of Pakistan (see Ahmad and Ludlow, 1987, for a description of the method). As we argued in section 5.7 this is used essentially as a price index to average appropriately the effect of price changes in order to find an indicator of their effect on the welfare of different groups.

We now consider the revenue potential of the reforms. First, we examine reforms which are 'approximately neutral' in that they raise the same revenues as the existing system (with its effective taxes). Second, we analyse reforms which would raise additional revenue.

'Approximately neutral' revenue reforms

The tax vectors t^v described in table 7.6 are constrained to satisfy $t^{e'}X = t^{v'}X = R$, where X is the vector of aggregate purchases in the pre-reform period. We calculate t^v as follows. Some entries are constrained to be the same as in t^e. We assume throughout that agricultural goods would carry the same rate of tax (post-reform) as they do now (as an exempt, but not zero-rated sector, agriculture could not reclaim VAT on inputs). In the six reforms of table 7.6, we assume that 'gur', 'cigarettes', 'bidis', and 'other food' would continue to be taxed as before. This could be achieved by excises. Replacing the revenues from all other taxes in the manner defined by the above equation yields a VAT at an equal proportional rate of 14.1% for reform I. For reform II we introduce an excise of 5% on 'meat' which is, from the analysis of reform and from the point of view of distributional characteristics, an attractive candidate for additional taxation at higher levels of inequality aversion. This would permit a reduction in the VAT of half a percentage point. A similar excise tax on 'milk' would permit another half a percentage point in the VAT rate (reform III).

A second set of assumptions posits a two-level VAT for each of the three reforms, with the lower rate of around 10% for a set of commodities with high-ranking distributional characteristics: 'edible oils', 'sugar' (see the discussion in Bird, 1987, concerning the taxation of sugar, which had traditionally been considered a good candidate for additional taxation), 'hygiene and medicine', and 'housing, fuel and light'. This increases the VAT rate on the remaining commodities by roughly 2 percentage points for the three reforms (see reforms Ia, IIa and IIIa). Having calculated tax

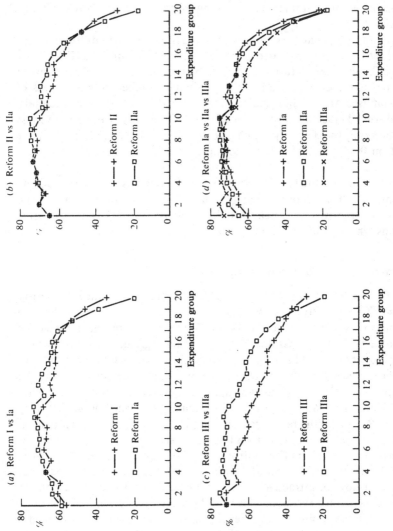

Fig. 7.2. Gainers and losers (equal revenue reforms). Households are grouped in terms of half-deciles of per capita expenditure. The vertical axis is the percentage of gainers.

vectors, t^v, defined in this way, we can then ask about their impact on different households and on revenue.

We begin our analysis of distributional impacts of the reforms in tables 7.6 and 7.7 by calculating gains and losses to households as if consumption were constant. As we have seen on a number of occasions previously, this would be correct if the changes were small. (We consider the calculations using equivalent variations, appropriate for non-marginal reforms, which are shown in table 7.9.) It appears that even reform I, with the equal proportional VAT, would make over 60% of households better off than in the current position (see table 7A.3a). The reduction in VAT rates, combined with a tax on 'meat' (reform II), appears to make more households better off, although the additional tax on 'milk' combined with a further reduction in VAT appears to make fewer people better off in comparison with the other reforms. However, there is a differential impact across different half-deciles. We observe that the middle income groups (half-deciles 4 to 13) gain most from reform I, and only for the top 10% do more than 50% of households lose. Reforms II and III are more egalitarian, in that a greater proportion of the poorest household groups gain. Thus, reform III, for which only 54% of all households gain (relative to around 61% for both reforms I and II), might be preferred in that a greater proportion of the bottom 20% are better off.

Figures 7.2(a–d) emphasise the differences between the equal revenue reforms. On the horizontal axis we have expenditure groups, with the percentage of gainers from the reforms on the vertical axis. The diagrams show the change in the percentage of gainers as we move from low to high expenditure groups. By focusing on equal revenue reforms we highlight the distributional effects of the change in rate structure. A central motivation for moving from the current tax system is to simplify the structure by introducing a less differentiated system. In going from reform I to reform III we increase the tax rate on commodities with relatively low distributional characteristics, i.e. those commodities to which richer groups allocate a high share of their expenditure. This enables us to set a lower rate for other commodities while keeping total revenue constant. A two-part VAT, along similar lines, is introduced in reforms Ia, IIa and IIIa compared to their counterparts (i.e. reforms I, II and III, respectively).

Examining the figures we can see that, on average, for each reform the percentage of gainers is higher in the poorer groups. So, in this sense, poorer groups are benefiting at the expense of richer groups for all reforms. Also, the more differentiated ('a' version) of each reform achieves 'greater redistribution' than its counterpart – note that to the left of income groups 18–19 for each reform, the 'a'-curve lies everywhere above its counterpart and, to the right of these groups, everywhere below.

Reform IIIa has the highest percentage of gainers in the poorest groups, with this percentage falling slowly at first but then more rapidly as one moves towards the richer groups. Figure 7.2d highlights this with the curve associated with reform IIIa being everywhere above those associated with reforms Ia and IIa for expenditure groups below 6–7, and below them for richer groups. On the other hand, reform Ia has percentage gainers increasing as we go from low to middle expenditure groups so that these latter groups are benefiting (at least in the sense of numbers who gain) more than the former from the transfer from the richer groups. This feature, although it exists, is not as prominent in reform IIa. Our interpretation of these results is reinforced by results presented in table 7A.5 which gives the average level of gain/loss across expenditure groups.

There are important sectoral differences in the impact of the reforms. While with each reform more rural households in total are made better off, more of the poorer urban households gain, particularly for reforms I and II. We have also conducted the exercise at the provincial level, although the results are not presented here. It would appear that rural/urban differences are rather more significant than the regional patterns, which roughly reflect the patterns of gainers and losers at the national level.

The two-tier VAT makes little difference in rural areas, given the consumption patterns, and particularly consumption of home-grown stocks. However, the effect of the two-tier VAT is to increase sharply the number of poor urban gainers and reduce the number of gainers among the top 5%.

We indicate in table 7A.5 the extent to which members of different expenditure groups gain or lose. We observe that, on average, for the equal revenue reforms described above, it is the top 10 to 20% that lose, although there are individual households that gain and lose in each half-decile. Whilst there are some gainers and losers within any group, there is a net gain for the poorer household groups in all reforms. This is most marked with the two-tier VAT, reform IIIa being the most attractive in this respect.

In practice, agricultural commodities would be exempt rather than zero-rated. In some cases effective subsidies on inputs might well cancel out the effects of taxes on inputs, and the agricultural sector might effectively be zero-rated for the most part, with a possibility of the wheat subsidy being maintained in some form. In this section we have assumed no change in the price of wheat. Further a movement from a positive effective tax on 'pulses' and 'maize' to effective zero-rating for the reasons mentioned above may not be plausible in all circumstances. However, calculating gainers and losers, keeping the positive effective tax on maize and pulses as the likely consequence of exempting this sector, rather than zero-rating it, does not greatly change the overall results. There are fewer gainers on average (down

Table 7.8. *Revenue consequences of the reforms*

Reform	'First round'	After demand shifts	Difference
		%	
I	10.45	11.72	+1.27
Ia	10.46	11.73	+1.27
II	10.44	11.58	+1.14
IIa	10.48	11.63	+1.15
III	10.49	11.58	+1.09
IIIa	10.46	11.54	+1.08
IV	11.16	12.80	+1.64
V	11.49	12.92	+1.43
VI	11.75	13.12	+1.37
VII	11.83	12.63	+0.80
VIII	11.53	12.34	+0.81
IX	12.54	13.91	+1.37
X	11.99	12.52	+0.53

Note: *All* percentages are percentages of total expenditure. Existing revenue is 10.47% of expenditure.

to 59% for reform I, as against almost 61% reported in table 7.6). The reduction in gainers is smaller for other reforms.

The revenue consequences of the different reforms, where we take account of the demand shifts as estimated through the LES systems for the different groups, are shown in table 7.8. After the demand shifts have been taken into account all changes from the effective tax to the new VAT rates show increased revenue. Reform IV which will lead to a 1.64% increase in revenue raised as a percentage of total expenditure looks attractive on both revenue and distributional grounds. Notice that an indirect tax which broadens the base would, in general, show total revenue greater than shown in the first round insofar as it leads to substitution away from newly taxed goods towards goods which are already taxed (where rates on goods already taxed are, on average, higher than the 'new' rate).

The VAT with additional revenue

Tax packages which can provide a substantial increase in revenue were described in table 7.7. In order to mitigate the distributional effects of the tax increases, we have concentrated on combinations of two-tier VAT structures, supplemented by the usual combination of excises, including the taxation of 'milk' and 'meat' in reforms V, VI, VII and IX.

Reform IV is a likely candidate for adoption, with a lower rate of 10% for 'edible oils', 'tea', 'housing, fuel and light', and 'clothing', and a standard rate of 20% (see table 7.7). On a 'first round' revenue calculation with consumption patterns unchanged, this would provide 6.6% additional revenue as compared with the current tax system and 50% of households would be made better off. The revenue calculated using the demand system represents 12.8% of expenditure as compared with an existing revenue around 10.5%. Thus the full effect of introducing reform IV would be an increase of revenue of around 22%.

Reform V maintains the 10% VAT only on 'edible oils', with a 15% rate for all other commodities, combined with an increased excise on 'bidis' (10%), and the 5% excise on 'meat' and 'milk'. This could raise 10% in additional revenue from indirect taxes ('first-round' calculation), but only 17% of households would benefit. However, the average loss for the poorest 20% of the population would be less than half of 1% of their expenditures, as against 1.6% for the top 5%. Reform VI is much the same as V, except that there is now a rate of 15% on all goods. An additional 5% excise is now levied on 'confectionery' and 'beverages', which were desirable candidates for additional taxation (from Ahmad and Stern, 1986, and the distributional characteristics above). This system could raise 12% in additional revenue ('first-round' effect) and around 10% of the population would be made better off: these would be largely concentrated in rural areas and amongst the poorest in the urban areas. The pattern of average losses by half-decile is still 'progressive': the richest 5% lose around 2% of their expenditures, and the poorest around 0.7% on average (see table 7A.5).

The treatment of the 'housing, fuel and light' consumption category is problematic in terms of tax classifications. Fuel and light for the poorest groups are principally wood and kerosene, which are relatively lightly taxed; and for the richer groups these include, *inter alia*, gas, petroleum and electricity. Thus, whilst we might wish to increase the tax on the items consumed relatively more by the rich, it might be neither feasible nor desirable to increase the tax on firewood, dung-cakes or (to some extent) kerosene. While in previous reforms we had allowed the tax on this sector to vary with the VAT, in reforms VII, VIII and X we set this to reflect a group of excises that would yield an average of 10% extra revenue ('first-round' calculation). While revenue increases only slightly for reform VII over reform VI, with a 20% VAT compensating for the reduced revenue from 'housing, fuel and light', the proportion of households gaining goes up to 23%. Again these are concentrated amongst the relatively poorer sections of the population.

A comparison of reform VIII with reform VII illustrates the effects of taxing 'milk'. While this tax could potentially add 3% in revenue, 10% of households who could have actually gained from reform VIII would be made worse off with the tax on 'milk'. This is an example of varying the tax on one commodity while holding others constant (subject, of course, to the limitations of the assumption of unchanged consumptions). The maximum revenue case we consider is that of a 20% VAT, with excises on 'housing, fuel and light' and 'bidis' held constant, but with the effective tax on 'edible oils' reduced to a 5% excise, in line with that proposed for 'milk' and 'meat'. This could raise 20% in additional revenue ('first-round' calculation) but most people would be negatively affected, albeit the rich more than the poor.

Using the modified LES estimates we again calculate the revenue effect of changing from the existing tax to the various reforms (see table 7.8). Note that in all cases the percentage of revenue raised rises after taking the demand patterns into account. Most striking is reform IV with a 1.64% increase over the 'first-round effects'. The lowest increase is reform X with only a 0.53% increase in revenue raised as a proportion of total expenditure.

Equivalent variations

The results displayed in tables 7A.3(a–c) and tables 7A.4(a–c) were based on unchanged consumptions and demand patterns. The assumption of unchanged consumption in the face of clearly non-marginal price changes, particularly in the revenue increasing cases, is, however, less than satisfactory. Here we examine the story of the earlier sections using the notion of equivalent variation (see section 5.7) for all the reforms considered above. The results are presented in table 7.9. However, since the results using the notion of equivalent variation use functions which are the same for broad categories of groups, we lose much of the detail of the earlier calculations.

It is apparent that the equivalent variations give similar results to the first-round approximations for gainers and losers for reforms Ia, IIa, IIIa. Reform IIIa again appears to be the most progressive. The others have the middle groups gaining more than the poorest, who are also net gainers. However, the differences between the equivalent variations and first-round effects are more marked for reforms I, II, III. This is because the price changes are more substantial in this case. Thus the linear approximation associated with taking first-round effects only is less satisfactory. Nevertheless the general picture is broadly the same.

The equivalent variations (see table 7.9) are estimated on the basis of step-wise ELES parameters evaluated for five sets of per capita expenditure

Table 7.9a. *Equivalent variations by half-decile for different reforms*

Per-capita expenditures half-deciles	I	Ia	II	IIa	III	Reforms IIIa	IV	V	VI	VII	VIII	IX	X
1	−1.458	0.231	−1.207	0.429	−1.291	0.350	0.777	−2.139	−2.394	2.098	2.435	−0.076	1.904
2	−1.445	0.381	−1.207	0.557	−1.386	0.397	0.787	−2.499	−2.810	1.956	2.453	−0.520	1.845
3	−1.437	0.472	−1.207	0.634	−1.443	0.425	0.792	−2.717	−3.062	1.871	2.464	−0.788	1.809
4	−1.431	0.540	−1.208	0.692	−1.486	0.446	0.797	−2.879	−3.250	1.807	2.472	−0.988	1.783
5	−1.714	0.848	−1.608	0.874	−2.065	0.432	1.563	−3.425	−3.834	2.492	3.330	−0.695	2.553
6	−1.739	0.868	−1.626	0.895	−2.090	0.456	1.482	−3.593	−4.037	2.410	3.288	−0.925	2.472
7	−1.761	0.887	−1.643	0.915	−2.112	0.477	1.409	−3.747	−4.224	2.334	3.250	−1.137	2.398
8	−1.783	0.905	−1.660	0.934	−2.135	0.499	1.336	−3.898	−4.407	2.259	3.212	−1.344	2.326
9	−1.510	1.725	−1.688	1.453	−2.553	0.596	2.622	−4.061	−4.768	2.574	3.892	−1.030	2.777
10	−1.542	1.739	−1.692	1.491	−2.571	0.628	2.513	−4.222	−4.967	2.528	3.895	−1.247	2.731
11	−1.587	1.759	−1.697	1.544	−2.596	0.674	2.360	−4.449	−5.249	2.464	3.900	−1.554	2.668
12	−1.626	1.776	−1.702	1.590	−2.618	0.713	2.228	−4.644	−5.491	2.408	3.904	−1.817	2.613
13	−2.767	1.044	−2.848	0.826	−3.559	0.161	1.749	−6.040	−6.761	2.684	4.060	−2.447	2.995
14	−2.894	0.974	−2.992	0.731	−3.747	0.040	1.482	−6.542	−7.340	2.400	3.893	−3.081	2.764
15	−3.018	0.906	−3.133	0.638	−3.930	−0.077	1.221	−7.030	−7.902	2.122	3.730	−3.697	2.539
16	−3.180	0.818	−3.316	0.517	−4.169	−0.230	0.881	−7.667	−8.636	1.761	3.517	−4.501	2.246
17	−5.309	1.177	−5.621	0.653	−6.427	−0.081	2.658	−10.414	−11.501	5.100	6.885	−3.687	5.595
18	−6.511	−0.288	−6.669	−0.682	−7.312	−1.178	0.179	−12.431	−13.612	2.990	4.858	−6.756	3.524
19	−8.683	−2.935	−8.561	−3.094	−8.911	−3.162	−4.301	−16.074	−17.427	−0.822	1.195	−12.300	−0.217
20	−17.347	−13.493	−16.111	−12.716	−15.292	−11.073	−22.174	−30.609	−32.643	−16.028	−13.414	−34.418	−15.143

Notes: (i) Changes in per capita consumption in rupees per month. These are expressed as percentages of expenditure in table 7.9b.
(ii) See table 7A.3a for definition of the groups.

Table 7.9b. *Equivalent variations as a percentage of expenditure*

Per-capita expenditures half-deciles	Reforms												
deciles	I	Ia	II	IIa	III	IIIa	IV	V	VI	VII	VIII	IX	X
1	−1.5	0.2	−1.2	0.4	−1.3	0.4	0.8	−2.2	−2.4	2.1	2.5	−0.1	1.9
2	−1.1	0.3	−1.0	0.4	−1.1	0.3	0.6	−2.0	−2.2	1.5	1.9	−0.4	1.5
3	−1.0	0.3	−0.8	0.4	−1.0	0.3	0.6	−1.9	−2.1	1.3	1.7	−0.5	1.3
4	−0.9	0.3	−0.8	0.4	−1.0	0.3	0.5	−1.8	−2.1	1.2	1.6	−0.6	1.1
5	−1.0	0.5	−1.0	0.5	−1.2	0.3	0.9	−2.0	−2.3	1.5	2.0	−0.4	1.5
6	−1.0	0.5	−0.9	0.5	−1.2	0.3	0.8	−2.0	−2.2	1.3	1.8	−0.5	1.4
7	−0.9	0.5	−0.8	0.5	−1.1	0.2	0.7	−1.9	−2.2	1.2	1.7	−0.6	1.2
8	−0.9	0.4	−0.8	0.5	−1.0	0.2	0.6	−1.9	−2.1	1.1	1.6	−0.7	1.1
9	−0.7	0.8	−0.8	0.7	−1.2	0.3	1.2	−1.8	−2.2	1.2	1.8	−0.5	1.3
10	−0.7	0.7	−0.7	0.6	−1.1	0.3	1.1	−1.8	−2.1	1.1	1.7	−0.5	1.2
11	−0.6	0.7	−0.7	0.6	−1.0	0.3	0.9	−1.8	−2.1	1.0	1.6	−0.6	1.1
12	−0.6	0.7	−0.6	0.6	−1.0	0.3	0.8	−1.8	−2.1	0.9	1.5	−0.7	1.0
13	−1.0	0.4	−1.0	0.3	−1.3	0.1	0.6	−2.1	−2.4	0.9	1.4	−0.9	1.1
14	−0.9	0.3	−1.0	0.2	−1.2	0.0	0.5	−2.1	−2.4	0.8	1.3	−1.0	0.9
15	−0.9	0.3	−0.9	0.2	−1.1	0.0	0.4	−2.1	−2.4	0.6	1.1	−1.1	0.8
16	−0.9	0.2	−0.9	0.1	−1.1	−0.1	0.2	−2.1	−2.3	0.5	1.0	−1.2	0.6
17	−1.3	0.3	−1.3	0.2	−1.5	0.0	0.6	−2.5	−2.8	1.2	1.7	−0.9	1.3
18	−1.3	−0.1	−1.4	−0.1	−1.5	−0.2	0.0	−2.5	−2.8	0.6	1.0	−1.4	0.7
19	−1.4	−0.5	−1.4	−0.5	−1.4	−0.5	−0.7	−2.6	−2.8	−0.1	0.2	−2.0	0.0
20	−1.5	−1.2	−1.4	−1.1	−1.3	−1.0	−1.9	−2.6	−2.8	−1.4	−1.2	−3.0	−1.3

Note: The table entries are changes in per capita consumption in rupees per month divided by the average expenditure per half-decile group.

groups at the group means, for urban and rural areas respectively. The use of these parameters generates average gains and losses for each expenditure group. This is similar to the average gain or loss estimated for each group in the first-round approximations described in previous sections and shown in table 7A.5. While it is possible, in principle, to generate a distribution of such gains and losses by household, the usefulness of such an exercise is limited by the fact that the demand parameters are group-specific rather than household-specific. For the purpose of exposition, therefore, we concentrate on the average gain/loss per expenditure group in assessing the effects of non-marginal tax changes.

One of the most interesting cases yielding additional revenue in the first-round approximations is that of reform IV. The first-round approximations suggested that 50% of households would be made better off with this tax change. The equivalent variations also confirm that this is likely to be a progressive reform. A substantial element in the gains made at the lower deciles relates to the relatively favourable treatment of 'edible oils', 'tea' and 'housing, fuel and light', all commodities which have high-ranking distributional characteristics (we have noted the problem with the treatment of the 'housing, fuel and light' sector in the previous subsection). Consequently, gains are displayed in all reforms in which the taxation of such goods is restricted, as illustrated further by reforms VII, VIII and X. Given that additional taxation is not imposed on 'housing, fuel and light' in reform X, and the excises on 'edible oils' are reduced, the equivalent variations for this reform suggest a relatively progressive sharing of the burden of the additional revenues, one that would be preferable to that imposed by the equal revenue reform I.

7.4 Concluding comments

We have in this chapter shown how two approaches can be made to work in the analysis of tax reform. The first to be applied was the theory of marginal reform which was used to identify desirable directions of movement from the status quo. There were three elements which governed that movement (i) the distributional characteristics of the goods which are candidates for increased or decreased taxation, (ii) the changing structure of consumer demand in response to taxation, and (iii) the relationship between market prices and shadow prices, which is important in capturing the consequences of changing demand structures. Amongst the different groups of assumptions considered in the analysis, the distributional characteristic played a particularly important role in governing the choice of directions for reform, provided that there is serious concern about the distribution of the costs and benefits of tax reform. The other elements played important roles too

and it must be emphasised that concentrating only on revenue consequences of reform as opposed to shadow revenue or the opportunity costs
'embodied' in the shifts of demand patterns can be very misleading. The
analysis helped identify important elements in the tax packages considered
in section 7.3 in our analysis of VAT and non-marginal reforms.

A number of developing countries have adopted the VAT in a relatively
short period of time with no loss of revenue. The analysis here suggests that
there is a strong case for a VAT in Pakistan. This would avoid many of the
difficulties facing the tax administration at present, and is likely to be easier
to administer in the long run. The benefits include, *inter alia*:
(i)   Non-distortionary taxation of inputs to domestic production;
(ii) Automatic remission of taxation for exports;
(iii) Possible lowering of tax rates with an increased tax base;
(iv) A possible incentive for self-policing and lower evasion which could be
      reinforced by computerised records;
(v)   When combined with a system of presumptive taxation for those who
      do not register it provides an incentive to keep proper accounts;
(vi) Provision of flexibility as the economy changes, in that frequent
      revisions for changes in the level of prices and relative prices would not
      usually be required; provision for high income elasticity can be built in
      by appropriate differentiation and it provides a straightforward means
      of increasing revenue across the board by the adjustment of only a few
      rates.

Although we have not been explicitly concerned with administration, the
benefits detailed above would be likely to offset the costs of adjustment and
transition. However, with respect to distribution, we have seen that the
VAT can also be designed to increase revenue in such a way that the rich
bear higher costs than the poor, some of whom might bear little cost or be
made better off.

We have seen the value of the analysis of reform in guiding the choice of a
desirable structure of indirect taxation. For policy-makers we have
illustrated how the evaluation of directions of reform might proceed,
without overly complicated models of the economy, and with the sort of
data that is now increasingly available (e.g. the programme of household
surveys being conducted by various international agencies, in addition to
national surveys conducted by many statistical offices around the world).
Finally, this section confirms that if it is seen as important to protect the
poor from damage in tax reform, then tax instruments can be designed to
meet this objective.

Appendix 7A.1

The ruling on the horizontal axes in figures 7.1(a–c) is that associated with the ranking of the social marginal costs of revenue when producer prices are proportional to shadow prices. The corresponding commodities are:

Figure 7.1a	*Figure 7.1b*	*Figure 7.1c*
(1) Edible oils	(1) Wheat	(1) Wheat
(2) Housing	(2) Tea	(2) Pulses
(3) Sugar	(3) Pulses	(3) Tea
(4) Other non-food	(4) Edible oils	(4) Edible oils
(5) Tea	(5) Sugar	(5) Sugar
(6) Clothing	(6) Rice	(6) Other foods
(7) Rice	(7) Other foods	(7) Rice
(8) Pulses	(8) Housing	(8) Clothing
(9) Other foods	(9) Clothing	(9) Vegetables
(10) Wheat	(10) Milk	(10) Housing
(11) Milk	(11) Vegetables	(11) Milk
(12) Vegetables	(12) Other non-food	(12) Other non-food
(13) Meat, fish and eggs	(13) Meat, fish and eggs	(13) Meat, fish and eggs

The ruling on the vertical axis is that associated with the ranking of the social marginal costs of shadow revenue using three separate tax vectors, i.e. effective taxes, shadow taxes (1) (generated using (WCF, ACF) = (0.9, 0.75)) and shadow taxes (2) (generated using (WCF, ACF) = (0.75, 0.5)). The rankings are those presented in tables 7.3b and 7.4b. Ranking number 1 represents the lowest in priority as a source for extra taxation.

Appendix 7A.2

Table 7A.1.

(a) *Spearman rank correlation coefficients for reform directions across inequality aversion parameters*

ε	0	0.5	1.0	2.0	5.0
	(i) *Effective taxes,* λ_i				
0	1.000				
0.5	0.698	1.000			
1.0	0.330	0.885	1.000		
2.0	0.291	0.857	0.989	1.000	
5.0	0.220	0.808	0.961	0.978	1.000

(ii) λ_i^v, $WCF=0.9$, $ACF=0.75$

0	1.000			
0.5	0.632	1.000		
1.0	0.500	0.950	1.000	
2.0	0.170	0.813	0.906	1.000
5.0	−0.100	0.582	0.764	0.934	1.000

(iii) λ_i^v, $WCF=0.75$, $ACF=0.5$

0	1.000			
0.5	0.654	1.000		
1.0	0.489	0.923	1.000	
2.0	0.330	0.863	0.950	1.000
5.0	−0.022	0.643	0.775	0.890	1.000

Note: The correlation coefficient for 13 elements with a significance level of 5% is 0.57.

(b) *Correlations of ranks across* λ_i^v *and* λ_i *for various* ε's

	λ_i^v		λ_i
	(a)	(b)	
$\varepsilon=0$			
(a)	1.000		−0.478
(b)	0.939	1.000	−0.363
$\varepsilon=0.5$			
(a)	1.000		−0.027
(b)	0.928	1.000	−0.154
$\varepsilon=1.0$			
(a)	1.000		0.368
(b)	0.961	1.000	0.225
$\varepsilon=2.0$			
(a)	1.000		0.648
(b)	0.928	1.000	0.423
$\varepsilon=5.0$			
(a)	1.000		0.874
(b)	0.961	1.000	0.758

Notes: (a) indicates a WCF of 0.9 and an ACF of 0.75.
(b) indicates a WCF of 0.75 and an ACF of 0.50.
(c) The correlation coefficient for 13 elements with a significance level of 5% is 0.57.

Table 7A.2. *Uncompensated own and cross-price elasticities*

	Wheat	Rice	Pulses	Meat	Milk	Veget	EdOils	Sugar	Tea	House	Cloth	OthFd	OthNF
Wheat	-0.236	-0.004	-0.003	0.002	-0.012	-0.002	-0.006	-0.005	-0.002	-0.001	-0.009	-0.005	0.005
Rice	-0.068	-0.600	-0.011	0.007	-0.039	-0.007	-0.021	-0.016	-0.006	-0.003	-0.030	-0.015	0.017
Pulses	-0.032	-0.006	-0.299	0.003	-0.018	-0.003	-0.010	-0.007	-0.003	-0.002	-0.014	-0.097	0.008
Meat	-0.150	-0.029	-0.024	-1.115	-0.087	-0.016	-0.047	-0.035	-0.014	-0.008	-0.066	-0.033	0.037
Milk	-0.078	-0.015	-0.012	0.008	-0.690	-0.008	-0.024	-0.018	-0.007	-0.004	-0.034	-0.017	0.019
Veget	-0.114	-0.022	-0.018	0.012	-0.066	-0.908	-0.035	-0.026	-0.010	-0.006	-0.050	-0.025	0.028
EdOils	-0.081	-0.016	-0.013	0.009	-0.047	-0.009	-0.693	-0.019	-0.007	-0.004	-0.036	-0.018	0.020
Sugar	-0.059	-0.011	-0.009	0.006	-0.034	-0.006	-0.018	-0.476	-0.005	-0.003	-0.028	-0.013	0.015
Tea	-0.065	-0.012	-0.010	0.007	-0.037	-0.007	-0.020	-0.015	-0.547	-0.003	-0.028	-0.014	0.016
Housing	-0.117	-0.022	-0.019	0.012	-0.068	-0.013	-0.036	-0.027	-0.010	-0.917	-0.051	-0.025	0.029
Clothing	-0.085	-0.016	-0.014	0.009	-0.049	-0.009	-0.026	-0.020	-0.008	-0.004	-0.708	-0.018	0.021
OthFd	-0.066	-0.013	-0.011	0.007	-0.038	-0.007	-0.020	-0.015	-0.006	-0.003	-0.029	0.581	0.016
OthNF	-0.148	-0.028	-0.024	0.015	-0.085	-0.016	-0.046	-0.034	-0.013	-0.007	-0.065	-0.032	-1.115

Notes: (i) Commodity titles correspond to those listed in table 7.1, note (iii), above.
(ii) The elasticities are those calculated by Ahmad and Ludlow (1987) for all Pakistan using the Micro-Nutrient Survey (1976) and a modified version of the linear expenditure system.
Source: Ahmad, Ludlow and Stern (1988), p. 300.

Table 7A.3. *Reforms I–IIIa: percentage of gainers in each group*

(a) *Total population*

Per capita expenditure groups	No. of households	Reform					
		I	Ia	II	IIa	III	IIIa
1	828	57.00	59.18	64.98	64.25	71.01	71.86
2	829	61.52	64.29	69.72	69.72	71.29	74.67
3	829	59.83	64.05	66.47	67.31	64.78	70.69
4	829	66.95	67.31	71.53	70.45	67.31	73.34
5	828	64.01	68.72	70.65	71.01	66.30	73.31
6	829	68.15	71.17	72.74	72.98	64.90	72.26
7	829	66.83	70.57	70.69	72.14	61.52	71.65
8	829	66.22	71.17	70.69	73.94	59.35	70.81
9	828	71.26	72.83	72.22	73.91	60.39	72.34
10	829	68.88	73.46	69.36	74.31	57.66	69.96
11	829	62.97	67.67	65.14	67.19	54.89	65.50
12	829	64.54	70.81	64.66	68.15	53.68	64.41
13	828	62.80	68.96	61.96	68.72	49.40	60.63
14	829	62.00	65.38	61.16	65.02	49.22	60.43
15	829	62.12	64.29	61.52	64.90	49.10	58.38
16	829	61.28	63.69	55.97	61.40	45.84	54.89
17	828	57.73	60.27	54.35	56.04	41.67	49.88
18	829	53.08	52.23	46.32	46.68	39.20	43.31
19	829	45.72	38.96	39.57	34.26	35.83	34.26
20	829	34.62	20.14	27.50	16.65	28.47	18.82
Total	16 575	60.87	62.76	61.86	62.95	54.59	61.57

(b) *Urban*

Per capita expenditure groups	No. of households	Reform					
		I	Ia	II	IIa	III	IIIa
1	372	66.67	80.38	70.70	82.26	56.18	76.61
2	373	70.24	84.99	72.92	83.38	53.89	77.48
3	373	70.51	83.11	72.65	83.91	51.74	75.60
4	373	69.17	78.82	70.24	81.50	46.38	72.65
5	373	72.39	84.72	73.99	83.38	49.06	73.46
6	373	69.17	80.97	68.90	80.97	45.84	70.24
7	373	66.49	79.09	64.08	75.34	44.77	65.15
8	373	64.34	76.68	61.66	71.31	43.43	63.00
9	373	62.20	76.94	59.52	75.60	39.95	61.66
10	373	60.86	73.19	58.98	70.51	40.75	58.45
11	373	61.39	70.78	57.91	66.49	37.80	55.23
12	373	60.32	67.29	58.71	68.10	40.75	56.57

Table 7A.3(b) (cont.)

Per capita expenditure groups	No. of households	Reform					
		I	Ia	II	IIa	III	IIIa
13	373	59.52	68.10	53.62	64.34	38.61	54.42
14	373	54.69	63.81	52.55	61.93	35.66	49.33
15	373	59.52	63.00	51.47	54.96	35.39	47.45
16	373	48.79	53.35	41.82	47.72	31.10	41.55
17	373	47.18	47.99	38.61	38.34	31.90	32.98
18	373	47.45	40.75	37.80	33.24	32.17	31.64
19	373	34.85	25.74	25.47	20.91	23.06	20.91
20	373	30.56	13.40	23.32	9.92	26.54	12.60
Total	7 459	58.81	65.65	55.74	62.70	40.25	54.85

(c) Rural

Per capita expenditure groups	No. of households	Reform					
		I	Ia	II	IIa	III	IIIa
1	455	56.04	58.46	63.08	63.74	72.97	72.09
2	456	57.89	57.02	68.64	63.60	72.15	71.71
3	456	60.96	62.50	68.86	67.98	73.03	74.12
4	456	57.89	59.87	67.11	63.82	68.42	69.08
5	456	59.87	60.31	65.35	64.25	68.42	71.93
6	455	66.15	62.86	70.99	66.59	71.65	71.65
7	456	62.06	60.96	70.18	65.79	70.83	71.49
8	456	65.13	65.79	70.61	68.42	69.74	71.71
9	456	65.13	63.16	70.83	65.13	70.18	68.20
10	456	64.91	64.69	71.05	66.89	67.54	69.30
11	455	68.13	68.79	73.63	71.87	70.77	73.41
12	456	69.96	65.35	71.49	67.32	69.08	71.93
13	456	68.64	66.67	70.61	68.64	67.11	71.27
14	456	60.31	58.55	66.45	61.40	63.60	65.57
15	456	64.91	63.38	67.11	63.82	63.38	64.91
16	455	65.05	63.96	66.59	64.40	61.54	65.05
17	456	63.38	57.24	64.69	61.62	61.40	63.82
18	456	65.79	59.43	63.38	59.43	59.21	57.89
19	456	60.09	53.73	58.33	52.41	55.70	54.61
20	456	48.90	35.09	48.25	35.96	49.78	41.67
Total	9 116	62.56	60.39	66.86	63.15	66.32	67.07

Notes: (i) Groups are sorted by per capita expenditure; group 1 is the poorest 5% on the basis of per capita expenditure while group 20 is the richest 5%.

(ii) I to IIIa are reforms which are 'approximately revenue neutral' – see text.

(iii) See table 7.6 for a description of the reforms, and the note to table 7.6.

Table 7A.4. *Reforms IV–X: percentage of gainers in each group*

(a) *Total population*

Per capita expenditure groups	No. of households	Reform						
		IV	V	VI	VII	VIII	IX	X
1	828	64.49	29.35	16.67	29.35	33.70	14.61	12.92
2	829	66.10	28.35	14.48	30.16	36.31	13.63	15.20
3	829	66.95	22.68	13.63	28.11	36.79	11.58	14.23
4	829	60.43	27.02	14.11	29.19	40.05	12.30	15.92
5	828	64.49	23.55	11.59	26.81	40.46	8.70	14.86
6	829	63.21	22.32	12.91	29.19	43.18	10.62	19.30
7	829	61.88	20.39	11.82	28.11	40.29	9.41	19.42
8	829	62.00	19.54	10.62	26.66	40.17	6.51	18.34
9	828	58.70	19.08	9.54	27.66	40.70	8.21	18.36
10	829	58.75	16.53	8.08	25.57	39.20	7.24	18.82
11	829	54.40	15.08	7.72	24.73	37.15	6.63	18.70
12	829	52.11	16.41	8.93	25.09	38.60	6.88	19.30
13	828	51.81	16.43	9.66	21.98	36.23	6.88	19.20
14	829	47.17	12.79	7.72	20.51	33.78	4.83	16.16
15	829	45.60	12.79	7.96	20.63	33.41	4.95	17.49
16	829	40.41	10.01	5.67	18.82	30.04	4.34	17.01
17	828	38.04	11.11	5.43	17.39	29.11	3.62	14.49
18	829	28.83	8.81	5.31	15.32	23.64	2.05	14.84
19	829	19.42	6.76	4.34	12.18	17.37	0.97	12.42
20	829	8.69	4.34	3.50	9.17	11.82	1.69	9.53
Total	16 575	50.67	17.16	9.48	23.33	34.10	7.28	16.33

(b) *Urban*

Per capita expenditure groups	No. of households	Reform						
		IV	V	VI	VII	VIII	IX	X
1	372	84.14	21.77	10.22	49.73	68.01	22.31	39.52
2	373	80.70	16.09	5.90	35.66	62.73	10.46	28.15
3	373	75.87	16.09	7.24	36.73	59.52	10.19	29.76
4	373	72.65	9.65	3.49	31.64	54.69	8.31	30.29
5	373	72.12	13.14	4.56	32.98	56.57	8.04	30.03
6	373	66.76	10.19	4.29	28.42	49.06	5.63	26.27
7	373	64.08	12.06	4.02	28.42	43.97	6.17	24.66
8	373	57.10	6.17	2.95	25.74	45.04	4.29	19.84
9	373	57.10	11.26	5.09	24.40	42.90	6.17	24.66
10	373	54.42	9.12	4.02	25.20	42.09	3.49	23.32
11	373	49.06	7.77	2.95	17.43	35.39	2.68	16.09
12	373	45.31	7.77	4.83	22.52	37.00	4.29	20.91
13	373	40.48	8.31	5.36	19.84	35.12	4.83	21.18
14	373	35.12	7.24	3.75	17.69	29.49	2.95	16.62

Table 7A.4(b) (cont.)

Per capita expenditure groups	No. of households	Reform						
		IV	V	VI	VII	VIII	IX	X
15	373	38.61	9.12	4.56	19.30	30.83	3.49	16.35
16	373	28.42	6.17	3.22	14.75	22.79	1.61	14.48
17	373	23.32	4.83	2.41	14.21	21.98	1.88	15.82
18	373	17.96	5.90	2.95	13.67	16.62	0.80	13.94
19	373	9.12	1.34	1.07	8.31	13.40	0.27	8.85
20	373	3.22	1.88	1.34	6.43	8.58	0.54	6.97
Total	7 459	48.77	9.29	4.21	23.65	38.79	5.42	21.38

(c) Rural

Per capita expenditure groups	No. of households	Reform						
		IV	V	VI	VII	VIII	IX	X
1	455	63.08	29.89	17.80	30.11	31.65	14.51	10.99
2	456	60.96	27.19	14.91	23.25	28.51	11.40	8.11
3	456	66.45	29.39	15.13	26.97	32.02	13.38	11.62
4	456	63.16	25.44	15.13	26.10	31.36	9.65	9.65
5	456	58.99	25.66	15.35	22.81	28.29	10.75	10.53
6	455	55.16	30.11	15.82	27.47	35.15	11.65	10.55
7	456	57.02	28.51	14.91	23.46	31.36	8.55	10.95
8	456	59.43	24.56	14.47	25.00	34.65	9.87	12.28
9	456	53.73	24.56	15.79	24.56	32.89	10.75	13.15
10	456	53.51	25.66	16.23	23.25	29.82	7.89	11.84
11	455	57.80	24.40	13.63	26.15	33.19	6.81	12.97
12	456	51.10	24.34	13.16	23.68	30.70	8.55	11.84
13	456	51.75	22.15	12.06	23.68	32.02	8.11	12.72
14	456	48.03	18.42	10.96	22.15	31.14	7.24	14.69
15	456	46.93	24.78	14.04	23.90	31.58	8.77	15.35
16	455	49.23	23.52	14.95	22.42	32.31	9.89	16.48
17	456	42.54	17.76	12.94	18.64	29.39	5.48	11.62
18	456	43.86	15.35	8.77	17.98	25.22	5.92	13.60
19	456	37.50	16.89	9.21	15.13	24.55	3.51	10.53
20	456	24.34	13.60	10.75	14.69	19.52	3.51	5.85
Total	9 116	52.23	23.61	13.80	23.07	30.27	8.81	12.19

Note: See tables 7.6 and 7.7.

Table 7A.5. *Average gains, maximum losses and maximum gains by per capita expenditure groups (Reforms: equal revenue reforms I to III)*

Per capita expenditure group	No. of households	Average loss/ gain	Maximum loss	Maximum gain
(a) Reform I		%	%	%
1	828	0.14	−4.79	5.50
2	829	0.22	−2.72	5.37
3	829	0.22	−3.57	5.02
4	829	0.28	−2.89	4.00
5	828	0.26	−2.43	3.40
6	829	0.30	−2.22	3.41
7	829	0.27	−3.36	3.46
8	829	0.27	−2.21	6.39
9	828	0.31	−4.42	4.16
10	829	0.26	−3.03	2.90
11	829	0.20	−4.56	3.60
12	829	0.23	−2.83	5.52
13	828	0.24	−2.18	4.56
14	829	0.19	−3.02	5.09
15	829	0.20	−3.25	4.51
16	829	0.17	−2.79	3.77
17	828	0.13	−2.98	6.76
18	829	0.01	−3.57	4.72
19	829	−0.13	−3.24	4.17
20	829	−0.41	−4.28	11.03
(b) Reform Ia				
1	828	0.24	−5.54	8.80
2	829	0.35	−4.02	6.92
3	829	0.37	−4.97	6.54
4	829	0.42	−4.40	5.39
5	828	0.43	−2.50	4.76
6	829	0.48	−3.46	4.51
7	829	0.45	−4.50	4.33
8	829	0.45	−2.90	8.26
9	828	0.50	−3.80	5.39
10	829	0.45	−3.87	4.00
11	829	0.36	−3.95	4.92
12	829	0.39	−3.46	6.52
13	828	0.42	−3.45	5.64
14	829	0.34	−4.39	7.00
15	829	0.35	−4.93	5.71
16	829	0.30	−3.97	5.32
17	828	0.22	−4.47	8.75
18	829	0.04	−5.18	5.73
19	829	−0.22	−4.78	5.47
20	829	−0.75	−6.40	13.46

Table 7A.5 (*cont.*)

Per capita expenditure group	No. of households	Average loss/ gain	Maximum loss	Maximum gain
(c) Reform II		%	%	%
1	828	0.31	−4.19	6.10
2	829	0.36	−2.39	5.81
3	829	0.33	−3.06	5.54
4	829	0.39	−2.66	4.31
5	828	0.35	−1.86	3.81
6	829	0.38	−2.05	3.61
7	829	0.35	−2.76	3.91
8	829	0.34	−1.83	6.93
9	828	0.38	−3.82	4.57
10	829	0.29	−2.65	3.07
11	829	0.25	−3.96	3.56
12	829	0.26	−2.29	5.97
13	828	0.26	−1.87	4.94
14	829	0.21	−2.78	5.24
15	829	0.23	−2.76	4.87
16	829	0.15	−2.33	4.06
17	828	0.10	−2.70	7.07
18	829	−0.03	−3.33	4.88
19	829	−0.20	−3.12	3.81
20	829	−0.46	−3.76	11.47
(d) Reform IIa				
1	828	0.38	−4.98	9.30
2	829	0.46	−3.70	7.30
3	829	0.45	−4.47	7.00
4	829	0.51	−4.08	5.66
5	828	0.50	−2.15	5.11
6	829	0.53	−3.34	4.67
7	829	0.50	−3.92	4.69
8	829	0.49	−2.53	8.72
9	828	0.54	−3.26	5.74
10	829	0.45	−3.51	4.07
11	829	0.38	−3.46	4.83
12	829	0.40	−3.19	6.92
13	828	0.41	−3.15	5.96
14	829	0.33	−4.16	7.08
15	829	0.35	−4.45	6.01
16	829	0.25	−3.50	5.56
17	828	0.17	−4.20	8.99
18	829	−0.03	−4.96	6.12
19	829	−0.32	−4.68	5.06
20	829	−0.82	−5.93	13.82

Table 7A.5 (*cont.*)

Per capita expenditure group	No. of households	Average loss/ gain	Maximum loss	Maximum gain
(e) *Reform III*		%	%	%
1	828	0.47	−3.79	6.50
2	829	0.44	−2.05	6.13
3	829	0.36	−2.72	5.89
4	829	0.39	−2.34	4.54
5	828	0.34	−2.00	4.08
6	829	0.33	−1.85	3.43
7	829	0.27	−2.36	4.20
8	829	0.26	−1.58	7.28
9	828	0.28	−3.42	4.84
10	829	0.18	−2.30	3.00
11	829	0.15	−3.56	3.79
12	829	0.15	−2.42	6.28
13	828	0.11	−2.16	4.94
14	829	0.07	−2.42	5.38
15	829	0.10	−2.44	4.82
16	829	−0.00	−2.16	3.94
17	828	−0.05	−2.40	7.42
18	829	−0.14	−3.40	5.21
19	829	−0.27	−2.94	4.06
20	829	−0.40	−3.49	11.83
(f) *Reform IIIa*				
1	828	0.61	−4.44	9.70
2	829	0.61	−3.24	7.65
3	829	0.54	−3.98	7.39
4	829	0.57	−3.57	5.90
5	828	0.54	−2.13	5.41
6	829	0.54	−2.88	4.51
7	829	0.48	−3.37	5.05
8	829	0.47	−2.07	9.12
9	828	0.50	−2.74	6.05
10	829	0.40	−3.03	4.07
11	829	0.34	−2.97	5.08
12	829	0.34	−2.96	7.28
13	828	0.31	−3.16	6.02
14	829	0.25	−3.66	7.24
15	829	0.28	−3.98	6.01
16	829	0.16	−3.23	5.41
17	828	0.09	−3.73	9.37
18	829	−0.07	−4.88	6.49
19	829	−0.32	−4.24	4.97
20	829	−0.68	−5.27	14.20

Table 7A.5 (*cont.*)

Note: Average loss/gain, maximum loss and maximum gain are the percentage change in expenditure under the reform. Average loss/gain is the average loss or gain (percent) of the households in the respective half-deciles occurring when changing from the existing tax to the reform. Maximum loss is the greatest loss (percent) that any household in that half-decile suffers under the reform. Maximum gain (percent) is the greatest gain that any household in that half-decile achieves under the reform.

Table 7A.6. *Average gains, maximum losses and maximum gains by per capita expenditure groups (Reforms: equal revenue reforms IV to X)*

Per capita expenditure group	No. of households	Average loss/ gain	Maximum loss	Maximum gain
(a) *Reform IV*		%	%	%
1	828	0.24	−3.60	3.53
2	829	0.22	−3.08	2.53
3	829	0.20	−5.53	2.46
4	829	0.13	−4.72	2.30
5	828	0.15	−3.77	2.62
6	829	0.14	−4.68	2.06
7	829	0.07	−5.92	2.03
8	829	0.08	−4.30	3.10
9	828	0.04	−6.08	2.99
10	829	0.03	−4.55	1.90
11	829	−0.07	−4.71	2.49
12	829	−0.11	−5.70	3.00
13	828	−0.11	−4.66	2.35
14	829	−0.21	−5.46	2.73
15	829	−0.24	−6.88	2.82
16	829	−0.34	−4.85	2.50
17	828	−0.45	−5.56	3.25
18	829	−0.66	−6.98	2.28
19	829	−1.04	−6.90	2.16
20	829	−1.91	−9.20	6.57
(b) *Reform V*				
1	828	−0.46	−5.69	4.60
2	829	−0.42	−3.35	4.55
3	829	−0.48	−4.03	4.32
4	829	−0.46	−3.85	3.77
5	828	−0.50	−3.01	3.18
6	829	−0.50	−3.10	2.71
7	829	−0.56	−4.26	2.96
8	829	−0.58	−2.55	5.70

Table 7A.6 (*cont.*)

Per capita expenditure group	No. of households	Average loss/ gain	Maximum loss	Maximum gain
		%	%	%
9	828	−0.57	−5.32	3.48
10	829	−0.67	−3.82	1.89
11	829	−0.74	−5.46	2.92
12	829	−0.74	−3.60	4.75
13	828	−0.77	−3.29	3.57
14	829	−0.83	−3.72	4.15
15	829	−0.83	−4.02	3.51
16	829	−0.93	−3.59	3.25
17	828	−1.00	−3.70	5.85
18	829	−1.14	−4.83	3.70
19	829	−1.33	−4.24	2.60
20	829	−1.63	−5.21	10.21
(c) *Reform VI*				
1	828	−0.77	−5.69	4.60
2	829	−0.72	−3.66	4.62
3	829	−0.78	−4.34	4.22
4	829	−0.75	−3.94	3.41
5	828	−0.79	−3.28	2.80
6	829	−0.79	−3.38	2.32
7	829	−0.85	−4.26	2.79
8	829	−0.87	−2.94	5.58
9	828	−0.86	−5.32	3.56
10	829	−0.94	−3.97	1.65
11	829	−1.01	−5.46	2.68
12	829	−1.02	−3.69	4.80
13	828	−1.05	−3.49	3.46
14	829	−1.12	−4.11	3.97
15	829	−1.12	−3.98	3.29
16	829	−1.21	−3.70	2.56
17	828	−1.28	−3.92	5.63
18	829	−1.41	−4.98	3.66
19	829	−1.59	−4.36	2.70
20	829	−1.83	−5.23	10.08
(d) *Reform VII*				
1	828	−0.80	−6.00	7.57
2	829	−0.72	−6.41	3.75
3	829	−0.71	−6.36	3.67
4	829	−0.72	−7.15	3.09
5	828	−0.67	−4.20	4.58

Table 7A.6 (*cont.*)

Per capita expenditure group	No. of households	Average loss/ gain	Maximum loss	Maximum gain
		%	%	%
6	829	−0.68	−5.60	2.58
7	829	−0.75	−6.70	3.11
8	829	−0.72	−5.86	2.41
9	828	−0.70	−6.09	3.16
10	829	−0.75	−5.18	2.62
11	829	−0.84	−5.88	3.04
12	829	−0.85	−6.27	2.41
13	828	−0.86	−6.12	2.61
14	829	−0.95	−6.16	2.99
15	829	−0.93	−7.34	3.68
16	829	−1.06	−6.03	3.61
17	828	−1.17	−6.93	3.07
18	829	−1.37	−8.00	2.37
19	829	−1.72	−7.23	3.20
20	829	−2.36	−9.43	6.55
(e) *Reform VIII*				
1	828	−0.71	−6.00	7.57
2	829	−0.57	−6.41	3.75
3	829	−0.50	−6.36	3.67
4	829	−0.48	−7.15	3.46
5	828	−0.43	−4.20	4.58
6	829	−0.40	−5.60	2.58
7	829	−0.44	−6.70	3.11
8	829	−0.41	−5.86	2.67
9	828	−0.38	−6.09	3.73
10	829	−0.41	−5.18	2.91
11	829	−0.50	−5.88	3.19
12	829	−0.51	−6.27	2.58
13	828	−0.48	−5.67	3.36
14	829	−0.57	−6.16	2.99
15	829	−0.56	−7.34	3.68
16	829	−0.67	−5.85	3.61
17	828	−0.78	−6.93	3.94
18	829	−1.02	−7.53	2.57
19	829	−1.40	−7.20	3.20
20	829	−2.14	−9.43	6.55
(f) *Reform IX*				
1	828	−1.41	−7.56	7.57
2	829	−1.29	−6.72	2.47

Table 7A.6 (*cont.*)

Per capita expenditure group	No. of households	Average loss/ gain	Maximum loss	Maximum gain
		%	%	%
3	829	−1.29	−6.69	3.03
4	829	−1.31	−7.52	1.88
5	828	−1.27	−4.71	3.76
6	829	−1.29	−5.95	1.34
7	829	−1.36	−7.55	2.89
8	829	−1.34	−6.06	2.24
9	828	−1.34	−6.39	2.19
10	829	−1.39	−6.05	1.81
11	829	−1.52	−6.30	1.91
12	829	−1.52	−6.54	1.87
13	828	−1.54	−6.33	1.49
14	829	−1.65	−6.25	1.90
15	829	−1.65	−7.55	2.08
16	829	−1.77	−6.34	2.03
17	828	−1.90	−7.05	2.32
18	829	−2.13	−8.17	1.43
19	829	−2.48	−7.46	0.99
20	829	−3.16	−9.52	6.37
(*g*) *Reform X*				
1	828	−1.54	−6.00	5.00
2	829	−1.33	−6.41	2.89
3	829	−1.22	−7.19	2.35
4	829	−1.18	−7.28	2.28
5	828	−1.10	−4.39	3.26
6	829	−1.02	−6.07	2.02
7	829	−1.07	−6.70	2.35
8	829	−1.01	−5.86	2.04
9	828	−0.98	−6.88	3.12
10	829	−0.98	−5.44	2.24
11	829	−1.06	−6.23	2.16
12	829	−1.06	−6.34	2.18
13	828	−1.00	−6.03	2.74
14	829	−1.11	−6.56	2.75
15	829	−1.06	−7.42	2.85
16	829	−1.17	−6.34	3.40
17	828	−1.23	−7.38	3.94
18	829	−1.44	−7.79	2.40
19	829	−1.75	−7.42	3.27
20	829	−2.36	−9.50	6.32

Note: See note to table 7A.5.

8 The taxation of land in Pakistan

8.1 Introduction

In this chapter we discuss four major options relating to the taxation of income from agriculture in Pakistan:

(i) an extension of the income-tax laws to agriculture;
(ii) the formal implementation of *ushr* (described below) as a tax on gross profit;
(iii) a tax on land or presumptive incomes from agriculture;
(iv) combinations of (ii) and (iii).

We shall be considering the merits of these four options with respect to incentives and distribution, uncertainty and insurance, and administration. Under (iv) we shall be considering three variants. We shall also discuss the attraction of both collecting and spending the revenue through a local administration.

Our primary concern is with the direct taxation of agriculture which, prior to the introduction of *ushr*, played a small and dwindling role in post-independence Pakistan. Where taxation of agriculture has occurred it has been largely through a price differential between domestic and international prices: this form of taxation now has much less importance. Indeed there are substantial subsidies on canal irrigation and electricity. Input subsidies including credit have also been provided to encourage the diffusion of high-yielding varieties of seeds and modern technologies. As we indicated in chapter 4 the methods and principles we have been applying have important lessons for agricultural pricing. Whilst one cannot analyse different aspects of taxation in complete isolation, our focus here is on direct taxation and we refer to the earlier chapters for pricing issues.

The direct taxation of land has a very long history in the sub-continent. As we emphasised in chapter 2, it was particularly prominent in Moghul times when it provided the bulk of Empire revenues and appeared to be of the order of 25 to 30% of national income (Kumar, 1982). It continued as a major source of finance until well into this century. We examine the history of the imposition of income-tax laws on agriculture in section 8.2, and highlight some experiments and discussions relating to this subject in the last hundred years or so. We assess briefly, and somewhat negatively, the potential for extending current income-tax laws to agriculture.

Ushr is paid as the result of a religious injunction and is an earmarked levy on gross output. There is an exemption limit of the equivalent of 948 kg of wheat per person and the levy applied in Pakistan is at 5% of output above this minimum. *Ushr* collections are, in principle, earmarked for 'protecting the vulnerable' and the collection and distribution are the responsibility of elected local committees. While it can provide for some of the major needs of social security expenditures at the local level, it is not formally an accrual to general revenues (whether provincial or central). In this sense *ushr* is in a somewhat different category from the other options. It has some attractive features, namely its earmarking (which may increase willingness to pay), moral or religious obligation, and the exemption limit determined in relation to a subsistence minimum (see section 8.5 below). The output basis allows one to avoid such problems as the differentiation of the rate structures according to land quality or poor harvests which are major difficulties with the land tax. *Ushr* is in principle designed to meet social expenditures on a 'class' of the vulnerable: the orphans, widows and disabled. Since its use has a widely respected purpose it is possible that this earmarking may make it easier to collect. This is an advantage which might be incorporated into other taxes, particularly locally raised, and we return to this issue in section 8.5.

Section 8.3 examines the arguments for basing taxation on productivity of agricultural land owned. In summary: there are only small disincentive effects, it provides for greater equity across different kinds of households, the base is generally easier to measure than other possibilities (such as output or income), the tax is close in spirit to the presumptive methods that might be effective for non-agricultural activities (see Ahmad and Stern, 1987b), and finally it can be integrated to fit well with other taxes, particularly the wealth tax on non-agricultural property. On the other hand a tax or levy such as *ushr* based on actual output has some desirable insurance properties (in bad years you pay less and in good years more) although the measurement of current output presents major problems. We consider different combinations of *ushr* and a land tax and conclude that, mainly for practical reasons, deductibility of *ushr* against the land tax would be the attractive option. Section 8.4 assesses the revenue potential and distributional consequences of possible land taxes. The favourable impact on distribution would be reinforced by the provision of social expenditures that are targeted towards meeting the requirements of the poor. The design and administrative implications of such a system are discussed briefly in section 8.5. The final section contains some concluding comments.

8.2 The historical context, income tax laws and problems with the existing system

Extensions of the income tax laws to cover agricultural incomes is a subject of some debate in Pakistan. A large proportion of the households in rural areas in Pakistan are peasant producers with small cash purchases. Under these circumstances, it might be very difficult to arrive at a reliable figure for net taxable income under the laws, since the cost of inputs, including labour, is deductible. Costs are difficult to determine, given the widespread use of family labour and other non-wage operating systems. Physical output itself is very difficult to observe, particularly since much of it is consumed directly. Even if physical outputs could be measured, valuation for tax purposes would not be easy since it is not evident which prices should apply – these vary considerably across seasons and between regions. Gross sales as a proxy for the value of output is not particularly helpful, since stocks can be adjusted in addition to variations in the amounts consumed. Thus there are formidable problems in determining both gross output and net income.

Taxable agricultural income is an elusive concept in all except a few highly commercialised countries, such as the USA and the UK. Even in France the authorities resort to presumptive methods to tax agriculture. Such methods assign a presumed income to the land and are therefore based on potential rather than actual outcomes. This would be associated with average productivities of a given type of land in a particular region over the years and is therefore closely linked to the value of the land. This is the base that would be particularly suitable in the case of Pakistan. The difficulties with other methods constitute only part of the argument in favour of such taxation and some other advantages are examined in section 8.3 below.

A brief digression on the history of agricultural income taxation in the sub-continent is helpful in understanding possibilities and difficulties. Income tax laws were introduced after the Crown took over administration from the East India Company in 1858. Mr James Wilson, the first Finance Member, imposed the income tax laws on non-agricultural and agricultural activities alike in 1860. However, on agriculture the levy was *presumptive*: it was assumed that profits from land were one-third of land revenue. Land revenue, where it was 'permanently settled', was a fixed yearly sum (see chapter 2). Persons paying land revenue of less than Rs 600 per year were exempt from agricultural income taxes. The Act expired in 1865, and was revived during the period 1869–73 to meet additional expenditures. Following the famine of 1876–7, there was a revival of direct taxation and a cess on land was imposed (see, e.g., Banerjea, 1930, Kumar, 1982, and Raychauduri and Habib, 1982).

Agriculture received complete exemption from the income tax during the period 1886–1935. There was, however, a consolidation of income tax laws in 1918, and there was a move to include net agricultural income in excess of Rs 1000 in the determination of the marginal tax rate on non-agricultural income. However, Mr Srikanth Ray, a rich landowner, moved an amendment to exclude what he regarded as an introduction of the agricultural income tax through the back door. It is interesting to note that the amendment 'was opposed by men of an advanced school of thought like M. A. Jinnah, Srinivas Shastri, T. Bahadur Sapu and B. N. Sharma' (Banerjea, 1930, p. 133). Notwithstanding the concerns of Jinnah and the others, in the resulting legislation (the Income Tax Act, 1922) agricultural income was exempted completely. In the Government of India Act of 1935, which is the basis of the taxation laws of countries in the sub-continent to this day, the taxation of agricultural income was made a provincial responsibility. Bihar was the first state to introduce this tax in 1938 and Assam followed in 1939, with Bengal in 1944, Orissa in 1948, and Mysore in 1955. Uttar Pradesh introduced such a law in 1948 and repealed it in 1957. Hyderabad tried it during 1950–6 and Rajasthan, 1956–60. It is reported that in Bihar and Orissa, the agricultural income tax amounts to less than 1% of state tax revenue. Uttar Pradesh and Rajasthan achieved 1% of state tax revenue but abolished it because of high collection costs. In Assam and West Bengal, however, there have been more substantial yields from the tax because of the tea plantations. Thus extensions of the income tax laws to agriculture, except where there are commercial activities such as plantations, does not appear to have been a fruitful source of additional revenue (see Joshi et al., 1968).

In Pakistan, as in the Government of India Act of 1935, the taxation of agricultural income has not been part of the Federal Legislative List. In East Pakistan (Bangladesh, since 1971) the provisions of the Bengal Agricultural Income Tax Act (Bengal Act VI of 1944) continued to apply. In the four provinces which constitute West Pakistan (which was one province during the period 1955–70), agricultural taxation remained a provincial subject. This was reflected in Article 47 of the 1973 Constitution, which placed 'Taxes on income other than agricultural income' as being part of the Federal List. There was an unsuccessful attempt to introduce an agricultural income tax, through the 1977 Finance (Supplementary) Act (I of 1977, 9 January 1977) which would have involved amending the 1922 Income Tax Act (clause vii of Section 4(3)) under which agricultural income has been exempted. This failed since it would have been a retrospective amendment to the Constitution.

The 'wealth tax' was introduced in Pakistan, on an individual basis, in the fiscal year 1963–4, but the value of agricultural land was not included. However, the Act was partially extended in 1969 to cover industrialists and businessmen who had been avoiding payment of income tax by attributing to agriculture income from other sources. In the Finance Minister's Budget speech of 1969 it was stated that the extension was intended to tax those who owned

large areas of agricultural land in as much as the wealth tax record of such assessees does not provide any material for cross-reference and verification in connection with the levy of income tax. It has, therefore, been decided to include, for purposes of Wealth Tax, the value of agricultural land in the wealth of a person who is *otherwise liable to Income Tax or Wealth Tax* [emphasis added].

Finance Minister's speech, 1969

Crops, trees and houses/buildings on agricultural land were excluded, and an exemption of Rs 100 000 was allowed. The basis for the determination of the value of agricultural land was ten times the produce index unit (PIU), a rough measure of the gross value of normal production per acre based on a judgement of land quality. These PIUs were estimated in connection with the rehabilitation of refugees (under the Pakistan Rehabilitation Act, 1956 (XLII of 1956) and the Baluchistan Rehabilitation Regulation, 1950 (II of 1950)). Thus apart from applying to a very small subset of land-owners (those who paid income or wealth tax on non-agricultural income or property) the wealth tax on agriculture was based on rather dated valuations of land.

It is interesting to note that the Wealth Tax (Amendment) Ordinance, 1979 (Ordinance XXXVIII of 1979) changed the base of the tax for non-agricultural immovable property from an individual assessee to the assessee, the spouse and any dependent children:

any immovable property *other than agricultural land*, owned by the spouse or any dependent children shall be deemed to belong to the assessee: provided that any immovable property so deemed to belong to the assessee shall not be included in the net wealth of the spouse or dependent child of the assessee . . .

However, the wording does not appear to rule out the option of separate assessment for tax purposes.

The fact that it is impractical to extend the income tax laws to agriculture does not imply that rich individuals involved in the agricultural sector should be favoured over less well-off households in non-agricultural activities. It is clear that during the last twenty years or so, in the post-

Green Revolution period, large farmers have had rapid increases in untaxed incomes. Land revenue degenerated into a system of harassment and corruption and one that did not raise very much revenue (Rs 226 million collected in 1980–1). The problems of exempting agriculture from the income tax do not consist only of the omission of some sources of revenue. Resistance to tax payment amongst non-agricultural taxpayers is encouraged. And there is evidence that industrialists and businessmen invested in agriculture to evade income taxes. The amendment to the wealth tax laws was an attempt to close this loophole. The exemptions together with the increasing role of black money and rising agricultural productivity have contributed substantially to the rapid rise in land prices, bestowing enormous capital gains to those lucky enough to have inherited or been given land, or to have acquired it many years ago.

The difficulties with alternatives, the historical record and the deficiencies of the current system all lead to a consideration of presumptive income based on agricultural holdings as the appropriate basis for taxation in agriculture.

8.3   The design of a land tax

The principles of land taxation were discussed in chapter 4. Here we examine the problems of designing a feasible land tax in the context of Pakistan. We consider, for different versions, the theoretical advantages, the practical problems of administration and the integration with *ushr*.

In principle the advantages of land taxation are that it has small costs in terms of disincentives, attractive distributional effects and a base which is measured with less difficulty than other bases. A disadvantage, in principle, is that if it is a fixed payment it would make no allowance for poor harvests – thus it contains no insurance element. A tax based on output, such as *ushr*, would embody an element of insurance. In theory, one would like a combination of the two (see, e.g., Hoff, 1989).

Let us examine how these principles apply to the situation in Pakistan. The basis of the tax, we shall suggest, should be the potential income of the land, i.e. one would seek a basis analogous to produce index units (PIUs) designed to reflect the quality of the land. These could be assessed periodically (every five years or so) and would not require the annual valuation of output. Annual valuation is likely to present insurmountable problems of administration. Given that the tax rate is likely to be fairly low (of the order of 7% of gross output at the maximum; see below) the disincentive to land improvement is likely to be minor. The productivity gains to irrigation for previously unirrigated land, for example, are likely to far exceed such a figure and such decisions would depend more on availability of canal schemes and finance rather than such a tax rate. None the less there would be a marginal effect and there is little available evidence to suggest how large this might be.

Given the very unequal distribution of land ownership in Pakistan the distributional impact is likely to be favourable relative to, say, most indirect taxes, particularly where an exemption limit is allowed which would relieve small farmers of payments. There would be substantial administrative savings from exempting small farmers in the reduction in the number of taxpayers. Some quantitative estimates are provided in the next section. On the other hand, an exemption limit gives the opportunity for larger farmers to divide their holdings within the extended family to reduce the tax burden. This is a perilous game for a landowner to play, however, as relatives might have a predilection to assert their own rights to the land. Indeed, litigation within families over land ownership is not uncommon. Generally there is a very powerful individual incentive to ensure that legal rights to land are properly established. One could make it a condition of continued ownership of a piece of land that land tax had been fully paid; if it had not, the state could take over the ownership of the land. There are few other taxes which allow this kind of administrative sanction.

In some ways it is the difficulty of evading land taxes, if administered with sufficient political backing, that makes that political backing so hard to come by. Opposition to a tax is at its most fierce where it cannot be evaded or avoided. Elimination of land taxes from the policy agenda would be a costly error for a community to make from the point of view of economic analysis. If revenue is to be raised one is better off having it raised in a manner such as the land tax which has the smallest distortions. But a group within the community *is* acting in its own best interests if it opposes a tax directed at them and shifts the burden to others. The problem of political acceptability is compounded where payment involves an assessee handing over money, as opposed to it being withheld before receipt, or where it is not concealed behind a price (as in many indirect taxes). There appears to be a 'cussed' law of taxation that the best taxes from the economic point of view are likely to raise the most hostility, and the land tax is perhaps the clearest example. Hence politicians like taxes to be as concealed as possible. Our task here, however, is to bring out the economic advantages and to show that it could work.

We have argued that the basis should be revised PIUs with an exemption limit. To avoid giving too much incentive to divide holdings, rates could be at a constant level on PIUs above the exemption limit. More detailed discussion of the operation is provided in the next two sections and here we consider the relationship with *ushr*. There are a number of possible ways of combining the two forms of taxation. We consider three here. These are (i) the crediting of *ushr* payments against land tax, (ii) a higher rate of land tax for those who have not paid *ushr*, and (iii) separation of *ushr* and the land tax so that both are collected without formal interaction.

We shall suppose that it would not be politically possible or theoretically or administratively desirable to make *ushr* the sole form of land taxation. As we have remarked, *ushr* is not part of the formal tax system and the religious groups would possibly not regard such a formal integration to be acceptable. Even if it were, it would be unattractive to make it the sole source of land taxation. Output measurement, as we have suggested, is very difficult and disincentives to apply inputs may be significant. Notice that the insurance attractions of an output tax depend on the measurement of the outputs of each individual farmer. It would be inadequate to index normal output for the climatic conditions since much risk is individual as well as systemic (see, e.g., Lanjouw and Stern, 1989). This problem will be a handicap to any serious attempt to provide an insurance element in agricultural tax policy.

We suggest that the first of the combinations, crediting *ushr* payments against the land tax, is likely to be the least problematic. It would simply require a statement from the *ushr* authorities as to the amount actually paid, which would be deducted from the land tax liability. Fraudulent pieces of paper might occasionally appear but it is, in principle, something which could be checked with the *ushr* authorities. If payments of *ushr* were thereby encouraged this would not be considered a problem and any feeling of unfairness by honest *ushr* payers that they were being doubly taxed would be mitigated. A disadvantage, in principle, is that the insurance element in *ushr* would be lost. The ultimate payment (by an honest taxpayer) would simply be the fixed land tax.

The second combination, that of *ushr* and land tax through a lower land tax for those who have paid *ushr*, would retain some insurance element. There would, however, be complications. One would have to know for the land tax whether *ushr* had been paid in *full*, and this may be difficult for the authorities to verify. In the preceding scheme it would be only the amount actually paid which would be certified. Further there would be the possibility of very big fluctuations in *ushr* and land tax payments since in a good year it would be attractive to pay land tax and in a bad year *ushr*. This would severely hamper the charitable activities based on *ushr*.

The third approach, the separation of a land tax and *ushr* with a low rate for the former, is likely to prove either unacceptable to taxpayers if the land tax is set too high, or unsatisfactory for revenue purposes if the rate of land tax is too low. If honest *ushr* payers (those who pay 5% of gross output apart from exemption) paid a further 7% land tax they would feel aggrieved and the scheme would probably be successfully opposed, notwithstanding

Table 8.1. *Land distribution and potential agricultural property- or land-tax base*

Acres	Ownership holdings		Operational holding			Base for land tax (12.5 acres exempt)				
	No. %	Area %	No. %	Farm area %	Cultivated area %	No. '000	Average holding acres	Total area '000 acres	Taxable base[b] '000 acres	Average tax rate[c] %
Under 1.0	8	—[a]	5	—[a]	—[a]	exempt				
1.0—< 2.5	19	3	13	2	2					
2.5—< 5.0	20	6	17	5	6					
5.0—< 7.5	15	7	17	9	10					
7.5—< 12.5	15	12	23	19	21					
12.5—< 25.0	13	19	17	25	26	499.5	16.57	8 276	2 032.97	1.9
25.0—< 50.0	6	17	6	16	18	229.7	31.92	7 333	4 460.77	4.6
50.0—<150.0	3	20	2	15	13	118.7	73.49	8 723	7 298.86	6.4
150 and over	1	17	—[a]	—[a]	6	24.8	301.77	7 484	7 174.00	7.3
	100	100	100	100	100	872.7			20 966.60	
Total (millions)	3.79	44.4 acres	4.07	47.1 acres	39.2 acres					

Notes: [a] Less than 0.5%.
[b] Taxable base determined with an exemption level of 12.5 acres.
[c] The average tax rate is $\tau \dfrac{(L_o - L_{ex})}{L_o}$, where L_o is land owned, L_{ex} the exemption limit and τ the land tax in rupees per acre.
Source: Government of Pakistan Agricultural Census Organisation (1980).

that a small fraction of those eligible pay *ushr* in full. If on the other hand the scheme were designed on the assumption that *ushr* was paid in full, then a rate of 2 or 3% for the land tax might be proposed. This would raise insufficient revenue to be worth the bother.

Income tax authorities have the power to use presumptive methods in assessing tax liability on non-agricultural income. Further, the enabling provisions for the short-lived capacity tax are still in place and permit excise tax administrators to assess liability on a number of 'reasonable' criteria. Thus the principles involved in our proposals already form part of the enabling conditions in the tax laws. Insofar as presumptive income is linked to the value of the land, this is similar to the provisions of the wealth tax.

We conclude from this discussion that the best combination for the Pakistan context would be a land tax based on PIUs (suitably revised), with an exemption level, and with deductibility of *ushr*. We examine the revenue and distributional consequences and some administrative considerations in the next two sections.

8.4 Potential revenues and distributional impact

Different versions of possible land taxes and their potential for generation of revenues, together with their effects on households in different circumstances, are examined in this section. The distributions of land ownership, farm-holdings and cultivated area in Pakistan from the Agricultural Census of 1980 (ACO) are shown in table 8.1. For some time, 12.5 acres has been popularly taken to be a 'benchmark' (for subsistence) holding in terms of such notions as a 'minimum scale' in Pakistan. Note that, in contrast, 5-acre holdings are considered large in parts of India and Bangladesh. In Pakistan the ACO reported that 77% of land ownership holdings were less than 12.5 acres, but that this accounted for less than 30% of the area owned. Similarly, for area operated, 75% of farms were less than 12.5 acres, accounting for 35% of the farm area, and 39% of the cultivated area.

An exemption of 12.5 acres of land (we discuss land quality below) would exclude around 3 million holdings and around 12 million acres. With this exemption around 870 000 holdings would, in principle, be subject to tax, and if the tax is applied only to land held in excess of the exemption limit, the taxable base is reduced to 21 million acres or around half the owned area.

An increase in the exemption limit to 25 acres would reduce the taxable base to 14.2 million acres. For an exemption limit of 50 acres, the base would be further reduced to around 9 million acres (see table 8.2). If the exemption limit is increased from 12.5 to 50 acres, and if a fixed revenue is to be raised, this would imply a 2.5-fold increase in the tax rate per assessable

Table 8.2. *Alternative exemption limits*

| | Exemption limit | | | |
| | 25 acres | | 50 acres | |
Acres	Taxable holding (average)	Taxable base (t_b) (acres '000)	Taxable holding (average)	Taxable base (t_b) (acres '000)
Under 25	———————————————— exempt ————————————————			
25% < 50	6.92	1 598.5	————— exempt —————	
50–<150	48.49	5 755.8	23.49	2 788.3
150 and over	276.77	6 863.9	251.77	6 243.9
Total		14 209.2		9 032.2

Note: If the exemption limit is L_{ex}, then the tax base for a household owning L_o is $L_o - L_{ex}$. The tax base is the sum of $L_o - L_{ex}$ over households for which this number is positive. Revenues are the land tax per acre times the base.
Source: Based on table 8.1.

acre, on average. The consequence would be a greater incentive to evade the tax.

In determining the level of land tax per assessable acre we conduct the analysis in terms of information for 1980–1 as the ACO figures relate to that year. Some updating for more recent years is also provided. For 1980–1, we estimate the gross value of output to have been approximately Rs 85 000 million (see Ahmad, Barrett and Coady, 1985). This yields an *average* output (per acre owned) of around Rs 2000 per annum (see table 8.3).

A tax on agricultural land at an average of Rs 150 per acre applied to 1980–1 holdings would have a potential yield of Rs 3145 million. A tax of Rs 150 per acre for 1980–1 would translate into Rs 250 per acre for 1987–8 and would yield around Rs 5200 million. The tax corresponds to a levy of 7.5% of the output from those acres above the exemption limit and a levy of 5% on total output. An average holding in the 12.5–25 acre group of 16.6 acres, would pay tax on 4.07 acres (thus, for 1980–1, Rs 610.5 on an average output of Rs 32 750, or an average tax rate of under 2%). In the 150+ acre group, the average landowner (owning 301 acres) would have an average tax rate of 7.3%, approaching the 7.5% limit. Thus the rate structure would not appear to be excessive, and through the exemption level the incidence is only on the relatively wealthy. If, for example, land is valued at Rs 25 000 per acre then no one with agricultural wealth of less than Rs 112 500 would be liable (compared with an exemption of Rs 300 000 for wealth purposes).

Table 8.3. *Potential revenues from a land tax*

	1980–1	1987–8
Gross value of output per acre (Rs)	1 973	3 424
Tax per acre (average) (Rs)	150	250
Implied revenue		
Base > 12.5 acres (Rs million)	3 145	5 242
Base > 25 acres (Rs million)	2 131	3 552
Base > 50 acres (Rs million)	1 355	2 258
Income and corporation tax (Rs million)	7 028	11 500
Provincial tax revenues (Rs million)	2 268	4 000
of which land revenue	226	
Federal development grants to provinces (Rs million)	2 328	

Source: (i) Revenue and grant figures from the Government of Pakistan, Ministry of Finance, *Economic Survey* (various).

(ii) Gross value of output has been calculated using the methods described in Ahmad, Barrett and Coady (1985).

The revenue of more than Rs 3000 million that could have been generated with full implementation may be compared with Rs 2268 million for total provincial tax revenues in 1980–1 or Rs 7000 million approximately that were collected on account of the income and corporation taxes in 1980–1 (see table 8.3) largely from the (smaller) urban population. The wealth tax yielded a paltry Rs 110 million. Thus, whilst the tax on agricultural land would, if fully collected, yield less than half the amount collected by the direct taxes on non-agricultural income, it would yield more than all provincial taxes (including land revenue) put together. The Rs 3227 million potential may also be compared with federal grants to provincial governments of Rs 2328 million on account of the development budget in 1980–1.

It is desirable to keep the definition of the base as simple as possible, and land owned can be clearly defined and documented. The land distribution in table 8.1 was generated by the 1980 Agricultural Census. Recall that Pakistan has already had major land reforms in the sixties and seventies and that many landowners have already taken evasive action, i.e. registering land in the names of friends and relatives. A tax with the low rates suggested will not have much impact on the registration of titles, as this can be a double-edged weapon (the title-holder might actually claim the land). However, this may happen to some extent, and would be more attractive if the land tax was considered too high. None the less, if land sales are encouraged this may not be altogether undesirable as land prices may be forced down (below what they would otherwise have been). If an assessee, spouse(s) and dependent children were to be treated as a single unit for the purpose of the determination of the exemption limit then this would increase the taxable base over the example in table 8.1.

The tax revenue has been calculated on the assumption that land-holdings for each household within each farm size group are the average for that farm size group. If land quality did not matter there would be no problem and the tax base would simply be the number of acres (in excess of the exemption limit) that a household owns. However, potential income is related to land quality and there may be substantial differences, for example, between an acre of irrigated and one of non-irrigated land. Produce index units (PIU) should be useful as weights, and could be designed so that the tax on the 'average' number of units per acre is equal to the average tax per acre, in the above calculations. In order to reduce disincentive effects, and to encourage improvements in productivity, the PIUs would need to be fixed for a duration of say five years. More frequent revisions would also be difficult in administrative terms.

8.5   Administration and the financing of local expenditures

In this section we examine some administrative aspects of a land tax (with crediting of *ushr* liability). We also examine possible advantages of linking the land tax raised to local expenditures and some implications for central revenues and expenditures.

The administration of the tax would be greatly facilitated if land records were computerised. Thus changes in ownership could be speedily known to the central record authorities. We suppose that individuals regard the establishment of ownership as sufficiently important for them not to change the records in order to evade a tax equivalent to only a small proportion of produce. Similarly, if the results of a more recent cadastral survey (the 1956 produce index units are outdated because, for example, of the effects of major investments in the Indus Basin which have occurred since the Mangla and Tarbela dams, as well as extended irrigation, both public and private) are also computerised, changes in the quality of land could also be gauged quickly, and the two files merged for the purpose of tax administration. The work involved would, no doubt, be substantial but corresponding surveys have been conducted in the past and information technology such as satellite monitoring and improved land assessment capabilities will in some respects make the task easier. There would also be advantages in a number of other respects (for example, legal, credit allocation or water charging) arising from up-to-date land records.

There may be considerable advantages in the earmarking of tax collections for social and economic investments in the areas in which the taxes are collected. To some extent this is supposed to happen with *ushr*, which is intended to be used for charitable poor relief. It is levied at a rate of 5% on the value of output: the levy is restricted to a base of 75% of the value of production, or two-thirds if tube-wells are not used, together with an exemption (see Jetha *et al.*, 1984). If *ushr* payments are made deductible from the land tax then this might also reduce the disinclination to pay *ushr* that has become apparent.

The linking with *ushr* itself provides an argument for raising and spending revenue locally. The former for administrative reasons – the two authorities could keep in close contact – and the latter so that any diversion from one to the other is not seen as a transfer out of the locality.

The spending of the revenues locally might also increase willingness to pay and the visible fruits of revenue spent locally might also put some moral pressure on people to make 'contributions'. Further, the central pool might be viewed locally as a bottomless sink drained by bureaucrats, defence ministers and the like. Earmarking may reduce diversion of funds by the Centre from the locality. Hence earmarking might help in raising revenue, ensuring that it is kept in the locality and that it is spent on the poor. This is also analogous to the earmarking of certain tax collections for social security purposes in developed countries.

The earmarking of funds for use where collected not only has implications for the general development of the rural areas, but also for transfers from the Centre to cover local expenditures on health, education and social infrastructure in these areas. Centre to Province transfers are substantial and if these could be reduced or eliminated a major burden on the central exchequer would be alleviated. The threat to so reduce these transfers according to a designated expected collection would provide a powerful incentive for the Provinces to collect. They would gain from more energetic collection and lose from less. If *ushr* were paid in full then it would amount to some 80% of the notional total land tax revenue leaving 20% for the locality if *ushr* payments are credited. For the smaller holdings *ushr* would exceed land tax liability for most years, as the *ushr* collections should be 5% of gross output, against nil land tax for 0–12.5 acre holdings, an average of 2% for the 12.5–25 acres group, and an average of 4.7% for the 25–50 acres category. Thus the crediting of *ushr* against the land tax would (if both were properly paid) imply no land tax payment (over and above *ushr*) for those owning less than about 50 acres. If *ushr* is used for local social security and relief and if we assume that it adequately meets that purpose then around 20% of the land tax revenue could be allocated for expenditures, such as investments in infrastructure or schools. In practice the land tax should be more efficiently collected than *ushr* (which is largely voluntary) so that the fraction should be considerably higher than 20%.

The definition of 'local' level would need to be examined. There would be some scope for 'pooling' of resources, as between *barani* (rain-fed) and irrigated areas of various districts and this may lead the argument towards larger areas. The chosen area should not, however, be so large as to dissipate the advantages of the visibility of and access to the *benefits* that such a scheme possesses.

8.6 Concluding comments

We have discussed different possible forms for the direct taxation of land and agricultural incomes in Pakistan. We conclude that there are strong economic and administrative attractions to a system that is based on potential output of land as measured by (revised) produce index units. There could be an exemption of around 12.5 acres for distributive and administrative reasons. *Ushr* payments would be debited against the payment. If, thereby, *ushr* payments increased then, given appropriate design, an effecive social security system for the poor might ensue.

The scheme would require a careful cadastral survey and up-dating of PIUs. This is both feasible and valuable for other reasons. The revenue would be substantial and the distributional impact favourable. The collection difficulties might be eased if collection were the responsibility of the locality which would also have the right to the revenue. Such a scheme could considerably reduce burdens on the Centre. There is no doubt that the tax could be administered, as the history of the sub-continent, from at least the early Moghul days until 1935, has shown.

The opposition is likely to be political since such a tax would be difficult to evade and would impinge on powerful groups which have been doing well under the existing system. For this reason the government might take it off the agenda. That is their decision. If they so decide then other sources of revenue and ways of taxing the relevant incomes should be found.

9   International contrasts

9.1 Introduction

In this chapter we present some experience from outside Pakistan with two objectives in mind. The first is to look at the lessons from other countries for three of the major themes of this book (i) the possible level of taxation and its balance across sources, (ii) different methods for indirect taxation, and (iii) the use of presumptive methods in the assessment of liabilities for both direct and indirect taxation. The second is to display the application of some of the techniques described in the earlier chapters to India. In so doing we show how they can be used to look at a range of questions not presented in our discussion of Pakistan. One of the purposes of the international comparison is to point to possibilities for practical reforms for Pakistan and to draw attention to potential problems.

The main focus of our examples will be India, as that is where our research first started and where similarities and contrasts are of the greatest immediate interest to Pakistan given their common history and similarities of geography and administration. We also draw on some of our (more limited) experience of Bangladesh and Mexico, as well as some broader trans-national studies conducted within the Fiscal Affairs Department (FAD) of the International Monetary Fund. The IMF's FAD has a unique knowledge of and international perspective on tax matters across countries (see, e.g., Tait, 1988, Goode, 1984, and Tanzi and Casanegra de Jantscher, 1989).

In the next section we look at the changing balance across sources of revenue in India and contrast it with that of Pakistan. In section 9.3 we consider indirect taxes in other countries, particularly the VAT but also trade taxes, and in section 9.4 we discuss presumptive methods. The application of some methods for the analysis of marginal reform to the balance of Indian taxes is presented in section 9.5 and section 9.6 provides concluding comments.

Table 9.1. *India: Tax/GDP ratios 1950–85*

	1950–1	1960–1	1970–1	1980–1	1984–5
Direct taxes	*2.4*	*2.7*	*2.5*	*2.6*	*2.7*
Corporate income tax	}1.8 {	0.7	0.9	1.0	1.3
Personal income tax		1.1	1.2	1.2	0.8
Land revenue	0.5	0.7	0.3	0.1	0.2
Indirect taxes	*4.1*	*6.3*	*9.3*	*13.0*	*14.3*
Customs	1.6	1.1	1.3	2.7	3.3
Central excises	0.7	2.8	4.4	5.1	5.2
Sales tax	0.6	1.1	2.0	3.2	3.5
Total	6.5	9.0	11.8	15.6	16.9

Source: Chelliah (1989), p. 159.

9.2 The balance of taxation in India

As we indicated in chapter 2, Pakistan's tax collections as a proportion of GDP at 11.2% in 1985 were not far from the average for the least-developed countries. And we have emphasised Pakistan's colonial history and tax laws, much of which it has in common with other countries of the sub-continent. But there are important respects in which the tax experiences of the countries differ. For instance, in Bangladesh the tax/GDP ratio was 4.2% in 1972–3, and this had increased to only 7.2% by 1985–6, some way short of levels attained in pre-independence India. The Indian performance, on the other hand, has been well above the average for the sub-continent in terms of the tax/GDP ratio, which had risen to around 17% by the mid-1980s.

Indian taxation, both in terms of tax/GDP ratios and the composition of taxes, has changed substantially from the position at independence (see table 9.1). While the direct taxes have remained more or less constant as a proportion of GDP, a declining contribution of land revenue has been compensated for by the increasing revenues from the corporate income tax. The personal income tax also contributed around 1.2% of GDP during the 1960s and 1970s, but there was a sharp drop in collections in the mid-1980s with the reductions in marginal tax rates designed to improve taxpayer compliance.

The most significant change in the pattern of taxation in India has been the increasing importance of indirect taxes, which contributed (almost)

Table 9.2. *India*: *Composition of tax revenue* (% *of total tax revenue*)

	1950—1	1960—1	1970—1	1980—1	1984—5
Direct taxes	36.8	29.8	21.2	16.5	15.2
Corporate income tax	} 27.7 {	8.2	7.8	6.6	7.8
Personal income tax		12.5	10.0	7.6	5.0
Land revenue	8.2	7.2	2.5	0.8	0.9
Indirect taxes	63.2	70.2	78.8	83.5	84.8
Customs	25.1	12.6	11.0	17.2	19.7
Central excises	10.8	30.8	37.0	32.8	31.0
State excises (liquor)	8.0	4.1	4.2	4.5	5.3
Sales tax	9.3	12.1	16.5	20.2	20.4

Source: Chelliah (1989), p. 160.

twice as much as a proportion of GDP in 1970–1 than in 1950–1, largely accounting for the extra 5% of GDP raised in 1984–5 over 1970–1. While India, more so than Pakistan, pursued an import-substitution policy from the early 1950s, she relied particularly heavily on a system of quantitative restrictions. This implied a drop in the relative importance of customs as a proportion of total tax revenue (see table 9.2). Almost the entire additional contribution to the indirect tax/GDP ratio was on account of domestic taxation until the mid-1970s, with union excises and state sales taxes both exhibiting substantial increases. However, with a gradual liberalisation of the trade regime, and a steady replacement of quantitative restrictions by tariffs in the late 1970s and 1980s, the relative importance of customs duties has increased.

A major constraint on tax policy in India has been the constitutional differentiation between the central and state governments over the power to tax final goods. Recall that under the Government of India Act of 1935 the provinces were granted jurisdiction over the taxation of final goods. This has led to an increasing reliance on excises as the major source of revenue for the central government. Excises in India and Pakistan take the old Commonwealth interpretation and are essentially taxes on domestic production. A consequence of this pattern of taxation has been cascading indirect taxes, with excises and customs duties on intermediate and capital goods as the main contributory factors (for details of calculations for India, see Ahmad and Stern, 1984 and 1987a). In order to mitigate some of the effects of this cascading, the Indian Government introduced a system, MODVAT, of rebating taxes under its control. This and related problems are discussed later.

Table 9.3. *Tax revenue and structure in sub-Saharan Africa, 1966–82*

	1966	1970	1978	1982
Tax revenue (% of GDP)	11.6	14.2	16.3	16.1
% of tax revenue				
Income	25.2	26.9	29.9	29.5
Domestic commodities	25.0	24.6	24.2	27.9
International trade	49.9	48.5	45.9	42.6

Source: Shalizi and Squire (1988), table 1.1, p. 3.

While the tax/GDP ratios in sub-Saharan Africa (see table 9.3) are similar to those in India, the structure of taxation, i.e. the contributions of various instruments to overall tax revenue, is closer to that in Pakistan. In Pakistan, as in sub-Saharan Africa, there is a major reliance on the taxation of trade for revenues (see Shalizi and Squire, 1988). Generally, in Latin America income and corporate taxes contribute to total tax revenues to a much greater extent than in either the sub-continent or sub-Saharan Africa and tax/GDP ratios have been attained which are closer to those of India than sub-Saharan Africa.

9.3 Indirect taxes

While indirect taxes are likely to continue to remain as the major source of revenue in developing countries in the foreseeable future, a number of issues remain which are of concern in a cross-country context. Clearly the type of indirect tax instruments employed affects not only revenues but also production incentives and efficiency, as well as distribution. There is often a tension between administrative ease and other objectives. Let us examine recent approaches to domestic and trade taxation in various countries.

9.3.1 *Domestic indirect taxation*

In many OECD countries general consumption taxes, such as VAT and the like, and excises (largely on alcohol, tobacco and motor spirits) contribute roughly equivalent amounts in terms of revenue, each of the two broad heads being around 5% of GDP on average (see table 9.4). There is an increasing utilisation of the VAT as a general consumption tax (the USA being a notable exception), with recent introductions being Greece, Spain, Turkey, Mexico, Indonesia and New Zealand. (For a listing of countries and rate structures of VAT, see table 9.5.)

The New Zealand VAT legislation (The Sale of Goods and Services Act, 1985) is considered to be one of the most comprehensive, and, as one of the more recent, benefits from the cumulative experience of a number of countries. It has been cited as a useful reference for other countries contemplating a VAT by Tait (1988) who points to its few exemptions and single rate. In New Zealand the intention in moving to a broad-based consumption tax was not only to raise revenues and reduce budget deficits, but also to reduce the rates of income tax. Apparently there was a view that the avoidance of the term 'value-added tax' would help limit hostility to the new measures.

Even though India provides an example of a low-income country that has managed to raise its tax/GDP ratio to levels more common in richer countries, it also illustrates the problems of an excessive reliance on limited instruments, and of constraints that prevent a rationalisation of the domestic tax structure. The recognition that the heavy use of excises is a major cause of the cascading of indirect taxes (see Government of India, Ministry of Finance, 1977, and Ahmad and Stern, 1983) and the inability of the central government to interfere with the state-level sales taxes have contributed to the introduction of a modified VAT or MODVAT levied on domestic manufacturing. The system is in practice a modification of the system of excise duties to include rebates for excises paid on inputs. This has led to a cumbersome set of provisions that are difficult to implement. Whilst some partial rebating has been achieved, the full advantages of a VAT-like system have not been evident in India so far, including the self-policing and other administrative advantages, as well as the gains from cross-referencing with respect to the income tax.

The Mexican experience of the introduction and implementation of the VAT is instructive, and reflects the importance of the political economy of a tax reform. During the 1960s, Mexico had a motley collection of excises, which included taxation of domestic production on a scale resembling that of the Indian sub-continent, as well as a sales tax on turnover which led to considerable cascading. In the mid-1960s, the Mexican Treasury began a consideration of the VAT: 'Nicholas Kaldor was imported and enclosed in Cuernavaca – to work secretly on a project of which a few limited copies were made' (Gil Diaz, 1988). This report was discussed with experts outside the government and with private sector representatives, who went to Europe to examine the experiences of those countries which had introduced the VAT. Their conclusion was that the tax would be inflationary, and the proposal was shelved. As Gil Diaz (1988) put it,

the private sector erred of course in arguing that a VAT would be inflationary, neither theory nor experience warranted such a view. It would have had a once-and-for-all effect on the price level since the turnover tax was not applied to imports and

Table 9.4. Receipts from main taxes as percentage of GDP at market prices, 1965, 1975 and 1984[a]

	Total taxes			Personal income taxes			Corporation income tax		
	1965	1975	1984	1965	1975	1984	1965	1975	1984
Sweden[b]	36	44	50	17	20	19	2	2	2
Denmark[b,c]	30	41	48	12	23	24	1	1	3
Belgium[b]	31	41	47	6	13	16	2	3	3
Norway[b,c]	33	45	46	13	14	11	1	1	8
Netherlands[b]	34	44	46	9	12	9	3	3	3
France[b]	35	37	45	4	5	6	2	2	2
Austria[b]	35	39	42	7	8	9	2	2	1
Luxembourg[b]	30	38	41	8	11	11	3	6	6
Italy[b]	27	29	41	3	4	11	2	2	4
Ireland[b]	26	32	39	4	8	12	2	2	1
United Kingdom[b]	31	36	39	9	14	10	2	2	4
Germany[b]	32	36	38	8	11	11	2	2	2
Finland[c]	30	35	36	11	17	16	2	1	2
Greece	21	25	35	2	2	5	—	1	1
Canada	26	33	34	6	11	11	4	4	3
Switzerland	21	30	32	6	11	12	1	2	2
Portugal	18	25	32						
Australia	24	29	31	8	12	14	4	4	3
New Zealand	25	30	31	10	16	18	5	3	3
United States	26	30	29	8	10	10	4	3	2
Spain	15	20	28	2	3	6	1	1	1
Japan	18	21	27	4	5	7	4	4	6
Turkey	15	21	14	4	7	6	1	1	2
OECD average[d]	27	33	37	7	11	12	2	2	3

Table 9.4. (cont.)

	Employees' social security			Employers' social security			General consumption			Excises, etc.		
	1965	1975	1984	1965	1975	1984	1965	1975	1984	1965	1975	1984
Sweden[b,c]	1	–	–	3	8	13	4	5	7	7	5	5
Denmark[b,c]	1	–	1	1	–	1	3	7	10	9	6	6
Belgium[b]	3	4	6	6	8	8	6	7	7	4	4	3
Norway[b,c]		2	3	3	8	7	7	9	8	6	7	8
Netherlands[b]	5	7	8	4	8	8	4	6	7	5	4	3
France[b]	2	3	6	9	11	13	8	9	9	5	3	4
Austria[b]	4	4	5	4	5	7	6	8	9	6	5	4
Luxembourg[b]	4	4	4	6	6	6	4	5	5	3	3	5
Italy[b]		3	3	1	11	10	4	4	6	7	4	4
Ireland[b]	1	2	2	2	3	4	1	5	8	11	9	9
United Kingdom[b]	2	2	3	5	4	4	2	3	6	8	5	5
Germany[b]	4	5	6	1	7	7	5	5	6	5	4	3
Finland[c]	–		5	1	3	3	6	6	8	7	6	6
Greece	1	1	1	1	2	3	2	5	5	7	6	8
Canada	1	3	3	2	3	3	5	4	4	4	4	5
Switzerland	2	3	3	2	5	5	2	2	3	4	3	3
Portugal	–			–	–	–	–	3	4	8	7	9
Australia	3	3	5	3	4	5	2	2	2	5	5	6
New Zealand	2	2	2	3	8	9	2	3	4	5	4	4
United States	1	2	3	2	3	4	1	2	2	4	3	2
Spain	–	1	–	–	1	1	3	3	4	3	2	3
Japan							–	–	–	5	3	4
Turkey							–	–	–	8	8	5
OECD average	2	2	3	3	5	6	3	4	5	6	5	5

Notes: Blank implies not available or non-existent.
– implies 0 or less than 0.5%.
[a] Countries ranking order by 1984 total tax to GDP ratios.
[b] Countries with a value-added tax as at 31 December 1984.
[c] Countries where receipts from employees' social security contributions on an income tax base are shown in 1100.
Source: Messere and Owens (1989).

Table 9.5. *Percentage VAT rates throughout the world*

	Date VAT introduced or proposed	VAT rates[a]	
		At introduction	On 1 January 1988
Argentina	Jan. 1975	16	9, 18
Austria	Jan. 1973	8, 16	10, 20, 32
Belgium	Jan. 1971	6, 14, 18	1, 6, 17, 19, 25, 33
Bolivia	Oct. 1973	5, 10, 15	10
Brazil[b]	Jan. 1967	15	9, 11
Brazil[c]	Jan. 1967		17
Canada[d]			
Chile	Mar. 1975	8, 20	16[e]
Colombia	Jan. 1975	4, 6, 10	4, 6, 10, 15, 20, 35
Costa Rica	Jan. 1975	10	8
Côte d'Ivoire	Jan. 1960	8	11, 11, 25, 35, 13
Denmark	July 1967	10	22
Dominican Rep.	Jan. 1983	6	6
Ecuador	July 1970	4, 10	6
France	Jan. 1968	6.4, 13.6, 20, 25	2.1, 4, 5.5, 7, 18.6, 33.3
Germany, Fed. Rep. of	Jan. 1968	5, 10	7, 14
Greece	Jan. 1987	6, 18, 36	3, 6, 18, 36
Guatemala	Aug. 1983	7	7
Haiti	Nov. 1982	7	10
Honduras	Jan. 1976	3	5, 6
Hungary	Jan. 1988	15, 25	
Iceland[d]	Jan. 1989	24	
Indonesia	Apr. 1985	10	10
Ireland	Nov. 1972	5.26, 16.37, 30.26	2.2, 10, 25
Israel	July 1976	8	6.5, 15
Italy	Jan. 1973	6, 12, 18	2.9, 18, 38
Japan[d]		3	
Korea	July 1977	10	2, 3.5, 10
Luxembourg	Jan. 1970	2, 4, 8	3, 6, 12

Madagascar	Jan. 1969	6, 12	**15**
Mexico	Jan. 1980	10	6, **15**, 20
Morocco	Apr. 1986	7, 12, 14, **19**, 30	7, 12, 14, **19**, 30
Netherlands	Jan. 1969	4, 12	6, **20**
New Zealand	May 1986	10	**10**
Nicaragua	Jan. 1975	6	**10**, 25
Niger	Jan. 1986	8, **12**, 18	**15**, 25, 35
Norway	Jan. 1970	20	11, 11, **20**
Panama	Mar. 1977	5	**5**
Peru	July 1976	3, **20**, 40	**18**
Philippines	Jan. 1988	10	
Poland[d]	Jan. 1986	8, **16**, 30	**8**, 16, 30
Portugal	Jan. 1986	...	7, **20**, 34, 50
Senegal	Mar. 1961–80[f]		
South Africa[d]	Apr. 1989	6, **12**, 33	6, **12**, 33
Spain	Jan. 1969	2.04, 6.38, **11.1**	3.95, 12.87, **23.46**
Sweden[g]			
Taiwan Province of China	Apr. 1986	5	5, **15**, 25
Thailand[d]	Jan. 1989		
Tunisia	July 1988	6, **17**, 29	
Turkey	Jan. 1985	10	12, **15**
United Kingdom	Apr. 1973	10	**15**
Uruguay	Jan. 1968	5, **14**	12, **21**

Notes: [a] Rates shown in bold type are the so-called standard rates applied to goods and services not covered by other especially high or low rates. Most countries use a zero rate for a few goods, and Ireland, Portugal, and the United Kingdom use it extensively to ensure that substantial amounts of goods and services are free of VAT.
[b] On interstate transactions depending on region.
[c] On intrastate transactions.
[d] Proposed or under discussion.
[e] June 1988.
[f] Senegal's VAT evolved from a limited manufacturers turnover tax with credits, and no precise date of introduction is given; it has only recently been extended to include services at rates of 7, 12.5, 17, and 50%.
[g] Effective rates.

Source: Tait (1988), pp. 40–4.

taxed exports, while the VAT proposed was of the consumption (destination) nature, applicable to imports, and with a zero rate on exports. It was not to be until the late 1970s that the Treasury was able to overcome the private sector's arguments that the VAT would be inflationary, on the grounds that a slight once-and-for-all increase in the price level would be more than compensated by the economic advantages and reduction in evasion of the net set of taxes.

The VAT adopted in Mexico has undergone three iterations. The introduction was at a basic rate of 10%, with exemptions for primary activities and some agricultural goods and basic foodstuffs. It facilitated the removal of 30 federal indirect taxes and 300 state excises, greatly simplifying administration with its broad base and simple rate structure. While the Treasury had estimated that a basic rate of 13% was needed to ensure that VAT revenues would be equivalent to the taxes replaced, in fact the lower 10% rate led to an indirect tax/GDP ratio in the year of the reform which was no lower than in the immediate pre-reform period. There was, however, a substantial increase in corporate income tax revenues, reflecting some of the advantages of the cross-referencing procedures of the VAT (see Gil Diaz, 1987).

The original VAT imposed was less than satisfactory in a number of respects. The legitimacy of the new tax was brought into question by exemptions being granted to sales through union stores. This, combined with legal stipulations requiring VAT liability to be shown separately from the price of a good (unlike the European practice), helped to increase consumer resistance to the tax. Another factor was the reduction in the base rate of VAT (6%) in the northern frontier states, so as to take into account the rates of sales taxes in nearby US cities. Further, while the rate structure of the VAT was to be set by the federal government, collections and the administration of the tax remained in the hands of the states, since the new tax had replaced largely state-level taxes. This made the enthusiasm with which the tax was collected very dependent on the revenue-sharing formulae adopted. During a transition year, state shares were based on a coefficient determined by past sharing arrangements with provision for revision in future years. In practice the original coefficients became impossible to change, given that those states which expected a fall in their shares withheld information, thereby according to Gil Diaz 'short-circuiting the whole process'. In effect the federal government kept increasing transfers to provinces, while keeping the overall proportions (or coefficients) constant, which led to complacency on the part of the states and a virtual doubling of federal transfers from 11% of tax revenues in 1979, to around 20% in 1986. The situation was not corrected until 1987, when the revenue-sharing arrangements were changed, allowing the states to keep 30% of VAT collections without a ceiling. This led to an immediate improvement in collections.

That the advantages of the simpler forms of the VAT can be dissipated with attempts to achieve excessive differentiation may be seen in the recent developments in the Mexican VAT. A first revision of the VAT entailed the enlargement of the sub-group of goods, within the food category, which were subject to a zero rate. This led to a slight decline in the indirect tax/GDP ratio. With the budgetary deficits of the 1981 and 1982 fiscal years, which coincided with the debt crisis, the incoming de la Madrid administration raised the base rate of the VAT to 15% for the 1983 fiscal year. To ensure political acceptability a 'symbolic' luxury rate of 20%, and a lower rate of 6% on medicines and some food items were also introduced. It was argued by the Under-Secretary of Tax Policy that the 'progressivity of the structure is miniscule compared to the administrative inconveniences the complex structure introduced. Besides the new general rate is probably high enough to make tax evasion extremely profitable, especially given the fragmented administration of the tax' (Gil Diaz, 1988). Despite these problems, the 1983 VAT collections were 3.25% of GDP, as against 2.8% in 1980.

Both the Mexican and Indian examples suggest that Pakistan is fortunate in that the administration of sales and excise taxes are under the (potentially) unified control of the central government. Thus a VAT implemented in Pakistan is less likely to face the problems that have been so evident in the more formal federal structures in India and Mexico, and thus has the potential to establish a buoyant and efficient tax instrument. And, as we showed in chapter 7, a VAT with exemptions and one (or at most two) rates, combined with a selective use of excises on final goods such as tobacco, motor spirits and alcohol, is distributionally attractive relative to the status quo.

9.3.2 The taxation of trade

We have seen that in the case of Pakistan, the taxation of trade, and particularly imports, forms one of the most convenient tax handles, and is thus likely to provide an attractive fall-back when there is a budgetary crisis. This short-run advantage in terms of revenue generation is in contrast to the negative effects on the domestic protective structure and incentives. Thus injudicious use of this instrument could have damaging consequences both for protection and the efficiency of domestic production, and be deleterious in terms of the longer-term prospects for revenue from domestic sources. This has been particularly striking in Bangladesh, which is even more dependent on the taxation of trade than Pakistan.

In Bangladesh, in the early 1980s, taxes on imports accounted for around 55% of tax revenues (see Government of Bangladesh, 1986). These taxes included customs duties, which ranged, on an *ad valorem* basis, from 2.5% to 400%, sales taxes on duty-inclusive values, a development surcharge at 2%, licence fees, and regulatory duties which ranged from 2.5% to 50%. The effect of the import tariff structure, combined with the pattern of imports, is such that almost half of the trade tax revenues are derived from raw materials and capital goods (for details, see Government of Bangladesh, 1986, table 15). This particularly heavy pattern of taxation of imported intermediate goods and raw materials has negative implications for the domestic users of such inputs, and places exporters (using these inputs) at a considerable disadvantage. Heavy import duties also lead to claims for rebates and export subsidies, which are more often than not on an *ad hoc* basis, with fertile prospects for fraudulent behaviour. Such problems are not confined to countries with the administrative difficulties of Bangladesh. Efforts to operate duty drawback schemes in countries with a reputation for good administration, such as Malawi, have not been particularly successful (see, e.g., Shalizi and Squire, 1988), and fraudulent rebates and subsidies are a major problem in the European Community.

9.4   Presumptive methods

The term presumptive taxation covers a number of procedures under which the 'desired' base for taxation (direct or indirect) is not itself measured but is inferred from some simple indicators which are more easily measured than the base itself. An important example already discussed in chapter 8 as a possible instrument in land taxation is the Pakistan produce index unit (PIU) as a measure of potential income from land. For a shop or restaurant the floorspace and position might be used as indications of sales. For a factory, electricity consumption, amongst other things, might be a suggestive indicator of output.

Presumptive taxation has a number of advantages. First, by reducing the discretion of the tax inspector in the interpretation of accounts it provides less scope for corruption and intimidation by tax officers and evasion by taxpayers. Second, it allows the taxation of groups with non-existent, poor or unbelievable accounts. Third, it is less damaging to incentives since an enterprise which over-performs relative to its presumptive indicators, in the sense that it has higher sales (or income) than is implicit in the presumptive formula, would not pay an extra tax. Thus it is generally a crude attempt to base taxation on taxable capacity.

According to Tanzi and Casanegra de Jantscher (1989) one of the first theoretical proponents of presumptive taxation was Einaudi (who was

President of Italy after the Second World War) in the 1920s, who based his generalisations on historical observations of the taxation of agricultural income in the Principality of Milan. He argued that if individuals were taxed on the basis of 'average' income, then there would be an incentive to produce above the average, since the additional income would be taxed at a zero marginal rate. The presumptive taxation of land (and other property) may proceed through first a reasonably accurate description of property values, and then an associated average rate of return. In the case of land, the requirement is for a fairly accurate cadastral survey. Presumptive methods for labour income are more difficult to establish.

The experiences of a number of countries with presumptive methods are described below. This draws heavily on Tanzi and Casanegra de Jantscher (1989), whose focus is property and labour income. A number of different bases for presumptive taxation have been considered or attempted. These include:

(i) *Changes in net wealth.* A number of countries have legislation which allows consideration of differences between the beginning and end of the year estimates of net wealth for tax assessment purposes. This method is not widely used, however, because of the difficulty in establishing net wealth at the two points in time.

(ii) *Value of particular assets.* The value of particular assets is often used as a presumptive base. In Chile, for those farmers without accurate records, income tax is liable to be assessed at 10% of the assessed value of the farm, with a possibility of challenge by establishing lower incomes. In Colombia, all taxpayers are liable for a minimum of 8% of net wealth, without the possibility of challenge. Where liquid assets are commonly held, this method discriminates against holders of property.

(iii) *Gross receipts.* A number of francophone countries have applied a fixed minimum corporate income tax, regardless of the size of the corporation or the volume of its activities. This presumptive tax can be credited against the regular corporate income tax liability, but with no refunds. A variant of this method (sometimes used in conjunction with the earlier presumption, the larger of the two applying) is to use a minimum percentage of gross receipts, ranging from 0.5% to 2.0%. The Colombian income tax legislation also provides for a tax on net income based on gross receipts which applies to all individuals (apart from the salaried) and corporations. As we noted in the discussion concerning *ushr*, the concealment of gross receipts is not likely to be a trivial matter. In Pakistan, enabling provisions exist which permit the authorities to use presumptive methods. The capacity tax experiment of the mid-1960s, which was an attempt to determine potential output rather than actual gross receipts, ran into implementation problems, particularly with the definition and estimation of capacity.

(iv) *Visible signs of wealth*. Visible signs of wealth are a common basis of presumption. In some countries, such as Brazil and Peru, it is up to the tax administration to decide which indicators to use. In France, Italy and some francophone African countries, the presumption is built into the tax code, with the cash income equivalent of the presumption carefully determined. Some of these indicators have included the main or secondary residence, racehorses, servants, yachts, planes and so on. While it may be difficult to codify the cash equivalent of some obvious signs of wealth in many countries, the method is often a useful indicator. None the less, care needs to be taken to ensure that it does not degenerate into a personal income generation activity for the tax collector.

(v) *Estimated assessments*. Estimated assessments are often used in the case of the self-employed and other 'hard-to-tax' groups such as professionals. In France the *forfait* system of presumption has developed. One variant of the *forfait* is to establish criteria, relating to physical inputs, use of labour, location and so on, which are discussed with representatives of relevant sectors prior to establishment of specific coefficients and indices. This method has been used, for instance, in Korea and also in Israel where it is known as the *tashiv* presumption and was established for those activities and individuals where book-keeping was difficult. It is sometimes the case that higher-income individuals conceal records in order to be assessed at the lower presumptive level. Partly in response to this problem, Ghana has established a fixed tax payment for certain activities. An analogy in Pakistan could be the use of licence fees for some occupations.

There are important lessons here for Pakistan. There are already enabling provisions for the use of presumptive criteria. The French variant of *forfait* using indicators may well prove a potent instrument. The valuation of assets such as land or residential property may well be another. However, the informational requirements for a wealth tax are likely to be prohibitive.

9.5 Directions of reform for India

In this section we describe the welfare analysis for India of changes in the relative contribution of different types of taxes, using the methods of analysis described in chapters 3 and 5 and in Ahmad and Stern (1987a). We examine within indirect taxes the balance between excises, sales taxes and customs duties. Customs and excises are predominantly Central taxes and sales taxation is primarily a State instrument. We do the analysis using the concept of the social marginal cost of revenue described in chapter 3 and developed in chapter 5. We also compare the estimated social marginal costs for indirect taxes with those from certain direct tax increases. To keep things simple (although it is not very satisfactory) we carry out our calculations under the assumption that producer prices and shadow prices are equal so that we may work with actual rather than shadow revenue. Thus we ask the question as to which of the broad headings are the most appropriate subjects for extra revenue, or, for a given revenue, in what direction should the balance of taxation be moving.

We begin by presenting the social marginal cost, λ_i, of taxing good i (see table 9.6). These results are analogous to those presented in chapter 7 for Pakistan. The formula for λ_i was presented in chapter 3 with examples of calculations provided in chapter 7. The effective taxes for India were calculated for eighty-nine sectors using input–output information and merged to nine to correspond to the estimates for the demand system which were available (see Ahmad and Stern, 1987a, for further details).

We showed in chapter 5 how the social cost associated with a group of taxes could be calculated. Here we shall apply this idea to the group of all excises, or of all sales taxes, or of all customs duties. If, for example, we make a small change with all excise taxes raised according to some given rule, we may calculate the resultant change in the effective tax on good i, which we call $\Delta t_{i(ex)}^e$. We may then calculate the social marginal cost of raising one rupee in this way as

$$\lambda^{ex} = \frac{\sum_h \sum_i \beta^h x_i^h \Delta t_{i(ex)}^e}{\sum_i \left(X_i + \sum_j t_j^e \frac{\partial X_j}{\partial t_i^e} \right) \Delta t_{i(ex)}^e} \tag{9.1}$$

with similar expressions for the social costs of raising one rupee via a uniform increase in import duties, λ^m, and via sales taxes, λ^{sa}. The results from carrying out these calculations are presented in table 9.7.

These social marginal costs may in turn be compared with the social marginal cost, λ^{PT}, of raising a unit of revenue through a uniform poll tax. It is easily seen, normalising β^h so that $\bar{\beta} = 1$, that

$$\lambda^{PT} = \frac{1}{1 - \bar{\delta}} \tag{9.2}$$

where $\bar{\delta} = \frac{1}{H} \sum_h \delta^h$ and

Table 9.6. *Welfare loss for indirect taxes*

	Effective tax	Levels of inequality aversion, ε									
		0	γ	0.1	γ	1	γ	2	γ	5	γ
1 Cereals	0.052	1.034	8	1.031	7	0.986	2	0.910	2	0.590	2
2 Milk and dairy products	0.009	1.004	9	0.970	9	0.706	9	0.483	9	0.100	9
3 Edible oils	0.083	1.067	6	1.049	6	0.897	4	0.741	4	0.338	5
4 Meat, fish, eggs	0.014	1.053	7	1.031	8	0.854	6	0.695	5	0.351	4
5 Sugar and gur	0.069	1.089	5	1.067	5	0.881	5	0.695	5	0.264	6
6 Other foods	0.114	1.135	4	1.114	3	0.951	3	0.804	3	0.464	3
7 Clothing	0.242	1.245	1	1.189	1	0.797	7	0.517	7	0.126	8
8 Fuel and light	0.274	1.163	2	1.152	2	1.063	1	0.968	1	0.678	1
9 Other non-food	0.133	1.145	3	1.087	4	0.717	8	0.487	8	0.176	7

Notes: (i) The welfare loss for commodity i, λ_i, represents the effects on all households (using the β^h corresponding to various levels of inequality aversion ε – see chapter 5) of an increase in the tax on the ith good sufficient to raise a rupee of government revenue. γ denotes the rank of the good by λ_i. A good ranked 1 would be such that a switch of taxation from it to any other good would increase welfare at constant revenue.

$$\lambda_i = \frac{\sum_h \beta^h x_i^h}{X_i + \sum_j t_j^e \frac{\partial X_j}{\partial t_i}}$$

(ii) The welfare weights, β_j, have been normalised so that the mean, $\bar{\beta}$, is one.

(iii) The effective taxes for India are calculated in a manner parallel to that for Pakistan described in chapter 6. They are expressed as a fraction of the consumer price.

(iv) The expenditure data come from Government of India (1978).

Source: Ahmad and Stern (1987a), table 11.4, p. 310.

$$\delta^h \equiv \mathbf{t}' \frac{\partial \mathbf{x}^h}{\partial m^h} = \sum_i \frac{t_i}{q_i} \frac{\partial (q_i x_i^h)}{\partial m^h} \qquad (9.3)$$

(where m^h is lump-sum income), i.e. the marginal propensity to 'spend' on indirect taxes. It should be intuitively clear that the cost of a unit of revenue is greater than one (with $\beta = 1$) since the gross lump-sum tax must be above one to allow for the loss of revenue from indirect taxes.

Our final comparison is with direct taxes. If a reform takes a small amount Δm^h directly from the lump-sum income of household h then the marginal social loss for the raising of a rupee is $-\Delta W / \Delta R$ where

$$\Delta W = \sum_h \beta^h \Delta m^h \qquad (9.4)$$

Table 9.7. *Welfare losses per marginal rupee associated with a 1% tax increase*

	ε			
Change	0	0.1	1	2
λ^{ex}	1.146	1.108	0.850	0.660
λ^{sa}	1.120	1.087	0.851	0.587
λ^{m}	1.172	1.120	0.773	0.538

Note: λ^{ex} is defined in equation 9.1 and the role of ε in chapter 5. $\lambda^{PT} = 1.1173$, where $\lambda^{PT} = 1/(1-\delta)$ and δ is 10.5%. The value λ^{PT} is the social marginal cost of raising extra revenue through a poll tax and δ is the average across households of the marginal propensity to spend on taxes. Recall that $\beta = 1$. See table 9.6.
Source: Ahmad and Stern (1987a), table 11.2, p. 302.

Table 9.8. *Welfare losses associated with income tax reforms*

	ε				
Reform	0	0.1	1	2	5
1 λ^{h}	1.143	1.082	0.594	0.245	0.004
2 λ^{T}	1.143	0.962	0.220	0.042	0.000
3 λ^{T}	1.143	0.834	0.045	0.000	0.000

Note: Reform 1: Marginal changes in exemption limits $\lambda^{h} = \beta^{h}/(1-\delta^{h})$. The household per capita expenditure figures for the calculations of β^{h} and δ^{h} (see equations 7.6 and 9.3) were based on income data for tax-paying urban households from official sources (see Ahmad and Stern, 1983).
Reform 2: Increase in all marginal income tax rates of 1%. λ^{T} is defined as equation 9.4 divided by equation 9.5.
Reform 3: Existing exemption limits, two upper tax bands increased by 5% (55%→60% and 60%→65%) with other marginal rates kept constant. Again, λ^{T} is defined as equation 9.4 divided by equation 9.5.
Source: Ahmad and Stern (1987a), table 11.5, p. 312.

$$\Delta R = -\sum_{h} \Delta m^{h} + \sum_{h} t' \frac{\partial x^{h}}{\partial m^{h}} \Delta m^{h} \tag{9.5}$$

We define a set of Δm^{h} for three different income tax reforms. We make the important assumption that changes in the taxes do not change pre-tax income. In any case we have no labour supply functions of any econometric seriousness so incentive effects would be impossible to quantify.

The three reforms and the associated marginal social losses concerning the personal income tax are summarised in table 9.8. These are (1) a marginal change in the exemption limit; (2) a 1% increase in the marginal income tax rates with the existing exemption limits; and (3) existing

exemption limits and marginal tax rates kept, with the exception of the two
upper tax bands, each of which is increased by 5%. With the exception of
the first case, we assume that the revenue comes from existing taxpayers,
and we use data from official sources on collection rates. We do *not* assume
that there is full enforcement of legal rates – we suppose simply that the
revenue collections are distributed across existing taxpayers in the manner
described. In the first case, we keep the old rates constant and move an
individual at the exemption limit into the system. For further details, see
Ahmad and Stern (1983 and 1987a).

We may now compare the social marginal costs from the different
sources. For $\varepsilon = 0$, or no aversion to inequality, the policy-maker would be
indifferent between the three methods of raising one rupee from the
personal income tax. With no labour supply responses and welfare weights
all equal to unity, λ^T becomes simply $1/(1 - \delta)$, where δ is the marginal
propensity to pay indirect taxes for this group: for $\delta = 12.5\%$ we have
$\lambda^T = 1.143$. $\lambda^h > \lambda^T$ (reform 2) $> \lambda^T$ (reform 3) for positive levels of ε. We re-
label λ^T (reform 1) as λ^h in the case of a change in the exemption limit to
remind us that we are dealing with a change in the income of one household
type only. The first inequality follows from the lower weight on the
expenditure of richer households that are brought into reform 2. Analogously, only the two groups with the highest per capita expenditure are
affected in reform 3. This argument abstracts from incentive and incidence
effects and assumes that the administrative costs of each reform are the
same: we explained above how these considerations could be introduced
into the analysis. A comparison of the corresponding columns of tables 9.6
and 9.8 suggests that, at moderate and high levels of inequality aversion ε,
say $\varepsilon \geqslant 1$, it would be preferable to raise an extra rupee from the personal
income tax rather than to use commodity taxes. At very low but positive
levels of ε, say $\varepsilon = 0.1$, in comparing λ^T with λ_i, we see that there would be a
lower welfare loss from raising the extra rupee in government revenue either
through increasing all marginal income tax rates (reform 2) or increasing
the marginal income tax rates for the highest two expenditure groups
(reform 3). For some commodities, however, $\lambda^h > \lambda_i$ at $\varepsilon = 0.1$; see, for
example, the λ_i for the first five food items in table 9.6. At $\varepsilon = 0$, $\lambda_i > \lambda^h$ only
for commodity groups (7) 'clothing', (8) 'fuel and light', and (9) 'other non-
food', and for other commodities $\lambda_i < \lambda^h$ or λ^T. This result shows the
importance of the distributional considerations and demonstrates that, at
very low levels of ε, extra tax on some commodities might be preferable to
additional income taxes, which are the reforms that are preferred at higher
levels of inequality aversion.

If there are differences in administration costs then, as we have seen, we
should compare $\lambda^h/(1 - \theta^h)$ and $\lambda_i/(1 - \theta_i)$, where θ^h and θ_i are the respective

administrative costs of raising one rupee from adjusting the exemption limit and the tax on the ith good. Thus, for example, if we compare the columns for $\varepsilon = 2$ in tables 9.6 and 9.8, we see λ^h at about 0.245 and λ_i at an average of around 0.68, giving λ^h/λ_i equal to 0.36. Hence if θ_i is zero, a marginal switch from commodity taxes to the income tax (by lowering the exemption limit) would be attractive provided that θ^h does not exceed 0.64 – in other words provided that the administration cost of raising an extra rupee from lowering the exemption limit does not exceed 64 paise. The corresponding borderline administration cost per rupee at $\varepsilon = 1$ (less aversion to inequality) would be lower, about 34 paise. Where aversion to inequality is substantial, it seems most unlikely that administration costs could be sufficiently high to reverse the attractiveness of a switch to income taxation by lowering the exemption limit.

The discussion is entirely in terms of actual revenue collections; hence the analysis includes the possibility of evasion, at least where pre-tax incomes are fixed.

The analysis here would be modified by disincentive effects, as was discussed in Ahmad and Stern (1987a). We cannot rule out the possibility that the effects on revenue could be strong: an extreme case would be where reducing rates actually increased revenue, although the absence of examples contrasts strikingly with the frequency of the suggestion. We cannot treat the issue numerically without explicit factor supply functions, and these are not available for India. We should also stress that the analysis is marginal. If substantial extra revenue is sought it may be impossible to find it among the higher income tax groups.

If we combine the calculations presented earlier with those discussed in this section, the position is the following (see tables 9.6–9.8). With no aversion to inequality and fixed-factor incomes, we would be indifferent among various ways of raising an extra rupee by the income tax and between these and a general increase in commodity taxes. Among commodity taxes we would, broadly speaking, concentrate extra revenue on goods with low demand elasticities. These are primarily foods (see table 9.6) and thus are goods subject to state (sales) taxes (see table 9.7). The position changes sharply, however, as soon as we bring in distributional considerations. For moderate levels of inequality aversion (for example, $\varepsilon = 1$), an extra rupee from the income tax becomes attractive, the marginal costs from an extra rupee from cereals becomes relatively high, and state (or sales) taxes are no more attractive than central taxes. With strong aversion to inequality ($\varepsilon = 5$), the argument for the income tax is very strong, cereals become very unattractive as a source of revenue, and import duties represent the most desirable general source of extra indirect tax revenue. The analysis of effective taxes showed (see Ahmad and Stern, 1987a) that among the sources of indirect taxes the central taxes (particularly the excise) are the worst offenders from the point of view of taxation of inputs.

Note that (tables 9.6 and 9.7) provided there is at least a small aversion to inequality the raising of revenue via the poll tax is less attractive than via indirect taxation (i.e. $\lambda^{PT} > \lambda_i$). This means that the direct tax system is not optimal in the sense required in the standard theorems. Indeed the results suggest that, if it were administratively feasible, it would be a welfare improvement to finance a uniform poll *subsidy* by raising indirect taxation.

We trust that the analysis of this section has shown that the methods developed in chapters 3 and 5 can be applied in a productive way to a wider range of problems than those considered in chapters 6 and 7. Together with the directions of reform identified, the methods can yield valuable suggestions for shifting the balance of taxation.

9.6   Concluding comments

In this chapter we have examined some international experience, primarily, but not exclusively, from India, with two aims in mind. The first was to identify lessons from other countries concerning possibilities and pitfalls in the reform of taxes in Pakistan. The second was to provide further and wider demonstration of the potential of the methods of marginal reform for the analysis of taxation in India.

We have seen that in many respects Pakistan lags behind other developing countries in the level and balance of its tax system. Its tax to GDP ratio is only average for its income category and trade taxes still play an excessive role. As we saw in earlier chapters (particularly chapter 6) this gives rise to major taxation of inputs and distortions of the price mechanism. The record of other countries, including India, shows that it is indeed possible to shift the balance of taxation within indirect taxes away from trade and towards domestic sources, in a manner such as VAT which avoids the taxation of inputs, and to increase the role of direct taxes. We saw further that Pakistan is in an important respect better placed than other countries, such as India or Mexico, to introduce a VAT, in that it is less constrained by a rigorous federal structure. In India this manifested itself as the problem of the allocation of sales taxation to the States, not the Centre, and in Mexico of revenue raising by the States being hampered by the incentive structures embodied in revenue-sharing. Nevertheless India and, particularly, Mexico have made major strides in the direction of a VAT.

Our discussion of the use of presumptive methods in other countries indicated not only that there was considerable scope for their application in Pakistan but also that it was important to keep simple the indicators to be used for inferring the taxable base. Their wider application would allow a considerable extension of the coverage of a number of taxes, direct and indirect, and provide a substantial assistance in the introduction of new ones such as a VAT or land tax.

The penultimate section of this chapter provided a demonstration of the use of marginal methods in the analysis of the balance of taxation in India. These generally supported the view that a shift towards direct taxation was desirable. They also showed that, if administratively feasible, a move towards a uniform subsidy financed by extra indirect taxation would increase welfare, confirming the sub-optimality of the direct tax and transfer system. This last result indicates that a crucial necessary condition for uniform taxes does not apply (see subsection 3.2.3). Further, the analysis of the reform of indirect taxation in India showed, as it did for Pakistan, the central role of distributional values in determining preferred directions for reform. We shall be putting some of the lessons of this chapter to work in formulating the reform package for Pakistan to be analysed in the next chapter.

10 Alternative sources of revenue for Pakistan

10.1 Introduction

In the previous chapters we have shown how the theoretical tools of public economics could be developed and applied to the Pakistan tax system. As always with applied work this involved a leap from the neat categories and results of the theory to the messy detail of a tax system as it is. In this chapter we make a number of further steps to respond to the challenge of providing a package of reforms based on the ideas of the theory and the empirical analysis of earlier chapters.

The grander task of designing a set of tax measures which might alleviate some of the major problems of the Pakistan revenue system means that the style of the analysis shows a break in a number of ways from the earlier chapters. First, we move immediately to the present and future rather than concentrating on years where data allow us to mount a more detailed analysis. Second, we bring in all the major tax tools rather than concentrating on indirect taxation. Third, borrowing and macroeconomic balance have to be considered. Fourth, administrative and political difficulties move closer to the centre of the stage. As a result of this broader scope the discussion will be less detailed in its consequentialist analysis of the possible reforms.

Notwithstanding these differences the argument and proposals are firmly rooted in the analysis and ideas of the earlier chapters. The proposals are strongly influenced both by the principles of tax design of chapters 3 and 4 and the difficulties of the existing system identified and measured in chapter 6 using the methods of chapter 5. In making the recommendations we have taken account of the analysis presented in chapter 7 of directions of marginal reform, of industrial priorities and of the incidence of non-marginal reform. We embody in the package the land tax analysed in chapter 8 and the international lessons from chapter 9.

Our analysis and recommendations in this chapter take the form of a set

Table 10.1. *Growth rates of GPD*

Period	Annual average real growth
	%
Pre-plan (1950–5)	3.1
First Plan (1956–60)	3.1
Second Plan (1961–5)	6.8
Third Plan (1966–70)	6.7
Non-plan (1971–7)	3.9
Fifth Plan (1978–83)	6.6
Sixth Plan (1984–8) (to 1987)	6.9

Source: Government of Pakistan, Ministry of Finance, *Economic Survey*, 1987.

of proposals designed to provide a revenue framework for the medium term. They are not designed to be implemented within a single year but they form a medium-term programme for reform which should be feasible over five years or so, so that a five-year plan period provides a natural time scale. There can be no doubt that the accumulation of revenue pressures on the one hand, and the cumbersome nature of the existing system, based on the colonial history and a motley collection of *ad hoc* measures since independence on the other, have brought Pakistan to the point where tax reform is an urgent priority.

In order to understand the context of the assessment of revenue and expenditure prospects we comment briefly on the growth experience in Pakistan. The growth rate of the Pakistan economy since independence in 1947 has been impressive, averaging over 5% per annum in real terms. This is despite a growth rate of around 3% during the 1950s, periods of political turmoil and external shocks, including wars with India, the dismemberment of the country and an influx of refugees. This robust performance notwithstanding, there are signs that a continuation of growth rates in excess of 6% per annum, achieved during the 1980s, may prove difficult to maintain in the medium term. A central problem is the emergence and widening of budget deficits in recent years, with a steep increase in domestic borrowing.

We concentrate in this chapter on possible measures which could both raise substantial revenue to help reduce these deficits and alleviate some of the inequities, inefficiencies and administrative difficulties of the current system. As we have seen there is an excessive role played by indirect relative to direct taxes. Direct taxes are inhibited by exemptions of large categories of income. Inefficiencies arise from the heavy reliance on customs duties and taxation of domestic inputs which discriminate between sources of production in a fairly arbitrary way and cascade through the productive system. We shall also explore here the possibilities for instituting a medium-term fiscal strategy for Pakistan, which links revenues and expenditures more closely than has been the case in Pakistan's past experience.

In section 10.2 we describe the pattern of financing of government expenditures, show how the deficits have emerged and consider possible targets for their limitation over a five-year period. Details of possible reform measures based on the analysis of previous chapters and prospects of additional revenue for each are presented in section 10.3. We do not examine government expenditures in detail but a discussion focusing on the link between revenues and expenditures is provided in section 10.4, together with a consideration of the possible establishment of a medium-term fiscal plan (MTFP). We discuss administration of revenues and expenditure control in section 10.5, and section 10.6 contains a summary of proposals.

10.2   Financing expenditures

The most striking feature of Pakistan's consolidated budgetary performance in recent years has been the emergence of, and steady increase in, a deficit of revenues over current expenditures. There was a surplus on the current acount of 2.6% of GDP in 1980–1, whereas 1986–7 shows a shortfall equivalent to 3.6% of GDP (see table 10.2). While revenues have fluctuated between 18% and 20% of GDP in the 1980s, current expenditures have increased steadily as a percentage of GDP during the period 1980–1 to 1986–7. The stagnation in revenues reflects the poor performance of tax revenue collections, particularly of the major tax heads. Thus, tax revenue, which was around 14% of GDP in 1980–1, had declined to 13% of GDP (revised figure) for 1986–7. And this was despite a four-fold increase in collections from surcharges (on petroleum and natural gas), which increased from approximately one-third of the collections of individual and company taxes to rough parity during this period. Although during the Fifth Five-Year Plan, the revenue surplus financed 12.4% of development expenditures, a deficit had appeared during 1982–3, the last year of the Plan, leading to a 5% cut in development expenditure (Government of Pakistan, Planning Commission, *The Sixth Five-Year Plan 1984–88*, p. 49). The current revenue deficit in the first four years of the Sixth Plan was approximately Rs 50 billion, or about 33% of development expenditures during this period.

The overall deficit in 1985–6 was above 9% of GDP compared with approximately 6% of GDP in 1980–1. It seems clear that maintaining deficits at recent levels over the medium term will generate severe problems.

Table 10.2. *Consolidated revenues and current expenditures: Federal and provincial governments*

	Revenues (1)	Tax revenue (2)	Current expenditures (3)	Revenue surplus on current account (4)	GDP (at market prices) (5)
(a) Rs million					
1972–3	9 675	7 498	9 422	253	67 492
1973–4	13 836	10 487	13 702	134	88 102
1974–5	16 883	12 840	18 679	−1 796	111 183
1975–6	20 333	15 588	20 500	−167	130 364
1976–7	23 573	17 715	21 911	1 662	147 748
1977–8	29 149	21 588	27 554	1 595	176 419
Non-plan	113 449	85 716	111 768	1 681	
1978–9	34 437	25 393	33 363	1 075	195 109
1979–80	42 146	32 947	38 861	3 285	234 528
1980–1	50 164	38 722	42 890	7 274	277 961
1981–2	55 760	42 877	51 020	4 740	321 840
1982–3	64 973	48 983	66 970	−1 996	362 165
Fifth Plan	247 481	188 972	233 104	14 377	
1983–4	80 571	58 062	83 953	−3 382	418 201
1984–5	89 812	61 087	101 025	−11 311	477 982
1985–6	109 790	72 449	122 954	−13 165	539 537
1986–7(r)	124 545	78 222	145 948	−21 403	602 188
(b) As a proportion of GDP					
1972–3	0.143	0.111	0.140	0.004	
1973–4	0.157	0.119	0.156	0.002	
1974–5	0.152	0.115	0.168	−0.016	
1975–6	0.156	0.120	0.157	−0.001	
1976–7	0.159	0.120	0.148	0.011	
1977–8	0.165	0.122	0.156	0.009	
1978–9	0.177	0.130	0.171	0.006	
1979–80	0.180	0.140	0.166	0.014	
1980–1	0.180	0.139	0.154	0.026	
1981–2	0.173	0.133	0.159	0.015	
1982–3	0.179	0.135	0.185	−0.006	
1983–4	0.193	0.139	0.201	−0.008	
1984–5	0.188	0.128	0.211	−0.024	
1985–6	0.203	0.134	0.228	−0.024	
1986–7(r)	0.207	0.130	0.242	−0.036	

Notes: (i) Revenues and expenditures are estimated gross of intra-governmental transfers. (r) is the revised estimate for 1986–7.

(ii) Col. 4 is col. 1 minus col. 3 and is called in the text the 'current surplus'.

Source: Ahmad and Stern (1987b), based on figures provided by the Planning Commission.

Table 10.3. *The financing of deficits*

	Sources of finance							Composition of financing		
	Revenue surplus on current account (1)	ADP (2)	Auton-omous bodies (3)	Non-bank sources (4)	External reserves (5)	Bank system (6)	Overall deficit/GDP (7)	bank (8)	Non-External (9)	Bank system (10)
				Rs million					%	
1972–3	253	4455	95	178	3670	259	0.061	4.9	88.5	6.6
1973–4	134	6506	122	1640	3864	746	0.071	2.7	62.0	11.3
1974–5	−1796	10754	216	1143	8785	2406	0.111	9.0	71.2	19.8
1975–6	−167	13558	416	−247	9461	4095	0.102	−1.9	71.5	30.4
1976–7	1662	16239	353	257	7630	6337	0.095	2.1	53.7	44.2
1977–8	1595	17121	522	2514	7237	5253	0.085	16.5	48.2	35.3
Non plan	1681	68633	1724	5485	40647	19096				
1978–9	1075	20485	975	1331	9216	7888	0.094	7.4	50.0	42.6
1979–80	3285	21805	1507	−1080	12543	5551	0.072	−6.9	73.6	33.3
1980–1	7274	25800	2019	3117	11374	2016	0.059	18.6	69.5	11.9
1981–2	4740	26469	1909	3041	11263	5516	0.061	14.8	57.4	27.9
1982–3	−1996	29384	2286	7933	14443	6719	0.081	27.2	49.4	23.5
Fifth Plan	14377	123943	8986	14342	58838	27690				

1983–4	−3 382	29 130	2 565	7 872	13 512	8 564	0.071	26.5	45.1	28.2
1984–5	−11 311	34 090	2 640	9 513	14 200	18 949	0.090	22.2	33.3	44.4
1985–6	−13 165	39 778	2 942	24 071	19 082	6 848	0.093	43.4	37.6	14.0
1986–7(r)	−21 403	44 469	2 788	28 241	23 081	11 761	0.105	44.8	36.2	19.0

Notes: (i) 'ADP' is the Annual Development Plan which includes expenditures by government organisations on investment. (r) is the revised estimate for 1986–7.

(ii) 'Autonomous bodies' consist mainly of certain public-sector corporations and other bodies and the entry in the table is the total operational surplus.

(iii) The overall deficit is (col. 2 – col. 1).

(iv) The last three columns represent the standard sources for the financing of deficits, respectively borrowing domestically, borrowing abroad and printing money. The banking system in Pakistan is nationalised and column (10) corresponds (following government accounting practices) to 'borrowing from the central bank', or monetisation.

Source: Ahmad and Stern (1987b), based on figures provided by the Planning Commission.

If financing is through domestic borrowing, as is currently the case, deficits will put strong pressure on real interest rates, to the long-run deterrence of private investment. The fiscal pressure is also having a damaging effect on public investment – the 1980s saw the Annual Development Plan (ADP) cut back from 9.3% of GDP to 7.4% in 1986–7. The shortage of revenue is also threatening government expenditures on social sectors such as education and health. And deficits, if continued and financed through borrowing from the central bank, are likely to encourage inflation which itself may harm business confidence. Inflation would moreover be a regressive form of government finance. The reduction in the real value of money balances held by households is like a tax, which tends to be borne disproportionately by the poor who have less access to protected forms of asset-holding. Further, government expenditures on interest payments on outstanding debt have been rising sharply, accentuating the problem of deficits.

While it is not easy to be specific about a level of the deficit that is acceptable, we can see from the effects described that the levels since the mid-1980s seem excessive. We see below that continued financing of current expenditures by domestic borrowing, given current interest rates and debt-to-GDP levels, will lead to a very rapid increase in both the level of debt and of debt service. For example, maintaining government (non-debt service) consumption and development expenditure (ADP) as well as tax and non-tax revenues, at a constant proportion of GDP, would lead to a $2\frac{1}{2}$-fold increase over the five-year period (see table 10.2) in the revenue deficit as a proportion of GDP (or a six-fold nominal increase), largely arising from additional interest payments. Thus, without a substantial reduction in the deficit (particularly on revenue account), serious problems are likely to arise. We examine these issues further in our discussion of medium-term fiscal policy in section 10.4.

An alternative to raising taxes is to cut expenditure. However, in recent years over 75% of current expenditures have been on defence and interest payments on debt, and the prospects for reducing either of these heads in the short run must be subject to considerable scepticism. If major parts of the Annual Development Plan do show a good rate of return, then its financing by borrowing would be much easier to justify than borrowing to meet current expenditures, which may be less likely to engender long-run growth and repayment potential. It is popularly argued that a reasonable medium-term objective might be the balancing of revenue and current expenditure, leaving capital expenditures to be financed by borrowing. This might be a convenient rule-of-thumb but would require very substantial efforts on both revenue-raising and expenditure control compared with recent years. One must be careful not to elevate it into an iron law required by theory or first principles. One could, for example, argue that major parts of ADP investment could not easily produce a financial rate of return sufficient to cover borrowing and should not be so required. Where they generate real incomes then their return may be best captured by the government through the general tax system rather than pricing. In this case we would be looking for tax revenues in the medium term to be contributing to the ADP as well as covering current expenditures. In other words, eliminating the current deficit is unlikely by itself to be sufficient, difficult as this may be, and the government should be looking for a significant surplus of current revenues over expenditure. And as far as financing options are concerned, it is the overall deficit that is of relevance, not just the deficit of revenues over current expenditures.

The overall deficit includes the ADP on the expenditure side, and the resources generated by public semi-autonomous bodies on the revenue side (which, however, declined from 0.7% of GDP in 1980–1 to 0.5% by 1985–6). Where nominal interest rates respond to inflation, and all interest payments are included as part of expenditures, there may be an accounting distortion in the overall deficit measure. This distortion is due to the fact that part of the increased interest payments are a compensation to bondholders for a reduction in the value of their bonds. Thus, it is often useful to correct for inflation by excluding the interest payments on government debt, or to focus on the 'operational' deficit (see also Buiter, 1983). However, Pakistan has not been a high inflation economy, unlike Brazil or Argentina, and there is less need to correct interest payments for inflation to assess underlying fiscal imbalances. In this chapter, we concentrate on the financing of the conventional 'overall' deficit, and the options include external resources including foreign aid, borrowing from the State Bank (as the central bank is known), and domestic non-bank borrowing. While the recourse to external resources has gradually declined over the years, major shortfalls in 1977 and 1984 were made up by increased borrowing from the central bank. However, financing constraints, and the failure to institute major reforms of the tax system, have led to a recourse to assistance by the International Monetary Fund in 1978, 1981–2 and 1988–90. In recent years, the reliance on domestic non-bank borrowing has increased greatly.

The early 1980s, with an overall deficit of around 6% of GDP in 1980–1, were the beginning of an extended period of substantial growth. It is reasonable, therefore, to suppose that the conditions ruling at the time were not inimical to sustained progress. While overall deficits were a little higher in the late 1970s, that was at a time when concessionary aid was also high, and it does not seem that this form of finance can be regarded as reliable in the current international climate. (The high deficits in the period 1974–6 were financed largely (over 70%) from external sources (table 10.3), amounting to over 7% of GDP. By 1984, external finance had declined to around 3% of GDP, while the magnitude of the deficit approached the levels of the mid-1970s.) Thus a target deficit of 5% of GDP for the overall fiscal deficit in the medium term seems reasonable. If the ADP were 8% of GDP, for example, the achievement of the target would allow $\frac{3}{8}$, or $37\frac{1}{2}$%, of development expenditure to be financed by government revenue leaving the remainder to be financed by borrowing and aid. This might be a prudent balance between the pressures of revenue and expenditure on one hand and the problems of inflation, borrowing and the availability of aid on the other. This would entail a surplus of 3% of GDP of revenues over current expenditures. This could not be achieved overnight and the careful sequencing of the approach to such a target would be part of a medium-term fiscal plan.

The Perspective Plan (1965–85) incorporated a target for reducing external resources to less than 5% of investment (or 1.1% of GDP) by the end of the Perspective Plan and envisaged a transition to 'self-sustained' growth by the terminal year, 1985. Notwithstanding the economic and political traumas that the country faced during the 1970s, foreign resources continued to provide around a quarter of investment in the mid-1980s (Government of Pakistan, Ministry of Finance, *Economic Survey*, 1987) or 3.8% of GDP in 1986–7. It is ironic that the objective of reducing foreign resources to around 1% of GDP may well be achieved, though not because Pakistan has achieved 'take-off' but due to the vagaries of the international environment.

Governments may resort to printing money to pay for their deficit and this is known as monetisation. How far this policy will be non-inflationary will depend on the real growth rate of the economy, the demand for money, and the elasticity of demand for real balances with respect to inflation and income growth (see, for example, Buiter, 1990). Evidence suggests that revenues generated through non-inflationary monetary expansion are fairly limited. Average rates of monetary financing have been of the order of 1% of GDP in developed countries, and less than 2.5% for developing countries. Even moderate money financing of the order of 1–2% of GDP has been associated with inflation in excess of 50% in many developing countries in the 1980–5 period (see, for example, World Bank, 1988). Pakistan's central bank has been traditionally 'conservative' in expanding credit to the government, apart from periods in the late 1970s and mid-1980s. In both these periods there has been an acceleration in inflation, associated with an expansion in money supply.

Recourse to domestic non-bank borrowing has been a feature of the last five or six years, rising from around 1% of GDP at the start of the decade to

4.7% in 1986–7. Given the rapid increase in internal public debt, accompanied by high interest rates (in 1986–7, 13.4% to 15.6% on various instruments), interest payments increased from 1% of GDP in 1979–80 to 2.5% by 1986–7. This additional expenditure will put further pressures to resort to deficit financing if additional taxation cannot be generated. While providing resources in the short run, there is a danger that sustained reliance on domestic borrowing will lead to additional pressures on budgetary resources and exacerbate the deficit. Given a short-term perspective, domestic borrowing might appear tempting to finance ministers as an attractive alternative to difficult decisions concerning the restructuring of the tax system. Therein lie the longer-term dangers that have been building up during the 1980s.

Our main focus here is not, however, the optimal level of the deficit as such, but, rather, an indication of revenue measures which could provide a substantial increase in the tax to GDP ratio over the medium term. If these efforts are pushed as hard as is deemed politically appropriate, or administratively feasible, then the government expenditure priorities, both current and developmental, would determine the level of overall deficit. We experiment with alternative expenditure profiles in this chapter to bring out the limitations on, and the consequences of, crucial decisions facing the government.

The principles that should guide the imposition of extra taxation have been described in the preceding chapters. In the remainder of this chapter we integrate the analysis concerning directions of reform with specific targets for revenue generation for the medium term. In section 10.3 we set out revenue options from existing tax instruments, together with some reforms and their revenue possibilities. The phasing of the revenue forecasts and possibilities of closer linking with expenditures through medium-term fiscal planning are discussed in section 10.4.

10.3 Proposals for revenue and reform

We shall examine in this section the main actual or potential sources of taxation and ask how they might be reformed or realised. Their revenue potential under both existing policies and possible reforms is examined. As a benchmark we take a tax profile for which it is assumed that policies are operated in such a way as to keep constant the fraction of each tax as a proportion of GDP. The benchmark figures for tax revenues as a proportion of GDP are presented in table 10.4 (base year). Given the phasing of the reforms described below, the associated tax/GDP contributions are depicted over a six-year period. For the purposes of the illustrations we have taken a five-year period following a base year of 1987–

8. Thus we are thinking of decisions being taken in the year 1987–8 and executed over the subsequent five-year period.

In the following subsections we discuss the phasing of individual tax measures. Note that the timings are hypothetical in that decisions to implement these measures would have been necessary in advance of the programme. It is to be emphasised that these are representative of likely outcomes over the medium term and need not be anchored to the regular Five Year Plans in any formal sense. We discuss trade tax revenues in subsection 10.3.1, domestic indirect taxes in 10.3.2, the taxation of income in 10.3.3, and the land tax and other revenues in 10.3.4 and 10.3.5 respectively. Overall tax-revenue prospects are summarised in 10.3.6.

10.3.1 The taxation of external trade

There has been an increasingly heavy reliance on customs duties in Pakistan's recent history with the result that rates of duty are now very high with the consequent problems of an erosion of the base, smuggling and increasing administrative problems. In addition, as we have seen in earlier chapters, customs duties bring with them serious distortions of incentives. Their main justification has to be in terms of convenience as a tax handle where there are few others. We shall argue that other handles are available for Pakistan in the medium term. The economic inadequacies of customs duties, together with their increasing administrative problems, lead us to the suggestion that they should not increase as a fraction of GDP and should decrease as a fraction of tax revenue. In the longer term they should be decreased as a proportion of GDP and ultimately be replaced by indirect taxation based on final goods. However, it would be unrealistic to suppose that alternative sources of revenue will build up sufficiently fast to allow customs duties to decrease as a fraction of GDP over the next few years. Within the constraint of maintaining revenues as a proportion of GDP, major readjustments are desirable in the treatment of external trade concerning balance across commodities, coverage, and a shift from quantitative restrictions to tariffs. Note that if total tax collections are projected to increase faster than GDP, then the share of customs duty collection in total tax revenue must decline.

If customs collections are to remain constant as a fraction of GDP, they must increase at a nominal annual rate of $(1+g)(1+\delta)-1$, where g is the projected real rate of growth of GDP over the plan horizon, and δ is the rate of growth of the GDP deflator (the inflation rate). Thus if g is 6% and δ is 5%, customs collections would have to increase by 11.3% per annum (or from an estimated figure of Rs 40 billion during the first year of a five-year plan to Rs 62.5 billion in the terminal year).

Proposals for revenue and reform

Table 10.4. *Revenue projections for a six-year period with proposed tax package*

	Base year	Year 1	2	3	4	5
Income and profits tax	0.019	0.019	0.025	0.026	0.027	0.028
Land tax	0.000	0.000	0.005	0.009	0.011	0.013
Total direct taxes	0.019	0.019	0.030	0.035	0.038	0.041
Customs	0.055	0.055	0.055	0.055	0.055	0.055
Sales/VAT	0.009	0.010	0.011	0.013	0.020	0.029
Excises	0.030	0.030	0.030	0.025	0.025	0.025
Surcharges	0.017	0.017	0.017	0.017	0.017	0.017
Other taxes	0.004	0.004	0.004	0.004	0.004	0.004
Total indirect taxes	0.115	0.116	0.117	0.113	0.120	0.129
Total tax revenues	0.138	0.139	0.151	0.153	0.163	0.175
Non-tax revenues	0.037	0.037	0.037	0.037	0.037	0.037
Total revenues	0.175	0.176	0.188	0.189	0.199	0.211
Autonomous bodies	0.006	0.006	0.006	0.006	0.006	0.006

Notes: (i) Projections calculated by authors.
(ii) We assume the tax package is decided in the base year and implemented sequentially as described in section 10.3.
(iii) Figures are proportions of GDP.
(iv) The base year 1987–8 was estimated using revenue proportions for 1986–7, which was made available to us by the Planning Commission in the autumn of 1987.

For customs duties to keep pace with GDP, then broadly speaking taxable imports should grow at the same rate as GDP if *ad valorem* rates are constant. To hold *ad valorem* rates constant, specific duties would have to be adjusted accordingly. Revenues might grow faster if imports of more heavily taxed goods grow more rapidly, if items on the restricted or banned list are permitted to be imported subject to duty, if rationalisation of the duty structure leads to a greater compliance, or if administration improves. While a full assessment would require a detailed model of the trade sector, it may not be overly optimistic to assume that customs collections will match GDP growth during the medium term.

It is difficult to evaluate the incidence of customs duties on different households with any precision, since most of the commodities subject to tax are intermediate goods, machinery and raw materials. In previous chapters, we showed in terms of 'effective taxes' how taxes on inputs fed through the production process into the price of domestically produced final goods. In

Ahmad, Leung and Stern (1984) we saw that for 1975–6 effective taxes on domestic production (of which customs form the major part) had an impact on different households which was roughly proportional to expenditure. In this sense they are not progressive. One would further need to evaluate the incidence of the taxation of foreign goods which are domestically consumed. For this one would require a survey which identifies, for example, the consumption of imported toothbrushes as distinct from domestically produced ones, as well as the extent of smuggling for such goods. We are not aware that such information exists for Pakistan, but this could be the subject of interesting research at a later stage.

Major reforms to customs are necessary to remove quantitative restrictions and rationalise the relationships between imports and the domestic production structure. Further, the removal of quantitative restrictions and their replacement with duties would increase revenue in the short term. But viewing tariffs as the most convenient tax handle is likely to be short-sighted and would adversely affect desired changes in trade and industrial policy. Given the revenue constraints and administrative difficulties on the one hand and the unattractiveness of customs duties from the standpoint of economic efficiency on the other, we have suggested that over the medium term customs duties should maintain their share of GDP but reduce their share of tax revenues. As taxation of final goods increases (through, e.g., a VAT) in the longer term, customs duties should decrease as a proportion of GDP.

10.3.2   Domestic indirect taxation

The analysis in earlier chapters suggests that major increases in indirect tax revenue should come from a replacement of the existing sales tax and the smaller excises by a VAT in the short to medium term. A VAT would take up to two years or so to design and implement, but it is quite feasible that it could yield an additional 1.5% of GDP in revenues by the end of the five-year period if experience of other developing countries is a guide. To raise this revenue from customs duties, assuming zero price elasticities for the corresponding imports, would imply an increase in the implicit tariff (i.e. revenue from customs duties divided by the base of 45% of imports) from 60% to 82% on average (with an even larger increase required if the price increases reduce imports). This would be undesirable, since it would further distort the pattern of production and intensify the problems of the haphazard incidence of these duties. Since nominal duties would have to rise very steeply (because elasticities are not, in general, zero) there might be further erosion in the base and additional tax evasion. In the rest of this section we concentrate on the reform measures suggested. The VAT might replace sales taxes and many of the excises but not all of the latter. There are special arguments such as health, externalities, merit goods and so on which indicate special treatment for certain goods, such as cigarettes. For those excises which are not to be subsumed under the VAT, for surcharges, and other indirect taxes, we assume that revenues will remain a constant fraction of GDP during the period of a medium-term fiscal plan.

The VAT

We consider here a fundamental reform of indirect taxation in Pakistan which would entail the introduction of a VAT. We envisage this as replacing the sales tax and the smaller excises. A few of the substantial excises and surcharges would remain (e.g. cigarettes and cement) where there are special reasons for singling out these goods. Over time, customs duties would be reduced as the VAT revenue builds up so that it becomes the major source of indirect tax revenue. As discussed in previous chapters, such a tax is consistent with the basic economic principles of efficiency, it can be designed with appropriate exemptions and rate structures to meet distributional and administrative concerns and experience from other countries shows that it can be administratively feasible.

All developing (and developed) countries have compliance problems and one cannot argue convincingly that Pakistan's administrative problems are overwhelmingly different from other poor countries. Indeed, in a number of ways administration in Pakistan is superior to that in many developing countries. We shall not provide a detailed review of the experience of other countries with a VAT since a useful collection of descriptions of that experience is provided by Tait (1988) and Gillis *et al.*, (1989). Our recommendations here and judgements of feasibility and timing are based on the lessons drawn from that experience. There are a number of different versions possible for a VAT in terms of definitions of base, methods of calculation of liability, and the administration of invoices and collection. These are all important issues but our main concern here is not to review these issues in detail. Rather we suggest the broad structure of a VAT from the point of view of base and rates, and comment briefly on how it could be introduced. It is interesting that the name VAT can be politically sensitive so that a creative title is sometimes necessary. We shall leave the name to the public relations experts and speak here of a VAT.

The VAT could be introduced over a two-year period. During the period of introduction, the VAT could be extended to sectors presently exempt from the sales tax, and a decision taken as to its extension to the wholesale stage. Once a decision is taken to introduce the VAT, considerable work will be required to fill in the details, including industry-level coverage, determination of exemption levels, treatment of the small-scale sector, administrative arrangements and the rate structure, including exemptions and zero-rating.

From the estimates of chapter 7, we observe that a revenue-neutral VAT could be designed to make the distributional impact progressive. On the basis of the discussion in chapter 7, one could suggest a basic rate of VAT of 10%, a luxury rate of 20%, exemptions for agriculture, and zero-rating of exports. An alternative is for a 15% basic rate, exemption for agriculture and zero-rating for exports. Appropriate differentiation (from distributional perspectives) for the overall tax system could then emerge from the combination of these structures and a set of excises. Small-scale and service sector enterprises would be able to choose not to come into the VAT network, but would then be subject to a presumptive tax on the basis of easily recognisable indicators. Legal provision for these presumptives already exists. More firms or individuals subject to presumptive taxation would come within the purview of the VAT, as record-keeping becomes more established.

An average rate of around 15% on taxable goods (given the two positive rates of 10% and 20%), applied to a base of 20% of GDP would yield around 3% of GDP in revenue. Such an estimate is based on the experience of other developing countries (see Tanzi, 1987). Turkey introduced a VAT in 1985, and quickly built to a base of 25% of GDP which, with a basic rate of 12%, now yields 3% of GDP. If the VAT is introduced in year 3 of the fiscal programme, replacing smaller excises and the sales tax, and allowing for an initial period of adjustment, one could envisage a combined excise/VAT revenue for that year to be at the level of sales tax/excise revenues for year 2. The expansion in VAT revenues should occur within a year, and the expansion of the base to 20% of GDP should yield around 3% of GDP five years or so from legislation. The experience of many countries is that, as sales expand with the growth of the economy, VAT revenues increase at a similar rate without the need for frequent rate adjustments. If the VAT applies to goods with, on average, income elasticities of demand greater than one, then revenue expansion at a faster rate than GDP is possible.

The VAT should, thus, provide the basis for a long-run expansion in revenues which, when the maximum coverage has been reached, would provide a source of revenue that would grow in line with GDP, avoid the cascading effects of the present system, encourage exports and domestic production, and which could have distributional features which are more attractive than the present system.

10.3.3 *Taxation of income*

As we saw in chapter 2, Pakistan's performance with the income and corporation taxes falls short of average collections achieved in other countries, even by the standards of the poorest group. And at around 1.9% of GDP in recent years, revenue is considerably below the collection of 2.7% of GDP which was achieved in 1980.

While we are not in a position to evaluate the extent of income and corporation tax evaded in Pakistan, estimates based on casual empiricism suggest, in all probability correctly, that this is substantial, despite a significant reduction in marginal tax rates in recent years. If there is not full indexation of personal income tax thresholds, then inflation is likely to raise additional revenues. But prospects for additional revenues appear to depend mostly on more efficient administration and better compliance, as suggested by the National Taxation Reform Commission. In addition, a removal of allowances, and the closing of loopholes, particularly by removing the *de facto* exemption for capital gains and preventing the possibility of disguising incomes as if from agriculture, would be helpful in increasing tax collections. While the capital gains tax itself may not raise substantial revenues, it should help income tax collections in making it more difficult to conceal an income source as a capital gain. On the other hand a land tax would provide major additional revenue, as well as helping income tax collections. Note that one of the advantages of the VAT is that it provides information that would be useful in improving income tax administration and, for this reason, could be administered by the same authorities to ensure efficient exchange of information on VAT and income tax records.

As with the personal income tax, the main problem with the corporate income tax is collection. On both administrative and economic grounds we would recommend a withholding tax on dividends. This tax payment would be set against corporate tax liability but would not be refundable. This has the twin advantages of speed, since corporate accounts and thus tax assessment are often very delayed, and greater sureness of collection, since often accounts are manipulated so as to show no liability. There would, for the honest firm, be no discrimination between distributed and undistributed profits, since the withholding tax is credited against the future liability. And the tax payment would also be credited against the income tax of the dividend recipient, and the dividend income would be included in his or her total income. This means essentially that the corporate and income tax systems would be much more closely integrated than at present and, as we argued in chapter 3, economic principles point us firmly in this direction. This simple reform would not pose severe administrative difficulties and could have substantial revenue potential. The present system exempts dividends and attempts to collect the corporate tax on profits. In principle, if the corporation tax and the marginal personal income tax were at the same rate it would be equivalent to our proposal. But our suggestions would make collection more timely and reliable since accounts are so often fraudulent and late. It is also more closely related to individual incomes. Further, 'business' expenses are often disguised payments to directors and senior staff. These should be carefully examined by the revenue authorities in order to plug a major loophole.

The revenue profile that we anticipate is that 1980 levels of revenue from the taxation of income could be achieved by the second year of the five-year period, with a rising proportion assumed to occur thereafter.

10.3.4 The land tax

As we argued in chapters 4 and 8 a land tax is attractive from the points of view of efficiency, equity and administration. It falls, if designed correctly, largely on the richer sections of the population, it has fewer disincentive effects than the use of other direct tax bases such as income or output, and the base itself is more easily measured. The main disadvantages are political, in that it is highly visible and falls on a group which is particularly powerful in Pakistan. Our purpose here is not to resolve these political difficulties but to draw attention to its other attractions and its revenue potential. If it is taken off the agenda for political reasons then this should be done explicitly: the revenue difficulties and problems with other sources will, of course, then be accentuated.

As discussed in chapter 8, our proposal is for a flat rate of tax on land with an exemption limit of 12.5 acres, which would ensure a fairly progressive incidence. Land quality would be taken into account by working with produce index units (PIUs), measures which are already in existence and could be revised to bring them up to date (PIUs have been used in connection with land revenues and settlement of land for refugees after partition). The flat rate would decrease the problems of progressivity associated with the subdivision of holdings within a family. No doubt the exemption level would encourage some families to subdivide, but it must be remembered that subdivision may be perilous for a household head. Families are not all unified entities in happy concord and the cousin, brother or son who is given some land with tax avoidance intent may well decide to regard the land as his own and leave the erstwhile head of household to fulminate. Our calculations of revenue potential are based on the land distribution figures from the Agricultural Census for 1980, and are discussed more fully in chapter 8. We expect that the land tax could be brought in quickly, say by year 1 of the plan, and yield revenue up to the full potential soon after. Our estimated projections (table 10.4), however, are conservative in expecting revenues to rise from less than half of the full potential in year 2 to three-quarters in year 3, approaching full potential towards the end of the plan period. In practice the phasing could be much quicker.

10.3.5 Other revenues

Other revenues involve a number of heads including, *inter alia*, income from public-sector corporations, earning from provision of government services such as posts and telegraphs and so on. This has not been a major focus of our research. Given that losses of public-sector corporations act in part like subsidies to their consumers, who are often the better off, there has been considerable pressure to reduce losses by raising prices. The revision of pricing for public-sector activities and services, to remove or considerably reduce losses, could be attractive on efficiency and revenue grounds and may not have adverse distributional consequences. This could be a fruitful area for further research.

10.3.6 Revenue profile

The revenue profile associated with the suggested measures is summarised in table 10.4. Assuming a 6% growth in GDP the table suggests that, if the reforms are instituted in the base year, additional revenues would be generated in year 2, increasing to an additional inflow of around 4% of projected GDP by year 5.

10.4 A medium-term fiscal plan

The formulation of a medium-term fiscal plan (MTFP) involves projections of revenues, expenditures and borrowing. Given estimates of two of these the third is the residual. Thus if the path of expenditures is regarded as fixed over the MTFP period, borrowing requirements are determined by the level of revenues that could be generated, i.e. they are the gap between revenues and expenditures during the forecasting period. A sensible approach to medium-term fiscal strategy in the Pakistan context is to start with the question: what revenue generation is possible over the reference period? We have been mainly concerned with this question in the preceding sections, and we treat our suggestions as the maximum it would be prudent to attempt to achieve in the medium term. Whilst our proposals, if implemented, would show a large increase, larger it might be argued than some governments may feel able to attempt, we shall see that it is still likely to leave major revenue problems.

The deficit in a particular year may be large due to unexpected expenditures or shortfalls in revenue, but may none the less not be a source of undue concern. In a MTFP one has to ask whether the deficits over a period of time are sustainable. This is because, in the medium term, expenditures are not fixed, and interest payments in particular are a function of the level of the deficit, borrowings and real interest rates. Thus expenditures and borrowing/deficits should be evaluated simultaneously, in relation to each other and to prospects for revenue generation.

In subsection 10.4.1, we discuss current expenditures briefly in relation to forecasting over the MTFP period. Potential expenditures and associated deficits are discussed in the context of a MTFP for Pakistan, along with projections for the five-year period in subsection 10.4.2.

10.4.1 Expenditures

The gap between revenues and current expenditures widened during the Sixth Plan period (as we have seen, a surplus on the current account was maintained for most years prior to 1983; see table 10.2). The share of tax revenues has stagnated around 13% of GDP during the 1980s. The increasing revenue deficit has been due to the failure of tax revenues to match the rapid increase in current expenditures. Expenditures on defence, debt servicing, social services and administration have increased faster than GDP during the 1980s, the first three heads accounting for two-thirds of current expenditure, and administration forming around 10% (see Government of Pakistan, Ministry of Finance, *Economic Survey*, various).

The increase in defence spending reflects Pakistan's geo-political situation, as well as additional pension and wage payments and the depreciation of the rupee. Prospects for reducing defence spending over the medium term, given the international environment, cannot be predicted with any degree of confidence and a civilian government is not a guarantee that defence spending will be lower than under a military regime. In any country, however, defence spending is limited by the resources available and spending here should not be immune from scrutiny. There is likely to be greater accountability of military spending with a renewed political process.

It might be assumed that a democratically elected government would be more likely to increase expenditures on the social sectors and to protect disadvantaged sections of society than to increase defence expenditure. The increase in spending on education and social services might be justified by pointing to Pakistan's inadequate social infrastructure. In recent years there has been an attempt to improve Pakistan's poor literacy rates by increased spending on education, and a decision of the Zia government to finance provincial expenditures on education above FY 1983–4 levels on a grant basis reflects the inadequate revenue-generating capabilities of the provinces. There has been some discussion of appropriate 'user charges' for education or health and these would no doubt require careful study. Some services, for example certain parts of the education system, are consumed in major part by the better off and a move to charge for services, while maintaining adequate provisions for the poor and needy, would ease the budgetary pressures on this account. It would also lessen the dependence of the Provinces on the Centre. At the same time there are many parts of health and education which are, or should be, consumed by the poor and they should be protected in any move towards user charges. As with defence, the undoubted needs in this area do not necessarily provide an automatic argument for raising expenditure faster than GDP and ambitions must be tailored to resources.

Increases in administrative expenditures are due largely to additional outlays on wages and pensions. There has also been a rapid increase in the numbers employed at various levels of government. The federal administration does seem to be aware of the costs (over and above salaries) of keeping its staff functional and efforts are made from time to time to limit such expenditures. Other increases in recent years include a Rs 2 billion unemployment fund, and a provision for the bad debts of the public sector. It would appear that careful consideration would be required before any increase in employment in general administration is permitted. There is no obvious reason, for example, why this should rise in proportion to population or GDP since there is a fixed cost element in any administration. Tax administration, on the other hand, may be a priority area for increasing both salaries and employment (see section 10.5).

There was some success in reducing the level of subsidies, which were 1.69% of GDP in 1985–6 compared with 1.76% in 1980–1. Subsidies on edible oils, sugar and cotton reflected cyclic movements in international prices. Movements in international markets have permitted the imposition of an export duty on cotton in September 1987. The subsidy on wheat has traditionally represented a means to protect the welfare of the poor. However, the move from subsidised rations to general subsidy for wheat has been associated with a burgeoning of the wheat subsidy since 1986. Research is needed on ways to target income security for the poor more efficiently, although the wheat subsidy in some form may well have an important role to play. Given the widespread diffusion of fertiliser use in Pakistan, and agricultural prices which are now close to world prices for most commodities, the case for a fertiliser subsidy is somewhat weakened, and should be examined in detail. While the export rebate has been abolished (a VAT would make life much simpler for exporters and the government), one of the remaining major subsidies in recent years has been the loss made by Pakistan Steel. Again this is an area which, in our opinion, would need further study. Appropriate user charges, particularly in the irrigation, energy and power sectors, could provide substantial extra revenue which might permit some expansion of current and capital expenditures.

Debt-service obligations have been discussed earlier, and are the result of a combination of a substantial increase of outstanding debt, largely from domestic sources, and a hardening of repayment terms. Although this variable is a function of the success the government may have in raising extra revenues, the existing situation is sufficiently serious to warrant the choice of overall level of debt and its annual servicing as key target variables for the Seventh Plan. Indeed, continuing deficits financed by borrowing put increasing pressure on expenditures because of the rising burden of debt-servicing. Thus debt and debt-service have played a central role in our forecasts below.

10.4.2 Medium-term fiscal planning for Pakistan

The full specification of a MTFP would involve the optimal or target paths for domestic and foreign borrowing for the Pakistan economy, within a fully articulated macro-model, incorporating the major interactions between the main variables. This is not a task which we have attempted. In this much more limited exercise, we use a system of standard macro-accounts (see Høst-Madsen, 1979, for details) and a set of simplifying projection assumptions to illustrate the probable consequences of particular configurations of expenditures and revenues, with respect to the overall level of debt and interest payments, over the MTFP. One can then examine the rate of change of the overall deficit (increasing rates of change suggest an explosive and unsustainable debt path) to reassess expenditure and tax policies. It must be emphasised that the formulation is not presented as a full model of the economy but simply as providing illustrative calculations to bring out the main trade-offs.

Let Y_t be GDP at market prices in year t; E_t, overall government expenditure; R_t, government revenue; and D_t, the overall deficit. Writing R_t^j for the revenue from the jth source in year t, we have $R_t = \sum_j R_t^j$. Using $E_t - R_t = D_t$, we have the basic accounting relation in the MTFP:

$$D_t + \sum_j R_t^j = E_t \qquad (10.1)$$

In the Pakistan context, we may write the overall expenditures in a year as the sum of the Annual Development Plan (ADP_t), the debt-servicing payments (DS_t) and other expenditures (J_t):

$$E_t = ADP_t + DS_t + J_t \qquad (10.2)$$

Thus, if overall expenditure is projected to grow at the rate of GDP, as is other expenditure, then a rising fraction of debt-service payments will lead to a fall in the ADP relative to GDP. This appears to have been the trend since the late 1970s (table 10.3). Interest rates are assumed constant in our calculations. Debt-service payments reflect both interest rates and outstanding debt. As debt rises in relation to GDP so will interest payments. To the extent that real interest rates increase as a result of additional government borrowing to meet deficits, the current expenditure figures will be underestimates. We assume, for simplicity and because it would be prudent, that borrowing from the banking system will not exceed current levels as a proportion of GDP. Given the uncertainty with respect to future external sources of finance, a similar assumption with respect to foreign borrowing may be overly optimistic, but is, nevertheless, made. Domestic (non-bank) borrowing is treated as a residual. Although thetre is some speculative evidence that the expansion of instruments for domestic borrowing in recent years has played a role in improving financial intermediation, and that private investment may not have been crowded out to an appreciable extent, it is also the case that there is discernible upward pressure on interest rates.

The effect of domestic borrowing on private savings and investment is an interesting and major research question. While the projections do not take into account the interactions between the two, it should be recognised that continued domestic borrowing may have an adverse effect on private investment, and consequently on growth rates.

Size of the public investment plan

One method of medium-term fiscal planning is to set a 'desirable' level for the overall deficit and then to match revenues and the given deficit to overall expenditures. For example, if revenues and deficit levels are constant as a proportion of GDP, a rising proportion of current expenditures in GDP will lead to a smaller proportion for the ADP. However, since we do not know what level of borrowing the government thinks appropriate, we have chosen to treat borrowing, and consequently overall debt, as residuals in an illustrative MTFP. Government current non-debt-service expenditures (J_t) are treated as a constant proportion of GDP. This leaves the ADP as a proportion of GDP to be specified. We have assumed that this ADP will be maintained at 7.7% of GDP over the

MTFP period. Note that our assumption that government investment is maintained at current levels in relation to GDP, together with the assumption that the growth rate will continue at the levels of the recent past, would be consistent with an extrapolation of incremental capital–output ratios and private investment rates at their past levels.

Projected deficits

A standard system of macroeconomic accounts is used to derive budget balances, balance of payments, monetary aggregates, private sector relationships and national accounts aggregates (for details see Høst–Madsen, 1979). Exports and imports are assumed to grow in line with GDP. As before we distinguish between the 'revenue surplus/deficit', which is the balance of current government revenues over non-development expenditures, and 'overall surplus/deficit' which includes all expenditure. We assume, as a rough approximation to historical experience, that GDP will grow at 6%. We consider two cases, A and B. They have the same expenditure profiles net of interest payments with, in each case, public investment (ADP) at 7.7% of GDP and other government (non-debt) expenditure (J_t) projected to grow along a profile forecast by the Planning Commission. The two cases are different on the revenue side: case A has revenue projections with the proposed tax package and case B maintains the benchmark tax structure with revenue from the different taxes being a constant proportion of GDP. The lower revenues in case B imply a faster growth in government debt and therefore higher debt-service payments. As a result, current expenditure, *including debt-service payments*, also grows more rapidly in case B.

Case A: With tax reform. The budget profile (table 10.5) with the tax reform measures shows that the current deficit is removed by the end of the five-year period, with the overall deficit declining steadily during this period. The domestic debt to GDP ratio continues to increase, though at a decreasing rate, and stabilises at 47% of GDP by Year 4 (debt to GDP ratios are not included in the tables). Government interest payments rise from 5.5% in the base year stabilising around 6.1% (of GDP) at the end, assuming interest rates are constant. Note that the interest rates assumed (e.g. 9% for domestic borrowing) have turned out to be on the low side relative to subsequent experience.

Case B: With present tax/GDP ratio. If projected expenditures are coupled with a tax-revenue profile based on the existing tax structure, on the optimistic assumption that the buoyancy of existing taxes is unity over the plan period then we see that the current deficit increases steadily as a

Table 10.5. *Budgetary implications of proposed tax package with public investment a constant fraction of GDP*

	Base year	Year				
		1	2	3	4	5
Current revenues	0.175	0.176	0.188	0.189	0.199	0.211
Direct taxes	0.019	0.019	0.030	0.035	0.038	0.041
Indirect taxes	0.115	0.116	0.117	0.113	0.120	0.129
Non-tax revenues	0.037	0.037	0.037	0.037	0.037	0.037
Current expenditure	0.206	0.208	0.210	0.211	0.211	0.211
Interest payments	0.055	0.057	0.059	0.060	0.061	0.061
Revenue surplus	−0.031	−0.032	−0.022	−0.021	−0.012	0.000
Public investment (ADP)	0.077	0.077	0.077	0.077	0.077	0.077
Overall deficit	0.107	0.109	0.099	0.098	0.089	0.077
Domestic non-bank	0.077	0.078	0.068	0.067	0.058	0.046
Banking system	0.009	0.009	0.009	0.009	0.009	0.009
External sources	0.021	0.021	0.021	0.021	0.021	0.021

Note: See notes to table 10.4. The difference between current revenues and the sum of direct and indirect taxes and non-tax revenues is accounted for by revenue from autonomous bodies.

proportion of GDP over the period, rising to 4.1% at the end of the period (see table 10.6). With public investment at 7.7% the end-year deficit would be 11.7%. The domestic debt to GDP ratio increases to 56% of GDP over the plan period. Government interest payments rise steadily to 6.5% at the end of the period and would go on rising. This assumes no increase in interest rates and it may become difficult to keep these down as debt and borrowing increase.

10.5 Administration

The elements of a MTFP have been described in the preceding section. Given the objective of sustained growth (albeit with equity) over the medium-term period, our primary concern has been with the increase of revenues. The existing pattern of reforms and expenditures appears unsustainable. What is required is a combination of *tax reform*, which ensures revenues while encouraging growth and protecting the poor and needy, a non-inflationary *monetary policy* without excessive recourse to

Table 10.6. *Unchanged tax structure with public investment a constant fraction of GDP*

	Base year	Year				
		1	2	3	4	5
Current revenues	0.175	0.175	0.175	0.175	0.175	0.175
Direct taxes	0.019	0.019	0.019	0.019	0.019	0.019
Indirect taxes	0.115	0.115	0.115	0.115	0.115	0.115
Non-tax revenues	0.037	0.037	0.037	0.037	0.037	0.037
Current expenditure	0.206	0.208	0.210	0.212	0.214	0.216
Interest payments	0.055	0.057	0.059	0.061	0.063	0.065
Revenue surplus	−0.031	−0.033	−0.035	−0.037	−0.039	−0.041
Public investment (ADP)	0.077	0.077	0.077	0.077	0.077	0.077
Overall deficit	0.107	0.109	0.111	0.113	0.115	0.117
Domestic non-bank	0.077	0.079	0.081	0.083	0.085	0.087
Banking system	0.009	0.009	0.009	0.009	0.009	0.009
External sources	0.021	0.021	0.021	0.021	0.021	0.021

Note: See notes to tables 10.4 and 10.5.

borrowing from the central bank, and control over *expenditures*. We comment briefly on some mechanisms for the central government which might be used to keep revenues and expenditures on track. The problems of administration of individual taxes have been considered in earlier chapters in the course of discussions of reform possibilities (see, for example, chapters 7 and 8).

10.5.1 Expenditure control

One method of relating expenditures to revenues, given public sector borrowing requirements, is an annual exercise within an MTFP. Examples of this type of procedure include those of the UK that have evolved since 1981, and the Gramm–Rudman proposals for the United States. The Gramm–Rudman law was designed with automatic expenditure cuts at the heart of the legislation. These cutting procedures should, in principle, be triggered when actual deficits exceed the targeted level. It is not clear that the specification of a target deficit and automatic cuts would be appropriate in a country like Pakistan, where the constitution and legal observance are less robust than in the USA.

The British experience is perhaps more relevant since detailed expenditure targets over a three-year period are discussed annually by the Treasury with government departments. This exercise also establishes the borrowing limits of the public-sector enterprises, and the expenditures of local governments. However, 'exogenous' payments such as the payments of debt interest and spending on social security are excluded. A feature of the British system that might be recommended for Pakistan is that expenditure targets be presented to Parliament two to three months before the Budget.

Provincial expenditures

For a MTFP to succeed in Pakistan, satisfactory methods for inter-governmental transfers need to be established. An additional source of revenue for local expenditures in our proposals is the land tax, which should make the task easier. A pre-condition for a successful MTFP in Pakistan is for a Finance Commission to review revenue-sharing arrangements between the Centre and the Provinces and local authorities periodically. Typically, in large federations, revenue-sharing formulae (usually incorporating estimates of provincial revenue generation, sharing of federal revenues from the income tax, sales taxes and so on, as well as an element of 'need' to assist backward regions) are determined every five to seven years. Once the sharing arrangements are determined, they should be strictly followed. Thus if a province has additional expenditure requirements, say to improve roads and sanitation in major urban areas, then the expenditure would have to be financed by a system of local rates, for example, or appropriate user charges. The consequence of pre-determining provincial transfers within an MTFP is that provinces would have to exploit local taxation potential to meet incremental expenditures, and could not assume that the federal exchequer would bail them out of any difficulty that might arise.

Other federal current expenditures

A public expenditure survey should be conducted annually, covering government spending departments and public-sector corporations, to elicit expenditure requirements for the next financial year and forecasts for the following two years or so. The current expenditure forecasts would then be assessed by the Finance Ministry, and adjusted so that totals match the current expenditure projections based on the MTFP path agreed by the Cabinet. A sub-committee of the Cabinet may have to adjudicate on conflicting demands, and the resulting set of expenditure estimates should be presented to Parliament some months prior to the Budget. The cash expenditure limits voted by Parliament would then be binding.

Although some of the machinery for a public expenditure survey to establish base-lines and targets is already in place given the procedures involved in arriving at the ADP, complete procedures including timing would need to be discussed in detail with the Ministry of Finance and the Central Board of Revenue in consultation with the Planning Commission.

10.5.2 Revenue planning

Administrative procedures would also have to be devised to ensure coordination of aid projections, disbursement and utilisation. Since this is the responsibility of the Economic Affairs Division, which is separate from the Planning Commission in large part, they would also have to be centrally involved in the MTFP, in addition to the Ministry of Finance and the Planning Commission.

The revenue projections for various taxes would be an integral element in the MTFP. We have indicated that overall revenue projections on the basis of current taxation are likely to be inconsistent with the requirements of adequate public investment and current expenditure combined with a sustainable borrowing requirement. The alternative revenue profiles, which would require Cabinet and Parliamentary approval, could however suffice to meet growth, security and social objectives.

The Five-Year Plans and the MTFP

The Five-Year Plans also entail iterative procedures similar to those which would be necessary for the MTFP, and there would be a need to coordinate the actions of the Planning Commission in this respect with those of the Ministry of Finance regarding current expenditures. The Annual Development Plan should also be presented to Parliament at the same time as the White Paper on current expenditures, so as to indicate the linkages between the two.

Statutory provisions and controls

An innovation within the prospective MTFP is that expenditures would be vetted by Parliament in advance of the Budget, which determines the balance between revenues and borrowing requirements. Expenditures would continue to be voted from consolidated funds, as at present, but there would be more systematic control of spending departments by various select committees. There should be severe sanctions for exceeding cash spending limits, and relaxation of the limits would be allowed only under exceptional circumstances.

If the kinds of procedures we have sketched were to be put into practice it is clear that a great deal of further detailed work would be required. Our concern is simply to indicate the kinds of considerations that are necessary and that some relevant international experience exists.

10.6 Summary of proposals

We have argued that the maintenance of current government revenues as a percentage of GDP together with the projected rising expenditures as a proportion of GDP would, if inflationary monetary policies are to be avoided, lead in the medium term to domestic borrowing which would soon become unsustainable. Further, given that the growth of revenues over the 1980s, with the accumulation of surcharges and *ad hoc* measures, has barely kept up with GDP, it is clear that the aim of maintaining the revenue to GDP ratio within the current system would itself be optimistic. This budgetary position together with the inefficient and inequitable existing tax structure makes tax reform an urgent priority.

The proposals set forth in this chapter could achieve a balance on the government current revenue account in a period of five years, allowing for increases in expenditure as a proportion of GDP. If, further, expenditures are restrained, the position of the early 1980s could be restored with government saving making a significant contribution to the finance of public investment.

In summary our tax proposals are as follows:

(i) *Customs*

(a) The removal of quantitative restrictions.
(b) A review of rates with a reduction in some of the very high rates and a closer linking with industrial policy.
(c) The maintenance of revenues as a constant fraction of GDP in the medium term.
(d) In the longer term, the reduction of customs duties as revenues from domestic taxation increase.

(ii) *Domestic indirect taxation*

(a) The introduction of a VAT up to the wholesale stage with eventual extension to the retail stage as experience develops.
(b) Exemption of agriculture from VAT. Zero-rating of exports with a resulting full reclamation of taxes on inputs.

(c) The choice of a two-rate VAT with a standard rate of 10% and a higher luxury rate. This would, if combined with appropriate exemptions (including the above), yield a distributional impact which is more progressive than the existing indirect tax structure. Alternatively, a simple 15% rate with adjusted excises which could yield both the revenue described and progressive distributional outcomes relative to the existing system.

(d) The retention of major excises such as those on tobacco, cement and petroleum for reasons of externalities (tobacco, petroleum), (de)merit goods (tobacco) and distribution (cement, petroleum), as well as for the reason of revenue.

(iii) *Income*

The tightening of administration, a closer integration of income and corporation tax, the removing of loopholes through agricultural income and the closer maintenance of 'business' expenses. Dividends should be taxed at source and credited against corporation and personal income tax liability. This would speed collection and reduce the scope for evasion. Income tax and the VAT should be administered by the same authority to benefit from the exchange of information.

(iv) *Land*

Consideration of a land tax based on produce index units (suitably updated) with an exemption level around 12.5 acres. Revenues would accrue to local governments, and would form the basis for social security and assistance at the local level

(v) *Presumptive methods*

A wide use of presumptive methods for both income and indirect taxes. Sales presumptions, for example, might be based on simple indicators of size and income presumptions related to visible assets or consumption.

(vi) *Public-sector pricing*

The appraisal of user charges and public-sector prices using the approaches and methods described in this book.

Together, we suggest, these proposals provide a rational and feasible way of generating extra revenue whilst promoting efficiency and equity.

11 Conclusions

11.1 Introduction

The purposes of this book have been, first, to provide principles and methods for the analysis of tax reform and, second, to apply those methods to tax reform in Pakistan, to identify improvements to the existing system and possible programmes for meeting revenue requirements in the future. Accordingly, we trust, these are the principal outputs of our work. We have tried to present both the principles and methods and the empirical analysis in a manner that can be applied to other problems, contexts and countries. Reforms were evaluated in terms of their consequences and we saw that this could lead quickly to analytical difficulty, but, wherever possible, we have tried to use simple techniques to cut through the complications. We should emphasise that the major difficulties come here, in the positive or predictive part of the enquiry, where we attempt to appraise policies in terms of their consequences, rather than in terms of a particular normative criterion. The techniques which we have been using are designed to examine in a coordinated and systematic way the implications of a reform for equity and efficiency in allocation across households, for government revenue, and for production allocations. These have been standard concerns in public finance and would be central to most investigations. As such our work follows in the public finance tradition which runs from Dupuit, Edgeworth and Wicksell to Musgrave and Samuelson.

The research methods we have used are those of tax reform, that is the identification of improvements from an existing state of affairs. This has, therefore, involved us in the detailed analysis of the status quo. Nowhere in this book, or in our research programme, has there been any attempt to calculate optimal taxes. Our use of the theories of optimal taxation has been in the examination of basic principles arising from the traditional concerns of public finance; for example, trade-offs between efficiency and equity, and the design of and balance between different tax instruments.

315

In analysing possible reforms and in formulating recommendations we have paid attention to the administrative capacity of the tax system and to political difficulties. Thus simplicity in administration, ease of measurement of tax base, availability of the information relevant for a tax, possibilities for evasion and corruption, and so on, have been important issues. We have not attempted to resolve political difficulties. A number have been indicated and it is not for us to insist on any solutions. That is a job for government. On the other hand, whatever the view of the role of government or the workings of the political system, one wants to know who gains and who loses from a reform, and that has been a central concern. Such an analysis should be a key input to the political process.

Some of our recommendations are not wildly at variance with policies that have been examined and occasionally proposed by tax missions or inquiries which may have used different approaches or less detailed methods. But that is not the point. We have not tried to invent a tax that no-one has thought of before. We have set out in our applied work to analyse possible reforms in a systematic way and to produce a coherent set of proposals based on a clear set of principles. We have seen that some apparently simple 'common sense' approaches produce arguments that are misleading or simply wrong. In tax policy, as elsewhere, it is only when we make the theory, principles and calculations explicit that we can evaluate properly the arguments for and against particular forms of action and that is what we have attempted to do. We hope that we have thereby provided a framework for further work on taxation in developing (and developed) countries.

We now summarise briefly the principles (section 11.2), methods (11.3), and possibilities for further research (11.4). Concluding comments are provided in section 11.5. A summary of our recommendations for Pakistan was provided at the end of the preceding chapter.

11.2 Principles

The derivation of simple guiding principles for tax design and reform was a principal objective of chapter 3 and these were summarised at the end of that chapter. We assemble them briefly here without the appropriate assumptions, qualifications, elaborations and examples which were provided in chapter 3.

(i) Where possible, lump-sum taxes and transfers, or close approximations, should be used to raise revenue and transfer resources. Possibilities are land taxes and subsidised rations.

(ii) It can be very misleading to look at one set of tax tools in isolation from what is happening elsewhere in the tax system. For example, we should not allocate redistribution to the income tax and revenue-raising to indirect taxes. Both types of tax affect resource allocation and distribution, and raise revenue.

(iii) As far as is possible the base for indirect taxation should be final consumption and not intermediate goods.

(iv) Public-sector prices should be set according to the same principles as indirect taxes: price equal to marginal social cost for intermediate goods (except where final goods cannot be taxed or there are special income distribution considerations) and marginal social cost plus an element of taxation for final goods.

(v) The appropriate criterion for the expansion of industries is, for the public sector, profitability at shadow prices of incremental output. The shadow prices are defined as social opportunity costs. Other criteria are reliable only where they generate the same outcomes as those of shadow prices.

(vi) Where producer prices and shadow prices coincide, indirect taxes should be guided by a trade-off between equity and efficiency amongst households. The outcome of this trade-off is not uniform proportionate rates for indirect taxes unless there is a well-functioning scheme for income support *and* there are closely similar preferences *and* these preferences have a special structure. Where producer and shadow prices diverge then one must add an upward adjustment to tax rates for goods with high shadow prices.

(vii) The main rationale for a corporate income tax, as opposed to a personal income tax, lies in taxing foreign incomes and monopoly rents. Where these aspects are not of major importance its primary focus should be as a means of collecting the personal income tax.

These principles are all derived within a single coherent framework. None of them can be regarded as obvious or be taken for granted, in that one can provide examples of 'rules' which have been enunciated which are in direct contradiction to them, or practical tax systems which clearly violate them. The derivation of guiding principles of this kind is one of the main objects of theory but it also warns us of the assumptions which require checking before one can proceed very far with the application or implementation of these rules. For example, the qualifications to the pricing rules stated in principle (iv) and the tax rules of principle (vi) are critical and should be examined carefully. And for brevity we have omitted a number of other important assumptions for the applicability of the rules (stated in chapter 3) which also require judgement and checking.

11.3   Methods

The purpose of the theory was not only to provide guiding principles for tax design but also to provide an organising framework for, and direct the detail of, the applied research. The principles point us towards the types of taxes that deserve close scrutiny and may lead to particular proposals. The methods allow us to scrutinise proposals in detail and identify those which are likely to yield improvements from the current position. The methods are directly consequentialist in that they are designed to bring out the consequences for households of a change and to evaluate those consequences in a systematic way.

The greatest analytical difficulties in the appraisal of policies generally lie in working out what the consequences of change will be, and this is particularly true of tax analysis. This difficulty is shared, or should be shared, by any attempt to look carefully at policy and is not unique to an analysis that adopts a particular set of criteria. The difficulty can be so great that many or most tax analysts stop a long way short of an explicit calculation of the consequences of the changes they are examining and offer instead a characterisation of anomalies or defects in the existing system together with an alternative based on simple principles of tax design. We would not argue that this latter approach should be jettisoned; indeed, it has in part guided us in the formulation of candidates for consideration in our own work. But the analysis should be pursued beyond this stage and there is an obligation on the policy analyst or advocate to make as precise as possible the consequences for participants in the economy of the changes being proposed. As increasing bodies of data become available the development of analytical techniques that take advantage of them becomes more productive. Indeed, the questions under examination and techniques of analysis should also lead and guide the data collection as much more becomes possible.

The methods we have developed and applied in this book are intended to help with the directly consequentialist analysis of policy change. We would emphasise four particular concepts or tools which have played a central role in our work: effective taxes; the use of household survey data; the social marginal cost of public funds; and shadow prices. The first and third of these represent techniques which we have conceived and developed ourselves, and the second and fourth constitute applications and extensions of existing methods and approaches. We comment on them briefly.

The original motivation for the calculation of effective taxes was the estimation of the revenue effects, flowing through demand shifts, of tax changes. However, our initial work (Ahmad and Stern, 1983) on India soon attracted the attention of policy-makers for two further reasons. First, it brought out the consequences of a rather complicated system of taxation of intermediate goods in terms of the overall effects on final goods and thus helped policy-makers understand what they were actually doing. This led to the realisation that many of the effects were unintended and undesired. For example, there was a subsidy for *khadi* (a simple cloth) whereas in fact the good was taxed through its inputs to a degree which more than offset the subsidy. Second, it led to a revision of the perceived degree of progressivity of the tax system. There were, and are, in India many taxes which are finely differentiated, with often an intention of taxing more heavily varieties consumed by richer groups. Taxes which fall on inputs, however, feed through the system in a way which would have been progressive only by chance and lead to taxes on goods which are more related to the structure of production and the ease of taxation of certain inputs than the incomes of the people who consume those goods. The main ingredients in the calculation of effective taxes were input–output tables and tax collections by commodity and these would be available for many countries.

Household survey data are invaluable if one is attempting to work out the distributional impact of policy change. It is particularly desirable for the researcher to have the data made available at the household level, for then one can investigate the impact of the changes on categories of households selected by the policy-maker and not some particular sub-aggregates pre-selected by statistical offices, where the concerns in defining the sub-aggregates may be only loosely articulated or based on considerations different from the current tax study. Often one has sub-aggregates only by groups defined by per capita household income or by urban versus rural. These categorisations are indeed important, but do not generally take one far enough. For example, in some contexts one would also be interested in the age of the different household members for the evaluation of household needs. In this case one would like to disaggregate households according to number and age of children. And breakdowns of the impact of policy changes by land ownership, region or caste may also be of central interest. It is only when one has access to data at the household level that the distributional impacts can be satisfactorily assessed according to the special concerns of a particular study.

The household data are used to calculate the effect of a policy change on the standard of living of the household. Generally, one is concerned to assess the effects of changes in prices and money incomes and thus a convenient tool is the indirect utility function (or its simple transformation, the expenditure function) which expresses household utility as a function of the prices it faces and the income at its disposal. The effect on household utility of a unit marginal change in the price of a good is then reflected by the amount consumed of that good – the more the household consumes the harder it is hit. Thus one calculates the monetary impact of marginal tax changes for each household in a simple manner from the expenditure patterns. Interpersonal comparisons come in only when these monetary impacts are compared across households. With non-marginal changes one measures the monetary changes by the equivalent variation (or something similar) which tells us what monetary loss to the household (were prices to be held constant) would be equivalent to the loss which would arise from the tax and price changes under analysis.

Interpersonal comparisons enter when we aggregate or compare monetary gains and losses for individual households, and these may be embodied in explicit welfare weights. We did not impose a unique set of weights but looked at different possibilities. We showed how they could be discussed and how the policy results depended on the welfare weights selected. Most explicitly, the welfare weights entered through our concept of the social marginal utility of income associated with a policy tool. This was defined as the effect on social welfare of a marginal tax change divided by the effect on revenue of the marginal change – hence it is the social cost of raising an extra unit of tax revenue via that tool. For an indirect tax this could be calculated in a fairly straightforward way using welfare weights and consumption patterns for the numerator (see equation (3.5)) and effective taxes and demand responses in the denominator. Once these social marginal costs are calculated one can then easily identify improving directions of tax reforms since one should shift revenue-raising on the margin from the higher to the lower cost instruments.

We emphasised in the analysis of the social marginal costs of funds just described that there was an important assumption involved in the method outlined, namely that shadow and producer prices were proportional. That is we were assuming that relative producer prices reflect relative social opportunity costs. Without this assumption the constancy of government revenue is an inadequate indication of the general equilibrium feasibility of a policy change. This is not to deny the government revenue constraint that generally is part of the model, but it is the case that the satisfaction of this, by itself, does not guarantee feasibility and the full set of adjustments associated with the re-establishment of equilibrium must be taken into account. The simplest and neatest way to do this is to use shadow prices –

defined in the only sensible and fully-consistent manner as the social opportunity cost of an extra unit of public supply. This summarises the full welfare impact, including all the general equilibrium repercussions, of extra demands which arise as a result of a policy change. The reform rule becomes that one should accept a policy change if the direct impact on household welfare exceeds the cost at shadow prices of the extra demands generated by the change. We showed that this idea could be expressed equivalently using shadow government revenue defined using the idea of a shadow tax, the discrepancy between market price and shadow price.

These ideas involved us in the calculation of sets of shadow prices for India and Pakistan, with the latter being presented here. These shadow prices would be useful in understanding a broad range of policy reforms, for example relating to trade and industrial problems, and not simply tax changes narrowly defined. As with effective taxes, we find that an analytical instrument established and calculated for a particular purpose has much wider applications. Our effective taxes have already been used by others and the same is true of the shadow prices. Hence it is not simply the methods themselves but some of the intermediate outputs of the analysis that are of value.

11.4 Further research

It is not unusual for a research programme to generate as many (or more) research questions as it answers and this is surely an example. There are a number of different kinds of research issue which arise. First, there are aspects of our own work which could, or should, with more time and resources, have been pursued in greater detail. Second, there are extensions of our methods to different, and possibly more complex, models. Third, there are the applications of our techniques to issues wider than taxation. Fourth, we have applications to other countries. And fifth, there are the data implications of the more extensive application of our methods. Guidance for data collection is not often included under further work or research topics but it is the job of economic analysis to direct as well as to respond to economic statistics collected by government agencies. We shall not attempt to be exhaustive on any of the groups of topics described, but shall simply try to illustrate some possibilities.

There are a number of important details of the tasks we have attempted which deserve substantial extra research work. We concentrate here only on aspects of the methods we have used and point to seven issues as examples: the treatment of competition between imported and domestically produced goods; the time path of adjustment of a shift away from trade taxes; the role of capital goods in the productive process; the shifting of taxes; the problems of particular industries; Centre–Province fiscal relations; and borrowing and financing of government expenditures. We discuss them in order. In basing our revenue calculations on the effective taxes on domestically produced commodities we have, as we indicated, assumed essentially either that increases in consumption come from domestic sources or that import taxes are the same as effective taxes. It is the former justification which is the stronger of the two in the sub-continent, although neither is very satisfactory. A more detailed analysis would face the issue of the competitiveness between the two types of good explicitly. Unfortunately the consumption breakdowns by source (domestic versus imports) are not easily available at the household level. And separate price information on the two components, which would be required to establish demand relationships, is likely to be very hard to come by.

There are a number of aspects of trade taxation which we should like to pursue in further detail, including the revenue effects of dismantling protection and the appropriate time-path for the shifts towards domestic indirect taxation, the further identification of genuine candidates for protection, the effects on prices of domestic competing consumer goods of reduced tariffs on imports, and the effects of changing protection on exchange rates.

For both Pakistan and India a substantial element of indirect taxation falls on capital goods. Thus an analysis which focuses only on current input–output flows will lose track of an important part of the indirect tax burden. There are two major problems, however, modelling and data. Outside steady state it is not easy to construct models which allow the conversion of taxes on capital goods into taxes on current flows of consumer goods; this conversion would be necessary to utilise demand responses in the analysis of revenue effects. And even where this is possible, or the steady-state assumption is made, the assembly of a matrix giving the vector of capital goods requirements for each output good is fraught with difficulty. We have made the steady-state assumption here and made a bold attempt at constructing the required matrix, but we would not pretend to be satisfied with either.

Our treatment of tax shifting has been very simple – we have assumed 100% shifting of indirect taxes for domestically produced products. This involves implicit assumptions about both domestic markets and the absence of competitive imports. One interpretation is perfectly elastic domestic supply (with no competitive imports), but other models can also yield a 100% shifting of costs. Shifting of an amount above or below 100% is possible in oligopolistic markets and will depend on the number of firms, their behaviour in relation to others, and the way in which the elasticity of demand changes along the demand curve. From this point of view, 100% shifting is not a polar case and may represent a convenient intermediate.

The acceptability of assumptions concerning the absence of competitive imports will depend on the good and the trading regime. For a good which is freely imported, subject to a tariff and identical to the domestic product, it will be appropriate to assume that the price is the world price plus the tariff. Changes in domestic taxation of the good will then affect the incomes of any factor specific to that good. Hughes (1987) has provided a valuable analysis of fuel taxes for three developing countries using this approach. For a discussion of the types of models (e.g. the Ricardo–Viner variety) which might be used in further work in this area, see Ahmad and Stern (1987a).

An analysis at a broad sectoral level is implied by the need to use both input–output data and estimates of demand systems. This means that important sectoral detail is lost. For an interesting application of these methods to sectors in Pakistan, see Coady (1991) on the fertiliser and other industries.

We have not said a great deal about Centre–Province relations. Pakistan has a federal structure with four provinces: Punjab, Sind, North-West Frontier Province, and Baluchistan. As in India there are constitutional restrictions on tax relations between Centre and Provinces. However, unlike India, these restrictions have played a much less prominent role, although they are of significance for a number of important subjects, particularly concerning the taxation of agriculture (see chapter 8).

The appropriate level of government borrowing was discussed in chapter 10, but it raises a number of important and fascinating issues of intertemporal allocation, risk and inflation which would involve a major further research investigation.

The second group of topics for further work concerns the extension of the methods to more complex models or those with a different emphasis. To some extent, of course, these topics overlap with the issues we have just been discussing in that the further analysis of some of the difficulties we have just identified would indeed involve greater complexity. However, the kind of model we have in mind here concerns issues which were not prominent in our detailed work. We focused here on input–output models and consumer demand. Also important for taxation are the structures of factor and output markets and production possibilities. The models pursued in this book were not tailored to deal with these issues. The approach of marginal reform can, however, be profitably applied; for a beginning, see Newbery (1987a) for an applied analysis of Korea, and Sah and Stiglitz (1987) for a discussion of some theoretical issues with a particular stress on labour markets.

For these further topics the effective tax analysis, which shifts the focus to final goods so that revenue calculations are eased, will become less significant. Most models which incorporate special features of output and factor markets would not have producer and shadow prices equal. Hence one can proceed either using a shadow price to summarise the general equilibrium effects of the repercussions of policy changes or carry the explicit calculation of these general equilibrium effects through the analysis. Strictly the results should be identical. However, for a discussion of model variation we would suggest that shadow prices might provide substantially greater flexibility. For example, we may be willing to hazard the guess that introducing a new feature into the labour market may have effects which can be summarised by a higher shadow price for labour. This can be checked in simple models which we can think of as laboratories for more complicated cases.

A third group of topics for further work would be to apply similar techniques to different issues. Of particular interest would be public-sector pricing, agricultural pricing and public-sector rationing and transfer programmes. The same types of techniques using marginal reform and shadow prices can be applied to all these problems. The public-sector pricing research could, in a number of respects, be very similar to that on taxation since a public-sector price increase is like a tax increase. Such work, however, would have to look much more closely at the structure of particular industries such as electricity, telephones, transportation and water. Work on agricultural pricing would have to focus on supply conditions and rural factor markets.

Public-sector rationing and transfer programmes can be analysed in terms of the social value of the benefits provided and the costs at shadow prices of demand generated by incremental incomes. There will, of course, be many other aspects to these programmes concerning various problems of administration and incentives, but the balance of social gains as described here and social costs of extra demands would be an important element in the story.

Work on other countries could, we hope, follow similar lines to those described here. We have worked most intensively on Pakistan but our ideas were originally developed during our work on India. Other countries would generate different perspectives, emphases and problems and doubtless the methods would be developed and improved in the process.

Finally, on further work, we should draw attention to guidance and requirements for data collection. Tax analysis requires that tax revenue data be associated with particular goods. The impact of the taxation of intermediates requires input–output data which separates domestic and imported inputs where possible, and also capital stock matrices. Incidence analyses require detailed household survey data on the consumption and production patterns. There is no doubt that these are heavy demands but they are not impossible. The requirements arise from the concern to follow through the effects of policy changes to their effects on households, a central objective in the consequentialist analysis of reform. Statistical authorities do ask for guidance on what should be collected and need to be convinced of the purposes of the exercise before releasing data which have been collected. It should not be too difficult to explain why these data are required and we were generally fortunate in the assistance we received.

11.5 Concluding comments

The principles and methods we have developed and discussed in this book represent an approach which can be applied across a broad range of policy problems and thus could form part of many research programmes or appraisals of policy. They should not be seen as narrowly specific to particular countries, time periods or social judgements. Simply put, the approach is to characterise the consequences of changes and then to evaluate them using explicit criteria. As such it might sound banal and unexceptional but in applied public finance the direct attempt to carry through the approach is not common. We have tried here to provide explicit principles and methods for carrying out that task.

The principles we reviewed in the theoretical parts of the book, particularly chapter 3, are basic to public finance and we summarised them in terms of some simple guidelines. These guidelines have fairly general applicability across countries and whilst they should not be seen as, and are not intended as, a standard package, they do point taxation firmly in particular directions, for example, indirect taxation towards final goods and away from excises on intermediate goods and tariffs. They emphasise the importance of seeing the tax, pricing and transfer systems as a whole and the dangers of analysing, for example, indirect taxes without an assessment of income support systems.

Similarly the methods and techniques which we developed, for example, effective taxes, the social marginal costs of funds and the use of shadow prices in tax reform, can be put to work in other countries too, and we hope to have shown the practitioner how this may be done. Thus our work is intended to provide principles and tools for the tax analyst or researcher to contemplate and use in a broad range of circumstances.

Finally, we should emphasise our conclusions for Pakistan as summarised at the end of the previous chapter. We have argued that the Pakistan tax system is urgently in need of reform and that there are packages available which, whilst far from perfect, could go a long way to alleviating many of the existing problems and distortions and provide a more equitable and efficient way of raising revenue for the future. The packages were based on the principles we have described and the techniques we developed together with an appreciation of the administrative difficulties Pakistan faces. We recommend them to Pakistan for serious consideration, just as we suggest the further application of the principles and methods we have developed.

References

Ahmad, E. (1987). 'Tax Regimes and Export Strategies with Reference to South Asia' in P. Streeten (ed.), *Beyond Adjustment*. Washington, D.C.: IMF.

Ahmad, E., S. Barrett and D. Coady (1985). 'Input–Output Matrices for Pakistan 1980–1', Discussion Paper no. 68, Development Economics Research Centre, University of Warwick.

Ahmad, E., D. Coady and N. H. Stern (1985). 'A Complete Set of Shadow Prices for Pakistan: Illustration for 1975/6', mimeo., University of Warwick.

(1988). 'A Complete Set of Shadow Prices for Pakistan: Illustration for 1975–76', *Pakistan Development Review* 27 (1): 7–43.

Ahmad, E., H-M. Leung and N. H. Stern (1984). 'Demand Response and the Reform of Indirect Taxes in Pakistan', Discussion Paper no. 50, Development Economics Research Centre, University of Warwick.

Ahmad, E. and S. E. Ludlow (1987). 'Aggregate and Regional Demand Response Patterns in Pakistan', *Pakistan Development Review* 26 (4): 645–55.

(1989). 'The Distributional Consequences of a Tax Reform: On a VAT for Pakistan', PPR Working Paper no. 238, World Bank, Washington, D.C.

Ahmad, E., S. E. Ludlow and N. H. Stern (1988). 'Demand Response in Pakistan: A Modification of the Linear Expenditure System for 1976', *Pakistan Development Review* 27 (3): 293–308.

Ahmad, E. and N. H. Stern (1983). 'The Evaluation of Personal Income Taxes in India', Discussion Paper no. 36, Development Economics Research Centre, University of Warwick.

(1984). 'The Theory of Tax Reform and Indian Indirect Taxes', *Journal of Public Economics* 25 (3): 259–98.

(1986). 'Tax Reform for Pakistan: Overview and Effective Taxes for 1975–76', *Pakistan Development Review* 25 (1): 43–72.

(1987a). 'Alternative Sources of Government Revenue: Illustrations from India, 1979–80', in D. Newbery and N. H. Stern (eds.), *The Theory of Taxation for Developing Countries*. Oxford: Oxford University Press.

(1987b). 'Fiscal Policy for the Seventh Five Year Plan', submission to the Pakistan Planning Commission.

327

(1989). 'Taxation for Developing Countries' in H. B. Chenery and T. N. Srinivasan (eds.), *Handbook of Development Economics*. Amsterdam: Elsevier Science Publishers.

(1990). 'Tax Reform and Shadow Prices for Pakistan', *Oxford Economic Papers* 42: 135–59.

Askari, H. and J. T. Cummings (1976). *Agricultural Supply Response: A Survey of the Econometric Evidence*. New York: Praeger.

Atkinson, A. B. (1977). 'Optimal Taxation and the Direct versus Indirect Tax Controversy', *Canadian Journal of Economics* 10 (4): 590–606.

Atkinson, A. B. and A. Sandmo (1980). 'Welfare Implications of the Taxation of Savings', *Economic Journal* 90 (359): 529–49.

Atkinson, A. B., N. H. Stern and J. Gomulka (1980). 'On the Switch from Direct to Indirect Taxation', *Journal of Public Economics* 14 (2): 55–64.

Atkinson, A. B. and J. E. Stiglitz (1976). 'The Design of Tax Structure: Direct versus Indirect Taxation', *Journal of Public Economics* 6 (1): 55–75.

(1980). *Lectures on Public Economics*. New York: McGraw-Hill.

Atkinson, A. B. and H. Sutherland (1988). *Tax-Benefit Models*, STICERD, Occasional Paper no. 10, Suntory-Toyota International Centre for Economics and Related Disciplines, London School of Economics.

Auerbach, A. J. and L. J. Kotlikoff (1987). *Dynamic Fiscal Policy*. Cambridge: Cambridge University Press.

Banerjea, P. (1930). *A History of Indian Taxation*. London: Macmillan.

Binswanger, H., Y. Mundlak, Maw-cheng Yang and A. Bowers (1985). 'Estimation of Aggregate Agricultural Supply Response from Time Series of Cross-Country Data', Working Paper 1985–83, Commodity Studies and Project Division, World Bank, Washington, D.C.

Bird, R. M. (1974). *Taxing Agricultural Land in Developing Countries*. Cambridge, Mass.: Harvard University Press.

(1987). 'A New Look at Indirect Taxation in Developing Countries', *World Development* (Oxford) 15: 1151–61.

Bliss, C. J. (1975). *Capital Theory and the Distribution of Income*, Advanced Textbooks in Economics, vol. IV. Amsterdam: North Holland.

Braverman, A., J. Hammer and C. Y. Ahn (1987). 'Multimarket Analysis of Agricultural Pricing Policies in Korea' in D. Newbery and N. H. Stern (eds.), *The Theory of Taxation for Developing Countries*. Oxford: Oxford University Press.

Buiter, W. H. (1983). 'Measurement of the Public Sector Deficit and its Implications for Policy Evaluation and Design', *International Monetary Fund Staff Papers* 30 (2): 306–49.

(1990). *Principles of Budgetary and Financial Policy*. Cambridge, Mass.: MIT Press.

Chalmley, C. (1983). 'Taxation in Dynamic Economies: Some Problems and Methods', World Bank, Country Policy Department; processed.

Chelliah, R. J. (1989). 'Changes in Tax Revenue Structure: A Case Study of India', in A. Chiancone and K. Messere (eds.), *Changes in Revenue Structures*. Detroit: Wayne State University Press.

Chenery, H. B. and T. N. Srinivasan (eds.) (1989). *Handbook of Development Economics*. Amsterdam: Elsevier Science Publishers.

Chiancone, A. and K. Messere (eds.) (1989). *Changes in Revenue Structures*. Detroit: Wayne State University Press.

Coady, D. P. (1991). 'Indirect Taxation and Pricing Policies in Developing Countries: The Case of Pakistan', Ph.D. thesis, London School of Economics.

Dasgupta, P. S., S. Marglin and A. K. Sen (1972). *Guidelines for Project Evaluation*. New York: United Nations Industrial Development Organisation (Vienna).

Deaton, A. S. (1979). 'Optimally Uniform Commodity Taxes', *Economic Letters* 2 (4): 357–61.

(1981). 'Optimal Taxes and the Structure of Preferences', *Econometrica* 49 (5): 1245–60.

(1987). 'Econometric Issues for Tax Design in Developing Countries' in D. Newbery and N. H. Stern (eds.), *The Theory of Taxation for Developing Countries*. Oxford: Oxford University Press.

Deaton, A. S. and J. Muellbauer (1980a). *Economics and Consumer Behaviour*. New York: Cambridge University Press.

(1980b). 'An Almost Ideal Demand System', *American Economic Review* 70 (3): 312–26.

Deaton, A. S. and N. H. Stern (1986). 'Optimally Uniform Commodity Taxes, Taste Differences, and Lump-Sum Grants', *Economic Letters* 20: 263–6.

Dervis, K., J. De Melo and S. Robinson (1982). *General Equilibrium Models for Development Policy*. New York: Cambridge University Press for the World Bank.

Diamond, P. A. (1970). 'Incidence of an Interest Income Tax', *Journal of Economic Theory* 2: 211–24.

Diamond, P. A. and J. A. Mirrlees (1971). 'Optimal Taxation and Public Production, Part I: Production Efficiency' and 'Part II: Tax Rules', *American Economic Review* 61 (1): 8–27 and 61 (3): 261–78.

Dixit, A. K. (1971). 'Short-Run Equilibrium and Shadow Prices in a Dual Economy', *Oxford Economic Papers* 23 (3): 384–400.

(1973). 'Models of Dual Economies' in J. A. Mirrlees and N. H. Stern (eds.), *Models of Economic Growth*. London: Macmillan.

(1984). 'International Trade Policy for Oligopolistic Industries', *Economic Journal* (supplement), 94: 1–16.

(1985). 'Taxation Theory in the Open Economy', Princeton University, Woodrow Wilson School. Published in A. J. Auerbach and M. S. Feldstein (eds.), *Handbook of Public Economics*, vol. I. Amsterdam: North Holland (1988).

Dixit, A. K. and V. Norman (1980). *Theory of International Trade*. Cambridge: Cambridge University Press.

Dixit, A. K. and N. H. Stern (1974). 'Determinants of Shadow Prices in Open Dual Economies', *Oxford Economic Papers* 26 (1): 42–53.

Drèze, J. P. and N. H. Stern (1987). 'The Theory of Cost–Benefit Analysis' in A. Auerbach and M. Feldstein (eds.), *Handbook of Public Economics*, vol. II. Amsterdam: North Holland: Elsevier Science Publishers.

Eshag, E. (1983). *Fiscal and Monetary Policies and Problems in Developing Countries*. Cambridge: Cambridge University Press.

Fei, J. C. H. and G. Ranis (1964). *Development of the Labour Surplus Economy.* Homewood, Ill.: Irwin.

Fischer, S. (1980). 'Dynamic Inconsistency, Cooperation and the Benevolent Dissembling Government', *Journal of Economic Dynamics and Control* 2: 93–107.

Gersovitz, M. (1987). 'The Effects of Domestic Taxes on Foreign Private Investment' in D. Newbery and N. H. Stern (eds.), *The Theory of Taxation for Developing Countries.* Oxford: Oxford University Press.

Gil Diaz, F. (1987). 'Some Lessons from Mexico's Tax Reform' in D. Newbery and N. H. Stern (eds.), *The Theory of Taxation for Developing Countries.* Oxford: Oxford University Press.

(1988). 'Reforming Taxes in Developing Countries: Mexico's Protracted Tax Reform', mimeo.

Gillis, M., C. Shoup and G. Sicat (1989). *The Value-Added Tax in Developing Countries.* Washington, D.C.: World Bank.

Giovannini, A. (1985). 'Savings and the Real Interest Rate in LDCs', *Journal of Development Economics* 18: 197–217.

Goode, R. (1984). *Government Finance in Developing Countries.* Washington, D.C.: Brookings Institution.

Government of Bangladesh (1986). *Bangladesh Fiscal Statistics.* Dhaka.

Government of India (1978). *NSS 28th Round 1973–74*, National Sample Survey. Delhi.

Government of India, Ministry of Finance (1977). *Report of the Indirect Taxation Enquiry Committee*, New Delhi.

Government of Pakistan, Agricultural Census Organisation (1980). *Agricultural Census*, Lahore.

Government of Pakistan, Central Board of Revenue (1986). *Pakistan Customs and Tariffs*, Islamabad.

Government of Pakistan, Federal Bureau of Statistics, *Foreign Trade Statistics* (annual). Karachi.

Government of Pakistan, Federal Bureau of Statistics, *Monthly Statistical Bulletin* (monthly). Karachi.

Government of Pakistan, Federal Bureau of Statistics, *National Accounts Statistics* (annual). Karachi.

Government of Pakistan, Ministry of Finance (1974). *Final Report of the Tax Commission.* Karachi.

Government of Pakistan, Ministry of Finance, *Economic Memoranda to the Budget* (annual). Karachi.

Government of Pakistan, Ministry of Finance, *Economic Survey* (annual). Islamabad.

Government of Pakistan, Planning Commission (1976). *Micro-Nutrient Survey.* Karachi.

Government of Pakistan, Planning Commission, *The Fifth Five-Year Plan 1978–83.* Karachi.

Government of Pakistan, Planning Commission, *The Sixth Five-Year Plan 1984–88.* Karachi.

Government of Pakistan, Planning Commission, *The Seventh Five-Year Plan 1988–93*. Karachi.

Guesnerie, R. (1977). 'On the Direction of Tax Reform', *Journal of Public Economics* 7: 179–202.

Habib, I. (1982). 'The Systems of Agricultural Production (Mughal India)' in T. Raychaudhuri and I. Habib (eds.), *The Cambridge Economic History of India*, vol. I. Cambridge: Cambridge University Press.

Harberger, A. C. (1962). 'The Incidence of Corporate Income Tax', *Journal of Political Economy* 70 (3): 215–40.

    (1974). *Taxation and Welfare*. Boston: Little, Brown.

Hausman, J. A. (1981). 'Labour Supply' in H. J. Aaron and J. A. Pechman (eds.), *How Taxes Affect Economic Behaviour*. Washington, D.C.: Brookings Institution.

Heady, C. and P. Mitra (1987). 'Optimal Taxation and Shadow Pricing in a Developing Economy' in D. Newbery and N. H. Stern (eds.), *The Theory of Taxation for Developing Countries*. Oxford: Oxford University Press.

Helpman, E. and P. R. Krugman (1985). *Market Structure and Foreign Trade: Increasing Returns, Imperfect Competition and the International Economy*. Brighton: Wheatsheaf.

Hinrichs, H. H. (1966). *A General Theory of Tax Structure Change during Economic Development*. Cambridge, Mass.: Harvard University Press.

Hoff, K. (1989). 'Land Taxes, Output Taxes and Sharecropping: Was Henry George Right?' Proceedings of a conference held in Anapolis, June 1989. To be published in A. Braverman, K. Hoff and J. Stiglitz (eds.), *Agricultural Development Policies and the Theory of Rural Organisation*. World Bank (forthcoming).

Hornby, J. M. (1968). 'Investment and Trade Policy in the Dual Economy', *Economic Journal* 78 (309): 96–107.

Høst-Madsen (1979). *Macroeconomic Accounts*. Washington, D.C.: IMF.

Hughes, G. (1987). 'The Incidence of Fuel Taxes: A Comparative Study of Three Countries' in D. Newbery and N. H. Stern (eds.), *The Theory of Taxation for Developing Countries*. Oxford: Oxford University Press.

Irfan, M. (1974). 'Shifting and Incidence of Indirect Taxes on Tobacco and Petroleum Products in Pakistan', *Pakistan Development Review* 13 (1): 66–87.

Islam, N. (1981). *Foreign Trade and Economic Controls in Development: The Case of United Pakistan*. New Haven, Conn.: Yale University Press.

Jeetun, A. (1980). 'Pakistan's Tax System: Structure Elasticity, Incidence and Fiscal Effect', Ph.D. thesis, Karachi University.

Jetha, N., S. Akhtar and G. Rao (1984). 'Domestic Resource Mobilisation in Pakistan (Selected Issues)', *World Bank Staff Working Papers* no. 632. Washington, D.C.: World Bank.

Joshi, T. M., N. Anjanniah and S. V. Bhende (1968). *Studies in the Taxation of Agricultural Land and Income in India*. New Delhi: Asia Publishing House.

Journal of International Economics (1983). 'International Factor Mobility: A Symposium', 14 (3/4), May.

Kay, J. A. and M. A. King (1986). *The British Tax System*, 4th edn. Oxford: Oxford University Press.

Kehoe, T. J. and J. Serra-Puche (1983). 'A Computational General Equilibrium Model with Endogenous Unemployment: An Analysis of the 1980 Fiscal Reform in Mexico', *Journal of Public Economics* 22 (1): 1–26.

Khan, S. R. (1974). 'An Estimation of the Shadow Wage Rate in Pakistan', *Pakistan Development Review* 13: 389–408.

King, M. A. (1977). *Public Policy and the Corporation.* London: Chapman and Hall.

(1980). 'Savings and Taxation', in G. M. Heal and G. A. Hughes (eds.), *Public Policy and the Tax System.* London: Allen & Unwin.

(1983). 'Welfare Analysis of Tax Reforms Using Household Data', *Journal of Public Economics* 21 (2): 183–214.

(1985). 'The Economics of Saving: A Survey of Recent Contributions' in K. Arrow and S. Honkapohja (eds.), *Frontiers in Economics.* Oxford: Basil Blackwell.

King, M. A. and D. Fullerton (1984). *The Taxation of Income from Capital: A Comparative Study from the U.S., U.K., Sweden and West Germany.* Chicago: Chicago University Press.

Kotlikoff, L. J. (1984). 'Taxation and Savings – A Neoclassical Perspective', Working Paper 1302. National Bureau of Economic Research, Harvard University, Cambridge, Mass.

Krugman, P. R. (1987). 'Is Free Trade *Passé*?', *Journal of Economic Perspectives* 1 (2): 131–44.

Kumar, D. (ed.) (1982). *The Cambridge Economic History of India*, vol. II. Cambridge: Cambridge University Press.

Kydland, R. E. and E. C. Prescott (1977). 'Rules Rather than Discretion: The Inconsistency of Optimal Plans', *Journal of Political Economy* 85 (3): 513–48.

Lanjouw, P. and N. H. Stern (1989). 'Agricultural Changes and Inequality in Palanpur 1957–1984', Development Economics Research Programme no. 24, London School of Economics. Also forthcoming in K. Hoff and J. Stiglitz (eds.). *Agricultural Development Policies and the Theory of Rural Organisation.* World Bank.

Lewis, W. A. (1954). 'Economic Development with Unlimited Supplies of Labour', *Manchester School* 22: 139–91.

Lipton, M. (1977). *Why Poor People Stay Poor: Urban Bias in World Development.* Cambridge, Mass.: Harvard University Press.

Little, I. M. D. and J. A. Mirrlees (1974). *Project Appraisal and Planning for Developing Countries.* London: Heinemann.

Little, I. M. D., D. Mazumdar and J. Page (1984). 'Small Manufacturing Enterprises: A Comparative Study of India and Other Countries', Development Research Department, World Bank, processed.

McFadden, D. (1973). 'On the Existence of Optimal Development Programmes in Infinite-Horizon Economies' in J. A. Mirrlees and N. H. Stern (eds.) *Models of Economic Growth.* London: Macmillan.

McLure, C. I. (1975). 'General Equilibrium Incidence Analysis: The Harberger Model after 10 Years', *Journal of Public Economics* 4: 125–62.

Meade, J. E. (1978). *The Structure and Reform of Direct Taxation.* (A report of a committee for the Institute of Fiscal Studies, chaired by J. E. Meade.) London: Allen & Unwin.

Messere, K. and J. Owens (1989). 'Long-term Revenue Trends and Current Tax Reform Issues in OECD Countries', in A. Chiancone and K. Messere (eds.), *Changes in Revenue Structures*. Detroit: Wayne State University Press.

Mirrlees, J. A. (1971). 'An Exploration in the Theory of Optimum Income Taxation', *Review of Economic Studies* 38 (2): 175–208.

Naqvi, B. (1975). 'Shifting of Indirect Taxes: A Further Study', *Pakistan Development Review* 14 (2): 174–84.

National Taxation Reform Commission (1986). *Final Report*. Karachi.

Newbery, D. M. G. (1974). 'The Robustness of General Equilibrium Analysis in the Dual Economy', *Oxford Economic Papers* 26 (1): 32–41.

—— (1986). 'On the Desirability of Input Taxes', *Economic Letters* 20: 267–70.

—— (1987a). 'Identifying Desirable Directions of Agricultural Price Reform in Korea' in D. Newbery and N. H. Stern (eds.), *The Theory of Taxation for Developing Countries*. Oxford: Oxford University Press.

—— (1987b). 'Agricultural Taxation: The Main Issues' in D. Newbery and N. H. Stern (eds.), *The Theory of Taxation for Developing Countries*. Oxford: Oxford University Press.

Newbery, D. M. G. and N. H. Stern (eds.) (1987a). *The Theory of Taxation for Developing Countries*. Oxford: Oxford University Press.

—— (1987b). 'Dynamic Issues' in D. Newbery and N. H. Stern (eds.), *The Theory of Taxation for Developing Countries*. Oxford: Oxford University Press.

Nurkse, R. (1953). *Problems of Capital Formation in Underdeveloped Countries*. Oxford: Blackwell.

Overseas Development Administration (1988). *Appraisal of Projects in Developing Countries: A Guide for Economists*, 3rd edition. London: HMSO.

Pakistan Institute of Development Economics (1985). 'Final PIDE Input–Output Table of Pakistan's Economy: 1975–76', Research Report no. 144, Islamabad.

Preobrazhensky, E. A. (1926). *Novaia ekonomika*. Moscow. Translated by B. Pearce as *The New Economics*. Oxford: Clarendon Press (1965).

Prest, A. R. (1972). *Public Finance in Under-Developed Countries*. Weidenfeld & Nicolson.

Radhu, G. M. (1965). 'The Relation of Indirect Tax Changes to Price Changes in Pakistan', *Pakistan Development Review* 5 (1): 54–63.

Raychaudhuri, T. and I. Habib (eds.) (1982). *The Cambridge Economic History of India*, vol. I. Cambridge: Cambridge University Press.

Robinson, S. (1989). 'Multisectoral Models' in H.B. Chenery and T. N. Srinivasan (eds.), *Handbook of Development Economics*, vol. II. Amsterdam: Elsevier Science Publishers.

Sah, R. K. and J. Stiglitz (1987). 'The Taxation and Pricing of Agricultural and Industrial Goods in Developing Economies' in D. Newbery and N. H. Stern (eds.), *The Theory of Taxation for Developing Countries*. Oxford: Oxford University Press.

Schultz, T. W. (ed.) (1978). *Distortions of Agricultural Incentives*. Bloomington: Indiana University Press.

Shah, S. M. S. and J. F. J. Toye (1979). 'Fiscal Incentives for Firms in some Developing Countries: Survey and Critique' in J. F. J. Toye (ed.), *Taxation and Economic Development*. London: Frank Cass.

334   References

334   References

Shalizi, Z. and L. Squire (1988). 'Tax Policy in Sub-Saharan Africa', Policy and Research Series, no. 2, World Bank, Washington, D.C.

Williamson, J. G. (1988). 'Migration and Urbanisation' in H. B. Chenery and T. N. Srinivasan (eds.), *Handbook of Development Economics*, vol. I. Amsterdam: Elsevier Science Publishers.

World Bank (1983). *World Development Report*. Oxford: Oxford University Press.

(1988). *World Development Report*. Oxford: Oxford University Press.

(1989a). *Medium Term Economic Policy Adjustments*. Oxford: Oxford University Press.

(1989b). *World Development Report*. Oxford: Oxford University Press.

Index

Printed in the United States
By Bookmasters